RESEARCH HANDBOOK ON CHINESE ENVIRONMENTAL LAW

RESEARCH HANDBOOKS IN ENVIRONMENTAL LAW

This highly topical series addresses some of the most important questions and areas of research in Environmental Law. Each volume is designed by a leading expert to appraise the current state of thinking and probe the key questions for future research on a particular topic. The series encompasses some of the most pressing issues in the field, ranging from climate change, biodiversity and the marine environment through to the impacts of trade, regulation, and sustainable development.

Each *Research Handbook* comprises specially-commissioned chapters from leading academics, and sometimes practitioners, as well as those with an emerging reputation and is written with a global readership in mind. Equally useful as reference tools or high-level introductions to specific topics, issues and debates, these *Handbooks* will be used by academic researchers, post-graduate students, practising lawyers and lawyers in policy circles.

Titles in the series include:

Research Handbook on Climate Change Adaptation Law
Edited by Jonathan Verschuuren

Research Handbook on Climate Change Mitigation Law
Edited by Geert Van Calster, Wim Vandenberghe and Leonie Reins

Research Handbook on Chinese Environmental Law
Edited by Qin Tianbao

Research Handbook on Chinese Environmental Law

Edited by

Qin Tianbao

Wuhan University, China

RESEARCH HANDBOOKS IN ENVIRONMENTAL LAW

Edward Elgar PUBLISHING

Cheltenham, UK • Northampton, MA, USA

Published by
Edward Elgar Publishing Limited
The Lypiatts
15 Lansdown Road
Cheltenham
Glos GL50 2JA
UK

Edward Elgar Publishing, Inc.
William Pratt House
9 Dewey Court
Northampton
Massachusetts 01060
USA

A catalogue record for this book
is available from the British Library

Library of Congress Control Number: 2014959499

This book is available electronically in the **Elgar**online
Law subject collection
DOI 10.4337/9780857931429

MIX
Paper from
responsible sources
FSC® C013056
FSC
www.fsc.org

ISBN 978 0 85793 141 2 (cased)
ISBN 978 0 85793 142 9 (eBook)

Typeset by Columns Design XML Ltd, Reading
Printed and bound in Great Britain by T.J. International Ltd, Padstow

Contents

Contributors

Chang Hong has held the position of Assistant Professor of International Law and the Law of the Sea at Xiamen University of China since 2014. She got her PhD degree in Trier University of Germany with an emphasis on the marine scientific research and the law of the sea.

Chen Shiyin has held the position of Lecturer of Law Department at Fuqing Branch of Fujian Normal University since August 2011. She is a PhD candidate on Environmental law at China University of Political Science and Law (CUPL) since September 2014. Shiyin focuses on environmental law and is author of several research articles in the field of environmental law.

Hou Jiaru holds the position of Professor of Environmental Law at the Civil, Commercial and Economic Law School of China University of Political Science and Law (CUPL) in Beijing. He obtained his PhD degree in Renmin University of China and LLM degree in Vermont Law School. His research areas include environmental tort law, international environmental law, environmental negotiation and environmental disputes resolution and civil law.

Jiang Xiaoyi has held the position of Associate Professor of Environmental Law at the Wuhan University China Institute of Boundary and Ocean Studies (CIBOS) the People's Republic of China since 2010. She defended her PhD on the topic of legal issues for implementing the clean development mechanism in the University of Western Sydney Australia in 2010. Xiaoyi is a young legal scholar focusing on research areas of international, comparative and national environmental law and policy. Her research and publications emphasize climate change issues. Since joining the CIBOS in November 2010, which is supported by Ministry of Foreign Affairs of the People's Republic of China, she has taught the course of international environmental law for graduate students and has also given her time to maritime environment issues.

Liu Nengye has been a Marie Curie Research Fellow at the School of Law, University of Dundee, UK since 1 September 2013. He defended his PhD on the prevention of vessel-source pollution, a comparative study between European and Chinese law at Ghent University, Belgium in

2012. Between 2012 and 2013 he was a postdoctoral fellow at Walther-Schücking-Institute for International Law, University of Kiel, Germany. Dr Liu has published widely in the field of international law of the sea and international environmental law. He serves as associate editor of the *Yearbook of International Environmental Law* (Oxford) and is a reviewer for various journals.

Qin Tianbao is Luojia Professor of Law, serves as the Director of the Research Institute of Environmental Law (RIEL) and the Associate Dean for the School of Law and is Professor of the China Institute of Boundary and Ocean Studies, Wuhan University, China. He is a legislative expert for China's Ministry of Environmental Protection and Ministry of Agriculture, and Hubei Provincial Parliament, an adviser of the Chinese delegation to negotiations on biodiversity and climate change issues. Professor Qin is the Secretary-General of Chinese Society of Environment and Resources Law (CSERL), a Member of IUCN World Commission on Environmental Law and of the Committee on the Legal Principles relating to Climate Change of the International Law Association. Currently, he is concentrating his research in the areas of laws and policies concerning biotechnology and biodiversity, water and ocean, trans-boundary environmental issues. Professor Qin is the author of several books and more than 60 articles in these fields.

Ren Shidan has held the position of Associate Professor at Southwest University of Political Science and Law in China since 1 July 2011. She defended her PhD on environmental law at Wuhan University in China in 2011. Dr Ren focuses on different topics of environmental law with an emphasis on the relationship between the environment and the poverty from the legal perspective.

Tou Xiaodong is the Dean of Law and Politics College, Wenzhou University. He has held the position of Professor of Environmental Policy and Law at the Faculty of Law at Wenzhou University since 1 November 2007. He received his Doctor's Degree on Environmental Law from Environmental Law Institute of Wuhan University, and has done his post-doctoral research in Macquarie University in Australia. He focuses on different topics of environmental law, with an emphasis on legal aspects of conservation of natural resources. Professor Tou has presided over more than ten provincial-level or above projects, such as National Social Science Fund, key projects of Zhejiang Philosophy and Social Scientific Planning, Humanities and Social Sciences Foundation of Ministry of Education of China, and so on. He is one of the young and middle-aged academic leaders in colleges of Zhejiang Province, one of the "151 Talents" of Zhejiang Province, vice-president of Zhejiang Environmental Law Society, Standing Committee of Environmental Law Society of China Environmental Science.

Wang Huanhuan is an Associate Professor in environmental law at School of Law at Sun Yat-sen University in Guangzhou, China. Her research interests lie in land contamination law, energy law and comparative environmental law. She earned a PhD in law from Wuhan University in 2010.

Yu Wenxuan is a professor and the Director of the Institute of Environmental and Resources Law, China University of Political Science and Law (CUPL) in Beijing, and is also the Director of the Research and Development Division of the Center for Legal Assistance to Pollution Victims (CLAPV). He was a visiting scholar at US Environmental Protection Agency and Vermont Law School from 2011 to 2012. Professor Yu specializes in environmental law and energy law and has published more than 70 academic papers and seven books. He led 20 research projects commissioned by Ministry of Education, Ministry of Justice, Ministry of Environmental Protection (MEP), State Forestry Administration, China Law Society, EU-China Biodiversity Program (ECBP), etc. Professor Yu serves as deputy secretary general of Environment and Resources Law Society, standing commissioner of the Committee of Environmental Law Branch of Chinese Society for Environmental Sciences, council member of Environment and Resources Law Society of Beijing Law Society. Professor Yu earned his doctorial and master degrees from CUPL, and joined Tsinghua University Law School as a postdoctoral researcher from 2007 to 2009. His doctoral dissertation "On Biosafety Legislation" was awarded "China National Excellent Doctoral Thesis" in 2009. He was selected into the "New Century Excellent Talents in University" program in 2012 by Ministry of Education.

Zhang Jianwei has held the position of Professor of Environmental Law at the Faculty of Law at Henan University since 1 October 2010. He defended his PhD on the government's environmental responsibility in 2007. He has been a visiting scholar in Sydney University and Ghent University. Professor Zhang focuses on different topics of environmental law, with an emphasis on legal aspects of climate change and governmental environmental responsibilities.

Zhang Shijun has been Professor of Environmental Law at the Law School of Shandong University of China since July 2005. He obtained his PhD Degree on Environmental and Resources Law at Law School of Wuhan University in 2005. He worked as a post-doctoral researcher at

Environmental School of Nanjing University from July 2007 to July 2009. From September 2009 to September 2010, sponsored by CSC, he worked as a visiting scholar at Law School of Maryland University of America. Shijun Zhang focuses on different topics of environmental law, especially on environment public interest litigation, environmental law enforcement, marine environmental law, and climate change. He published his monograph "Study on the Standing in Environmental Public Interest Litigation" in 2011.

Zhao Xiaobo (Bob Zhao) is a Lecturer in law at the School of Law and Justice, the University of Southern Queensland (USQ). He received his PhD degree in law from the University of Western Sydney (UWS) in 2012 sponsored by the Chinese Scholarship Council. Prior to join USQ, he worked as a Lecturer at the Shanghai University of Finance and Economics. His research interest focuses on the Chinese Environmental Law, comparative contaminated land law and environmental torts, etc. His monograph titled *Developing an Appropriate Contaminated Land Regime in China: Lessons Learned from the US and UK* was published by Springer in 2013. He is also the author and co-author of several peer reviewed journal articles and book chapters.

Zhou Chen has held the position of Assistant Professor, Master Supervisor of Environmental Policy and Law in the Law School of Xiamen University China since 1 May 2013. She defended her PhD on technology transfer regime under the UN Framework Convention on Climate Change and Chinese legislations on 30 January 2013, under the program of Tilburg University the Netherlands (funded by the Chinese Scholar Council). Between 2009 and 2013, she gained practical experience as research fellow of Tilburg Sustainability Center, and legal researcher of Dutch consultancy ClimaXmi. Chen focuses on different topics of environmental law, with an emphasis on legal aspects of climate, energy policies and WTO regime.

Table of environmental legislation

Nature Resources and Energy Regulations Laws

Main Regulations and Rules

Ecology Conservation Laws

1. Introduction

Qin Tianbao and Zhou Chen

1.1 OVERVIEW

'The domain of environmental law and policy extends to any place where the earth is modified by human action.'[1] China is not, of course, an exception. In line with the global trend of improving the environment by legal tools, China plays an important role and its efforts have aroused great concern not only from developing countries, who are considered major players in the current game, but also in the broader international community.

From the geographic perspective, China is an integral part of the earth environment and bio-circle. It is self-evident that on the issue of environment protection, no one country can completely account for itself. In the very recent past, for instance, there was widespread recognition that rapid economic growth and progressive urbanization accompanied by escalating GHG emissions, excessive energy consumption and local environmental degradation dominate many developing countries.[2] Because China is the largest developing country in the world it is difficult for it to escape from the tensions of modernization and environment issues that face these countries.

Like many southern countries, China is confronted with a fundamental challenge in pursuing continuous economic development while avoiding the accompanying environmental degradation.[3] In the past few years, GDP growth has been at the expense of an excessive extraction of natural resources, driving China to an historical turning point. To supply the

[1] See Alan Miller, James Leape, Christopher Schroeder and Robert Percival, *Environmental Regulations Law, Science and Policy,* Aspen Publishers, 2006, p. 3.

[2] See Fei Teng and Alun Gu, 'Climate change: National and local policy opportunities in China, climate change modeling and policy', 74 *Nota di Lavoro*, 2007, p. 2, available at http://www.feem.it/Feem/Pub/Publications/WPapers/default.htm.

[3] See Chris Deal, 'Climate change, technology transfer: Opportunities in the developing world', *ASME WISE Intern*, 2007, p. 2.

world with products, most of the environmentally toxic enterprises are established in China, heavily polluting local environments.[4] China is now suffering from serious air pollution, water problems and soil contamination. The failure to protect the environment not only threatens public health, but also incurs significant social and economic costs. By way of an example conventional air pollution has become so serious in China, that it kills possibly 400,000 to 750,000 people per year and accounts for about 5.78 per cent of Chinese GDP.[5] Recently China's capital city Beijing was reported as suffering the worst air pollution in recent memory: smoggy haze.[6]

Nevertheless, China's own distinctive features affect its attitude towards environmental issues. It has the world's largest population, has harsh natural conditions, a relatively small area of cultivated land, few water resources and heavy pollution.[7] The need for self-sufficiency has exerted enormous pressures on the ecosystem. In addition, specific environmental settings vary from region to region, particularly between south-east and north-west.[8] All of these factors, to a greater or lesser extent, affect the progress of addressing these biological problems in any terms including those of law. From the viewpoint of history, China, like many other ancient civilizations, reveals considerable understanding of the need for ecological balance, rooted in the efforts of people centuries ago to survive and prosper in agrarian and pastoral societies.[9] As advanced by the ancient philosopher Dong Zhongshu, this set of beliefs, called Tian Ren Gan Ying (the interaction of heaven and man), pinpoints the correlation and interaction between natural environment and human activities.[10] According to him, extreme weather and other dislocations in

---

[4] See Jiajun Wen, 'Climate change and China: Technology, market and beyond', report for Focus on the Global South, occasional paper, 2009, p. 15.

[5] 'Costs of pollution in China', World Bank and State Environmental Protection Administration PRC, 2007, pp. xvii.

[6] See Frank Langfitt, 'China's air pollution: Is the government willing to act?', 24 May 2013, available at http://www.wbur.org/npr/186246634/Chinas-air-pollution-is-the-government-willing-to-act.

[7] Haiyan Wang, 'An introduction to environmental law and policy', *Environmental Policy and Law*, **34**:4–5, 2004 p. 193.

[8] This depends on many factors such as latitude, precipitation, wind patterns, coastal conditions and economic activities in particular districts.

[9] The earliest ecological wisdom has been reflected in the *I Ching: Book Of Changes*. It aims to provide for the government's ownership of natural resources to ensure feudal society order.

[10] See Jonathan B. Wiener, 'Climate change policy and policy change in China', 55 *UCLA Law Review* 2008, pp. 1819–22.

the natural order were considered portents of misgovernment. In the meanwhile, it is commonly known that the Chinese legal tradition is based on the philosophy of Confucius, which contrasts radically with the western system of 'legalism'. Confucianism, the system of human governance with an emphasis on moral education and social harmony, has been dominant in China for a very long time.[11] Yet, the rise of an industrial and urbanized society in recent times has challenged this approach. Law proves for sound environmental management and governance, particularly when it comes to modern environmental problems. Legal tools have thus attained greater importance gradually and have become a considerable factor in the political, economic and social transformation of the country.

1.1.1 History of Chinese Modern Environmental Law

Environmental problems are not novel. Instead, they are, in particular those that heavily influence human beings' survival and development, the byproduct of modernization.[12] Recently, the Chinese leadership has become aware of local environmental situations, which indicate that China has suffered, and is suffering, great damage from its environmental problems, but, at the same time, it could gain greater net benefits from a good environment policy.[13] In 1983 Chinese policy-makers promulgated environmental protection as a basic national policy.[14] The five principles of Chinese environmental law have been set out as a guide for the domestic environmental legislations, including: (i) sustainable development; (ii) prevention first; (iii) rational development; (iv) the beneficiary bears the development burden; and (v) public participation. In fact, the progress of modern environmental legislation in China has undergone three important periods.

---

[11] See Derek Bosworth and Deli Yang, 'Intellectual property law, technology flow and licensing opportunities in the People's Republic of China', *International Business Review* 9, 2000, p. 455. Governments operate in a cultural/social context that emphasizes hierarchy, order, knowledge (and adhering) to one's place in the scheme of things.

[12] Li Qijia, 'The development of Chinese Second Generation's environmental law', 24 April 2010, available at http://yangzx.fyfz.cn/b/606199.

[13] See Wiener, note 10 above, p. 1813.

[14] See Wang Jin, *Environmental Law*, Beijing University Press, 2011, p. 45.

1.1.1.1 The general evolution

Establishing period The first period, starting from 1949 (when the People's Republic of China had just been established) to the 1960s is regarded as the 'establishing period'. The new political, economic and legal order had to be set up immediately.

Pioneering period From 1966 to 1977, China had experienced the 'Cultural Revolution' and social chaos nationwide, there was, therefore, hardly any significant progress made in environmental legislation. This second period is the so-called 'pioneering period'. China's environmental law evolved only slowly during these periods, because of the 'Great Leap Forward' policy that aimed to revitalize the economy and environmental protection was, therefore, simply not on that agenda.[15] 'Only few environmental interests can be located, such as in the regulation on mineral resources and factory safety, including provisions on water pollution prevention and waste disposal.'[16] Despite this, it should be borne in mind the severe floods and droughts that took place at the end of the 1960s. China had then signed the 1972 United Nations Stockholm Declaration on the Human Environment, and issued a decision on environmental protection and improvement.[17]

Surging period The third period is in essence the real development of modern environmental law, which began in 1978 and continues to the present day. In this time phase, China's environmental law is characterized as systematization that will ultimately develop into an independent sector.[18] Straight after the attendance at the Stockholm Conference on

---

[15] The 'Great Leap Forward' policy was an economic and social campaign by the Communist Party of China (CPC) from 1958 to 1961. The campaign was led by Mao Zedong and aimed to rapidly transform the country from an agrarian economy into a communist society through rapid industrialization and collectivization.

[16] See Stefanie Beyer, 'Environmental law and policy in the People's Republic of China', *Chinese Journal of International Law,* **5**:1, 2006, p. 191.

[17] This decision constituted the impetus for the environmental legislation in the subsequent era of China's policy of openness and economic reform adopted by Deng Xiaoping in 1978.

[18] In 1979 the National People's Conference (NPC) issued *PRC Environmental Protection Law (for Trial Implementation)*, where three industrial pollution control programs were established: (i) environmental impact assessment; (ii) effluent and emission discharge fees; and (iii) the 'treble simultaneity'. It was

Human Environment,[19] China essentially set itself on the road to environmental legislation. As a milestone, in 1978, the *PRC Constitution (1978)*, in its article 26, mandates environmental protection as a specific constitutional component and one of the important responsibilities of the state.[20] Rapid growth over the following three decades fostered the formation of a detailed environmental legal system. Among them, the enactment of *PRC Environmental Protection Law (1989)*, is viewed as the most remarkable exercise in local lawmaking.[21] With the guidance of both *PRC Constitution (1982)* and *PRC Environmental Protection Law (1989)*, in a relatively short period, China has built quite an extensive set of pollution prevention and control legislation.[22] However, the formal legislation has hardly been translated into effective controls. Pressing environmental problems still exist. In fact, environmental degradation is an increasingly serious issue. Two major reasons account for this: (1) at the very beginning, China constructed its environmental laws by trying to transfer the western solution, for instance, directly transplanting the western laws into existence, without fully taking consideration of indigenous legal, political and social situations;[23] (2) the local economic

---

a landmark of Chinese environmental protection and a sign that environmental law in China had become an independent law sector.

[19] The United Nations Conference on the Human Environment, met in Stockholm 5–16 June 1972, to consider the need for a common outlook and for common principles to inspire and guide the peoples of the world in the preservation and enhancement of the human environment. More information of Stockholm Conference on Human Environment is available at http://www.unep.org/Documents.Multilingual/Default.asp?documentid=97&articleid=1503.

[20] PRC Constitution, art. 26: '[t]he state protects and improves the environment in which people live and the ecological environment. It prevents and controls pollution and other public nuisance'.

[21] From the first 'Environmental Protection Law (for Trial Implementation)' enacted in 1979, there have been over 30 years in Chinese legislative construction on environment issues.

[22] For instance, Marine Environmental Protection Law (1982), Water Pollution Prevention and Control Law (1984), Air Pollution Prevention and Control Law (1987), Grassland Law (1985) and Water Law (1988) etc.

[23] The Air Pollution Prevention and Control Law (1995), Solid Waste Pollution Prevention and Control Law (1995), Water Pollution Prevention and Control Law (1996), Noise Pollution Prevention and Control Law (1997), Regulation on Nature Reserves (1994), Coal Law (1996), Flood Control Law (1997), Energy Saving Law (1997), Damage from Earthquake Prevention and Control Law (1997), Forest Law (Revised in 1998) and Land Management Law (1998), Marine Environmental Protection Law (Revised in 1999), Air Pollution Prevention and Control Law (Revised in 2000), Safe Production Law (2002),

development under the ‘Reform and Open’ policy deepens in this time phase.[24] Especially during the second half of the 1990s, economic growth remained the priority, and a great number of environmental damages crises were emerging. The country did not only confront environmental problems, such as soil erosion, deforestation and desertification typically associated with a developing and overpopulated agricultural society, but also those of an industrialized country having to deal with a welter of pollution and resource exhaustion. In this period, many environmental laws, regulations and rules were revised and updated in order to strengthen the effectiveness of compliance.[25] In addition, it is worthwhile mentioning that central government authority was slightly decentralized and regional authorities enacted significant environmental legislation.[26] Only recently, China has been confronted with emerging environmental problems, ranging from energy exhaustion to climate mitigation and adaptation.[27] These constitute additional pressures for local legislative construction, challenging top legislatures at large. In general, great achievements have been made on environmental legislation, for instance, institutional arrangements and environmental liability have been strengthened. In 2011, the new round amendment to the *PRC Environmental Protection Law (1989)* (EPL) was incorporated into the current legislative plan.

1.1.1.2 The newly revised EPL

On 24 April 2014, the Beijing Government approved changes to the state’s EPL for the first time in 25 years. This lately revised law will

---

Environmental Impact Assessment Law (2002), and Radioactive Pollution Prevention Law (2003), etc.

[24] This policy was initiated by Deng Xiaoping in the late 1970s. It emphasized speedy development by raising efficiency, relaxing the cumbersome planning and bureaucratic controls that had hobbled performance, and making the system more responsive to popular demands.

[25] For instance, Water Pollution Prevention and Control Law, Marine Environmental Protection Law, Air Pollution Prevention and Control Law and Mineral Resources Law, etc.

[26] Wang Canfa, ‘Chinese environmental law enforcement: Current deficiencies and suggested reforms’, *Vermont Journal of Environmental Law*, 8, 2006, p. 194.

[27] See Jolene Lin, ‘Climate governance in China: Using the “Iron Hand”’, in Benjamin J. Richardson (ed.), *Local Climate Change Law: Environmental Regulation in Cities and Other Localities,* Edward Elgar Publishing, 2012, pp. 1–3.

come into force on January 1, 2015 and apply to almost every article of the current law in due course.

Background and process The progressive amendment was launched three years ago when China was suffering perennially severe pollution on a national scale, in particular in respect of water and air pollution. 'Since *PRC Environmental Protection Law* was passed in 1989, the country has become the world's second-largest economy and its biggest carbon emitter; decades of breakneck economic growth have left many of its rivers decimated and its cities perennially shrouded in smog.'[28] Taking smog as an example, Beijing and the surrounding regions often compound the particulates, known as a very unhealthy PM 2.5, these cities are also home to a large number of coal-burning power plants and industries including steel and cement that also burn coal.[29] Water pollution is another vital threat: rivers, a long list of both familiar and unfamiliar names, dried up at a worrying rate. The water environment is a source of utility, animal habitat and the ecologic sub-system, the security of which has gradually come to be regarded as crucial and taken into Chinese policy and law agenda: preventing the degradation of rural country water environment has become top of the list of priorities.

As a matter of fact, water and air pollution manifest the effects of the last 30 years industrialization in China. Of all potential pollutions, water and air pollution tend to trigger public crises, arousing great concern both at international and national levels. Right at the beginning of 2014, Lanzhou, a heavily industrialized city of 3.6 million people in the north-western province of Gansu, warned that potable water had been found to contain dangerous levels of benzene: a cancer-inducing chemical.[30] It was not only the panic among residents that undermined

---

28 See Jonathan Kaiman, 'China strengthens environmental laws', Chinese Legal Database, 25 April 2014, available at http://www.theguardian.com/environment/2014/apr/25/china-strengthens-environmental-laws-polluting-factories.

29 In Beijing, the situation is a little different: apart from the traditional industrial pollutants, car exhaust emissions significantly increase year-by-year, the situation was made worse by a local cold winter and the geographically mountainous environment.

30 According to the local authorities, benzene in tap water was 20 times above national safety levels (10 micrograms). Initial investigation showed that the high levels of benzene were caused by industrial contamination at one of the two culverts that transfer raw water from a sedimentation plant to the water treatment plant. The water supply company, Lanzhou Veolia Water Co, is majority-owned by the city government and was working to redirect to its water treatment plant water which usually went to a power plant. After the accident

government accountability, but also great concern was expressed on how to implement pollution control laws in a more integrated manner. The comprehensive EPL thus calls for the synergy objectives such as the supplying of city water, pollution treatments and government motors. Over the past years, domestic public heath and environment accidents have emerged, which urge, directly or indirectly, the legislatures to seriously review, re-evaluate and improve the existing EPL. In the meanwhile, Chinese environmental legislation is often produced in an attempt to meet international trends.[31]

The new amendment to EPL is essential. Despite the official start in 2011, the preparations were being made as early as the middle of the 1990s. From the 1995–2012 National People's Congresses (the Chinese highest legislative agency), 78 themes forwarded by 2,474 Representatives which are particularly concerned with revising the 1989 EPL.[32] The proposed themes reflect the appeals covering various social fields such as enterprises, NGOs and academics, with representatives from districts including Taiwan and Hainan.[33] The demonstrable amendment progress proves formidable; tensions can be seen where local and central authorities meet and where sectional interests intertwine (i.e., natural resources and environment protection organs). Wherever there are conflicts, there is likely to be a compromise. The divergence on the extent and scope of revision therefore remains throughout the drafting and reviewing process. The legislative agency for instance insisted on slight adjustments, while the voices from the grass roots and academics insisted on big changes that are likely to touch some core problems, such as the right to environment, state liability and penalties for polluters.[34] After the four reviews, the long-awaited expected EPL was eventfully approved at the

---

happened, officials warned citizens not to drink tap water for the next 24 hours. For more information, available at http://www.huffingtonpost.com/2014/04/11/lanzhou-water-benzene_n_5131728.html.

[31] See Wang Jin, *The Theoretical Basis of Chinese Environmental Law*, People Court Press, 2006, p. 27.

[32] 'Analysis on the newly revised environmental protection law', *Legal Education*, 28 April 2014, available at http://www.chinalawedu.com/web/21611/wa2014042809084585824759.shtml.

[33] Ibid.

[34] During this process, scholars like Cai Shouqiu, Wang Canfa and Wang Shuyi presented their disagreement for the 'limited amendment', the principal tone set by the drafting agency. It was agreed that that too many compromises under the limited amendment would result in a meaningless and obsolete legal document. See Jiang Wenzhang, 'Principles to amendment is unfixed yet, the new EPL will be postponed', *Economic Observing*, 27 April 2012.

11th Meeting of the Standing Committee of the Seventh National People's Congress on December 26, 1989, promulgated by Order No 22 of the President of the People's Republic of China on December 26, 1989, and effective on the date of promulgation.

Main contents, difficulties and open problems The revised law is deemed 'the strictest law' aimed at safeguarding the Chinese currently degrading the natural environment and continuous sound development.[35] There are three changes in this revision. Above all, stricter obligations are imposed on enterprises to prevent and control pollution. According to the 1989 EPL, enterprises should undergo environmental impact assessments before commencing construction projects; the new law also expands the scope of projects and clarifies the legal consequences of non-compliance.[36] On this basis, it further compels enterprises to establish environmental protection responsibility systems that specify the responsibilities of persons-in-charge. Any enterprises that fail to eliminate pollution in due course may be ordered to suspend or shut down its operations. And, punishments are tougher for environmental offences with the introduction a of daily penalty system. In addition to this, more specific requirements are introduced with regard to pollution-discharge licenses, emergency-response plans and environmental-information disclosure (which will be discussed in more detail later). Secondly, in the public policy, government is meant to support the development of the environment industry and encourage enterprises to take environmental-protection measures. It is important that, for the first time, the law has established clear requirements for ecological protection with the simple emphasis in official rhetoric: 'The new law says that economic and social development should be coordinated with environmental protection, and it encourages studies on the impact environmental quality has on public health, urging prevention and control of pollution-related diseases.'[37] Under the basic policy of ecological protection, greater authority and flexibility is given in the event of implementation: for instance in closing-down and detaining the illegally polluting devices. Thirdly, China is becoming closer to the rest of the world by setting out public interest litigation. The theoretical basis behind public interest litigation is the

---

[35] 'China enacts the strictest environmental protection law', *Xinhua News*, 24 April 2014, available at http://news.xinhuanet.com/legal/2014-04/24/c_1110399677.htm.

[36] Environmental Protection Law(1989), art. 13.

[37] NPC Standing Committee chairman Zhang Dejiang said. See Kaiman, note 28 above.

right to the environment which, in China, is the latest emerging field that has yet to achieve a great improvement. To realize the right to environment on a down-to-earth ground, the revised law expands the scope of plaintiffs on the basis of current civil litigation procedures, which provides a legal channel for citizens and community groups to participate in environmental protection. A social organization is allowed to appeal to the court for acts that pollute the environment, damage the ecology, and harm public interest if it meets the conditions of several requirements.[38] According to the preliminary estimates, nearly 300 social organizations in China meet these requirements.

These changes reflect the government's will in the establishment of the Ecologic Civilization; it also means great challenges, particularly as far as implementation and enforcement are concerned. The term 'ecological protection', for instance, highlights a full-dimensional protection of the ecologic system and a holistic approach is thus needed to provide a better protection for air-ground, sea-land. The revised EPL in its overall structure, however, weighs pollution control more than ecologic protection as it transitionally is. The imbalance is likely to be corrected with upcoming single laws especially relevant to natural resources protection, as well as to the better understanding of the term 'environment'. Another example refers to enforcement measures: the environmental protection agency, which has the principal supervision and management of protecting the environment in China, is conferred with executive powers by the new law. Similar provisions appear in the *PRC Water Pollution Prevention and Control Law (2008)*, but result in a very limited influence.[39] It is therefore reasonable to question the effectiveness of enforcement measures taken by environmental protection agency. In the new context, the agency may be subject to administrative liability and/or public litigation,[40] due in reality to inadequate capability or willingness. As for public

---

[38] The 2014 Environmental Protection Law, art. 58. For example, the social organization must be registered in the civil administrative department of the local government, and the organization must have specifically engaged in public environment protection activities over five consecutive years without any violations.

[39] See Chang Jiwen, 'Highlights, difficulties and disappointments of the revised EPL', *China Environment*, 5, 2014.

[40] It is easier to solve the difficulties of carrying out enforcement measures among the small-and-middle enterprises, such as detaining, removing their polluting devices or even shutting them down, however, when it comes to some large, state-owned enterprises, environmental protection agency have to confront many obstacles to take the due measures because of the lack of countervailing powers.

interest litigation, many more details need to be formulated afterwards in the aspects of court procedures, burden of proof and the distribution of compensation. To solve this, the specialized rules for implementation or judicial interpretation will be promulgated in accordance with the 2014 EPL. It can be also seen that the amendment adopts a gradual approach to fulfill the principle-environmental democracy, by excluding the status of individuals in lawsuits.

In the spite of improvements, some key issues remain untouched in the new amendment to EPL. As aforementioned, the law has not confirmed and declared the rights to environment. However, at the international level, both the theory and practice about the rights to environment have been well developed. China on the one hand introduces certain basic rights such as the right to know, public participation and organizational rights to litigation, but, on the other hand, refuses to write the terms of the right to the environment in the final version of draft EPL. Nevertheless, as an individual and collective right, the right to environment is assumed to be foregone in the name of less tangible, spiritual values, enforcing substantive and procedural environmental rights, and even conflict resolution. With the clarification and development of environmental right, the space for bottom-up public supervision, particularly through the use of law and the courts, is and will be continuously widened.[41]

Moreover, the new law fails to frame the current governance system in which there is no clear division between a uniform and a sectional environment supervision and management. Namely, the intertwined interests among sectors fail to be coordinated in an effective manner. However, it is impossible for one amendment to adopt all sorts of opinions, handle every new phenomenon and to solve each single remaining problem. As a periodical important step, the 2014 EPL has made constructive achievements and will be discussed in this *Handbook* as needed.

1.1.2 The Evolution of Chinese Institutional Construction

In China, the progress of institutional construction concerning environment protection is not completed over night. Instead, it has experienced a prolonged, arduous time period. We can very briefly recall this progress from the viewpoints of legislature, administration and judiciary.

---

[41] Despite no comprehensive statistics on environment-related claims, court reports indicate that the number of claims relating to air, water and land pollution is increasing.

1.1.2.1 Overview – Three branches

Legislative branch At the central level, the highest body of the State is the NPC, which has the authority to enact all basic laws like environmental protection laws and to supervise their implementation in reality. Due to the limited conferences held by the NPC (once a year), most legislative activity is conducted by its Standing Committee who has the competence to pass laws except basic laws, and to interpret those basic laws. In China, the chief executive organ – the State Council – is authorized to enact administrative regulations pursuant to national and constitutional law. So far, a considerable number of administrative regulations as well as departmental regulations have been developed by the State Council administrative department of environmental protection individually or jointly with other relevant ministries, commissions and departments.

At the local level, provinces, autonomous regions and municipalities have local legislative powers, by which they allocate mandatory environment targets into the city and county level and for industrial sectors and major businesses in a consistent manner.[42] Considering the scope of this handbook, we will mainly focus on those statutory efforts made on a central scale and highlight those regional legislations of particular importance.

ADMINISTRATIVE AGENCY The administrative structure of China is the so-called centralistic system, as declared by the *PRC Constitution*.[43] Environmental governance is predominantly arranged in a five-tier hierarchical structure: central government, provincial, prefectural, county and township. The Beijing Government is at the top of this structure, issuing vertical directives to its branches throughout the country. As will be fully discussed in Chapter 2,[44] this top-down deployment has been instrumental in galvanizing local government action on environmental protection and pollution control, which historically have not been a priority.

In 1972, The State Council established a project-based institution: the Water Conservation Working Group became responsible as the first water pollution control project. On this basis, two years later a specialized

---

[42] The environment targets set by government at the top are obligatory. Sub-national governmental agencies are only authorized to establish local standards where no national standard exists, while more stringent standards should be established.

[43] PRC Constitution, art. 3.

[44] Chapter 2, Brief introduction to Chinese legal system.

institution: the Environment Protection Working Group was set up under the authority of the State Council. In the following ten years, the State Council's Environment Protection Working Group took charge of conducting, implementing and coordinating environment protection activities nationwide. In 1981, together with the State Family Planning Commission, it issued the Rules on Management of Construction Project and thus applied environment impact assessment (EIA) and the 'Three Simultaneous' system into approval for relevant projects.[45] Then, there was an apparent change: during the Sixth-Five Plan, China first integrated environment protection into the nation's social-economic development. The State Council's Environment Protection Working Group was therefore merged with several other organs such as the State Urban Construction Administration and State Construction Engineering Administration, ultimately resulting in the Ministry of Urban and Rural Construction and Environmental Protection. Along with the fact that environment protection was promulgated as a basic national policy, China had set up Environment Protection Agency (EPA) which is, in its very nature, subsidiary to the State Council. To enhance environmental legislations and implementation, the NPC then established the Environment and National Resource Protection Commission for coordinating all legislative activities in a comprehensive, systematic manner. By the end of the 1990s, China had conducted a reformation of the State Council, and simultaneously upgraded EPA into the State Environment Protection Administration (SEPA) in order to restrict and counter against the overheating of economic growth. From then on, China entered a revival era of environmental legislation and implementation. In 2008, the central government made a crucial decision to promote the SEPA into the Ministry of Environment Protection (MOEP). Instead of the subsidiary organ to the State Council, the MOEP in itself is a integral part of the State Council, which means the government duty of environment protection has been strengthened in planning, policy-making, implementing, coordinating and problem-solving. Nowadays, the MOEP plays the most significant role in environmental governance and implementation.

JUDICIAL COURT A judiciary aiming at dispute settlement is a powerful guarantee for environmental justice. In China, a four-level court system is

[45] 'Three Simultaneous' is the extension of the EIA. It is a term of art in Chinese environmental law. It means that for all new projects and for the modification or expansion of existing projects, the facilities to prevent pollution and other public hazards and other environmental protection facilities must be designed, developed and put to use simultaneously with the principal project.

in existence, including Basic Courts, Intermediate Courts, Provincial High Courts, and the Supreme People's Court. This system is vertical, led by the Supreme People's Court that itself is vested with the power to decide concrete cases and also with extensive interpretative powers. Below the national level, it consists of local people's courts and of courts having exclusive jurisdiction over cases involving disputes over maritime, forest, railway and military issues.[46] In general, they follow the principle of two instances of trails for final adjudication. As is commonly known, China belongs to civil law system in which cases play a marginal role. As a basic principle, no courts, except the Supreme People's Court, are authorized to interpret laws and are confined to the implementation process.[47] All these local courts are subject to, and supervised by the Supreme People's Court. The specific application of laws conducted in the judicial proceedings of the Supreme People's Court has binding force on all courts.

Court proceedings are perceived as a last resort. However, green litigation in China is a difficult business. As far as environmental law is concerned, it may authorize enforcement not only against private polluters, but also against the government agency responsible for administrating the environmental laws.[48] Environmental cases thus involve civil, criminal and administration litigation. For a long time, most of environmental litigation traditionally fell under the jurisdiction of the civil court in China.[49] But in 2007, the situation was fundamentally changed when the first environmental law division was established in Guiyang municipal intermediate people's court of Guizhou Province.[50] At the time of writing, more than 90 environmental courts have been established on a national scale and 11 of them have been in operation long enough for

---

[46] The Supreme People's Court in Beijing supervises the administration of justice by all subordinate 'local' and 'special' people's courts. These Courts of Special Jurisdiction comprise the Military Court of China (military), Railway Transport Court of China (railroad transportation) and Maritime Court of China (water transportation), and the Forest Court of China (established in forest areas particularly).

[47] Apart from the Supreme People's Court: its judicial interpretations are legally binding, which is equal to legislation.

[48] See Jonathan R. Nash, *Environmental Law and Policy*, Aspen Publisher, 2010, p. 28.

[49] This is because the traditional practice in the Chinese court system is to direct cases to separate civil, criminal or administrative divisions.

[50] The State Council's 'Decision on the Implementation of Scientific Development and Strengthening of Environmental Protection' specifically mentioned the 'promotion of environmental public interest litigation', 2005.

preliminary analysis of their experiences to be possible: two in Guizhou Province, one in Jiangsu Province, and eight in Yunnan Province.[51] While the traditional practice in the Chinese court system is to direct cases to separate civil, criminal or administrative divisions, these environmental courts have adopted new rules that allow them to accept and process *all* environmental cases in the aspects of standing, jurisdiction, and remedies, among other things.[52]

There is hardly any tradition of settling regulatory issues through courts and most polluters do not even acknowledge that violating environmental laws and regulations is a legal offence.[53]

In sum, it can be found that the Chinese environment protection under the current institutional construction is complicated, fragmented and sometimes disordered. Some institutions were established temporarily in the absence of a long-term plan. However, there is a general tendency that environment protection becomes more and more important in the China's central governance and legal construction. By virtue of the regime, the combination of legislative and executive powers, three branches are assumed to cooperate more closely and consistently in order to achieve a uniform environmental objective.

1.1.2.2 The combination of legislative and executive powers

Describing the Chinese current institutional system is not social ideology, but because of the necessity of capturing the big picture in which environmental laws are generated, developed and carried out. 'The Combination of Legislative and Executive Powers' provides the necessary

---

51 Environmental courts have also been established since mid-2009 in Zhangzhou, Fujian Province, available at http://www.enlaw.org/bmgl/wrfz/2010 05/ t20100525_21984.htm; in Tuorong, Fujian Province available at http://www.ndzrw.cn/sygl/dtxx/201003/117213.htm; in Nanjing, Fujian Province available at http://www.enlaw.org/bmgl/wrfz/201006/t20100606_22023.htm; in Liupanshui, Guizhou Province available at http://www.legaldaily.com.cn/zfb/content/2010-03/04/content_2072929.htm?node=20609; and in Qingdao, Shandong Province available at http://www.enlaw.org/bmgl/wrfz/201004/t20100414_21747.htm.

52 See Alex L. Wang and Jie Gao, 'Environmental courts and public interest litigation in China', *Court Innovation*, **3**:1, 2010, p. 39.

53 The principal mediating organs are the local environmental protection bureaus and the pollution monitoring stations, although most conflicts continue to be resolved through less formal mediation mechanisms in which the precise determination of rights and liabilities is less important than achieving a solution acceptable to all parties within a context structured by law, social custom, and economic reality.

political atmosphere and regime basis for Chinese environmental protection. Compared with the western 'Separation of Three Powers',[54] the Chinese regime – the combination of legislative and executive powers – was deeply embedded in traditional culture (highly centralized), recent history (revolution), and political claims of 'people are master'. Under this regime, the Congress as an elected representation agency has full powers, by which the state integrates law/decision-making into implementation/enforcement in a highly consistent term. The distinctive characteristics of this regime are: (1) the relational identity of Congress and administrative agency; (2) the unidirectional function of powers; (3) the highest status of representation agency.[55]

When it comes to environment protection legislation and practices, the typical regime 'Combination of legislative and executive powers' has a huge influence and the start and fast development of relevant legislation undoubtedly benefitted from this highly uniform system of power. The modern generation of environmental laws in China has been largely promoted by governments, in contrast to the environmental laws of most of its counterpart countries, in which civil society and democracy play an equally important role.[56] The absence of grass roots requests governments and their representation agency actively addressing environment problems that were, in fact, not very urgent because of poor industry in that special period.[57] Since then, governments have played a leading role in the environmental law making. In the meantime, China's sustainable development and environmental protection is deployed top-down. By virtue of the combination of legislative and executive powers, the obstacles to implementing and enforcing environmental laws both at central and local level could be reduced. Taking the legal branch as an example, China has a system of civil law in which cases play a marginal role. As a basic principle, Chinese courts are not authorized to interpret

---

[54] 'The separation of powers' often imprecisely used interchangeably with the balance of powers principle, is a model for the governance of a state (or who controls the state). The model was first developed in ancient Greece. Under this model, the state is divided into branches, each with separate and independent powers and areas of responsibility so that the powers of one branch are not in conflict with the powers associated with the other branches. The typical division of branches is into a legislature, an executive, and a judiciary. Nowadays, this high degree of separation of powers is found worldwide, including Chinese Hong Kong.

[55] Chapter 2. Brief introduction to Chinese legal system.

[56] Li Qijia, 'The speech on the inter-generation development of Chinese environmental law', *Shanghai University of Finance and Economics*, 2009.

[57] Ibid.

laws and are confined to the implementation process. Because of the limited role of the courts, one successful experience cannot be directly applied to another case: this leads to much inconsistent enforcement in practice. At the regional level, governments particularly have a considerable influence on the People's Court. 'It is not unusual for one court to fail to cooperate in the enforcement of the judgments made by higher and similar level courts. Few rules and guidelines are in place to manage the inconsistencies and conflicts that occur.'[58]

1.1.3 Striking Chinese Characters

There are several fundamental characters about the legal system of which we must be aware before we embark on our analysis of Chinese environmental law.

Despite its youthful framework, the Chinese environmental law system is rather broad and vague and thus appears boundless. Most environmental laws have been in existence for quite a long time, and while the general and broad system of environmental law in China remains complex, its understanding is further confounded by periodic statutory amendment, ongoing changes to existing regulations, and the continuing introduction of new ones. In principle, its current system of environmental laws consists of: (1) legislation addressing comprehensive environmental protection; (2) specialized legislation for pollution prevention, natural resource protection and conservation and; (3) the ratification of international conventions and treaties concerning environmental protection.[59] A comprehensive list of environmental legislation is to be found in the Legal Table at the beginning of this *Handbook*.

It is noticeable that Chinese environment law is in particular policy-oriented. Instruments including plans, strategies, and directives, are frequently used to set national goals for environmental protections related to aspects, to be discussed later, like natural environment conservation,

---

[58] See Derek Bosworth and Deli Yang, 'Intellectual property law, technology flow and licensing opportunities in the People's Republic of China,' *International Business Review* 9, 2000, p. 474. The local governments' heavy influence on the courts is not limited to financial matters; in addition to the fact that court operating expenses are funded by local district authorities, local citizens also join the judge as 'people's assessors' in hearings, and local party officials generally have a significant impact on the jurisprudence and career advancement.

[59] In a broad sense, this system also includes the expansion of environmental protection into other areas of legislations like litigation laws, trade laws, administrative laws.

pollution control and prevention, and resource saving. Concurrently policy arrangements are centred on Hu Jintao's official doctrines of 'Harmonious Society' and the 'Scientific Development Concepts'.[60] The latest Xi-Li administration just forwarded the new strategies of 'Five In One Pattern' and 'Establishment of Beautiful China'.[61] To achieve these, governments have continued to roll out five-year plans and in recent years a start has been made on integrating environmental goals in these plans.

Compliance weakness is a continuing bottleneck.[62] Although recently China has been actively developing its environmental law system and has made massive achievements, relevant adherence is far from being effective and efficient. Legislative objectives remain unachieved for the ecosystem is deteriorating as a whole, even with localized areas of improvements. Most recently, the Chinese Government has identified inadequate enforcement as one of the key factors in the deteriorating environmental situation. The 11th and 12th Five-Year Plans strategically emphasized the need to strengthen environmental enforcement and compliance assurance.[63] As a consequent phenomenon, the ineffectiveness has been affected by a wide coverage of elements including regulatory, administrative and practical ones. In this regard, this *Handbook* will review the current environmental regulations in a comprehensive manner so that statutory coherence as well as conflicts tend to be examined as expected.

On a related point, public participation is but limitedly played although increasing step by step. Unlike the Western world and Japan, where modern environmental law has emerged,[64] the role of the grassroots has

---

[60] The 'Harmonious Society' and 'Scientific Development Concept' serve as guidelines indicating a shift from 'promoting all-out economic growth to solving worsening social tensions'. See Xing Zhigang, "Plan unveiled to build harmonious society", *China Daily*, 12 October 2006, p. 1, available at http://www.Chinadaily.com.cn/China/2006-10/12/.

[61] In the Eighteen Report, it aims to promote the strategic adjustment of economic structure, promote the integration of urban and rural development, ecological civilization mentioned as a new height. More information is available at http://www.gov.cn/18da/.

[62] Part IV: Compliance and Enforcement.

[63] China.org.cn, Green strategy, available at http://english.gov.cn/2006-02/08/content_182528.htm.

[64] See Li Qijia, 'The second generation of modern environmental law', Academic Report In Shanghai University of Finance And Economics, 2009. According to Li, local citizens, in the Western world and Japan, are key participators to conducting modern environmental protection activities and

been historically ignored in China, particularly in policy-making and implementation and, in general, public participation appears weak.[65] Many citizens in China suffer from environmental problems relating to water, air and solid waste pollution. They are often unaware of their environmental rights or lack knowledge about how to defend them. Nevertheless, this situation has been reversed slightly. The frequency and seriousness of pollutions accidents recently have violated the normal life of people, arousing their awareness of their environmental rights. Appeals on environmental issues are increasing. As far as the relevant statistics are concerned, in 2007, National Environmental Disputes complaints and petition letters surpassed 70 million and reached 80 million by 2009.[66] The growing environmental awareness as well as the ability to challenge environmental rights essentially promotes thc recent development of environment law, due to the fact that they aim to improve the access to environmental justice. Indeed, 'public participation requires a balance between economic interests and environmental protection'.[67]

China's efforts to protect environment and regulatory establishment are embedded in the international society's actions. As well recognized, China plays a proactive role in environmental diplomacy. Driven by a perception of itself as a 'responsible big country', China is now the party of a wide range of Multinational Environmental Agreements (MEAs) which cover nearly all important domains such as marine protection, climate change, biodiversity and trans-boundary movements of hazardous wastes, etc. The progress of framing those MEAs into the domestic legal system in part enhances the quality of local legislations. As a matter of fact, the several advances of environmental legislations and/or amendments happened as a result of China's accession to international environment conferences. Likewise, Chinese endeavours in environment protection and relevant legal construction will certainly contribute to the global efforts of improving the earth stewardship.

---

related legislations. To a large extent, they drive this process by spontaneous behaviours as well as the cooperation of authorized governments.

[65] See Wang Canfa, note 26 above, p. 172. Public participation can improve local administrative and legal transparency in implementation. For instance, it can promote the multidirectional flow of information in disclosure and encourage transparent communication with external actors.

[66] China Environment Forum, Event on Environmental Public Interest Law, 29 November 2012, available at http://www.wilsoncenter.org/article/event-environmental-public-interest-law-China.

[67] Wang, above note 65, p. 172.

1.2 WHAT IS MEANT BY THE 'HANDBOOK'?

Defining the term 'handbook' presents certain difficulties. However, as a starting point, we can tackle it by distinguishing what is not a handbook.[68] At the moment, there are several academic works on Chinese environmental law, but no such efforts aim at an overarching framework of Chinese environmental law. In this term, it could be concluded that the handbook is a combination of theories with practices of Chinese environmental law, and with a focus on the introduction and necessary comment on relevant laws and regulations and their latest developments.

The *Chinese Environmental Law Handbook* is intended to serve the needs of environmental academics and practitioners by providing comprehensive guidance on the complex array of Chinese main land environmental laws and implementing regulations that environment professionals from both domestic and international must know, or master for the purposes such as research, consulting, compliance and learning. Moreover, the *Handbook* aims also to strike a balance between practical preoccupations and critical or theoretical reflection.

1.3 SCOPE AND STRUCTURE OF THIS HANDBOOK

1.3.1 Scope

As aforementioned, the *Handbook* is designed as a whole to provide readers with both a 'bigger picture' of Chinese environmental law and a more in-depth understanding of its preoccupations. The normative statues enacted at a central level are thus a major focus of this book rather than regional legislations, unless the latter prove to be of particular importance and completely necessary to explain certain problems. Also considering the scope of this *Handbook*, we are rather cautious to indentify, assess and incorporate personal opinions in the process of analysis. The book benefits from the expertise of a significant number of authors.

1.3.2 Structure

In total, the book has been structured into 19 distinct chapters, each of which essentially corresponds to a particular domain of environment protection like general issues, pollution control, natural conservation,

---

[68] See James F. Berry and Mark S. Dennison, *The Environmental Law and Compliance Handbook*, McGraw-Hill, 2000, pp. 5–9.

liability and international environmental issues. This form of organization should enable readers to easily locate the laws and regulations governing a particular issue.

Chapter 1 – Introduction, as a starting point, this section describes the context of China's environmental policies and laws. Discussion is mostly on the historical evolution and institutional structure. Several essential characters are then presented in order to offer readers more common sense and better understanding. In addition to this, Chapter 1 also serves to explain the purpose and scope of this book by exploring what constitutes a 'handbook', the general structure of the entire book and specific rational behind it.

Chapter 2 presents a brief introduction to the Chinese current legal system, which provides a general picture of both the statutory and institutional arrangements in concurrent China. This Part is theoretically important for the *Handbook*, since it sculptures a basic setting in which Chinese environmental laws are generated, developed, exercised and implemented.

Starting from Chapter 3, the subsequent chapters focus on specific domains of Chinese environment protection activities: pollution control and prevention, natural resources conservation and climate mitigation and adaptation. Above all, Chapters 3, 4, 5, 6 and 7 deal with pollution control laws, consisting of five chapters which explain laws promulgated to control the adverse impacts of certain types of human activities (i.e., industrial and municipal) on the environment. Certain pressing issues are comprehensively and constructively discussed in this chapter, for instance air pollution, soil pollution, water unitization and ocean pollution.

Besides, traditional pollutions such as solid waste, toxic and harmful substance, on which legislations are also described herein. A host of critical regulatory instruments for instance environmental standards, Discharge Permit System (DPS), 'Three Synchronizations' ('3S') and Environmental Impact Assessment (EIA) are to be surveyed accordingly. This part is a center of domestic environmental laws.

Chapter 8 is a full discussion of Chinese legislative efforts at addressing climate change. China was reported to surpass the US and became the largest emitter in the world. Its domestic endeavors to reduce GHG emissions have certainly drawn great attention worldwide. Chapter 8 examines the latest climate and energy policies and legislation in a systematic manner. Several vital initiatives launched at the moment are also mentioned in the chapter in order to provide full information on the relevant implementation and enforcement.

The following chapters address various environmental elements conservation with the aim of enhancing their ecological functions. There are in total six chapters (Chapters 9 to 14), each of which essentially corresponds to a particular type of environmental medium (i.e., land, fresh water, forest, minerals and biodiversity) or specialized area presently highlighted (i.e., protected area). A great emphasis is placed on the ecological function of environment elements in these chapters. Taking ocean as an example, Chapter 3 discusses the heated marine pollution sources and relevant measures in China, while Chapter 10 highlights the marine ecological conservation as well as marine living resources, in particular in key sea areas.

Chapter 15 is entitled Environmental liability. With a normative survey, it is time to focus on a real world scenario: compliance and implementation. The key to comply with and implement environmental laws is environmental liability. Over the last 30 years, a relatively mature environmental liability system has been established in China during its long march towards the 'rule of law'. In this chapter, three main forms of environmental liabilities – civil liabilities, administrative liabilities and criminal liabilities – are discussed in substantial detail.

Using Chapter 15 as a base, Chapter 16 further explores the dispute settlement mechanism arising from environmental rights and obligations current in China. Both litigious methods and alternative disputes resolutions (ADRs) are examined comprehensively in this chapter, which also reviews the substantive and procedural provisions relating to civil actions and administrative actions prescribed by the laws, regulations and governmental documents. In particular, it places the discussion on Chinese continuous attempts to create environmental courts as well as the potential problems concerned.

Chapters 17 and 18 shed light on the international perspective and rounds out the coverage of the *Handbook* with a discussion of international environment law and China's position. To date it is no doubt that China has an important role to play in environmental geopolitics, and MEAs continuously constitute an important source of the Chinese legal basis of environmental protection. In this regard, Chapter 17 looks at the broad and general policies in the environment-related foreign affairs like principles, strategies, plans and standpoint and attitude, while Chapter 18 focuses more on legal issues such as MEAs and their domestic integration.

The final chapter, Chapter 19 concludes the book by generalizing some fundamental points in China's environmental laws. Based on this, there are certain positional tendencies to be traced in this demonstrative progress which we are particularly pleased to share.

2. The Chinese legal system

Wang Huanhuan

2.1 OVERVIEW

A modern legal system with a complicated structure is becoming established in China, a country with dramatic social, economic, cultural and political changes. It is totally new compared with the legal systems in traditional China before the liberalization and even the first three decades after the liberalization.[1] The Cultural Revolution from 1966 to 1976 overwhelmingly undermined the unstable and fragile legal system that existed. How to fill the legal vacuum generated in the ten years was brought onto the priority list of the country, especially since the Reform and Opening in 1978. After that, China has strongly embraced the notion that a solid legal system is required for further development. The revival and improvement of the legal system further accelerated with the Opening and Reform proceeded and China's entry into WTO (World Trade Organization) in 2001.

Retrospectively, establishment of the Chinese modern legal system is quite a different process from that of the western countries. On the one hand, it has only spent 30 years or so to accomplish most of the process. On the other, it is mainly pushed by state power[2] and thus proceeds step by step according to the legislative planning. Yet, it is hard to conclude that legislation in China is totally blind to the demands of legal reform within the social development process. After labouring for several decades, the White Paper on Socialist Legal System with Chinese Characters issued in October 2011 announced that the 'legal system with Chinese characteristics' has been established in China. The declaration is backed by the formulation of the Constitution and 240 pieces of laws,

---

[1] Several observers have pointed out the differences, see Eric W. Orts 'The rule of law in China', *Vanderbilt Journal of Transnational Law*, **34**: 43–115, 2001; Volker Behr, 'Development of a new legal system in the People's Republic of China', *Louisiana Law Review*, 67, pp. 1161–80, 2007.

[2] Many papers clearly explored the process, see Albert H. Y. Chen 'Towards a legal enlightenment: Discussions in contemporary China on the rule of law', *Pacific Basin Law Journal*, **17** (126), 1999.

706 pieces of administrative regulations, as well as more than 8,600 pieces of local decrees regulating the society in a broad spectrum.

This chapter aims to provide an overview of the current fledgling, although thriving, legal system, or legal institutions – statutes, courts for instance – in a broader sense, in China with emphasis on environmental law where appropriate. The issues, such as how laws are promulgated, which laws are currently in effect, who is responsible for the execution of laws and how the judiciary system works in China are the main topics. Specifically, the chapter proceeds as follows. Part 2 begins with a structural description of laws currently in effect in accordance with the customized division of the legal system. Then, Part 3 reviews the legislative branch including the allocation of legislative power, the legislation procedure and the rules resolving conflicts of legal norms. Then the chapter will examine the judiciary system containing the courts and procuratorates in China. Finally, the role of the executive branch in China's legal system will be analyzed.

2.2 CURRENT LEGAL FRAMEWORK

The legal system in China is, similar to other countries with civil law systems, 'an organic, comprehensive and unified whole consisting of well-defined divisions or branches of law into which all laws maybe classified in an exhaustive manner'.[3] However, the division of current laws distinguishes one from the other among observers.[4] In March 2011, Wu Bangguo, Former Chairman of Standing Committee of the National People's Congress (NPC), stated in the work report of the Standing Committee submitted at the Fourth Session of the Eleventh NPC that China's legal system has seven major branches. The categorization is viewed as the official method especially when it is reaffirmed by White Paper on Socialist Legal System with Chinese Character issued by Information Office of the State Council in October 2011.

---

[3] Albert H. Y. Chen, *An introduction to the legal system of the People's Republic of China*, Butterworths Asia: Singapore, 1992, p. 185.

[4] Zhang Zhiming, 'The establishment of legal system in China in transition', *China Juris.* 2009(2): 140–58.

2.2.1 Constitutional Law System

The constitutional law system contains 39 pieces of laws (16 per cent of current laws) including *the PRC Constitution (1982)* and related laws. The *PRC Constitution (1982)* is the fundamental source of state authority.

China has historically enacted Constitutions of 1954, 1975, 1978 and 1982. The *PRC Constitution (1982)* is currently in effect. It has four chapters (138 articles) articulating the general principles of the country and the legal system, the basic rights and duties of the citizens and the structure of the state. Notably, the constitutional principles for socialist China such as rule of law, Four Basic Principles as well as Opening and Reform are incorporated. Constitution in China has a serial of amendments passed in 1988, 1993, 1999 and 2004. As the Preamble of the Constitution provides, the Constitution is 'the fundamental law of the state and has supreme legal authority'. Article 5 further states: 'All state organs, the armed forces, all political parties and public organizations and all enterprises and institutions must abide by the Constitution and the law … No organization or individual is privileged to stride beyond the Constitution or the law.' Among others, the 2004 amendment added the provisions concerning protection of private property rights and human rights, as well as the improvement of social security.

The related constitutional laws aiming to guarantee the enforcement of the Constitution and the operation of state power mainly consist of four parts: (1) organic laws such as Election Law, Organic Law of the NPC, Organic Law of the State Council, Organic Law of Court, Organic Law of the procuratorate, Legislation Law and Rules on Standing Committee of NPC provide for the establishment, structure, duties and basic operating rules of the governmental organs; (2) Law on Ethnic Autonomous Region, Basic Law of Hong Kong Special Administrative Region (SAR), Basic Law of Macau SAR, Organic Law on Villager Committee articulating the legal regimes on Ethnic Autonomy, Special Administrative Regions and Citizen Autonomy in China; (3) laws concerning the sovereignty, land and national security including the Law on National Flag and Law on Nationality; and (4) law on citizen's basic political rights such as Election Law.

2.2.2 Administrative Law System

The administrative law system dealing with government agencies and their responsibility has 77 pieces of laws (33 per cent of current laws). They could be categorized as general administrative law and specific administrative law. General administrative law includes: (1) organic law concerning the establishment, roles, powers and duties of administrative agencies and their personnel; (2) law concerning regulatory power of government agencies involving administrative permit, punishment, supervision and so forth; and (3) law of administrative remedy involving the administrative litigation, reconsideration, and state compensation. Specific administrative laws are those regulating affairs including public and national security, statistics, post, customs, military affair, education, science and technology, culture, sanitary, sports etc.

In 1989, China enacted the Administrative Litigation Law allowing citizens to bring lawsuits challenging specific administrative action. Later in 1994, the State Compensation Law was enacted to address state liability covering the claimants, liable organs of the compensation and the scope, procedure of administrative and criminal compensation. The Administrative Review Law was then formulated to provide for intra-agency review of administrative actions. Another important administrative law is the Administrative Penalty Law passed in 1996 which provides the procedure of punitive measures imposed by administrative agencies. The administrative Licensing Law, adopted in 2003, aims to set up a general framework for administrative licensing.

2.2.3 Civil and Business Law System

The civil law system in China functionally encompasses various legal mechanisms covering property rights, marriage, inheritance, adoption, protection of intellectual property rights, tort, etc. Commercial law encompasses such titles as company, tickets, insurance, securities and guarantee in the sphere of business transactions is another branch within the system.

In 1986, the General Principles of Civil Law was promulgated. Despite the generality conveyed by the title, it is the most basic and comprehensive law in the field in the past two and half decades.[5] It contains 156 articles including chapters on basic principles and objectives, the status of natural persons, the status of legal persons, civil behaviour, civil rights and civil liability. In 1999, the Contract Law was enacted merging the former Economic Contract Law, Foreign Contract Law and Technology Contract Law to unify the concept of contract into the civil law line. After intense discussion, the NPC in 2007 passed the Property Law followed by the enactment of Tort Law. It is noteworthy that a unified

---

[5] Only two articles were slightly revised by the 'Decision by the NPC Standing Committee on amending several laws' in 2009.

civil code codifying existing laws providing consistent provisions is under draft. However, when it will enter the legislative agenda is still unclear.

The Company Law (1993, revised in 2004 and 2005) is one of the major commercial laws to regulate corporate governance including the creation, structure, operation, dissolution, and related issues of limited liability companies and joint stock companies. The new Company Law in 2005 revised approximately 90 per cent of the provisions attempting to decentralize the regulatory power of the state over companies, to abolish complicated approval procedure of setting up joint stock companies, to accomplish corporation governance structures, and to strengthen the protection of shareholders' rights. The objective of the new company law is enhanced by the reform on commercial registration system promoted since 2014.

2.2.4 Economic Law System

The goal of establishing a market economy in China requires a uniform and impartial rule of law economy. Economic law in China, accordingly, mainly copes with the influences over practitioner of the market and the market itself exerted by the state. According to theoretic investigation, it mainly regulates:

> vertical economic relations or economic management relations between higher level and lower level of the planned sector of the economy as well as some horizontal relations that are closely related to vertical economic relations such as contracts entered into in furtherance of state plans. In addition, some internal structures of economic organizations as well as organizations related to foreign economic activities, such as Sino-foreign joint ventures, also fall within the category of economic law.[6]

The system with 60 laws and a large amount of regulations and local laws bestrides the following spectrum: (1) laws on macroeconomic regulatory tools such as Budget Law, Audit Law, Law on the People's Bank of China, Price Law, Individual Income Tax Law, and Law on Supervising Commercial Banks; (2) laws on market and competition rules including Antimonopoly Law (2007), Law on Protection of Customers' Rights, Law on Product Quality, Advertising Law, Law on Bid Invitation and Bidding, Government Procurement Law, and Investment

---

[6] Daniel C. K. Chow, *The Legal System of the People's Republic of China in a Nutshell* (Second edition), West Academic Publishing, 2009, pp. 330–1.

Fund Law and so forth; (3) laws promoting Opening-up and international trade including Law on Joint-venture, Law on Foreign Corporations, and Foreign Trade Law; (4) laws boosting industrial development, for instance, Agriculture Law, Railway Law, Electricity Law, Coal Law, Construction Law, Real Estate Law, Harbour Law; and (5) laws on standardization and uniform technical rules including Standardization Law, Statistics Law, Mapping Law, etc.

Anti-unfair competition law enacted in 1993 witnesses China's transition from planning economy to market economy. It encompasses prohibition for unauthorized use of trade names, packaging or trade dress thereby causing confusion, commercial biding, false or exaggerated advertising, unauthorized use of trade secrets, and smear campaigns. Price Law of 1997 aims at establishing a market-oriented pricing mechanism under the macroadjustment of the state. It therefore regulates price competition and improper pricing activities including price fixing, predatory pricing and price discrimination.[7] The Foreign Trade Law is designed to fulfil China's international commitment in cross-boundary trade.

2.2.5 Social Law System

Up to the end of August 2011, China had enacted 18 social laws regulating labour protection, social security, social work and charity to guarantee equality and justice of the society. To note, Labour Law, Labour Contract Law, Labour Union Law, Employment Promotion Law, Law on Working Safety, Law on Safety in Mines, Law on Prevention and Control of Occupational Disease, Law on Mediation and Arbitration of Labour Dispute are enacted to integrate regulations on labour protection, labour sanitary and safety, occupational training, and labour dispute resolution, labour supervision to protect the rights of workers. Social Security Law, Law on Protection of Disabilities, Law on Protection of Juveniles, Law on Protection of Aged People's Rights, Law on Protection of Women's Rights aims to provide service or benefit for those falling into the disadvantageous condition of property, disability, unemployment, old age and others. Law on Donation for Public Interests, Law on Red Cross Foundation, and Law on Social Relief are under deliberation recently.

---

[7] Salil K. Mehra and Meng Yanbei 'Against antitrust functionalism: reconsidering China's Antimonopoly Law', *Virginia Journal of International Law*, **49** (2): 380–429, 2008.

Labour Contract Law (in effect in 2008) is enacted to emphasize the importance of the labour contract system, to specify the rights and obligations of the employee and employer and to protect the rights of workers in signing, implementation, and termination of labour contacts. It also affirms the irreplaceable role of labour unions in labour relations. The requirements that employers should contribute a certain share to the social security account of the workers and should offer a wage above a minimum wage are other noteworthy points enshrined. Another important law newly passed within the civil law system is the Social Security Law (entered into force from 1 July 2011), it is the first comprehensive law to address social security and related regulatory matters. In addition to consolidating current rules, the law also contains some pivotal principles and provisions. For example, it clarifies, for the first time that the social security system in China contains five mandatory types of insurances. It also regulates the transfer of individual social security accounts and liabilities of the employer for breaching social security law.

2.2.6 Criminal Law System

The Criminal Law was adopted in 1979 and received a major revision in 1997 supplemented by another eight amendments in December 1999, August 2001, December 2001, December 2002, February 2005, June 2006, February 2009 and February 2011 sorted by date. The Criminal Law has two parts: general provisions and specific provisions. The general provisions mainly deal with basic principles of criminal law, definition of criminal offence, types, level and application of criminal sanction. Criminal offence is defined as an act that endangers the society and thus punishable according to law. The act could be intentional or sometimes, out of negligence. The principal types of sanctions, as one of the two categories, include public surveillance, criminal detention, fixed-term imprisonment, life imprisonment and death penalty. The supplementary types of sanctions, on the other hand, are fines, deprivation of political rights and confiscation of property. The seriousness of the consequences of an act could be measured by a fixed amount of currency or several criteria, which will trigger the application of criminal law. The specific provisions provides 452 specific offenses after the 2011 Amendment ranging from crimes of counterrevolution and crimes of endangering public security to crimes of undermining the socialist economic order, crimes of infringing rights of the person and the democratic rights of citizens, crimes of property violation, crimes of obstructing the administrative of public order, crimes of endangering national defence, crimes of bribe, crime of dereliction of duty, and crime of the serviceman's violation of duty.

2.2.7 Procedure Law

China has three major procedure regimes, the civil procedure law led by Civil Procedure Law surrounded by Arbitration Law and a serial of judicial interpretations on evidence, mediation, and execution of judgments; the administrative procedure law including Administrative Procedure Law, Administrative Review Law and the procedural provisions in other administrative substantive law; and the Criminal Procedure Law in the criminal litigation system.

The Civil Procedure Law has four parts. The first is general provisions providing the jurisdiction of courts, trial panel, litigants, evidence and other requirements; the second stipulates the trial procedures ranging from ordinary trial, summary process, appeal, and specific types of suits; the third states the enforcement procedure of the judgments, and the fourth articulates special procedures for foreign parties. The basic procedure for hearing cases is as follows: in a trial of first instance, there is court investigation and crossing debate followed by judgment. A case might enter into appeal process upon decision of the parties. Pre-trial mediation is encouraged to efficiently solve civil disputes.

The Criminal Procedure Law was passed in 1979 and revised in 1996. It is the main regulatory basis for investigation, prosecution, adjudication and sentencing of criminal cases. The public security organs are involved in the initiation and investigation stages of most cases, and the procuratorate investigates some cases and handles the prosecution phase of all criminal cases. Courts are in charge of criminal trials. The proceeding of the trial is similar to that of the civil litigation.

The Administrative Procedure Law is designed to allow ordinary citizens to bring lawsuits in front of the courts against administrative agencies for specific administrative actions including administrative sanction, administrative compulsory measures, violation of commercial autonomy, permitting, refusal to perform duties, state compensation, illegally imposing duties to citizens, and other infringements of 'other personal and property rights'. Another remedy for illegal or inappropriate administrative decisions is to resort to internal administrative review in accordance with the Administrative Review Law.

Recently, the Civil Procedure Law and Criminal Procedure Law have been revised while the Administrative Procedure Law has been listed on the revision agenda of NPC. The key points of the revision of the Civil Procedure Law are regimes concerning summary procedure, evidence, pre-trial procedure, public interest litigation, judiciary affirmation of outside mediation, re-trial, and enforcement of adjudication. The provision on public interest litigation has far-reaching significance for environmental public interest litigation and has been complemented by Article 58 of Law on Environmental Protection. The major revision of the Criminal Procedure Law aiming to harmonize criminal penalty and human rights protection mainly involves the evidence, defence, investigation measures, compulsory measures, trial process, enforcement, and special procedure. The revision of the Administrative Procedure Law will put more emphasis on protection of citizens' rights against administrative power, making general administrative decisions challengeable, and on the possibility of increasing litigants.[8]

It is noteworthy that environmental law is included in the administrative law system in this official division of current law, largely due to the overwhelming command-and-control-regulation instruments employed in current environmental laws. In fact, contentions about whether environmental law should be independent or affiliated to other branches of law had already arisen in the 1980s. Many scholars attempted to prove its independence arguing that environmental law had expanding laws and regulations, comprehensive regulatory instruments, unique legal doctrine, while embracing a coherent aim of environmental protection.[9] Later in 1997, The Discipline Catalogue of Postgraduate Degree Awarding jointly issued by National Education Commission[10] and Academic Degrees Committee of the State Council classified environmental law as independent discipline of second tier under the major of law. However, the white paper provoked the controversy again already eased after the independence environmental law gained in legal education and academic research. The variation of the division approach underestimates the importance of environmental law regulation or even ignores other regulatory doctrines such as unique environmental liability regime, environmental criminal law, and economic or cooperative forms of regulation

---

[8] Ying Songnian, 'Key points in revising Administrative Procedure Law', *Legal Daily*, 25 August, 2011.

[9] Wen Boping, 'Environmental should be an independent division of law', *Legal Magazine*, 1980 (2); Cai Shouqiu, 'The independency of Environmental Law as a Division of Law', *Legal Research*, 1981(3); Xu Xiangmin and Gong Gu, Thinking on Environmental Legal System, *Legal Forum*, 2009 (2).

[10] The National Education Commission was replaced by the Ministry of Education in 1998.

and accordingly overestimates the traditional instruments in administrative law regime. It might cause confusion and restrictions to development of environmental law, its academic research and legal education.

2.3 LEGAL BRANCH[11]

Laws in China may take the form of laws, regulations, decrees, rules, and decisions to name a few. Differing from sharp separation of legislative, executive and judicial powers in many western countries, legislative authority in China is allocated among many organs. The NPC and its Standing Committee are accorded the supreme legislative power. Meanwhile, other organs, such as the State Council and subordinate departments, the People's Congress and government of provinces and other authorized cities, People's Congress and government of Ethnic Autonomous Region, and Central Military Commission and its divisions share the legislation power in a certain sphere. Therefore, this part mainly examines legislatures and legislation procedure after discussion on hierarchy of legal norms in China.

The *PRC Constitution (1982)* is the fundamental law within the legal system providing for the basic rights and duties of citizens and the structure of the state. It is seen as the 'mother law' setting roots and outlines for other legal norms. Basic laws regulate the most pivotal areas of the state including criminal and civil affairs, organization of state agencies are enacted by the NPC. The Standing Committee promulgates laws such as Nationality Law, Bankruptcy Law, Marriage Law, and Education Law falling into the type of 'other laws'. Administrative regulations are made by the State Council. Local decrees are enacted by local people's congresses. Departmental rules and local rules are respectively issued by department of the state or by local people's government.

Since the hierarchy of laws is directly determined by the levels of legislative organs, the more superior the organ is, the higher level and broader validity the law has. The following parts will examine the legislative power of a variety of authorities entitled by the Constitution and Law on Legislation.

---

[11] The arrangement of the following three parts focusing on the legislative, judicial and executive branch cannot easily be equal with the equilibrium of the three power forms. As a matter of fact, the judicial and executive powers both originate from the legislative branches, say the People's Congress and its Standing Committee at different levels.

2.3.1 State Legislation

2.3.1.1 National People's Congress

The Constitution and Legislation Law endow the NPC, the highest organ of state power and national legislature with a broad range of powers to decide the most fundamental issues in the country. The Congress consists of delegates elected by provinces, minority autonomous regions, municipalities and the army meeting once a year. As for law-making, it has the power: to amend the Constitution; to enact basic laws; and to enact other laws if necessary.[12] Clearly, its power in amending the Constitution represents its supreme legislative power. Once an amendment bill is submitted by the Standing Committee or one-fifth of the delegates, the Constitution can be revised with a two-thirds majority vote. The NPC is also entitled with the power to supervise the implementation of the Constitution.

Apart from enacting and amending basic laws, the NPC also has the authority to enact and amend 'other laws' on two occasions: first, laws on the power and working procedure of the NPC and on other important issues mainly concerning rights and duties of the citizens. As for the second occasion, the 'other laws' such as Organic Law of the Villager Committee and Law on Administrative Penalty, generally fall within the authority of the Standing Committee, however, they are, de facto, enacted by the NPC when listed on the legislation agenda of the NPC.

---

[12] Laws in China, as the most important source of the legal system, are divided into 'basic laws' and 'other laws' enacted and revised, generally by the NPC and its Standing Committee respectively. The only criteria to distinguish whether a law is 'basic law' or 'other law' is the importance of the issue regulated rather than the legislator. The major reason is that occasionally the NPC might enact and amend 'other laws' while the Standing Committee might amend 'basic' laws when necessary. According to art. 8 of the Legislation Law, the following areas can only be regulated by laws: (1) national sovereignty; (2) creation, organization and duties of People's Congress, government, People's Court, and People's Procuratorate at all levels; (3) ethnic autonomous region, special administrative and citizen autonomy; (4) criminal and criminal penalty; (5) derivation of citizen's political rights, compulsory measures and punishment relating to constrain of personal freedom; (6) expropriation of non-state-owned property; (7) basic civil regime; (8) basic economic regimes and regimes relating to finance, tax, custom, and international trade; (9) litigation and arbitration; and (9) others. One of the main criticisms challenging the exercising of state legislative authority is that the boundary of the 'basic laws' and 'other laws' is ambiguous.

The NPC also has the authority to amend or abrogate any laws enacted by its Standing Committee and to nullify any autonomous decree or specific rule in Ethnic Autonomous Region approved by its Standing Committee which contravene Constitution or the second paragraph of Article 66 of Legislation Law, stated in Article 88 of Legislation Law.

As one of the special committees of the NPC, the Environmental Protection and Resources Conservation Committee takes charge of research, deliberating and drafting bills on environmental and natural protection. It is under the leadership of the Standing Committee when the NPC is not in session.

2.3.1.2 Standing Committee of the National People's Congress

The Standing Committee is the permanent body of the NPC. When the NPC is not in session, the Standing Committee exercises the supreme legislative power supervised by the NPC, without, however, going beyond the limitations set by the Constitution and Legislation Law or the authority of the NPC.

First, the Standing Committee of NPC has the power to interpret the Constitution and laws. The interpretation power embraced by the Standing Committee is pivotal as the validity of interpretation is the same as that of the Constitution and laws. Secondly, the Standing Committee has the power to enact and amend 'other laws' except those enacted by the NPC itself. The Standing Committee is also empowered to partly amend the basic laws enacted by the NPC when the NPC is not in session as long as the amendment does not contravene the basic principles of the basic laws.

The amending process of the *PRC Environmental Protection Law (2014)* sheds light on the legislative proceedings of the NPC, Standing Committee and special committee. After a long-lasting contention about whether to abolish or revise *PRC Environmental Protection Law (1989)*, the Standing Committee finally approved the revision outline brought by Environmental Protection and Resource Conservation Committee in 2011. In the same year, that Committee delegated the Ministry of Environmental Protection to draft the amendment. The amendment bill was finally voted and approved by the Standing Committee after soliciting public participation twice and a reading four times. In fact, even though the Law on Environmental Protection is top of the pyramid of environmental legislation, it still lacks the form of 'basic law' because it was adopted and revised by the Standing Committee.

2.3.1.3 State Council

The State Council is the supreme administrative organ implementing the Constitution and laws. Historically, it was not equipped with legislative power until the Constitution (1982) came into force. According to Article 56 of the Legislation Law and Article 89 of the Constitution (1982), the State Council was entitled to enact administrative regulations when: (1) necessary to implement law;[13] (2) required by its responsibility stipulated in Article 89 of the Constitution;[14] and (3) delegated by the NPC or its Standing Committee. Note that the State Council has been delegated with the power to enact regulations on taxation[15] and to enact interim rules or regulations regarding the economic reform and open-up affairs.[16] The delegation actually implies transference of state legislative power rather than creation of new administrative legislative power.

Aside from the power to enact administrative regulations, the State Council also has the power to submit bills to the NPC and its Standing Committee. It facilitates the State Council to propose a bulk of bills, amounting 70 per cent of all the laws enacted by the NPC and its Standing Committee since 1979.

2.3.1.4 Departments of the State Council

Ministries, commissions, the People's Bank of China, the Auditor-in-General and other directly subordinated organs of the State Council have the power to adopt departmental rules within their respective jurisdictions to implement laws and administrative regulations, decisions and orders of the State Council without contravening them. 'Departmental rules' here is a general term that might take the form of rules, decisions, opinions, measures, orders and notice. As Daniel C. K. Chow has observed, departmental rules are generally detailed and technical rules when the entity issuing the rules are the primary ones involved in applying a particular law, and can also serve as explanations or interpretations of existing laws or administrative regulations.[17]

---

13 Many laws specify that their implementation should be the responsibility of the State Council.

14 In fact, art. 89 of the Constitution provides a broad spectrum of duties performed by the State Council.

15 The Seventh Session of the Sixth National People's Congress in 1984.

16 The Third Session of the Sixth National People's Congress in 1984.

17 Chow, note 6 above, pp. 153–4.

2.3.2 Local Legislation

Local legislation in China refers to the promulgation, modification and nullification of local decree, local rules, autonomous regulation and rule, as well as the laws in the Special Administrative Region.

2.3.2.1 Local decrees

The competent organs to enact local decree are People's Congresses and their Standing Committees of the provinces, Ethnic Autonomous Regions (EAR hereafter) and municipalities directly subordinate to the central government, as well as the People's Congresses and their Standing Committees of large cities. 'Large cities' are capital cities of provinces and EAR, cities approved by the State Council as 'large cities' and cities where Special Economic Zones (SEZ hereafter) are located.

Local decrees can, in the first place, be enacted to implement laws and administrative regulations at national level, especially where the laws and regulations are too general to regulate the situations and features of the area. They can also, in the second place, be issued to regulate regional affairs where state legislation is unnecessary. In addition, the Legislation Law leaves room for a local decree to regulate a certain issue if no national law exists. However, it will become invalid if it contravenes new national laws that later come into force.[18] Local decrees should not go against the Constitution, laws and administrative regulations. As for the procedural requirement, local decrees at provincial level should be filed to the Standing Committee of the NPC and the State Council for recording. Decrees enacted by the People's Congresses and their Standing Committees at municipality level should, by contrast, get prior approval by Standing Committees of the People's Congress of provinces and EAR.

The authority to enact local decrees can also be acquired by delegation from the Standing Committee of the NPC. In the past three decades since the Reform and Open-up in 1978, People's Congresses and their Standing Committees in Guangdong and Fujian Province have been delegated with the authority to enact economic laws in a particular area. Subsequently, People's Congresses and Standing Committees of the SEZs in Hainan Province, Shenzhen, Xiamen, Shantou and Zhuhai were also delegated to make local decrees. The delegation aims to give priority to experimental practices in the SEZ to construct the socialist market

---

[18] Legislation Law, art. 64.

economy and to the 'getting on track with international community'.[19] It is worth mentioning that the local regulations in SEZ only take effect within the geographic boundary of the SEZ.

2.3.2.2 Local rules

Local rules are made by the governments of provinces, EARs and 'large cities' to: (1) implement laws, administrative regulations and local decrees; and (2) specifically administer affairs within the duties of local governments ranging from economy, education, science, culture, sanitary, sports, construction, finance, public security, and ethnic issues stipulated by the Constitution and organic laws of local government.

2.3.2.3 Decrees in Ethnic Autonomous Regions

People's Congresses of the EARs are especially empowered to enact general autonomous decrees and specific autonomous decrees to cope with special societal, political and cultural issues and to protect rights of ethnic people. Ethnic Autonomous Prefectures and Ethnic Autonomous Counties equivalent to ordinary cities and counties also have the power to enact two types of decree. A general autonomous decree is a collection of comprehensive legal norms dealing with basic affairs in the EAR while a specific autonomous decree focuses on a particular facet of the autonomy.

In order to maintain the privilege and flexibility given to EAR, the autonomous decree must have different rules from that in national laws and regulations emphasizing its special situation provided that it is consistent with the fundamental principle of laws and administrative regulations, without changing legal norms set by the Constitution, EAR Law and other specific regulations or rules on EAR. Also, autonomous decrees in EARs will not take effect without approval of Standing Committees of the NPC. Similarly, autonomous decrees at Ethnic Autonomous Prefectures and Ethnic Autonomous Counties level should get approval by Standing Committee of Provincial People's Congresses.

2.3.2.4 Laws in Special Administrative Region

There exists a sub-legal system in the Hong Kong SAR and Macao SAR under the 'one country, two system'[20] guideline after the reversion of

---

[19] Orts, note 1 above, p. 45.

[20] As for the formation of the guideline, please see Jin Huang and Andrew Xuefeng Qian 'One country, two system, three law families and four legal regions: the emerging inter-regional conflicts of law in China', 5 *Duke J. Comp. & Int'l L.* 289, p. 289, 1995.

Hong Kong and Macao to China. Hong Kong and Macao SARs were equipped with unique power to legislate independently to maintain stability. The power is superior to any other local legislatures since the former legal systems in the two regions are basically independent.

According to the Basic Law of Hong Kong SAR and Macao SAR, the Congress has the power to pass laws on any criminal, civil, and commercial affairs other than that on national defence and diplomacy. However, the Congress of Hong Kong SAR is able to promulgate laws to facilitate the enforcement of national laws on national defence and diplomacy, among other things. The Congress in Hong Kong and Macao SAR can also submit a bill on amendment of Basic Laws to the NPC. The initiative should have a two-third vote of the Congress and endorsement by the chief administrative officer.

2.3.2.5 Conflict among legal norms and the solving rule

Conflicts among different legal rules occur because there are multilevels of legislature with ambiguous power divisions at national and local level, among the NPC and its Standing Committee and the State Council, and among varied departments of the State Council. Moreover, the dramatic economic prosperity and social transition has also brought about conflicts among legal norms.

The Legislation Law was designed to build up a hierarchy to clarify the validity of various law-making authorities by deciding which law prevails when conflict occurs. In principle, legal norms at lower levels should not contravene those at upper levels. Departmental rules and local decrees generally have the same legal validity and thus should be applied respectively within their own scope. However, there is no fixed rule to solve the inconsistency when the two regulate the same issue. Article 86 of the Legislation Law stipulates that: (1) the State Council has the authority to decide to apply local decrees if it considers the local decrees prevail over the departmental rules; if it thinks the opposite, the State Council should refer the issue to the Standing Committee to decide; and (2) the State Council has the authority to decide which one should be applied when conflicts happen among departmental rules or between departmental rules and local rules.

In accordance with the Legislation Law, laws, administrative regulations, local decrees, general autonomous decrees, specific autonomous decrees, departmental and local rules should be modified or invalidated when: (1) they are enacted beyond the authority of the legislatures; (2) they contravene the legal norms at upper level; (3) because of inconsistency between the provisions of different rules governing one and the same matter, the provisions of one side be altered or anulled;

(4) departmental or local rules have inappropriate provisions which should be modified or invalidated; and (5) there is procedural illegality.[21] The NPC has the power to change or repeal inappropriate laws enacted by its Standing Committee as well as the autonomous decrees approved by it. The Standing Committee of the NPC has the power to repeal administrative regulations and local decree when they contravene the legal norms at higher levels and to repeal autonomous decrees approved by the Standing Committee of People's Congress of provinces, EARs and municipalities directly subordinated to the central government. The State Council has the power to change or repeal inappropriate departmental or local rules. The People's Congress at provincial level has the authority to amend or repeal the inappropriate local decrees enacted or approved by their Standing Committee. The Standing Committee of Local People's Congress has the power to repeal inappropriate rules passed by government at the same level. Inappropriate rules made by government at local level can be repealed by the provincial government. Lastly, delegation of legislation might be withdrawn if the authorized entities abuse the delegation.[22]

2.4 JUDICIAL BRANCH

The judicial branch of the legal system in China is mainly composed of courts and procuratorates responsible for the enforcement of laws.[23] Unlike their counterparts in many western countries, their establishment originates from the authority of People's Congresses at varied levels. Also, they lack the power of constitutional scrutiny. In terms of the structure of the judicial system, courts and procuratorates are divided into four levels and two trials are needed to finalize a case. The supreme people's court and supreme people's procuratorates have the power of legal interpretation on the application of laws.

2.4.1 Courts

According to the *Constitution (1982)*, courts are the judicial organs of China. As the main places for dispute settlement, they adjudicate cases openly and independently. The court system is divided into four levels

---

21 Legislation Law, art. 87.

22 Ibid., art. 88.

23 Public security organs and judicial administration organ partly play a role in the judicial system as well.

with a sum of 3,557 courts[24] deployed as the Supreme People's Court at national level, Higher People's Courts at provincial level, Intermediate People's Courts at municipal level, and Basic People's Courts at county or district level. When it comes to interior structure of court, it is usually divided into civil, economic, criminal, administrative and enforcement divisions. Court personnel comprise the President, Vice-Presidents, chief judges, associate chief judges, judges and clerks. Each court also has a Judicial Committee composed of the Presidents, Division Chiefs and experienced judges. Cases are usually adjudicated by collegiate panels consisting of three to seven judges, the number must be odd. Simple civil cases, economic cases and minor criminal cases can be heard by a single judge. There is also a permanent Judicial Committee in each division responsible for deliberating complicated cases and to summarize judicial experiences.

2.4.1.1 Basic People's Court

Basic People's Courts, generally located in counties or cities outside districts, municipal districts and autonomous counties, usually hear cases of first instance. A Basic People's Court has jurisdiction over criminal, civil and administrative cases at first instance, except those under the jurisdiction of courts at higher level or specialized courts. The court may set up several People's Tribunals with the same judiciary as Basic People's Courts in big towns or populous townships. If a Basic People's Court considers that a case heard is of major importance and should go for trial to a court at a higher level, it may transfer the case to the appropriate organ.

2.4.1.2 Intermediate People's Courts

Intermediate People's Courts are established in capital cities of provinces or EARs, other municipalities with districts, EARs, or within the municipalities directly subordinated to the State Council. The jurisdiction of Intermediate People's Court are cases of first instance within the category set by laws and decrees, cases of first instance transferred from Basic People's Courts, and appealed and protested cases from a lower court. When an Intermediate People's Court considers that a criminal or civil case heard is of major importance and requires trial by court at higher level, it may transfer the case to the appropriate court.

---

[24] A statistic from 2007. See Yuanxiang, 'The road to justice', *Guangming Daily*, 6 November 2008.

2.4.1.3 Higher People's Courts

The Higher People's Courts are courts of provinces, autonomous regions and municipalities directly under the State Council. The internal structure is almost the same as that of the Supreme People's Court. The Presidents of higher courts are appointed by People's Congresses at provincial level. The judges are appointed by standing committees of the Provincial People's Congresses.

Higher People's Courts deal with cases of first instance within the category set by laws and decrees, cases of first instance transferred from people's courts at lower level, cases of appeals and of protests lodged against judgments and orders of people's courts at lower level, and cases of protests lodged by People's Procuratorates.

2.4.1.4 The Supreme People's Court

The Supreme People's Court, located in Beijing, is the highest judicial organ in China. Its jurisdiction is superior to all lower and special courts, and it serves as the supreme appellate court. The President of the Supreme People's Court is elected by the NPC and its Standing Committee with a term of five years and may serve for no more than two consecutive terms. The Standing Committee of the NPC appoints and dismisses Vice-Presidents, heads and associate heads of divisions, and judges in the court.

The court has more than 200 judges who meet in smaller tribunals to decide cases. The court has a criminal division, a civil division, and an economic division. It may have such other divisions when deemed necessary. Recently, the Supreme People's Court declared that a special environmental adjudication division be set up to hear civil cases on environmental pollution or natural resources disputes, to review environmental civil cases heard by local courts and to issue judicial explanations on environmental issues.

The main responsibilities of the Supreme People's Court are hearing cases with the most far-reaching influences, appeals or protests against adjudication of Higher People's Courts and specialist courts, as well as cases it deems necessary to take to trial. It also has the power to supervise judiciary in local People's Courts and specialist courts. In addition, it has the power of judicial interpretation in terms of application of laws.

2.4.1.5 Specialized courts

According to the *Constitution (1982)* and Organic Law of the People's Court, specialized judicial organs including military courts, maritime courts, railway and transport courts, forestry courts, oil courts, etc, with jurisdiction over a certain area can be established within the judicial system. As clearly designated in the Constitution, military courts are established within the People's Liberalization Army (PLA) in charge of criminal cases within PLA and economic disputes when both parties are servicemen. They comprise an inherently closed system with three levels: basic military courts, military courts of mega military areas and military court of the PLA. The Maritime Courts, equivalent to intermediate people's courts in terms of judicial level, primarily adjudicate maritime cases. They are founded in coastal cities such as Tianjin, Dalian, Shanghai, Ningbo, Guangzhou, etc. Their appellate courts are High People's Courts in suit. The railway transport courts handle criminal, civil and other cases occurring within the process of railway transportation. They have two levels, i.e., the intermediate railway transport court and the railway transport court respectively equivalent to people's courts at intermediate and basic level. Its appellate court is the High People's Court where the Railway Bureau is located. Forestry courts and land reclamation courts are mainly located in the districts with advanced forestry or agriculture such as Heilongjiang Province. In contrast with ordinary courts, the jurisdiction of specialized courts might cover several administrative regions. Because of the influences from the departments, local oil, forestry or agriculture officials, China is attempting to incorporate these 'departmental or corporative' courts, mainly railway transport courts, forestry courts, oil courts among others, into corresponding local courts.[25]

2.4.2 Procuratorate System

2.4.2.1 Structure of procuratorates

As legal supervision organs exercising the power of prosecution in China's legal system, the setting of procuratorates basically parallels the court system consisting of the Supreme People's Procuratorate and the local People's Procuratorate including those of provinces, autonomous regions and municipalities directly subordinate to State Council, branches of provincial procuratorates and those of autonomous prefectures and

[25] For example, according to Opinion on Reform of Courts and Procuratorate of Railway Transport jointly promulgated by Supreme People's Court, Supreme People's Procuratorate, Ministry of Finance, Ministry of Railway and so forth. The railway transport courts and procuratorates should be separated from railway transport enterprises and transferred to local courts. The process then accelerated with the reform of Ministry of Railway.

cities directly under the provincial governments and people's procuratorates of counties, cities, autonomous counties and municipal districts.

As for the interior structure of procuratorates, most noteworthy are the procuratorial committees, a component in each people's procuratorate, since they are obliged to discuss and decide important cases and other major issues led by the chief procurator, in line with the principle of minority-subordinate-to-majority. If the chief procurator disagrees with the majority's decision on an important matter, it is will be referred to the Standing Committee of the People's Congress at the corresponding level for final decision.

2.4.2.2 Function of the procuratorates

The People's Procuratorates, according to the Organic Law of People's Procuratorate in China, play an important role in criminal cases. They are obliged to collaborate with courts and public security organs to complete proceedings in criminal cases. First, they exercise procuratorial authority in cases of treason, of attempts to split the country and of other major crimes that violate state policies, laws, administrative regulations and decrees. Secondly, they investigate cases involving graft, infringement of citizens' democratic rights, violation of duty and other cases which they deem necessary to handle directly, and decide whether to arrest the offenders and initiate public prosecution. Thirdly, they review cases investigated by the public security organs and state security agencies and decide whether to approve arrest and to prosecute; supervise the investigation activities of public security organs and state security agencies to determine whether violation of law has occurred; also, they initiate and support public prosecutions of criminal cases and supervise the criminal trials of the people's court to determine whether the laws are complied with. In addition, the procuratorates are the main organs to supervise law implementation in China. They have the power to supervise the verdicts and sentences of the people's courts in criminal cases. In cases where they find definite errors, protests will be initiated. They also supervise the execution of sentences in criminal cases and the activities of prison's guards and houses of detention to determine whether they abide by the law. Civil and administrative litigations are also under their supervision. In addition, procuratorates in China are responsible for protecting a citizen's legal right to file complaints or petitions against administration activities violating the law, to investigate those infringing citizens' rights, and to deal with the citizens' accusation.

2.4.2.3 Specialized procuratorates

Along with the specialized courts, there also exists several specialist procuratorates supplementary to the main procuratorate system. The military procuratorates are special organs for legal supervision in the Chinese People's Liberation Army. They exercise procuratorial authority in cases of dereliction of duty and other criminal offenses committed by serviceman. The railway procuratorates in all regional railway bureaus and sub-bureau commit railway-related functions of legal supervision. Similarly, departmental or corporative procuratorates are gradually merged into procuratorate at local levels.

2.4.2.4 Specialization of judiciary of environmental protection

After Qingzhen in Guizhou Province launched the first environmental courts in 2007, courts at different levels are enthusiastic in creating special tribunals to address environmental matters. Up to July 2013, 134 special environmental courts or tribunals had been established in all levels of local courts.[26] They generally take the form of independent environmental adjudication division (Huan Bao Shen Pan Ting), Environmental People's Tribunal (Huan Bao Fa Ting), Environmental Collegiate Panel (Huan Bao He Yi Ting), and Environmental Circuit Court (Huan Bao Xun Hui Fa Ting).[27]

The specialization in environmental justice in China also propels the change in other judicial organs. For instance, Environmental Supervision Branch in People's Procuratorate of Guizhou Province and Safeguard Branch for Environmental and Biological Safety in Public Security Bureau of Guizhou Province have been established to accompany the environmental adjudication division within the High People's Court in that province. The comprehensive reform of the judiciary concentrating on environmental problems is deemed as a first step to substantively promoting the access to environmental justice and development of environmental public interest lawsuit in China.

---

[26] Special Environmental Tribunal is established in China Supreme People's Court, 21st *Business Herald*, 3 July 2013.

[27] Zhang, Bao and Zhang, Minchun, Specialized Environmental Courts in China: Status Quo, Challenges and Responses. *Journal of Energy & Natural Resources Law*, Vol. 30(03).

2.5 EXECUTIVE BRANCH

The legislative power of the competent governments or their constituents is supplementary to their primary function – to implement legal norms. Under system in China, as observed by Chow, all sovereign state power resides in the central level authorities and the power that is enjoyed by provincial level authorities and below is delegated power from the central level authorities.[28] When it comes to the structure of the governments, even though the core personnel of governments are elected by the corresponding People's Congresses and their Standing Committees, they are also under the leadership of governments at upper levels.

2.5.1 State Council

The State Council, that is, the Central People's Government, is the executive organ at national level within the legal system. It is composed of the Premier, the Vice-Premiers, the State Councillors, the Ministers, the Auditor-General and the Secretary-General, the Governor of the People's Bank of China. The Premier of the State Council is nominated by the President, reviewed by the NPC, and appointed and dismissed by the President. Other members of the State Council are nominated by the Premier, reviewed by the NPC or its Standing Committee, and appointed and removed by the President. In the State Council, a single term of each office is five years, and incumbents cannot be reappointed after two successive terms.

The State Council is responsible for carrying out the principles and policies of the CPC as well as the regulations and laws adopted by the NPC, and dealing with such affairs as China's internal politics, diplomacy, national defence, finance, economy, culture and education. Under the Constitution, the State Council exercises the power of administrative legislation, the power to submit proposals, the power of administrative leadership, the power of economic management, the power of diplomatic administration, the power of social administration, and other powers granted by the NPC and its Standing Committee. To date, it is composed of 25 Ministries and Commissions, one Special Organization directly under the State Council, 16 organizations directly under the State Council, four administrative offices under the State Council, and several institutions directly under the State Council such as the Xinhua News Agency.

---

[28] Chow, note 17 above, p. 87.

At national level, nearly 15 Ministries or Bureaus share the responsibility for regulating environmental and natural resource issues. The Ministry of Environmental Protection is the lead regulatory agency undertaking a general responsibility for making policy, setting environmental standards and for execution of environmental protection laws and policies. The other agencies are responsible for certain specific scopes of administration. For instance, land protection, management of minerals and marine environment protection is primarily under the administration of the Ministry of Agriculture. Forest conservation and management of national park and forestry protected areas fall under the responsibility of National Forestry Bureau. Due to the diverse distribution of regulatory powers among the departments, the leading environmental protection agency is hard put to act as the comprehensive administration authority. Hence, under the background of 'super-ministry' reform in the State Council, the former State Environmental Protection Administration was replaced by the Ministry of Environmental Protection in 2008. However, observers point out that the upgrading of the leading environmental protection agency 'cannot solve the horizontal authority disputes among different departments or the vertical conflicts within framework of environmental protection sector',[29] mainly because the reform rarely involved the re-allocation of responsibility re-allocation and coordinative mechanism.

2.5.2 Local Governments

China has 22 provinces, five ethnic autonomous regions, and four municipalities directly subordinated to the State Council. The governors of the provinces and autonomous regions and mayors of the centrally governed municipalities are appointed by the State Council after approval of the NPC. The provinces and autonomous regions are divided into cities, autonomous prefectures, counties, and autonomous counties; and counties and autonomous counties are divided into townships, ethnic townships and towns. The municipalities are directly subordinated to the State Council, large cities and autonomous regions are divided into districts and counties; and autonomous prefectures are divided into counties, autonomous counties and cities.

The leading environmental protection agencies and other related regulatory agencies are respectively set up at all three levels of local

---

[29] Mark Qiu, and Li, Honglin, "China's Environmental Super Ministry Reform: Background, Challenges and the Future" (September 24, 2008). *Environmental Law Reporter*. Available at SSRN: http://ssrn.com/abstract=1273230.

government. However, the name and regulatory scope might vary among different regions. For example, Human Settlement and Environment Commission replaced the Environmental Protection Bureau in 2009. The new agency adopts new coordinative mechanisms to avoid the rigid division of regulatory power. Administrators of three related agencies including Housing and Construction Bureau, Water Affairs Bureau and Meteorological Bureau simultaneously act as vice-chairman of the Commission. Besides, major decision related to environmental protection of the three bureaus should also get approval from the Commission.

2.6 CONCLUSION

In general, the legal system in China is largely a civil law system where centralized and systemized statutes are the main sources of law, but it should also be borne in mind that contemporary China has a unique cultural, political, and economic context when exploring the legal system and its functioning. In other words, 'Law in China presents a mosaic of traditional legal conceptions, the strong historical influences of Western colonialism and Marxist theory, and strenuous current efforts to adapt to the legal requirement of a fast-changing global economy.'[30] How to harmonize the attitudes towards westernization and conserving tradition is another critical issue to note since 'these conflicting attitudes toward adopting western-based legal concepts continue to create tensions as China continues to modernize its legal system'.[31] In sum, China's legal system is recovering from the lawlessness of cultural revolution. Tremendous progress has been made including the gradually improved legal institutions and 'rule by law'. However, how to evolve from 'a system of law' to a 'rule of law' will be the main issue to cope with in the following years.

---

30 *Supra* note 19.

31 Chow, note 17 above, p. 66.

3. Air pollution prevention law

Yu Wenxuan and Chen Shiyin

Atmosphere is one of the fundamental elements of the environment. It provides the appropriate temperature and safe living environment for humans. Unfortunately, industrialization and other human activities throughout the whole world have polluted the atmosphere, resulting in the air pollution, referred to as 'the introduction of chemicals, particulate matter, or biological materials that cause harm or discomfort to human beings or other living organisms, or cause damage to the natural environment or built environment, into the atmosphere'.[1] Air pollution is among the most urgent problems in China.

Air pollution is caused by both natural phenomena and human activities. In the modern age the main sources of air pollution are human activities. These activities mainly include: (1) household pollutants, including those produced during cooking, heating, bathing, etc.; (2) industrial pollutants, from industrial production, especially the soot, dust, organic and inorganic compound discharged from heat power plants, iron and steel plants, chemical factories and cement mills, etc.; (3) agricultural pollutants, such as SO_2, NO_2 and PM1O, which are produced by straw burning; and (4) traffic pollutants, such as NO, hydrocarbon and lead, etc. discharged from cars, trains, boats and airplanes. To resolve these problems, legislation must include measures to mitigate these pollutants.[2]

In China, the overall air quality in cities has been improved compared with the past several years, but some areas are still severely polluted. For the year 2013, the air quality monitoring[3] in 74 cities[4] showed that 4.1

---

1 See 'Air pollution', available at http://en.wikipedia.org/wiki/Air_pollution, last visited January 10, 2012.

2 See Ke Zhou et al. (eds), *Law on the Protection of Environment and Resources*, pp. 139–140 (2d ed., China Renmin University Press, 2010) (2007).

3 The monitored items include SO_2, NO_2 , PM10, PM2.5, O_3 and CO_2.

4 These cities and three other regions were chosen by Ministry of Environmental Protection (MEP) to be monitored in the first stage of implementing the latest version of Ambient Air Quality Standards, See the Implementation Plan for the First Stage Monitoring of the New Ambient Air Quality Standards, available at http://www.zhb.gov.cn/gkml/hbb/bgt/201205/t20120524_230080.htm, last visited August 10, 2014.

percent of these cities met the new Ambient Air Quality Standards,[5] and 71 cities exceeded the latest Standards. None of the counties and cities in the regions of Beijing-Tianjin-Hebei and Pearl River Delta met the Standards; and only Zhoushan, an island city in Yangtze River Delta, met them.[6] The annual averaged days of haze nationwide were 35.9, an increase of 18.3 days over the previous year.[7] A 2013 research study showed that 44.4 percent of 473 counties and cities were affected by acid rain, accounting for 10.6 percent of China's total territory, mainly along the Yangtze River and south of the middle and lower reaches of it.[8]

In recent years, automotive emissions have become one of the major pollutants, especially in urban areas. In 2012, data monitors recorded approximately 21.176 million tons of SO_2 and 23.378 million tons of NO_X in China. The data declined by 4.52 percent and 2 percent respectively compared with those in 2011.[9] The statistics from China Vehicle Emission Control Annual Report (2013) showed that in 2012 CO_2 and HC discharged from cars respectively accounted for more than 70 percent of the total CO_2 and HC emissions; and NO_X and PM emitted by cars made up more than 90 percent of the total discharged from all kinds of motor vehicles.[10]

3.1 EXISTING AIR POLLUTION PREVENTION LEGISLATION IN CHINA

The legislation and its implementation have played a key role in controlling air pollution in China. Originally the legislation focused on air pollution in workplaces; but over the years laws have been passed covering many aspects of this field, see Table 3.1 below.

---

[5] The latest version of it is GB3095-2012.

[6] See *The Report on China's Environmental Status (2013)*, available at http://jcs.mep.gov.cn/hjzl/zkgb/2013zkgb/201406/t20140605_276521.htm, last visited August 10, 2014.

[7] Ibid.

[8] In the monitored 473 counties and cities in 2013, 27.5 percent of these counties and cities suffered from acid rain of more than 25 percent per year, and 9.1 percent of these counties and cities suffered from acid rain of more than 75 percent per year, ibid.

[9] Ibid.

[10] *China Vehicle Emission Control Annual Report (2013)*, available at http://www.zhb.gov.cn/gkml/hbb/qt/201401/t20140126_266973.htm. last visited August 10, 2014.

Table 3.1 *Existing air pollution prevention legislation in China*

	Title	Issuing Authority (-ies)	Date issued	Notes
Laws	*PRC Air Pollution Prevention and Control Law*	Standing Committee of NPC	04-29-2000	The fundamental law on air pollution prevention in China.
Administrative Regulations	*The Administration Regulations of Ozone Depleting Substances*	State Council	04-08-2010	The Regulations mainly to establish the legal framework for limiting the production, sale, use, import and export of ODS.
Departmental Rules	*The Supervision and Administration Measures of Automobile-exhaust Pollution*	MEP	08-15-1990 (2010 Amended)	The measures to control automobile exhaust pollution are as follows: (1) supervising exhaust pollution of new automobile, the engines, and imported motor vehicles; and (2) ensuring the automobile maintenance industry meets emission standards.
	The Administration Measures of Burning Prohibition and Comprehensive Utilization of Straws	MEP; MA; MF; MR; MT; CAAC	04-12-1999	Burning of crop straw is prohibited in some areas. The governments at all levels are required to take steps to make full use of crop straw.
	The Administration Measures of Imports and Exports of the Ozone Depleting Substances	MEP; MC; GAC	01-21-2014	The Lists of Import and Export of Controlled ODS in China are formulated. The import and export of ODS in the lists must be officially approved.
	The Provisions on the Standards for Compulsory Retirement of Motor Vehicles	MC; MPS; MEP	12-27-2012	Motor vehicles have to be scrapped under certain conditions, one of which is excessive pollutants emission.
	The Administration Measures of the Comprehensive Utilization of Coal Ash	SDRC; MST; MIIT; MF; MLR; MEP; MHURD; MT; SAT; GAQSIQ	01-05-2013	Encourage the comprehensive utilization of coal ash during the process of collection, storage, transport and separation.

Local Regulations* (Beijing as an example)	*The Regulations of Prevention and Control of Air Pollution in Beijing*	Beijing Municipal People's Congress	01-22-2014	The special measures mainly include joint prevention and control of air pollutants by the government, total control target of priority pollutants, and control of motor vehicle pollutions, etc. In addition, the liabilities are more detailed than the *Law on the Prevention and Control of Air pollution.*
Environmental Standards	*Ambient Air Quality Standard (GB3095-2012)*	MEP; GAQSIQ	02-29-2012	Environmental Standards consist of national standards (GB), industrial standards (HJ) and local standards (DB). Local standards evolve the standards that are not prescribed in national standards and industrial standards.
	Indoor Air Quality Standard (GB/T 18883-2002)	MEP; GAQSIQ	11-19-2002	
	Integrated Emission Standard of Air Pollutants (GB16297-1996)	MEP; GAQSIQ	04-12-1996	
	Emission Standards for Odor Pollutants (GB 14554-93)	MEP; GAQSIQ	08-06-1993	
	Emission Standard of Air Pollutants for Thermal Power Plants (GB 13223-2003)	MEP; GAQSIQ	12-30-2003	
	Technical Regulation for Ambient air Quality Assessment (on trial) (HJ 663 – 2013)	MEP	09-22-2013	
	Integrated Emission Standards of Air Pollutants (DB11/501 – 2007)	Beijing Municipal Environmental Protection Bureau; Beijing Municipal Administration of Quality and Technology Supervision	10-31-2007	

Note:
* Local legislation refers to the local regulations and rules made by local legislatures combining actual condition of different regions, in order to implement the related Laws better. Local legislation, in the broad sense, includes local regulations and local governmental rules.

3.1.1 Evolution of Legislation

Air pollution prevention legislation in China began in 1950s, mostly focusing on the protection of environmental health and the prevention of occupational diseases in the workplace, especially in mining enterprises. In 1956, the State Council promulgated the Decision on Preventing the Harm of Silica Dust in Factories and Mines. In 1973, the State Planning Commission[11] issued the Planning of Preventing Silica Dust and Toxic Substances in Enterprises. PRC Environmental Protection Law (for trial implementation) was enacted in 1979, which stipulated legal principles, systems and measures to prevent and control the air pollution. Then, in the 1980s, the focus for the prevention and control of air pollution in China shifted to optimizing urban energy structure and coal processing. Several regulations and standards were promulgated in this period, including the Regulations on Prevention and Control Industrial Pollution by Technological Upgrading (1983, the State Council), the Regulation on Technical Policies of Prevention and Control of Coal-based Air Pollution (1984, the Environmental Protection Commission of the State Council), the Interim Measures on Developing Civil Use Briquette (1987, the State Council) and others. The special legislation for air pollution prevention was promulgated 1987. The Standing Committee of the Sixth National People's Congress passed and implemented the PRC Air Pollution Prevention and Control Law in 1987, with two amendments in 1995 and 2000.

Also, the authorities controlled the emissions of pollutants through environmental standards. In 1962, the State Planning Commission and the Ministry of Health jointly issued the Hygienic Standard for the Design of Industrial Enterprises (GBJ1-1962).[12] Additionally, the State Planning Commission, the State Construction Commission and the Ministry of Health released the Tentative Standard for Discharging Three Industrial Wastes (GBJ4-73)[13] in 1973. This Tentative Standard established the discharge standards for SO_2, CO_2 and 11 other categories of hazard substances, as well as 'Three Simultaneous'[14] and other important legal systems. For example, the Emission Standard of Boiler Dust (GB3841-1983) and its subsequent standards regulated the pollutants discharged by motor vehicles and by industrial production. At present,

---

11 It is now The National Development and Reform Commission (NDRC).

12 It was replaced by GBZ1-2010.

13 'Three industrial wastes' include waste water, waste residue and waste gas.

14 It refers to how the supporting facilities for controlling air pollution should be designed, built and used at the same time with the principle projects.

the two main environmental standards include the Ambient Air Quality Standard (GB3095-2012) and the Comprehensive Emission Standard of Air Pollutants (GB16297-1996).

3.1.2 Legal Framework and Main Contents

The legal framework and main contents of the PRC Air Pollution Prevention and Control Law in China can be summarized as the following eight aspects:

3.1.2.1 Supervision and management

PRC Air Pollution Prevention and Control Law stipulates the supervision and management techniques for the prevention and control of air pollution. The main points include: (1) Governments at all levels are responsible for ambient air quality in the areas under their jurisdiction. They are obliged to develop plans and policies and take effective measures to make the air quality meet the environmental standards; (2) the local and central environmental protection agencies conduct unified supervision and management of prevention and control of air pollution in the specific region for every one of them; and (3) other relevant departments supervise and manage the air pollution control within their responsibilities.

3.1.2.2 Pollution caused by coal

Coal is the most important energy resource in China, as it plays a significant role in the energy structure of China. On the other hand, the use of coal results in the significant coal-based air pollution. To address this issue, the Standing Committee of the National People's Congress enacted several laws to control the coal-based air pollution, beginning with PRC Coal Industry Law in 1996. Also, the National Development and Reform Commission in 2007 approved The Several Opinions on Accelerating the Ceasing of Small Thermal Power Units and relevant articles in other laws to further address the coal-based air pollution. Furthermore, the implementing plan related to governing SO_2 pollution produced by coal-burning entities as part of the Eleventh Five-Year Plan for National Economic and Social Development. According to these legislations, the main measures of prevention and control of coal-based air pollution mainly include the following aspects:

a. Processing. The measures prohibit the mining of collieries with excessive toxic or harmful substances, such as radioactivity, arsenic, etc.[15] Also, the legislation restricts the mining of high-sulfur or high-ash coal.[16] The measures promote coal washing and dressing in the coal process.[17] In addition, the coal boiler should meet the environmental standards prescribed by the state. To eliminate outdated equipment and technologies, manufacturing, selling and importing substandard boilers is not allowed.[18] Thus, the enterprises have a legal duty to install facilities to reduce the sulfur and ash in coal and decrease the emission of SO_2 and oxycarbide through these pollution-reduction and new technology measures.

b. Heating. Residents previously used small coal boilers or stoves for heating, which also caused severe air pollution. The centralized heating provides a good solution. The centralized heating facilities are developed in coal heating areas using the boilers with high-efficiency and low-pollution and other supporting facilities, which cut down the pollutants caused by coal-burning heating.[19]

c. Clean energy. The government creates policies that encourage and support the use of low-sulfur, low-ash coal and clean energy. Furthermore, these policies limit zones in the key cities to using clean energy only, such as natural gas, LPG, power from wind and water, and prohibits the sale and burning of high-polluting fuel. Additionally, these policies apply to energy sources used in cooking. It is required that clean energy is used in catering services, especially in large- and medium-sized cities. Other users of domestic cooking in urban areas of large- or medium-sized cities – those not designated as coal-prohibited areas – must use sulfur-fixed briquettes of coal or other clean energy as fuel. The policies require that domestic cooking reduce the direct consumption of coal as a fuel and shall do so within a prescribed but gradual time limit.[20]

d. Obligations of enterprises. If coal-fired power plants and other large or medium-sized enterprises continue to discharge over-standard pollutants, then supporting facilities for desulfurization and dust removal must be installed, and other measures for controlling the discharge of sulfur dioxide or for dust removal must be adopted.[21] In addition, coal-burning enterprises operating in densely inhabited

15 PRC Air Pollution Prevention and Control Law (2000), art. 24, para. 4.
16 Ibid., art. 24, para. 1.
17 Ibid., art. 24, para. 2.
18 Ibid., art. 27.
19 Ibid., art. 30.
20 Ibid., arts 9 and 26.
21 Ibid., art. 30.

areas are required to take measures against firing and dust in order to prevent air pollution when the enterprises store coal, gangue, coal cinder, coal ashes, sandstone, lime soil or other materials.[22]

3.1.2.3 Pollution caused by vehicles and vessels

The main pollutants discharged by cars and vessels include oxynitride, SO_2, CO, and lead. To prevent and control the air pollution caused by vehicles and vessels, the Supervision and Administration Measures of Automobile-exhaust Pollution was jointly issued by State Environmental Protection Agency,[23] the Ministry of Public Security, the National Import and Export Commodity Inspection Bureau, the General Logistics Department of the Chinese People's Liberation Army, the Ministry of Transport and China Automobile Industry Corporation in 1990. Additionally, the Control Standards for regulating hazard substances in diesel and gasoline[24] include:

a. Technical requirements. According to the Control Standards, no company or individual shall manufacture, sell or import motor vehicles and vessels that discharge excessive pollutants.[25] If motor vehicles do not meet the emission standards at the time they are manufactured, they cannot be driven on the road. Motor vehicle repair companies shall carry out repairs to make the motor vehicles meet the discharge standards prescribed in the relevant Standards.[26]
b. Fuel oil quality. The central and local governments support the production and consumption of superior fuel oil and adopt measures to reduce the air pollution by harmful substances. The production, import and marketing of leaded gasoline should be prohibited within a time limit prescribed by the State Council.[27]
c. Vehicles and vessels testing. The relevant administrative departments test motor vehicles and vessels emissions annually. The relative departments of communications, fishery and other competent authorities may authorize annual emission tests of qualified

---

22 Ibid., art. 31.

23 It was renamed 'Ministry of Environmental Protection' in 2008.

24 For example, Emission Standard of Air Pollutant for Gasoline Transport (GB 20951-2007); Limits and Measurement Methods for Emissions from Light-duty Vehicles (GB 18352.3-2005); Limits and Measurement Methods for smoke at Free Acceleration from Agricultural Vehicles (GB 18322-2002), etc.

25 PRC Air Pollution Prevention and Control Law (2000), art. 32.

26 Ibid., art. 33.

27 Ibid., art. 34.

motor-vessels for their exhaust fumes in accordance with the relevant regulations. The administrative departments of environmental protection, e.g., local or provincial Environmental Protection Bureau (EPB), or MEP, may conduct random tests for pollution discharge of any actively parked motor vehicles.[28]

3.1.2.4 Exhausted gases, dusts and fetors

Exhausted gases include mercury vapor, fluoride, chlorine, and zinc oxide. In China, certain laws require that industrial production must recycle inflammable gas and reduce the waste gas.[29] Companies that discharge sulfide-bearing gas must be equipped with desulfurizing installations or adopt other measures for desulfurization.[30] The discharge of gases and aerosols containing radioactive substances must not exceed the discharge standards prescribed in relevant Standards.[31]

Another problematic pollutant in Chinese air quality is dust, a particulate matter particularly PM2.5, that can be inhaled into lungs. Therefore, enterprises that discharge dust must adopt measures to remove such dust or, at least, the dust must undergo purification treatment. To combat the dust pollution problem, the government will also take measures such as the responsibility system for afforestation; strengthening the administration of construction operations; expanding the area of paved ground; controlling the collection of debris and waste using clean transportation measures in order to prevent the increase in brownfields corresponding with economic development increase in the per capita possession of green land; reducing the size of bare land and surface dirt; and preventing and controlling the dust pollution in the urban areas.[32] As a result, the Ministry of Environmental Protection enacted the new version of Ambient Air Quality Standard (GB3059-2012). PM10 and PM2.5 are strictly restricted in this new Standard, the level 1 concentration limits[33] for them are 50μg/m³ and 35μg/m³ respectively in 24-hour average, and the level 2 concentration limits are 150μg/m³ and 75μg/m³ in 24-hour average.

Additionally, the government passed a provision controlling the emission of fetor. Fetor means a strong offensive smell, which is harmful to human beings. High concentration fetor may cause pneumonedema and

---

[28] Ibid., art. 35.
[29] Ibid., art. 37.
[30] Ibid., art. 38.
[31] Ibid., art. 39.
[32] Ibid., art. 43.
[33] The level 1 is applied to first category of functional areas of ambient air quality, which are explained with details in section 8, Environmental Standards.

even death. Enterprises that discharge fetor must take measures to protect residents living nearby. And it is illegal to burn asphalt, asphalt felt, rubber, plastics, leather, garbage and other materials that may produce toxic or harmful smoke or dust or fetor in densely inhabited areas and other areas that need special protection.[34]

3.1.2.5 Pollution caused by straw burning

As agriculture comprises a large portion of the economy, China produces a great deal of straw for livestock and energy uses. Unfortunately, the population disposes of the straw by open-air burns, thus adding to the poor air quality. To deal with this problem, in 1999, The State Environmental Protection Agency, the Ministry of Agriculture, the Ministry of Finance, the Ministry of Railways, the Ministry of Transport and Civil Aviation Administration of China jointly passed the Administrative Measures of Prohibiting Burning Straw and Its Comprehensive Utilization. Moreover, in 2011, the National Development and Reform Commission, the Ministry of Agriculture and the Ministry of Finance released the Implementing Scheme for Comprehensive Utilization of Crop Straw during Twelfth Five-Year Plan for National Economic and Social Development to further strengthen the straw burning pollution controls.

The Administrative Measures of Prohibiting Burning Straw and Its Comprehensive Utilization prohibits the open-air burning of straw that will contribute to air pollution or dust in designated areas – in densely inhabited areas, areas around airports, areas in the vicinity of main traffic arteries or areas designated by the local people's government. According to the PRC Air Pollution Prevention and Control Law, local EPBs have the authority to order violators to stop the illegal act and, if serious, impose upon them a fine of not more than 200 yuan.[35]

3.1.2.6 Ozone layer protection

China ratified the Vienna Convention for the Protection of the Ozone Layer in 1989 and the Montreal Protocol on Substances that Deplete the Ozone Layer in 1991. Because of these new treaty obligations, China made several regulations on ozone layer protection, such as the Regulation on Administration of Ozone Depleting Substance (2010, the State Council), the Administration Measures for Importing and Exporting Ozone Depleting Substance (1999, SEPA), the China's National Scheme

---

[34] PRC Air Pollution Prevention and Control Law (2000), art. 40 and art 41, para. 1.

[35] Ibid., art. 42, para. 2 and art. 57, para. 2.

of Phasing Out Ozone Depleting Substance (1999, SEPA), and the China's Lists of Importing and Exporting Controlled Ozone Depleting Substance (Sixth batches).[36] The government encourages and supports the production and use of substitutes for the ozone-layer-depleting substances and guarantees that the output of the ozone layer depleting substances will reduce gradually. Enterprises that produce or import ODS must, within a certain time limit, carry out the production and import in accordance with the approved quotas.[37]

3.1.2.7 Energy saving and emission reduction

Energy saving and emission reduction is one of the most important approaches to achieving the goal of a low-carbon society. In 2012, the State Council released the Twelfth Five-Year Plan for National Economic and Social Development Comprehensive Work Program of Energy Saving and Emission Reduction. In this Plan, reduction targets were established, e.g., the whole country's total COD emissions would be 234,760,000 tons, reduced by 8 percent; the total ammonia nitrogen emissions is 2,380,000 tons, cut by 10 percent; the total SO_2 emissions would be cut by 8 percent to achieve total amount control target 20,864,000 tons; and all NO_X discharge would be down to 20,462,000 tons. The large proportions of these total emissions were distributed to various regions, and the rest of them were reserved for implementing pilot projects of emission trading.[38]

In addition, the General Office of the State Council promulgated the Several Opinions on Further Strengthening Energy Saving and Emission Reduction and Accelerating Structural Adjustment in Iron and Steel Industrial in 2010. It is a policy document, especially established for iron and steel industrial on energy saving and emission reduction, in which the relevant administrative departments were assigned tasks, e.g., the Ministry of Environmental Protection is in charge of investigating illegal activities involving environmental protection.

---

[36] The first batch was released in 2000, and the second batch in 2001, the third batch in 2004, the forth batch in 2006, the fifth batch in 2009, the sixth batch in 2012.

[37] PRC Air Pollution Prevention and Control Law (2000), art. 45.

[38] See Twelfth Five-Year Plan for National Economic and Social Development Comprehensive Work Program of Energy Saving and Emission Reduction. http://www.gov.cn/zwgk/2011-09/07/content_1941731.htm, last visited 20 June, 2012.

3.1.2.8 Environmental standards

The environmental standards regarding air pollution prevention and control mainly consist of standards for air quality standards and air pollutant discharge.

First, the air quality standard refers to the highest pollutants concentration in a unit volume of air permitted by the law. The current national level standard is the Ambient Air Quality Standard (GB3095-2012), which classifies functional areas of ambient air quality into three categories. The first category includes nature reserves, scenic spots or places of historical interest, and other places that need special protection. The second consists of residential areas determined by town planning, mixed areas of commerce, transportation and residents, cultural areas, general industrial zones and rural areas. The last category is the particular industrial zone. Different standards would be applied to each category. Additionally, provincial or governments at the same level may establish local standards for items not specified in the national standards. The standard of air environment quality is an objective criterion to judge each functional area on its level of pollution. Also, the national or local governments can use these legal grounds to directly determine the standard value of air pollutant emission.[39]

One of the most important environmental standards in China is the Integrated Emission Standard of Air Pollutants (GB16297-1996), which defines the pollutant concentration or quantity discharged from air pollution sources with the purpose of achieving a specific air quality standard. Provincial or the same level governments establish local emission standards for those not specified in the national standards. Because the national standards set the minimum, the lower-level governments may set more stringent local standards. In turn, they would report these stricter standards to the administrative department of environmental protection under the State Council for their records. Thus, in these local areas with more stringent environmental pollution standards, the company or individual that discharges pollutants must abide by the local criterion.[40]

---

39 PRC Air Pollution Prevention and Control Law (2000), art. 6.

40 Ibid., art. 7.

3.1.3 Special Measures

Besides the basic environmental legal systems – such as environmental protection planning, environmental impact assessment, 'three simultaneous' – China also stipulates some other special measures to protect air quality.

3.1.3.1 Key cities and 'two control zones'

The State Council designates key cities in accordance with their urban master plans, environmental protection plans and the situation of air quality in these cities. Under these criteria, the key cities[41] mean the cities that require special treatment due to their severe air pollution. Also, special provision (clause 2 of article 17) within the PRC Air Pollution Prevention and Control Law (2000) designates key cities for the prevention and control of air pollution for municipalities directly under the Central Government, provincial capitals, coastal open cities and key tourist cities. The tailored design of the legal system matches the aerial variations of the pollution levels across China, to avoid high-cost and inefficient pollution-control standards as a result of indiscriminate treatment on air pollution by a one-size-fits-all approach. Besides, these key cities usually have large-scale populations, a relatively developed economy and more severe air pollution than other cities. Therefore, the designation of key cities should improve the air quality of China and also favor the efficient use of the economic strengths of China's developed areas.[42]

The 'Two Control Zones' mean the acid rain control areas, where acid rain has occurred or will probably occur, and the SO_2 pollution control areas that are seriously polluted by sulfur dioxide. The Ministry of Environmental Protection approves the 'Two Control Zones', which determine if the zone's local air pollution, and meteorological, topographical, soil and other natural condition will be polluted by discharges from other areas. In 1998, the State Council approved the Delimitation Plan of 'Two Control Zones', and proposed control targets and solutions.

3.1.3.2 Total control target and discharge permission

The total control target means the particular region should achieve the total control target through reducing emissions and the reducing quantity

---

[41] Currently there are 113 such key cities in China, see *The Report on China's Environmental Status (2010)*, http://jcs.mep.gov.cn/hjzl/zkgb/2010zkgb/., last visited January 17, 2012.

[42] PRC Air Pollution Prevention and Control Law (2000), art. 17.

is required by regulations.[43] Local governments implement total control targets in some areas in China, only in particular zones that cover 'two control zones' and the regions not meeting the standards of prescribed air quality. The local government in these areas must check and approve the total emission and issue licenses for emission to the pollutant discharging companies.[44] The discharge permission would be issued on the basis of an allocated total control target for a region. Then the aforementioned emission trading can be implemented by trading discharge permissions.[45]

3.1.3.3 Monitoring

The Ministry of Environmental Protection established environmental monitoring institutions and monitoring network, formulating unified methodology[46] for monitoring, clarifying and evaluating the situation of air pollution, and providing technology, methodology and statistics for prevention and control of air pollution. In the monitoring network, the MEP and other relevant departments share the work and cooperate with one another to collect data and materials to provide the fundamental support for air quality announcements, air pollution reports and plan-making for air pollution prevention.[47]

3.2 CHALLENGES FOR CHINA'S AIR POLLUTION PREVENTION LEGISLATION

To address climate change as a developing economy, China confronts multiple pressures ranging from the developing economy, eliminating poverty, reducing GHG discharges. However, China attaches great importance to coping with these issues, and fully realizes the importance and urgency of responding to them through serious measures to curb the air pollution. While the current legislation plays a positive role in preventing and controlling air pollution as well as improving air quality, China faces multiple challenges in the following areas:

---

[43] See *Tutorial of Environmental Protection Law* 229 (Han Depei et al. eds., Law Press 5d ed. 2007) (2d ed. 2003).

[44] PRC Air Pollution Prevention and Control Law (2000), art. 15.

[45] At present, this is not a comment practice. Some Provinces are making pilot efforts.

[46] Such as the method standard for determination of SO_2, CO_2, TSP, etc.

[47] PRC Air Pollution Prevention and Control Law (2000), art. 22.

3.2.1 Regulatory Scope

The regulatory scope of air pollution control laws and regulations in China is improving, but the following three respects are not within the regulatory scope:

3.2.1.1 PM2.5

For a long time, China mainly monitored sulfur dioxide, NO_X and inhalable particulars: air visibility, haze, and photochemical smog were not included within the regulatory scope. These new types of pollution, very different from traditional coal-burning pollution, are actually a photochemical pollution featuring PM2.5, and they lead to serious human health problems. China's approach to these pollutants changed in 2012. The emission limit of PM2.5 was set in Ambient Air Quality Standards (GB3095-2012). Key areas, such as Beijing-Tianjin-Hebei, Pearl River Delta and Yangtze River Delta, etc., municipalities directly under the Central Government and provincial capitals must implement the new standards in 2012; 113 key cities and model cities for environmental protection are under an obligation to comply with the standards from 2013. It will come into force nationwide on 1 January 2016.[48]

3.2.1.2 Mobile pollutions

China has no air pollution control regulations on mobile pollution sources, including airplanes, trains and non-road vehicles. These kinds of air pollution sources have become one of main causes of pollution, much like the aforementioned air pollution particles.

3.2.1.3 NO_X

According to the *Bulletin of China's Environmental Status* (2010), the amount of NO_X discharge has increased annually surpassing that of sulfur dioxide. Although acid rain pollution in China is comprised mostly of sulfuric acid, NO_X has gradually contributed more to acid rain. In order to fundamentally change this problem, NO_X discharge must be effectively controlled. The fine particulate matter not only causes acid rain, but also contributes to air pollution, endangers human health, and decreases air visibility. Large-to-medium-size cities, such as Beijing, Guangzhou, Shanghai, Hangzhou, Ningbo, Nanjing, Chengdu and Wuhan, have relatively high concentrations of nitrate dioxide. In some

---

[48] See The Notice on Implementing Ambient Air Quality Standards by the Ministry of Environmental Protection, http://www.gov.cn/zwgk/2012-03/02/content_2081004.htm, last visited 20 June, 2012.

cities, the NO_X pollution even causes an increase of concentration in ozone and thus gives rise to photochemical smog pollution. For instance, the concentration of ozone has often exceeded standards in Beijing, Guangzhou, Shenzhen, etc. The current law fails to explicitly control NO_X, which makes the law enforcement quite difficult.

3.2.2 Coordination Between Laws

With regard to pollution control deadlines, the existing law provides that the discharged pollutants exceeding national and local environmental standards must be treated within a time limit.[49] But PRC Environmental Protection Law stipulates that those enterprises and public institutions, which cause serious pollution, must conduct treatment within a time limit.[50] There is another example. As to the over-standard discharge, the existing law mandates that environmental protection administrative departments issue a fine for exceeding the limit.[51] While PRC Environmental Protection Law stipulates that enterprises must pay this over-standard discharge fees according to the relevant regulations and treat this pollution.[52] The different rules for pollution control deadline and penalty to over-standard discharge in the PRC Environmental Protection Law (1989) and the PRC Air Pollution Prevention and Control Law (2000) bring difficulties for environmental protection departments to enforce the legislation.

3.2.3 Legal Regimes

The command-and-control approach has long been the major legal mechanism for air pollution prevention and control in China. The legal systems use methods such as a total control target, discharge permission, pollution control deadline, and the 'three simultaneous'. The command-and-control approach played an important role for more than 30 years, which was helpful for air quality improvement. In order to make a successful implementation of the Eleventh Five-Year Plan for National Economic and Social Development, mandatory emissions-cutting measures enacted by central and local governments have proven effective to achieve low-carbon goals. While the command-and-control approach has had remarkable effect in the short term, they often encounter significant

49 PRC Air Pollution Prevention and Control Law (2000), art. 48.
50 PRC Environmental Protection Law (1989), art. 29.
51 PRC Air Pollution Prevention and Control Law (2000), art. 48.
52 PRC Environmental Protection Law (1989), art. 28.

problems such as high-cost, low-efficiency and unsustainability.[53] The most poignant example highlights the problem of power rent-seeking. With a command-and-control approach, law enforcers have the authority to decide whether or not to inflict the administrative punishment on polluters. As a result, this situation could entice law enforcers to participate in power-for-money deals during the enforcement of environmental laws.

Meanwhile, some important legal regimes should be established or improved. For example, the joint pollution prevention and control in key areas, the total control target system, and the emission-trading system have been widely implemented in practice. Some regions have already successfully established local regulations[54] and have practical experiences on these issues. But there are just local administrative decrees to promote and implement these legal systems. Another example is related to motor vehicle pollution, which lacks effective regulation on vehicle fuel, auto-fuel additive, and clearing agents. With the number of motor vehicles sharply increasing recently in China,[55] the government has to address the related pollution issues; otherwise any efforts to control air pollution will be in vain.

3.2.4 Liabilities

The existing law on liabilities stipulates a very low level of pollution discharge fee, which is far below the real cost of treatment. As a result, this low fee discourages enterprises from investing in pollution treatment and preventing discharges of pollutants. In other words, the low penalties cause enterprises to only pay pollution discharge fees and fines rather than invest more in pollution treatment facilities. Besides, the existing law does not have any articles regarding compliance with the license for pollution discharge. Discharge permission was provided in Article 15 of

---

53 See Hu Yuan, Zheng Shaohua, "From Governmental Control to Social Governance: Focusing on Revision of the PRC Air Pollution Prevention and Control Law", 32 *Modern Law Science*, 150, 150-6(2010); Qin Tianbao, "A Comparative Study of Law on Prevention and Control of Air Pollution between China and USA", 14 *Environment Protection of Inner Mongolia*, 11, 11-3(2002).

54 For example, the *Guidance on Experimental Works of Emission-trading of Zhejiang Province* (2009).

55 The vehicle number escalated from 118,157,000 to 190,062,000 during the Eleventh Five-year Plan period. See *China Vehicle Emission Control Annual Report* (2011).

the PRC Air Pollution Prevention and Control Law (2000), but in its Chapter VI, Legal Liability, no provisions about violating licenses can be found.

It should also be noticed that in the existing laws, most of the legal liabilities are administrative responsibilities. In the *PRC Air Pollution Prevention and Control Law*, only one provision relates to civil liability: Article 62, which is inadequate to punish polluters.[56] Partly due to rent-seeking in execution of administrative regulations, any administrative law enforcement fails to provide the 'teeth' to air curb pollution.

3.3 RECOMMENDATIONS FOR IMPROVING AIR POLLUTION PREVENTION LEGISLATION

The problems discussed above can be resolved through the expansion of regulatory scope, coordination between relevant legislations, improvement of legal regimes and liabilities.

3.3.1 Regulatory Scope

The stipulations on pollutions caused by power plants, toxic substances and motor vehicles should be improved; also, ozone layer conservation and climate change should be taken into account.

3.3.1.1 Power plant pollution

Because coal-burning pollution contributes to the main source of air pollution, stricter control measures on pollutants discharged by coal-burning power plants should be adopted. Specifically, these power plants and other large-to-medium-size coal-burning plants should install matched facilities or take other effective measures for dedusting, desulfurization, and denitration if they discharge dust, sulfur dioxide or NO_X

---

[56] Article 62 of PRC Air Pollution Prevention and Control Law (2000) provides:

> Any company that has caused an atmospheric pollution hazard shall have the responsibility of removing the hazard and of making compensations to the companies or individuals that have suffered direct losses. Any dispute over the liability to make compensations or the amount of compensation may, at the request of the parties, be settled by the administrative department of environmental protection; if a party refuses to accept the decision, it may bring a suit before a people's court. The party may also bring a suit before the people's court directly.

exceeding emission standards. Thus, the law must take this issue into account in order to effectively solve this problem.

3.3.1.2 Toxic substances pollution

Because coal still remains the most important industrial fuel in China, coal-burning air mercury pollution looms large. Thus, any related coal-processing provisions should include the prevention and control of mercury pollution. These reforms will help respond to the increasingly serious mercury pollution arising from coal production and burning. As for air pollution caused by other harmful and toxic substances, further legislation should prohibit mining coals carrying radioactive, arsenic, mercury or other toxic and harmful substances exceeding standards as prescribed in the relevant environmental standards.

3.3.1.3 Motor vehicle pollution

We suggest providing measures that would include incentive and supportive provisions. For instance, giving priority to developing public transportation, encouraging developing and utilizing those low-pollution or pollution-free motor vehicles and boats, all attach importance to producing and selling clean vehicle fuel. We also suggest enhancing the monitoring of motor vehicles in conjunction with strengthening the inspection of fuel additive and clearing agents would enhance the control of air pollution with both sticks and carrots. Besides, expanding the range of vehicles with increased discharge standards should also include aircrafts and motor boats, as they contribute significantly to the air pollution problem by motor vehicles.

3.3.1.4 Ozone layer conservation and climate change

On the international scene, more attention has been paid to increased attention, such as establishing regulations in response to ozone layer conservation and climate change. In China, the policies and actions responding to climate change should be embodied in legislation. The state should encourage enterprises to adopt advanced techniques, facilities, and emission-decrease as well as recycling techniques so as to decrease green-gas discharge.

3.3.2 Consistency

Further legislation should also focus on the inconsistent provisions on the same issue in relevant laws. One obvious example is pollution control deadline. The existing articles about pollution control deadline should be in accordance with the provisions of the PRC Environmental Protection

Law (1989). Further legislation should clearly define the time for pollution control. Based on these clear stipulations can the environmental protection authorities order polluters to make restricted production, limited pollution discharge, suspending production as well as renovation. Another example is over-standard discharge. Further amendment to the PRC Air Pollution Prevention and Control Law should stipulate penalties in the chapter 'Legal Liabilities' and ensure they are severe enough to encourage compliance.

3.3.3 Legal Mechanisms

As discussed above, some of the command-and-control approaches should be improved according to the environmental management needs. But obviously command-and-control approach in itself is not enough to implement the requirements of sustainable development. Further legislation should also focus more on market-based approaches and public involvement.

3.3.3.1 Joint prevention and control

Regional compound air pollution has frequently emerged in big cities. Owing to the particular formation and circulation of air pollution, every single city lacks the capability to control these air particles. As a result, the joint pollution prevention and control model, refers to the integrated planning, unified monitoring, unified supervision, uniform assessment and coordination between different regions, has been introduced and successfully proceeded in Pearl-delta Region, Yangtze River Region, and Beijing-Tianjin-Tanggu Region, etc.[57] This model should be provided in the further revision of the PRC Air Pollution Prevention and Control Law.

3.3.3.2 Total control target

Because of the increasing number of pollution sources and total emission amounts, and the local limited air capacity, air quality still remains serious. The first paragraph of Article 15 of PRC Air Pollution Prevention and Control Law (2000) clearly stipulates that the total control target is only applicable to those areas whose air quality fails to meet the standards as prescribed in the related environmental standards. Also, the acid rain as well as carbon dioxide monitor zones, as delimited by the

---

[57] See the Twelfth Five-year Plan on Joint Prevention and Control for Air Pollution in Key Areas (Draft). http://wenku.baidu.com/view/417dd46aa4517 7232f60a25f.html last visited 20 June, 2012.

State Council, place an extreme restriction on the scope of validity of the total control target: the effectiveness of total control target is thus greatly decreased. Considering the fact that the total control target for main pollutants has been widely implemented, and it proved to be successful in water pollution and control, total control target measures must be applicable to the air pollution prevention and control in urban and regional level, not just in the existing restricted areas.

3.3.3.3 Emissions trading

Some provinces have begun to conduct emission trading in recent years.[58] It has been incorporated into the Eleventh Five-year Plan of National Environmental Protection and Comprehensive Working Program of Energy Saving and Emission Reduction. Therefore, it is suggested promoting incentive provisions in new or reformed legislation. Although, China needs much reform in order to establish a national legal system of emission trading that contains a support monitoring system for emission sources, a distribution system of allowances, markets for emission trading etc.

3.3.3.4 Public involvement

The enhancement of public environmental awareness and the emerging of environmental NGOs[59] demonstrate the excellent conditions for developing public participation and increasing concerns. The public gives assistance to environmental law enforcement through avenues such as self-governance in their respective neighborhoods or organizations and by filing environmental public litigation. As a result, the public's right to participate in environment management should be included in further legislation for controlling, mitigating, and preventing air pollution. And the most important is to design the proper approach for the public to participate in air pollution control, including supervising the air pollution information, voicing their opinions on relevant polices and construction projects, and enjoying the right to claim compensation for air pollution.

3.3.4 Liabilities

Law-makers should provide legal liabilities in response to compulsory articles in existing laws and regulations. Besides economic punishment,

---

[58] Such as Jiangsu, Piking, Chongqing, Zhejiang, Shanxi, etc.

[59] Such as, Center For Legal Assistance To Pollution Victims (CLAPV) (http://www.clapv.org/); Global Village (http://www.gvbchina.org.cn/); Friends of Nature (http://www.fon.org.cn/), etc.

the law should incorporate more administrative penalties and compulsory measures so as to make the law more implementable. The law should also further clarify such important issues as victims' rights to claim compensation for the loss incurred, exemptions, dispute-resolution approaches, polluters' burden of proof, and representative suits. Thus reforming laws will definitely promote environmental civil suits and the implementation of environmental laws.

It should be emphasized that the legal liability system should move from supporting powerful enterprise interests to pollute to a system that encourages these same enterprises to clean up their act and creates rights for the public to seek justice for environmental torts. Pollution victims, through the courts and watchdog institutions such as NGOs or local communities, can help supervise air polluters in order to protect their own interests. Compared to administrative law enforcement in environmental protection, individuals have stronger motivation to seek relief. Thus, this individual incentive to assist in the monitoring process overcomes the weakness of the impetus shortage of law enforcers in environmental administration. More provisions on civil liability should be included in existing legal liability. They should consist of several policies, such as qualification for claimants in environmental torts, range for compensation of pollution victims, responsibilities of polluters and approaches of compensation.

4. Water and oceans law

Liu Nengye

4.1 WATER POLLUTION

4.1.1 Introduction

Water pollution is a serious problem in China. The Ministry of Environment Protection of the People's Republic of China (MEP) has indicated that in 2009, 39 percent of state-monitored rivers were so polluted that they were unsuitable for human contact. Of the 26 state-monitored lakes, only 42.3 percent were not polluted. Moreover, 55 percent of underground water in China is non-potable.[1]

Water pollution accidents have occurred with increasing frequency in recent decades. For example, in 2005, 1,406 environmental pollution accidents were reported to the MEP, of which 49.2 percent were water pollution accidents.[2] Serious accidents occur almost every year. For example, on 13 November 2005, an explosion occurred at a petrochemical plant of Jilin Petrochemical Corporation in Jilin Province, China. The explosion led to a spill of an estimated 100 tons of toxic substances made up of a mixture of benzene, aniline and nitrobenzene. The pollutants entered the Songhua River and a plume of contamination started flowing downstream to Russia.[3]

In May 2007, Lake Tai, the third largest freshwater lake in China, was overtaken by a major algae bloom and was contaminated by cyanobacteria. As a result, at least two million people living among the canals,

---

[1] 'Fresh Water', 2011 *China Environment Bulletin*, Ministry of Environment Protection (in Chinese).

[2] S. X. Zhou, (2008), 'Guan yu Shui wu ran Fang zhi Fa (Xiu ding Cao an) de Shuo ming' [An Overview on the Amendments to the PRC Water Pollution Prevention and Control Law], Standing Committee of National People's Congress Gazette, 2 (268), 226–230. (in Chinese)

[3] United Nations Environment Programme, *The Songhua River Spill China*, December 2005, Field Mission Report.

rice paddies and chemical plants around the lake had to stop drinking or cooking with their main source of water.[4]

On July 12, 2010, the Fujian environmental authorities confirmed that a sewage leakage from the Zijinshan Copper Mine had caused serious pollution in the Tingjiang River, one of the largest waterways in Fujian Province. The company did not announce the pollution until nine days after the leaking started on 3 July.[5] Most recently, authorities in Guangxi Province in Southern China detected high levels of cadmium in the Longjiang River, after investigating reports of hundreds of dead fish in Hechi City on 15 January 2012. Cadmium spill on Longjiang River threatened water supplies to several Chinese cities with millions of inhabitants.[6]

The question therefore is whether current Chinese law is sufficient to effectively address water pollution in the country. This part describes the current Chinese legal framework and the challenges that China faces.

4.1.2 Legislation

4.1.2.1 PRC Environmental Protection Law

The PRC Environmental Protection Law (EPL) was established in 1989.[7] It briefly addresses the prevention of water pollution. Article 17 provides that the government at various levels shall take measures to protect regions where major sources of water are stored. On 24 April 2014, China's New Environmental Protection Law (2014 EPL)[8] was adopted, entering into force on 1 January 2015. The 2014 EPL replaced the 1989 EPL, with the hope of combating China's serious environmental problems. However, as a statute of general applicability, the EPL does not provide much detail on the creation and implementation of a regime for controlling water pollution. Rather, the EPL creates a framework of core

---

4 'In China, a lake's champion imperils himself', *New York Times* 14 Oct 2007, www.nytimes.com/2007/10/14/world/asia/14china.html?pagewanted=all.

5 'Zijin Mining's Pollution Spill', www.china.org.cn/business/2010-12/13/content_21531729.htm.

6 'Cadmium Pollution Contained in S. China River', www.china.org.cn/environment/2012-01/29/content_24496235.htm.

7 PRC Environmental Protection, Standing Committee of National People's Congress Gazette, 6 (1989) 16–21.

8 中华人民共和国主席令第9号 [Decree of the President of P. R. China (No. 9)], 中华人民共和国环境保护法 [PRC Environmental Protection Law], 24 April 2014.

principles to guide environmental protection. The details of the provisions are to be expanded in subsequent environmental protection legislation.[9]

4.1.2.2 PRC Water Pollution Prevention and Control Law

Water pollution happens when toxic substances enter water bodies such as lakes, rivers, oceans and so on, getting dissolved in them, lying suspended in the water or depositing on the bed. This degrades the quality of water.[10] The most important legislation in China addressing water pollution is the PRC Water Pollution Prevention and Control Law (WPPCL).[11] The WPPCL was first adopted in 1984. It was revised in 1996 and 2008.

The Chinese economy has been developing rapidly in recent decades. Chinese legislators acknowledge, however, that the discharge of pollutants into water has not been effectively controlled.[12] Recognition of the lack of effective control is the driving force for the amendments to the WPPCL. The 2008 WPPCL contains eight chapters with 92 articles. The chapters come under the following headings: (1) General Principles; (2) Standards and Planning for the Prevention and Control of Water Pollution; (3) Supervision and Management for the Prevention and Control of Water Pollution; (4) Measures for the Prevention and Control of Water Pollution; (5) Protection of Drinking Water Sources and other Special Waters; (6) Dealing with Water Pollution Accidents; (7) Liabilities; (8) Miscellaneous.

"The WPPCL is applied to the prevention and control of pollution in rivers, lakes, canals, channels, reservoirs and underground water under China's jurisdiction".[13] The WPPCL has established several measures to cope with water pollution. Environment impact assessment is necessary for the construction of projects or other facilities that directly or indirectly discharge pollutants into water.[14] Water pollution prevention and control facilities must be designed, built and operated at the same time as the

---

[9] Tyler, Z (2006), 'Transboundary water pollution in China: an analysis of the failure of the legal framework to protect downstream jurisdictions', *Columbia Journal of Asian Law*, **2** (19), 586.

[10] Water Pollution, Worldwide Fund for Nature (WWF), http://wwf.panda.org/about_our_earth/teacher_resources/webfieldtrips/water_pollution/.

[11] PRC Water Pollution Prevention and Control Law, Standing Committee of National People's Congress Gazette, 2 (2008) 215–25.

[12] See n. 2 above.

[13] 2008 WPPCL, art. 2.

[14] Ibid., art. 17(1).

construction of the project. The water pollution prevention and control facilities must be checked by the Environmental Protection Administration (EPA). The project will not be allowed if the water pollution prevention and control facilities are not deemed acceptable by the EPA.[15] The government shall set the standard for total amount of certain pollutants that can be discharged into water. In a region where the discharge of pollutants have exceeded the total amount set by the government, the EPA must suspend Environment Impact Assessment for construction projects that have the potential to discharge more pollutants.[16] This means no new project would be allowed to be established. The Act provides that the MEP can publicize a list of provinces which have not achieved the standard for controlling the discharge of pollutants into water bodies. The EPA of provincial government shall supervise its local branches at city level.[17] A company must obtain a permit from the EPA before discharging industrial wastewater and medical sewage into water. This permit is also applicable for sewage treatment plants.[18] Companies that discharge pollutants into water must register with the EPA, providing information about their pollutant discharge facilities, treatment as well as categories, amount and concentration of pollutants.[19] For those companies that are identified by the EPA as big polluters, they are required to install equipment for monitoring the discharge of pollutants.[20] In addition to discharge permits, companies have to pay a pollutant discharge fee to the EPA. The EPA must use the money to prevent and control water pollution.[21] The EPA is entitled to conduct on-site inspections of companies that discharge pollutants into water.[22]

The WPPCL also sets specific measures to prevent and control different types of water pollution. The discharge or dumping of oil, acid alcohol, alkaline alcohol, toxic sewage, radioactive waste or sewage, industrial and urban waste into water is prohibited.[23] Hot or contaminated sewage must be treated before being discharged.[24] Specifically, the WPPCL focuses on the prevention and control of industrial, urban, rural and vessel-source water pollution. The WPPCL uses command and

---

15 Ibid., art. 17(3).
16 Ibid., art. 18.
17 Ibid., art. 19.
18 Ibid., art. 20.
19 Ibid., art. 21(1).
20 Ibid., art. 23.
21 Ibid., art. 24.
22 Ibid., art. 27.
23 Ibid., arts 29, 30 and 33.
24 Ibid., arts 31, 32.

control measures to deal with industrial pollution. The Law declares that the government shall require companies that may cause water pollution to improve their technology and adopt preventive measures to reduce water pollution.[25] The National Development and Reform Commission (NDRC) of the State Council is authorized to publish a list of banned technology and equipment that may cause serious water pollution. Small-scale paper-making, leather-making, printing and dyeing, dyestuff, coking, sulfur refining, arsenic refining, mercury refining, oil refining, electroplating, pesticides, asbestos, cement, glass, steel and thermal power projects that seriously pollute water environment and do not conform with the state industrial policies will not be approved.[26]

With respect to urban water pollution, WPPCL provides that local governments must bear the responsibility for building and maintaining sewage treatment network facilities.[27] Urban sewage treatment plants can charge polluters for their services. The pollutants discharge fee paid to the EPA will be waived for companies that pay the service fee.[28]

The WPPCL pays special attention to the use of pesticide when considering water pollution in rural areas. The management of transportation, storage and disposal of overdue pesticide shall be under control by the WPPCL.[29] The government shall provide support for building treatment plants for farms. However, it is the farms' responsibility to ensure sewage discharge meet the standards set by the EPA.[30]

On the issue of vessel-source pollution, China has adopted the PRC Marine Environment Protection Law and the Regulation on the Prevention and Control of Vessel-Source Pollution (2009). However, it was previously not clear which kind of discharge standard a seafaring vessel needed to obey in inland waters. The 2008 WPPCL provides that seafaring vessels must follow discharge standards set for inland waters when they are in a river or an inland port. The dumping of garbage from vessels is completely prohibited. The ban also applies to the discharge of oily waste and residue.[31] Ports, docks and ship-building yards are required to have enough reception facilities to receive vessel-source pollution. In addition, the conduct of any of the following operations shall, be reported to the Maritime Safety Administration for approval or

---

25 Ibid., art. 40.
26 Ibid., art. 42.
27 Ibid., art. 44.
28 Ibid., art. 45.
29 Ibid., art. 47.
30 Ibid., art. 49.
31 Ibid., art. 52.

permission beforehand: (1) cabin washing, cabin cleaning, residual oil discharging and oily water collecting by a vessel in the port waters; (2) the operation of ship-to-ship transfer of bulk liquid cargo apt to cause pollution damage; and (3) the operation of ship dismembering, ship salvaging, ship building or repairing in the sea, or any other surface or under-water ship construction or repairs.[32]

The 2008 WPPCL has an entire chapter (Chapter 5) dedicated to the protection of drinking water sources and special water bodies.[33] Water pollution accidents have been a frequent occurrence in recent decades causing severe drinking water problems in both urban and rural areas. The government is concerned that water pollution accidents could result in social unrest.

Compared to the 1996 WPPCL, the 2008 WPPCL provides much more detail about the establishment of drinking water source protection zones (DWSPZ). Local governments are required to put clear signs and warnings at the boundary of the DWSPZ.[34] It is forbidden to set any sewage outfalls in the DWSPZ.[35] Within the first-class DWSPZ, the building reconstruction or extension of any project irrelevant to the protection of water source or water supply facilities is prohibited. Projects unconcerned with the protection of water source or water supply facilities must be shut down or demolished by local government. Moreover, aquaculture, tourism, swimming, fishing or other activities that might result in water pollution are banned.[36]

Within the second-class of DWSPZ, the building, reconstruction or extension of any project that may cause water pollution is also disallowed. Projects that have been built must be closed or demolished by local government. Aquaculture, tourism, swimming, fishing or other activities in the second-class DWSPZ shall take measures to prevent water pollution.[37]

Chapter 6 of the 2008 WPPCL addresses water pollution accidents. In 2007, the National People's Congress adopted the Emergency Response Law.[38] The 2008 WPPCL refers to the Emergency Response Law's

---

32 Ibid., art. 55.

33 Special water bodies mean water in place of interests, important fishing areas and other water area that has special economic or cultural value. Ibid., art. 64.

34 Ibid., art. 56(4).

35 Ibid., art. 57.

36 Ibid., art. 58.

37 Ibid., art. 59.

38 Emergency Response Law of P. R. China, Standing Committee of National People's Congress Gazette, 6 (2007), 535–43.

provisions on preparation, disposal and restoration measures in the case of a water pollution accident.[39] It is the responsibility of companies that may cause water pollution to adopt a contingency plan.[40] Moreover, when a water pollution accident occurs, the company must take emergency measures and report to the EPA. The EPA then shall report to local government.[41] Pollution caused by fishing vessels shall be reported to Fisheries Agency, while other vessel-source pollution shall be reported to the MSA.[42]

Chapter 7 of the 2008 WPPCL sets administrative, civil and criminal liability over water pollution. There is only one article (art. 69) which addresses the liability of the EPA and other relevant government authorities. If the EPA fails to issue an administrative license or other approval document in due time, punishments shall be imposed on the person in-charge and other directly liable persons.[43] Administrative fines are the most common tool for punishing polluters. For example, any entity that refuses to accept the supervision or inspection conducted by the EPA or falsifies in the process of supervision or inspection will be fined no less than 10,000 yuan and no more than 100,000 yuan.[44]

The 2008 WPPCL also provides fines without limits on the maximum amount. For example the discharge by any company of water pollutants beyond the state or local standards or that which exceeds the allowed total discharge volume of major water pollutants would be to incur a fine of not less than twice, but no more than five times, the amount of pollutant discharge fee.[45] If a water pollution accident is minor the fine for the polluter shall be calculated on the basis of 20 percent of the direct losses caused by the accident. However, if the accident is major, the fine shall be calculated on the basis of 30 percent of the direct losses caused by the accident.[46] In addition to fines, paper-making, leather-making, printing and dyeing, dyestuff, coking, sulfur refining, arsenic refining, mercury refining, oil refining, electroplating, pesticides, asbestos, cement, glass, steel and thermal power projects that seriously pollute the aquatic environment and do not conform with the state industrial policies shall be shut down by the local government.[47]

---

[39] 2008 WPPCL, art. 66.
[40] Ibid., art. 67.
[41] Ibid., art. 68(1).
[42] Ibid., art. 68(2).
[43] Ibid., art. 69.
[44] Ibid., art. 70.
[45] Ibid., art. 74.
[46] Ibid., art. 83.
[47] Ibid., art. 78.

Any party whose rights and interests are damaged by a water pollution accident is entitled to require the polluter to eliminate the damage and claim compensation for their losses.[48] The 2008 WPPCL introduces strict liability for polluters. It is provided that for damages caused by water pollution accidents, polluters shall assume the burden of proof in establishing a lack of causation between the actions of the alleged polluter and the damage suffered.[49] If there are a number of parties whose rights and interests are affected in a water pollution accident, the Law enables the parties to take joint action.[50]

The 2008 WPPCL briefly refers to the Criminal Law of the P. R. China for imposing criminal liability over water pollution.[51] It does not however refer to any specific provision of the Criminal Law. Furthermore, it says nothing about the criteria for applying criminal liability. This makes it difficult to impose criminal liability in practice.

4.1.2.3 Regulations and implementing rules

Ministries and Commissions under the State Council are authorized to issue rules within their respective jurisdiction in order to implement laws and regulations.[52] State Council administrative regulations and departmental rules form the backbone of the Chinese legal system. They not only provide detailed implementing rules for NPC laws, but also indicate the governing principles of law in areas where national legislation does not exist.[53] After the adoption of the 1984 WPPCL and the amendments of the WPPCL in 1996, Regulations were issued by the State Council in 1989 and 2000. Although the WPPCL was recently revised again in 2008, the 2000 Regulation on the Implementation of the Water Pollution Prevention and Control Law[54] is still valid. It is anticipated that a new implementing rule for the 2008 WPPCL will be issued by the State Council. Nevertheless, to date there is no indication that any legislative process is in place for the purpose of developing a new implementing rule.

---

[48] Ibid., art. 85.
[49] Ibid., art. 87.
[50] Ibid., art. 88.
[51] Ibid., art. 90.
[52] The PRC Constitution, art. 90.
[53] P. Keller, 'The National People's Congress and the making of national law', in Otto, J. M. et al (eds), *Law-Making in the People's Republic of China*, The Hague: Kluwer Law International Law, p. 79.
[54] Regulation on the Implementation of the Water Pollution Prevention and Control Law, State Council of P. R. China Gazette, 15 (2000), 5–9.

4.1.3 Institutions

The Ministry of Environmental Protection is the major competent department responsible for water pollution in China. The MEP and its local branches (EPA) implement and enforce the WPPCL. China's environmental protection administration is not a centralized system. The EPA is affiliated with local governments and guided by the MEP. The 2008 WPPCL provides that the EPAs at or above the county level shall supervise and administer the prevention and control of water pollution.[55] For example, the EPA above county level is entitled to issue a water pollutant discharge permit. The MEP also plays an important role in the national and regional law-making process regarding the prevention and control of water pollution.

The 2008 WPPCL charges the Maritime Safety Administration (MSA) with the authority of supervision and administration for the prevention and control of water pollution from vessels. As will be discussed in the second part of this chapter, the MSA establishes offices along China's coast and major rivers such as Yangtze River and Yellow River. The offices along the coast are directly led by the MSA Headquarters in Beijing, while those branches along rivers are affiliated with local government.

The departments in charge of water resources, state land and resources, health, construction, agriculture and fishery under the government at or above the county level as well as institutions in charge of protecting water resources in major river basins shall, within their respective scope of duties and functions, exercise supervision and administration over the prevention and control of water pollution. Major river basins refer to Yangtze River, Yellow River, Huai River, Hai River, Pearl River, Liao River and the Lake Tai. In these areas, the Ministry of Water Resources establishes special authorities to manage water-related affairs. Nevertheless, the role of those special authorities is to date not clear, which will be further discussed below.

4.1.4 Challenges

4.1.4.1 Institutional matrix

Although the MEP and the EPA are the competent departments assigned to deal with water pollution, as pointed out above several other authorities are involved. It is the intention of Chinese legislators that the environmental protection administrations could play a leading role and coordinate different authorities to work on the prevention and control of

---

[55] 2008 WPPCL, art. 8.

water pollution. In practice, relations between the EPA and other authorities are problematic. For example, according to the Ministry of Water Resources, water resources departments are competent to manage all water resources in China. The demarcation of competences between water management and water pollution prevention and control is however unclear under Chinese law. Therefore, both the water resources departments and the EPA adopt their own water planning. Moreover, the two authorities have established separate water monitoring systems and publish different reports about the environmental quality of monitored rivers and lakes. This is confusing and a waste of resources.

Similar issues arise between the EPA and the Ministry of Constructions. It is the responsibility for the Ministry of Constructions and its local departments to supervise and guide the construction of wastewater treatment plants in urban areas. Furthermore, the constructions departments are in charge of providing water to people in cities. The capacity of wastewater treatment plays an important part in the prevention and control of water pollution. However, the EPA has no authority to ask for the establishment of more wastewater treatment plants: it is estimated that currently most Chinese cities are not capable of fully treating wastewaters before discharge into rivers and/or lakes.

4.1.4.2 River basin management

As mentioned above, the Ministry of Water Resources has established basin commissions for each of the seven major river basins. These commissions conduct basin-wide water management, mainly of large, trans-provincial rivers or lakes on behalf of the Ministry of Water Resources. China is trying to integrate all water-related administrative responsibilities into a single water agency. With the aim of enhancing the capacity for integrated water resources management this agency would be in charge of unified surface water and groundwater management both in rural and urban regions.[56] However, basin commissions established by the Ministry of Water Resources are not a competent government authority to implement and enforce the WPPCL. They are not associated with the MEP and cannot coordinate the work of EPA. The question therefore remains as to the best way to enhance the role of basin commissions to achieve effective integrated water management and to address issues of water pollution prevention and control.

---

[56] B. Griggs, J. Peck, and Y. Xue (2008–09), 'Comparative water law and management: the Yellow River basin in western China and the state of Kansas in the western United States', *Kansas Journal of Law and Public Policy*, 18, 441.

4.1.4.3 Government failures and lack of public participation

Government failure to act properly is one of the leading causes of present Chinese environmental problems, including water pollution.[57] The government plays the key role in addressing water pollution in China. Environmental protection administrations are weak in the vast countryside areas. This explains why the current regime works better on the prevention and control of industrial water pollution but plays a limited role in addressing rural water pollution.

Command and control measures are common strategies found in Chinese legislation for the prevention and control of water pollution. Market incentives are rarely used. Furthermore, as a general problem for Chinese environmental law, the lack of public participation is also seen in the prevention and control of water pollution. Enhanced public participation should therefore be taken into account in future revisions of the law. This will enhance the accountability of government and ensure it functions in accordance with its mandate.

4.2 MARINE POLLUTION

4.2.1 Introduction

China is a coastal country with 18,000 km of mainland coastline and 6,900 islands with an area larger than 500 m^2 each. The total sea areas claimed under China's jurisdiction is about 3 km^2. This includes the Bohai Sea and the sea areas in the Yellow Sea, East China Sea and South China Sea. More than 1,500 rivers flow into the sea through broad drainage areas.

China's sea areas are also home to abundant marine biodiversity. There are 22,629 recorded species and various types of marine ecosystems such as mangroves, coral reefs, coastal wetlands, sea grass beds, islands, bays, estuaries and upwelling lay the foundation for the economic and social sustainable development for the coastal areas.[58]

According to *Bulletin* of China's Marine Environmental Status of China for the year of 2012 published by State Oceanic Administration (SOA), 67,880 km^2 of sea areas under China's jurisdiction was below the

---

[57] M. Y. Wang (2008), 'China's pollutant discharge permit system evolves behind its economic expansion', *Villanova Environmental Law Journal*, 19, 117.

[58] 1. General Review, *Bulletin* of China's Marine Environmental Status of China for the year of 2010, State Oceanic Administration of P. R. China.

Sea Water Quality Standard Category IV.[59] The dominant pollutants were inorganic nitrogen, active phosphate and petroleum.[60] The main polluted areas were located at the coastal areas of the northern Yellow Sea, Liaodong Bay, Bohai Bay, Laizhou Bay, Yangtze River estuary, Hangzhou Bay, Pearl River estuary and coastal waters close to some big and medium cities.[61]

The Chinese economy has grown extremely fast in the last few decades, with the marine environment deteriorating at the same pace. Can relevant Chinese law play a positive role for the protection of marine environment? This part provides an overview of Chinese legal framework on the prevention and control of marine pollution. Challenges for current regime are identified as well.

4.2.2 Legal Framework

4.2.2.1 China's maritime zones

The 1958 crisis over the offshore islands, Jin Men and Ma Zu (Quemoy and Matsu), occasioned a major formal declaration by the Government of P. R. China: the "Declaration on China's Territorial Sea".[62] China then adopted the Law of the Territorial Sea and Contiguous Zone[63] in 1992 and the Law of the Exclusive Economic Zone and Continental Shelf[64] in 1998. China first issued its baselines (part of mainland coast and the Paracel Islands) in 1996.[65] In 2012, China declared baselines of the

---

[59] 1. Quality of Marine Environment, *Bulletin* of China's Marine Environmental Status of China for the year of 2012, State Oceanic Administration of P. R. China.

[60] Ibid.

[61] Ibid.

[62] The 1958 Declaration provides that: (1) the breadth of China's territorial sea shall be 12 nautical miles. This breadth applied to territories of China, including Taiwan and its surrounding islands, and the islands in the South China Sea; (2) the straight base line method was adopted for establishing the territorial sea limit; (3) Bohai Bay and Qiongzhou Strait were Chinese internal waters; (4) no foreign military vessels or aircraft may enter China's territorial sea and the air space thereabove without prior permission. Declaration on Territorial Sea of P. R. China, State Council Gazette, 27 (1958), 575.

[63] Territorial Sea and Contiguous Zone Law, State Council of P. R. China Gazette, 3 (1992), 69–70.

[64] Exclusive Economic Zone and Continental Shelf Law, Standing Committee of Natioanl People's Congress Gazette, 3 (1998), 275–7.

[65] Government of People's Republic of China Declaration on Baselines, State Council, 15 May 1996.

Diaoyu/Senkaku Islands in dispute with Japan.[66] The extent of the China's territorial sea measures 12 nautical miles from the baseline of the territorial sea. China's baseline of the territorial sea is designated with the method of straight baselines, formed by joining the various base points with straight lines.[67] The exclusive economic zone of China is an area beyond and adjacent to the territorial sea extending to a distance of 200 nautical miles from the baselines from which the breadth of the territorial sea is measured.[68]

4.2.2.2 PRC Marine Environmental Protection Law

The development of marine environmental protection law in China has largely followed the work in the general area of environmental law. In addition, China first adopted the PRC Marine Environmental Protection Law (MEPL) in 1982 soon after signing the 1982 United Nations Convention on the Law of the Sea (UNCLOS).[69,70] The UNCLOS entered into force in 1994, China ratified it in 1996. As a consequence China revised its MEPL in 1999.[71] A further reason for the amendment to the MEPL was an attempt to cope with the deterioration of China's marine environment in recent decades.

According to the UNCLOS, "pollution of the marine environment" means the introduction by man, directly or indirectly, of substances or energy into the marine environment, including estuaries, which results or is likely to result in such deleterious effects as harm to living resources and marine life, hazards to human health, hindrance to marine activities, including fishing and other legitimate uses of the sea, impairment of

---

[66] Government of People's Republic of China Declaration on Baselines of Diaoyu Islands, 10 Sept 2012.

[67] Territorial Sea and Contiguous Zone Law of P. R. China, art. 3.

[68] Exclusive Economic Zone and Continental Shelf Law of P. R. China, art. 2.

[69] 'United Nations Convention on the Law of the Sea', (1982) 21 (6) *International Legal Materials* 1261–354.

[70] For detailed comments on the MEPL 1982, see Silk, M. (1985) 'China's Marine Environmental Protection Law: The dragon creeping in murky waters', Occasional Papers/Reprints Series in Contemporary Asian Studies, n.6.

[71] For new amendments to the 1999 MEPL compared to 1982 MEPL, see Zou, K. Y. (2001) 'People's Republic of China: curbing marine environment degradation, China's new legislation', *International Journal of Marine and Coastal Law*, 16, 347–60; Explanations on the Draft of Amendments to the PRC Marine Environmental Protection Law, Environment and Natural Resources Committee of the Standing Committee of National People's Congress, 22 June 1999.

quality for use of sea water and reduction of amenities.[72] Sources of marine pollution include land-based, dumping, vessel-source, seabed activities and atmospheric sources.[73] The 1999 MEPL establishes specific chapters to deal with land-based marine pollution (Chapter 4), pollution from coastal construction projects (Chapter 5), pollution from marine construction projects (Chapter 6), dumping (Chapter 7) and vessel-source pollution (Chapter 8). In addition, the MEPL 1999 consists of another five chapters regarding general provisions (Chapter 1), supervision and administration of marine environment (Chapter 2), marine ecological conservation (Chapter 3), legal liabilities (Chapter 9) and supplementary provisions (Chapter 10). The 1999 MEPL is applicable to internal waters, territorial seas and the contiguous zones, exclusive economic zones and continental shelves of the People's Republic of China and all other sea areas under China's jurisdiction.[74] Generally speaking, China avoids enforcing the MEPL in disputed sea areas such as the East China Sea and South China Sea. If marine pollution that occurs in sea areas under China's jurisdiction is caused by activities in sea areas beyond China's jurisdiction, the 1999 MEPL shall apply as well.[75] It is provided that the government shall establish the standard for the total amount of pollution that can be disposed in key sea areas.[76]

In Chapter 2 of the 1999 MEPL, it is provided that national and local marine environment quality standards shall be one concern for establishing national and local water pollutant discharge standards from landbase. In key sea areas, the determination of water pollutants discharge standards shall also take into account the standards to control the total amount of pollutants into sea areas.[77] Nevertheless, the control of water pollution and the control of marine pollution remain separate under Chinese law. This creates problems for effective protection of marine environment and will be discussed below.

In the area of marine conservation, the State Council and local governments at the provincial level shall adopt effective measures to protect typical and representative marine ecosystems such as mangroves, coral reefs, coastal wetlands, islands, bays, estuaries, important fishery

---

72 UNCLOS, art. 1(4).

73 Ibid., arts 207–212.

74 1999 MEPL, art. 2, para 1.

75 Ibid., art. 2, para 3.

76 In 2002, State Oceanic Administration published the National Marine Functional Zoning, 30 sea areas in Bohai Sea, Yellow Sea, East China Sea and South China Sea are listed as key sea areas.

77 1999 MEPL, art. 10.

waters. Where marine ecosystems with important economic and social values that have been damaged, efforts shall be made to renovate and restore them.[78] Article 22 of the 1999 MEPL establishes criteria for the establishment of marine protected areas: (1) typical marine physiographic areas, representative natural ecosystem areas as well as areas within which natural ecosystems have been damaged to some extent, but may be recovered through efforts of protection; (2) sea areas with rich marine biodiversity, or the areas with rare and endangered marine species; (3) sea areas, seashores, islands, coastal wetlands, estuaries, bays with special protection values; (4) sea areas where marine natural heritage of great scientific and cultural values are located; and (5) other areas which call for special protection.

Land-based sources contribute approximately 80 percent of global marine pollution.[79] Chapter 4 of the 1999 MEPL was formulated with the aim of addressing this problem. The location of sewage draining outfalls shall be determined in accordance with marine functional zoning, marine dynamic conditions and relevant regulations, and shall, after scientific assessment, be reported to the EPA at city level or above for approval. The EPA is required to seek opinions from State Oceanic Administration (SOA), Maritime Safety Administration (MSA) and the Fisheries Administration before giving final approval for setting pipelines for discharging pollutants into sea areas. The construction of new sewage draining outfalls in marine nature reserves, important fishery waters, coastal historic sites and scenic spots is prohibited under the Act.[80] The EPA and Water Resources departments at provincial level are authorized to ensure water quality of estuaries.[81] However, the 1999 MEPL does not address the issue of inter-departmental coordination and cooperation.

The 1999 MEPL provides different restrictions on the discharge of different types of pollutants into sea areas. The discharge of oils, acid liquids, alkaline liquids, hypertoxic waste liquids and wastewater containing high and medium radioactivity into the sea is *prohibited.* The discharge of wastewater containing low radioactivity into the sea shall be *restricted.* The discharge of wastewater containing persistent organic matters and wastewater containing heavy metals shall be *strictly*

---

78 Ibid., art. 20.

79 UN General Assembly, Oceans and the Law of the Sea, Report of the Secretary-General of 18 August 2004, A/59/62Add.1, 29, para. 97.

80 1999 MEPL, art. 30.

81 Ibid., art. 31.

controlled.[82] Medical sewage carrying pathogens and industrial wastewater are not permitted to be discharged into sea areas before being properly treated to meet relevant discharge standards.[83] The discharge of industrial wastewater and sewage containing organic and nutrient matters into bays, semi-closed seas and other sea areas with low capacities of self-purification shall be strictly controlled.[84] This can be seen as the legal basis for the Chinese Government's actions on the pollution prevention and control of Bohai Sea, such as the "clean sea campaign (2001–2005)".[85] Chapter 4 addresses land-based pollution. It provides that the transfer of hazardous wastes through the passage of China's internal waters and territorial seas is prohibited. For the transportation of hazardous wastes through the passage of other sea areas under the jurisdiction of China, vessels must obtain the approval from the MEP.[86]

Chapter 5 addresses pollution from coastal construction projects, such as paper mill, chemical plant, printing and dyeing, tannery, electroplating, brewery, oil refinery and ship-dismantling. Chapter 6 concerns marine construction projects, such as oil exploitation platforms. Environmental impact assessments must be conducted and approved by the EPAs before the establishment of any new coastal project.[87] For the construction of a new marine project, an environmental impact assessment must be conducted and approved by the SOAs beforehand.[88] Moreover, environment protection installations of the coastal/marine construction projects shall be designed, built and commissioned together with the principle part of the construction project.[89]

Dumping is regulated by Chapter 7 of the 1999 MEPL. Dumping into any sea areas under China's jurisdiction is not allowed without a permit from the SOA.[90] The list of wastes that can be dumped into the sea shall be drafted by the SOA in consultation with the MEP and approved by the State Council.[91] Furthermore, dumping areas shall be designated by the

---

82 Ibid., art. 33.
83 Ibid., art. 34.
84 Ibid., art. 35.
85 Bohai Sea is a semi-closed sea completely within China's jurisdiction. However, the campaign failed to improve the marine environment in the Bohai Sea.
86 1999 MEPL, art. 39.
87 Ibid., art. 43.
88 Ibid., art. 47.
89 Ibid., arts44, 48.
90 Ibid., art. 55.
91 Ibid., art. 56.

SOA with the approval of the State Council.[92] It is noted that the SOA can designate a temporary dumping area. The SOA only needs to consult with the MSA and Fisheries Administration.[93]

Maritime transport is only responsible for about 12 percent of the total marine pollution.[94] However, this pollution often affects more than one state. Furthermore, shipping is an activity with intensive communication between different states and individuals and is regulated by international conventions.[95] However, international conventions that China ratified cannot be directly applied and therefore need to be transformed into domestic legislation.

Chapter 8 deals specifically with vessel-source pollution. According to Article 62(1) of the 1999 MEPL, no vessels or their related operations may discharge into the sea areas under the jurisdiction of the People's Republic of China any pollutants, wastes, ballast water, vessel garbage or other harmful substances in violation of the provisions of this law. The MEPL itself does not clarify the discharge standards. In practice, the MSA follows the latest standards set by the International Convention for the Prevention of Pollution from Ships, 1973 (MARPOL) and its amendments.[96] The 1999 MEPL requires all ships to possess anti-pollution equipment. Moreover, ports, harbors, loading stations and shipyards are to be equipped with reception facilities.[97] The 1999 MEPL provides that the carriage of hazardous goods must be approved by the competent authority, namely the MSA.[98] It also calls for the establishment of an oil pollution insurance and compensation fund.[99] The MSA may exercise enforcement measures on ships and marine installations if a casualty on the high seas causes serious pollution damage or poses the threat of pollution damage to sea areas within China's jurisdiction, in accordance with Article 221 of the LOSC (measures to avoid pollution arising from maritime casualties).[100]

---

[92] Ibid., art. 57.

[93] Ibid.

[94] International Shipping Facts and Figures – Information Resources on Trade, Safety, Security, Enviornment, Maritime Knowledge Center, International Maritime Organization, 2011, p. 24.

[95] E. J. Molenaar, *Coastal State Jurisdiction over Vessel-Source Pollution*, The Hague: Kluwer Law International, 1998, pp. 18–19.

[96] Interviews with MSA staff (Dalian, Qinghuangdao, Tianjin, Yantai, Qingdao, Shanghai, Ningbo, Guangzhou, Shenzhen and Haikou).

[97] 1999 MEPL, art. 62(2).

[98] Ibid., art. 67.

[99] Ibid., art. 66.

[100] Ibid., art. 71.

The 1999 MEPL provides three kinds of liabilities: administrative liability, civil liability and criminal liability. Administrative liability is the most commonly used tool in the form of warnings and fines. It only provides that whoever causes pollution damage to the marine environment shall remove the pollution and provide compensation for any losses incurred. For damage to marine ecosystems, fishery resources and marine protected areas which result in heavy losses, the SOA is authorized to claim compensation in court on behalf of the state.[101] The 1999 MEPL sets out the elements of criminal liability in Article 91. Paragraph 3 of that article provides the only link between the 1999 MEPL and the Criminal law.[102, 103] It provides that in cases of significant pollution of the marine environment resulting in major damage (great loss of public or private property/bodily injury or death of another person), criminal liability shall be imposed according to applicable law.[104] The Standing Committee of the National People's Congress indicates that this article was added to the 1999 MEPL in accordance with Chapter 6, Section 6 on Crimes of Impairing the Protection of Environment and Resources in the Criminal Law.[105] In the Criminal Law, there is no specific offence for marine pollution. It seems that Article 338, "Considerable Accident with Environmental Pollution" is the most likely offence that fits with the 1999 MEPL. However, Article 338 of the Criminal Law was revised in 2011.[106] "Great loss of public or private property/bodily injury or death of another person" is no longer a precondition to attributing criminal liability for environmental damage.[107]

---

[101] Ibid., art. 90.

[102] M. G. Faure and J. Hu (2006), *Prevention and Compensation of Marine Pollution Damage: Recent Development in Europe, China and the US*, Alphen aan den Rijn: Kluwer Law International, p. 68.

[103] Decree of the President of P. R. China (No. 83), Criminal Law of P. R. China, Standing Committee of Natioanl People's Congress Gazette, Issue No. 2, 1997. (in Chinese).

[104] It is noted that 1999 MEPL uses the same terms as the Chinese version of UNCLOS, such as "significant pollution" and "major damage."

[105] The major revisions of the 1999 MEPL, www.people.com.cn/zgrdxw/news/200004/04/lf30302.html (in Chinese).

[106] Decree of the President of P. R. China (No. 41), Eighth Amendments to the Criminal Law, Standing Committee of National People's Congress Gazette, 2 (2011).

[107] Criminal Law, art. 338:

> In violation of the regulations of the State, discharges, dumps or treats radioactive waste, waste containing pathogen of infectious diseases, toxic substances or other hazardous waste, thus causing a major environmental

4.2.2.3 Regulations and implementing rules

The State Council has adopted several regulations regarding marine pollution. These include the Regulations on the Prevention and Control of Land-Based Marine Pollution (1990),[108] the Regulations on the Prevention and Control of Marine Pollution from Coastal Construction Projects (1990, as revised in 2007),[109] the Regulations on the Prevention and Control of Marine Pollution from Marine Construction Projects (2006),[110] the Regulations on the Administration of Dumping into the Sea (1985)[111] and the Regulations on the Prevention and Control of Vessel-Source Marine Pollution (1983, as revised in 2009).[112] It is noteworthy that regulations on land-based pollution and dumping have not been revised for more than 20 years, even though the amendments to the MEPL were conducted in 1999: Thus Chinese law is therefore quite weak when trying to deal with the largest source of marine pollution.

The implementing rules issued by ministries or governments at provincial level are too numerous to be listed here. For example, as of 30 November 2009, there existed a total of 596 implementing rules issued by the MSA that were in force.[113] A series of rules were adopted by the Ministry of Transport after the entry into force of the Regulation on the Prevention and Control of Vessel-Source Marine Pollution. These include the Implementing Rules on the Insurance for Civil Liability of Damage by Vessel-Source Oil Pollution,[114] the Rules on the Prevention and Control of Marine Pollution from Ships and Relevant Operating Activities,[115] the Rules on the Contingency Plan and Contingency Response of

---

pollution, shall be sentenced to fixed-term imprisonment of not more than three years or criminal detention and shall also, or shall only, be fined; if the consequences are especially serious, he shall be sentenced to fixed-term imprisonment of not less than three years but not more than seven years and shall also be fined.

[108] Decree of the State Council, No. 61, 1 August 1990 (in Chinese).

[109] Decree of the State Council, No. 507, 25 Sept 2007 (in Chinese).

[110] Decree of the State Council, No. 475, 19 Sept 2006 (in Chinese).

[111] Decree of the State Council, 6 March 1985 (in Chinese).

[112] Decree of the State Council of the P. R. China, No. 561, 30 Sept 2009 (in Chinese).

[113] Announcement No. 8, 2009 of China MSA, the List of 596 Valid Maritime Safety Rules (in Chinese).

[114] Decree of the Ministry of Transport, No. 3, 2010 (in Chinese).

[115] Decree of the Ministry of Transport, No. 7, 2010 (in Chinese).

Vessel-Source Marine Pollution[116] and the Rules on the Investigation of Vessel-Source Pollution Accidents at Sea.[117]

4.2.2.4 Institutions

There used to be several authorities involved in law enforcement in sea areas under China's jurisdiction. These include the Sea Police of the Border Control Department of the Ministry of Public Security; the MSA of the Ministry of Transport; the State Fisheries Administration of the Ministry of Agriculture; the SOA; the Bureau of Anti-Smuggling of the China Customs; and China Sea Rescue and Search Administration of the Ministry of Transport. In 2013, the 12th National People's Congress adopted the Institutional Reform and Functional Change Plan for State Council. According to the Plan, a new China Coast Guard was established, which incorporated Sea Police, State Fisheries Administration, China Marine Surveillance (SOA) and Bureau of Anti-Smuggling at Sea.[118] The China Coast Guard is affiliated with the SOA and under technical guidance of the Ministry of Public Security.

As Zou Keyuan points out, it is a common practice of Chinese law-making that most of the laws and regulations have a provision stating the competent authority for the implementation of the legislation. It is clear that the authority that is designated as a competent authority for the implementation of a particular piece of legislation will enjoy enforcing power.[119] Article 5 of the 1999 MEPL sets out the competencies of different departments for the protection of the marine environment. The MEP shall provide guidance, coordinate and supervise nation-wide environmental protection work. The MEP shall be responsible for the prevention and control of marine pollution from land-based and coastal construction projects. The MSA is authorized to deal with vessel-source pollution. However, marine pollution caused by fishing vessels falls within the jurisdiction of the Fisheries Administration.[120] The environmental protection department of the military is in charge of marine pollution caused by military vessels. The SOA is in charge of the supervision and administration of the marine environment. The SOA is

---

[116] Decree of the Ministry of Transport, No.4, 2011 (in Chinese).

[117] Decree of the Ministry of Transport, No. 10, 2011 (in Chinese).

[118] Standing Committee of National People's Congress Gazette, Issue No. 2, 2013 (in Chinese).

[119] K. Y. Zou (2002), 'China's Ocean policymaking: Practice and lessons', *Coastal Management* 40, 152–6.

[120] With only one exception that pollution in non-fishing ports caused by fishing vessels will be under the jurisdiction of the MSA.

also responsible for organizing survey, surveillance, supervision, assessment and scientific research of the marine environment. They are also responsible for the prevention and control of marine pollution caused by marine construction projects and dumping.

4.2.3 Challenges

4.2.3.1 Implementing MEPL in disputed sea areas

China has maritime boundary disputes with its neighboring countries, including Japan, North Korea, South Korea, Vietnam, the Philippines and Indonesia.[121] Moreover, in the East China Sea, there is a dispute between China and Japan over the sovereignty of the Diaoyu islands (Chinese name)/Senkaku Islands (Japanese name). The islands are currently controlled by Japan. China, however, claims these islands on the basis of Article 2 of the 1992 Law on the Territorial Sea and Contiguous Zone. In the South China Sea, China has islands sovereignty disputes with Vietnam, Malaysia and Philippines over the Nansha Islands (Spratly Islands).[122] In total, nearly 1.5 m km^2 of sea areas claimed by China overlap with claims made by neighboring countries. Concerns have been raised by the rest of the world over whether China will enforce its marine environmental protection legislation in the disputed sea areas.

4.2.3.2 Gaps in current legislation

In 2011, China experienced the worst oil spill disaster from offshore oil exploitation platforms in its history. In the Bohai Bay oil spill disaster, ConocoPhillips China (managing company of oil exploitation platforms), a subsidiary of the U.S.-based oil company ConocoPhillips, reported that oil and mud leaking from two of the company's platforms in the Penglai 19-3 oilfield totalled 2,500 barrels.[123] The disaster not only caused serious pollution in almost 7 percent of China's Bohai Bay, it also brought to the surface numerous questions relating to the sufficiency of China's current regime for oil pollution. The questions for current legislation include: (1) which party shall be sued? The oil field is owned

---

[121] K. Y. Zou (2001), 'China's exclusive economic zone and continental shelf: Developments, problems, and prospects', *Marine Policy*, 25, 77–8.

[122] For details, see K. Y. Zou (2005), 'Implementing the United Nations Convention on the Law of the Sea in East Asia: Issues and Trends', *Singapore Yearbook of International Law*, 50–52.

[123] Oil spill in China's Bohai Sea rises to 2,500 barrels: http://news.xinhuanet.com/english2010/china/2011-08/12/c_131045663.htm

by the state-owned China National Offshore Oil Corporation and managed by ConocoPhillips China; (2) Who can bring the case to the court? fishermen? local government? NGOs? Or maritime authorities (in this case State Oceanic Administration (SOA))? (3) What is the legal basis for claiming compensation under Chinese law? (4) This disaster was caused by human elements, could criminal liability be imposed on individuals who are responsible for this disaster? None of these questions are adequately addressed under current legislation.[124] The head of SOA conceded during the 2012 National People's Congress Meeting that the MEPL is not sufficient to deal with land-based pollution and marine biodiversity loss. Moreover, there is a gap in the MEPL for the prevention and compensation of ecological damage to marine environment.[125] An amendment to the 1999 MEPL seems to be necessary in the near future.

4.2.3.3 Separation of the control of water pollution and marine pollution

Under the current Chinese legal regime, there is a separation of the prevention and control of freshwater pollution and marine pollution. In theory, the EPA is authorized to prevent and control freshwater pollution. It is also the appropriate authority to guide, coordinate and supervise marine environmental protection. In practice, the EPA has neither the capacity nor the human resources to deal with land-based marine pollution, while the SOA has no authority over pollution that flows from land into the sea. The current arrangement therefore is not effective in coping with a soaring increase of land-based pollution.

4.3 CONCLUDING REMARKS

China is facing serious problems of water and marine pollution and Chinese law does intend to deal with the problem. The WPPCL provides comprehensive measures to prevent and control water pollution. However, several problems exist, including a lack of coordination between the MEP and the Ministry of Water Resources Management, government failure to act in countryside and lack of public participation.

---

[124] N. Y. Liu (2013), 'Criminal liability for vessel-source pollution in China: Law and practice', *International Journal of Marine and Coastal Law*, 28, 528–9.

[125] Head of State Oceanic Administration says law amendments are necessary for the protection of marine environment, http://news.xinhuanet.com/politics/2012-03/13/c_111647302.htm (in Chinese).

Regarding marine pollution, the MEPL is the major legislation; but it is doubtful that China will enforce it in disputed sea areas with its neighboring countries. Furthermore, 2011 Bohai Bay oil spill disaster brought to the surface numerous questions relating to the sufficiency of China's current regime for oil pollution. For example, gaps in the MEPL for the prevention and compensation of ecological damage to marine environment need to be addressed in the near future.

Moreover, it is noted that the most significant cause of marine pollution is from land-based sources, and this pollution is principally carried into the sea.[126] Nevertheless, China has established two separate regimes on the prevention and control of water pollution and marine pollution. However, this separation of two regimes under Chinese law then becomes an obstacle for the effective prevention of marine pollution.

---

[126] Freestone, D. and Salman, S. (2007), 'Ocean and freshwater resources', in Bodansky, D. Brunnée, J. and Hey, E. (eds), *Oxford Handbook of International Environmental Law*, Oxford: Oxford University Press, p. 360.

5. Soil protection law

Tou Xiaodong

The soil pollution problem in China is becoming increasingly serious because of the long-term, extended and high-energy consuming economic growth. In 2004, Sun Tieheng, an academician of Ecology Institute of Chinese Academy of Science, found that the severity of soil pollution in China had been underestimated.

The major findings of his study are summarized as follows: around 20m hectares of cultivated land had been polluted by cadmium, arsenic, chromium, lead and other heavy metals and that accounted for about one-fifth of the total cultivated land of China. Of cultivated land 10m hectares was polluted by industrial "three-waste", and the acreage of cultivated land irrigated by effluent had reached over 3.3m hectares. The grain production of the whole nation was diminished by more than 10m tons a year due to heavy metal pollution, while 12m tons of grain was similarly polluted; resulting in total economic losses of at least 20bn yuan (RMB) a year. As well as the cultivated land pollution, soil or land in industrial, mining and urban areas in the country had also been seriously polluted. Economic losses caused by other types of soil pollution such as pesticide and organic pollution, radioactive pollution and pathogen pollution were hard to estimate. Soil pollution had directly led to the decline in food quality, and the contents of cadmium, chromium, arsenic, lead and other heavy metals in grain, vegetables, fruits and other foods were over the content standards or near critical level in some places. As well as affecting the quality of food, soil pollution had also affected other qualities of agricultural products. For example, sewage irrigation had already resulted in the phenomena that the vegetables tasted worse, were more perishable or even emitted unpleasant peculiar smells in some places. The storage quality and processing quality of agricultural products could not meet the requirements of intensive processing because of soil pollution.[1] In a word, soil pollution in China has already influenced the quality of cultivated land,

[1] Zheng Zixuan. 2004. "Environmental and Resources Protection Committee recommended National People's Congress to legislate, soil pollution control law has quickened". *Guangzhou City of China*: *Nanfang Daily* (March 9th): B01.

the safety of food and the health of the people. In addition, due to soil pollution, China's agricultural products' competitiveness in the global market weakened and exports dropped sharply. Even worse, material and energy output to the environment by the polluted soil can cause pollution to air and water and damage to biological diversity, aggravate pollution of the entire environment and then threaten the national ecological safety.

The present situation of soil pollution compels us to take legislative measures, without which, soil pollution will be difficult to reverse and maybe beyond recovery. Irrational soil utilization must be regulated through legislation and the implementation of relevant soil pollution control laws. In terms of current applicable legislation on soil pollution control in China, from the historical point of view, legislation of this sort is getting more and more attention and becoming more and more specialized. Across the board, various provisions are still scattered, systemless and inconsequential, abstract so difficult to implement, and many critical systems are in place. Thus, generally speaking, existing legislation cannot cope with the increasingly intense situation of soil pollution. At the same time, it does not meet the quantitative requirements of controlling and managing the soil specially and synthetically. It is, therefore, imperative to promote special legislation on soil pollution control and achieve a system and pertinence for soil pollution control.

5.1 THE DEVELOPMENT OF LEGISLATION ON SOIL POLLUTION CONTROL IN CHINA

5.1.1 Stage of Principled Legislation on Soil Pollution Control (1979–86)

In China, the earliest explicit mention of protecting the soil and preventing soil pollution in legislation is Article 10 and Article 21 of PRC Environmental Protection Law (for Trial Implementation) of 1979. Article 10 states: "Use the land reasonably according to local conditions, improve the soil, increase vegetation, and prevent soil erosion, soil sealing, salinization, desertification and soil and water loss." Article 21 states: "Develop high-efficiency, low-toxicity and low-residue pesticide actively. Extend biological control and comprehensive prevention. Use sewage to irrigate reasonably. Avoid pollution of soil and crop." Thereafter, Article 10 of the PRC Constitution set out the principled regulation: "use the land reasonably", and the 1986 PRC Land Management Law made an analogous provision. These are all early laws and most of them were principled declarations without any definite system or regulation.

This may be explained because of the generally better environment and less serious environmental pollution then.

5.1.2 Stage of Decentralized Legislation on Soil Pollution Control (1987–2004)

The PRC Water Pollution Prevention and Control Law (promulgated in 1984, revised in 1996 and 2008); the PRC Air Pollution Prevention and Control Law (promulgated in 1987, revised in 1995 and 2000); the PRC Solid Waste Law (promulgated in 1995, revised in 2004); the PRC Radioactive Pollution Prevention Law (promulgated in 2003); and other specific pollution control laws" enactment and revision provided special regulations. Regulations on the Control over Safety of Dangerous Chemicals (promulgated in 1987, revised in 2002); Regulations on the Control of Pesticides (promulgated in 1997, revised in 2001); Rules on Management of Industrial Pollution Source Monitoring (Temporary) (promulgated in 1991); Administrative Measures for Urban Living Garbage (promulgated in 1993, revised in 2007); Rules on Management of Restricted Use of Pesticides (promulgated in 2002); Rules on Prevention and Control of Environmental Pollution by Wasted Hazardous Chemicals (promulgated in 2005); and other administrative rules and regulations provide the basis for further control of soil pollution. Just like fallen leaves return to the roots, pollution including air pollution, water pollution, rubbish or waste and widely used fertilizers and pesticides in agricultural cultivation, will fall to ground and lead to soil pollution. In other words, all pollution has the potential to be a source of soil pollution. Therefore, although laws, rules, regulations do not include specialized legislation on soil pollution, they are also norms applicable to soil pollution control.

5.1.3 Stage of Great Importance Attached to Legislation on Soil Pollution Control (2005–now)

During this stage, the national policy took soil pollution control legislation seriously and came to a pinnacle. In November 2005, National Environment Protection Bureau promulgated the National Environmental Protection Rules Construction Plan of the Eleventh Five-Year Plan which pointed out that there was no legislation on soil pollution control and it should be formulated as soon as possible. In December 2005, the State Council promulgated the decision on applying the Scientific Outlook on Development ([2005] 39) that clearly put forward the issue of pollution control in rural environmental protection, environmental law perfection and the development of science and technology. The fourth session of tenth National People's Congress on 14 March 2006 passed the Eleventh Five-year Program for National Economy and Social Development of People's Republic of China (PRC), in which second section of the sixth chapter clearly pointed out "strengthen rural environment protection, carry out situation investigation on national soil pollution and control soil pollution comprehensively". These state policies mainly established the fundamental key of specific legislation on soil pollution control and built the appropriate policy atmosphere for soil pollution control legislation. The National Environment Protection Bureau and Ministry of Land and Resources promulgated the National Soil Situation Investigation and Special Work of Pollution control in December 2004. In early 2005, central finance established a special fund for the federal soil situation investigation and special work of pollution control and prior arranged RMB 20,000,000 as start-up capital. In 2006, it invested more and arranged RMB 130,000,000 as a special fund. With the deployment of the domestic soil pollution situation investigation, relevant investigation reports on soil pollution situation will be announced in succession and the actual situation of soil pollution in China will gradually become clear, which will help lay the foundation for soil pollution control legislation. Furthermore, it is worth mentioning that Shenyang Environment Protection Bureau and Shenyang Planning and State Land Resource Bureau jointly issued the Shenyang Administrative Measures for Remediation and Restoration of Polluted Area Environment (Trial) on 25 May 2007, with six chapters and 32 sections in total, including supervision of polluted areas, evaluation and identification of insanitary areas, control and restoration of polluted areas and legal liability. It is the first special legislation on control and restoration of polluted areas and provides a sample of reference for central government to make special laws. The abovementioned measures began to be enforced from 1 June. Promulgation of the Soil Pollution Control Law cannot be accomplished in one day, however, and the measures can serve as a trial period before the release of Soil Pollution Control Law. In this way, we can test the effects throughout the period to offer some inspiration for central legislation.[2] If we connect the special provisions of soil pollution prevention during enterprises' relocation in Announcement about Accomplishing the Work of Environment Pollution Prevention during Relocation of Enterprises by National Environment Protection Bureau (1 June 2004) and the system of

---

[2] Wang Zaixiang. 2008. "Legislation review on soil pollution prevention in China". *Wuhan City of China, Law Review* (3): p. 79.

soil environment risk assessment and polluted soil recovery established in Zhejiang Regulation of Prevention and Control of Environmental Pollution by Solid Waste (March 29 2006), we can find that departmental policy and local regulation paid more and more attention to the problem of soil pollution prevention and also showed a tendency of specialization.

Overall, so far as soil pollution control legislation is concerned, it can be said that relevant laws, administrative rules, local statutes and departmental regulations generally made provisions of soil pollution control from three aspects: first, from the aspect of agricultural environmental protection which mainly prevents soil pollution by using fertilizer, pesticide and sewage irrigation; second, from the aspect of regulations on "three wastes" prevention, mainly preventing soil pollution from released sewage, wastewater and unreasonable dispose of solid waste; and third, from the angle of the specially protected natural region and cultural sites. The basic function is to protect the soil in these regions from pollution by human activities while protecting the unique areas environment.

5.2 SPECIFIC SYSTEMS INVOLVED IN EXISTING LEGISLATION ON SOIL POLLUTION CONTROL

China's current regulations, despite being dispersive, numerous and jumbled, contain much that could contribute to soil pollution control. The following are an introduction to some of the law systems.

5.2.1 Supervision and Management System of Soil Pollution

According to the current regulations, land management authorities, construction authorities, agriculture authorities, environment protection authorities, quality supervision authorities and water authorities all have supervisory powers. The PRC Land Management Law, the PRC Agriculture Law, the PRC Solid Waste Law, and the Law on Quality and Safety of Agricultural Products all provide the relevant authorities with power. However, there are few stipulations about the division of supervision powers, although some local rules and measures have more explicit conditions in this aspect. The second chapter in Shenyang Administrative Measures for Remediation and Restoration of Polluted Area Environment specifically stipulates the powers of various departments in the control and restoration of polluted area. Article 16 in the Regulation on Prevention of Environmental Pollution by Solid Waste of Zhejiang Province provides that the people's government at or above the county level should enact a plan for soil pollution control, organize investigations of the soil pollution situation and adjust the function of seriously polluted and difficult to restore cultivated land. The Contingency Plan for '1·21' Leakage Accident of Benzene promulgated by municipal government of Taiyuan City of Shanxi Province regulates the method of division of responsibilities and cooperation of the Agriculture Bureau, the Environmental Protection Bureau and the Cityscape and Sanitation Bureau in the process of disposal of polluted soil.[3] Especially Article 12 of Administrative Measures for Environment Remediation and Restoration of Polluted Area of Shenyang City provides that environmental protection authorities, planning authorities, land and resources authorities, minerals authorities, construction authorities and other relevant authorities should establish a joint supervision system of evaluation and remediation of contaminated sites. The joint supervision system may be the development direction of soil pollution supervision and management system in the future. This is also decided by the diversity of sources of soil pollution and the departmental and regional segmentation of soil legislation.

A. Monitoring, evaluation and reporting system of soil pollution Soil pollution monitoring, reporting and assessment are the basis for knowing the quality and pollution status of soil, and also a precondition for soil pollution control. There are many recent laws that involve monitoring, reporting and assessment of soil pollution, but they are scattered and unsystematic. The main laws and regulations related to soil monitoring are as follows: the Rules on Management of Industrial Pollution Sources Monitoring (for Trial Implementation) (February 22 1991) provides management measures for monitoring industrial pollution sources which may pollute soil; Article 24 in the Rules for Implementation of PRC Water Pollution Prevention and Control Law (March 20 2000) provides: "In cases of using industrial and municipal effluent to irrigate, agriculture management department of people's government at or above the county level should monitor water quality and soil and agricultural products regularly after irrigation, take corresponding measures to prevent underground water and agricultural products from being polluted"; Article

---

[3] The concrete content of this regulation is:

> … the government of Jinyuan district is in charge of the organization of the whole work, the agriculture bureau of the municipal government of Taiyuan City is in charge of collaborating with the government of Jinyuan district, the environmental protection bureau of the municipal government of Taiyuan City is responsible for the monitoring, the cityscape and sanitation bureau of the municipal government of Taiyuan City is responsible for the contact of the work of polluted soil burning.

12.9.7 in the Technical Code for Medical Waste Chemical Disinfection Centralized Treatment (Trial) (February 8 2006) and Article 12.9.7 in the Technical Code for Medical Waste Microwave Disinfection Centralized Treatment (Trial) (February 8 2006) separately require that the soil environment around chemical disinfection treatment plants and microwave disinfection treatment plants should be monitored systematically; Clause 28.8 in the Administrative Measures for Urban Living Garbage provides:

> Regular supervision and measurements of environmental impact including impact on water, air and soil should be carried out according to requirement; tests and evaluations of domestic waste treatment instruments should be done in terms of performance and environment protection index and the results should be reported to local construction (environmental hygiene) department.

Relevant laws with soil evaluation and reporting include: Article 28 in the PRC Land Management Law (revised in 2004) require an assessment of land graduation, and Article 15 in the Implementation Regulations for Land Management Law in 1998 concretely provides a system for implementing assessment of land graduation; Article 18 in the PRC Air Pollution Prevention and Control Law (April 29 2000) provides:

> The competent department of environmental protection management under the State Council jointly with relevant departments, according to weather, landform, soil and other natural conditions, can designate areas already or may produce acid rain and other areas seriously polluted by sulfur dioxide as acid rain control region or sulfur dioxide pollution control region after being approved by State Council;

Clause 7.4 in the Rules on Management of Restricted Use of Pesticides (June 28 2002) provides: "Research reports issued by applicable technology department should be offered if it makes crops suffering harm caused by accumulation of extensive residual pesticides"; Articles 10 and 14 in the Rules on Prevention and Control of Environmental Pollution by Wasted Hazardous Chemicals (August 30 2005) provides that the soil and underground water in an area where dangerous chemicals are produced should be tested and an ecological risk evaluation report must be compiled accordingly. Article 3, Section 3, Part 1 in the Technological Policy for Mine Ecological Environment Protection and Pollution control (September 7 2005) jointly promulgated by the National Environmental Protection Bureau, the State Land Source Ministry and the Health Ministry required that a database of mining areas' basic situation should be established; Article 15 in the Quality and Safety of Agricultural

Product Law (April 29 2006) provides that the regions are prohibited from growing produce where there are toxic and harmful substances in the soil that are therefore not suitable for specific crop production.

B. Remediation and restoration system of soil pollution The control of soil pollution is a dynamic process and there are no specific laws stipulating concrete measures about it although there are some relevant regulations. Laws relating to soil pollution control include: Clause 52.3 in the Rules on Management of Safety of Dangerous Chemicals (January 26 2002) provides that closure, separate measures and wash-infection measures should quickly be taken to the actual and possible harms to earth caused by accidents; Clause 4.1 in the Cleaning Technological Specification of Solid Waste in Bottom of Three Gorge Reservoir (Trial) (June 13 2005) requests that polluted soil in the bottom of Three Gorge Reservoir should be cleared up or given innocuous treatment; the '1·21' Benzene Leakage Pollution Incident Contingency Plan promulgated on January 22 2006 by Taiyuan municipal government of Shanxi Province puts forward polluted soil incineration and soil reciprocal transplantation measures.

Laws relating to soil pollution restoration include: Article 24 in the Rules for Implementation of the PRC Water Pollution Prevention and Control Law (March 20 2000) providing that relevant measures should be taken to avoid polluting soil, underground water and agriculture products in cases of using industrial and municipal effluent to irrigate; the Announcement about Insist on Managing Saving and Intensive Sites by Law to Support Building Socialistic New Countryside (No. [2006] 52 document promulgated by National Ministry of Land and Resources) promulgated by National Ministry of Land and Resources stipulates: "Newly cultivated land should fully use stripped plough layer soil"; Clause 8.2 in the Cultivated Land Requisition-Compensation Balance Examining Methods promulgated by National Ministry of Land and Resources provides: "Construction units occupying cultivated land by authority should strip plough layer soil of occupying cultivated land, to use for land development and consolidation project or soil improvement"; Articles 32 and 35 in the Land Management Law (2004) requests that government take measures to improve soil; Article 3, Section 4, Part 6 in Technological Policy for Lake Reservoir Eutrophication Prevention jointly promulgated by the federal Environment Protection Bureau, the Ministry of Agriculture, the Ministry of Water Resources, the Ministry of Communications and the Ministry of Science and Technology on May 10 2004 provides that ecological protection technology in agricultural area should improve soil structure to strengthen soil's own erosion resistance ability. The China Water Saving Technology Policy Outline (April 21

2005) requests that technology should be used to improve soil structure and its water and nutrient-holding ability; Article 17 in Zhejiang Regulation of Prevention and Control of Environmental Pollution by Solid Waste (March 29 2006) established a restoration system of impure soil; the Land Reclamation Regulation promulgated by State Council on November 8 1988 provides land reclamation methods; and the Interim Measures for Land Reclamation Project Management in Comprehensive Agricultural Development promulgated by Ministry of Land and Resources on December 29 2002 concretely provides for management of land reclamation projects in comprehensive agricultural development.

C. Responsibility system for soil pollution As there is no special soil pollution legislation, the stipulations about responsibilities for soil pollution are scattered throughout relevant laws and regulations. Regulations at central government level include: Article 58 in PRC Solid Waste Law (December 29 2004) providing for administrative legal responsibility for polluting the environment (including soil) by the improper disposal of solid waste; Clause 25.1 in the Rules on Prevention and Control of Environmental Pollution by Wasted Hazardous Chemicals (August 30 2005) provides organizational responsibility for soil monitoring of those who do not monitor according to the rules; Article 338 in the Criminal Law (March 14 1997) provides criminal responsibility for discharge dumping or disposal of hazardous waste violating state regulations that causes serious environmental pollution accident, Article 342 provides criminal responsibility of violating soil management law and causing destruction of huge amounts of cultivated land.

Regulations at local government level include: Article 52 in the Zhejiang Regulation of Prevention and Control of Environmental Pollution by Solid Waste provides for administrative rightful responsibility for not disposing of polluted soil by the requirements; Chapter 5 in the Shenyang Administrative Measures for Remediation and Restoration of Polluted Area Environment provides for legal responsibility – mainly administrative legal responsibility) of the violator in the procedure of remediation and restoration of polluted areas in Article 3.

D. Treatment cost system of soil pollution There are few laws and regulations that provide a fund for the burden of soil pollution control clearly; and regular practice is that "who pollute, who pay and control." But the government shoulders the burden when the person in charge cannot afford to pay or cannot be found. Article 3 in the Announcement about Accomplishing the Work of Environment Pollution Control during Relocation of Enterprises promulgated by National Environment Protection

Bureau (June 1 2004) provides the principle of "who pollutes pays."[4] Clause 17.3 in the Zhejiang Regulation of Prevention and Control of Environmental Pollution by Solid Waste makes supplementary provisions of governmental responsibility when the polluter in charge cannot pay or if their identity is not certain, and it is mainly the formal confirmation of customary practice.[5] Article 11 of the Shenyang Administrative Measures for Remediation and Restoration of Polluted Area Environment further defines the principle of cost sharing which can serve as reference for future legislation. The Land Reclamation Regulation provides for sharing and using of land reclamation costs. Chapter 5 in the Administrative Measures for Land Development and Reclamation of Benxi City in Liaoning Province (March 20 1998) specifically provides for land reclamation and development funds: although the range of land development and reclamation fund is limited, it offers innovative experiences for providing soil pollution remediation funds in the future.[6]

5.3 DEMANDS FOR PERFECTING RELEVANT LAWS AND REGULATIONS AND ENACTING SPECIAL LAWS AND REGULATIONS ON SOIL POLLUTION CONTROL RAISED BY CURRENT SITUATION

5.3.1 Special Legislation on Soil Pollution is Absent and Relevant Provisions on Soil Pollution Control are Scattered and Unsystematic[7]

The issue of soil pollution control is mentioned in the PRC Environmental Protection Law; the PRC Land Management Law to PRC Water Pollution Prevention and Control Law; PRC Air Pollution Prevention and

---

[4] This article provides: "To the environmental pollution problems caused by remained pollutants, original production and business units are responsible for controlling and restoring soil's function."

[5] This article provides: "The cost of cleaning and disposing polluted soil should be taken by unit or individual; the cost is taken by people's government at or government above the county level when person in charge is not definite or has no ability to take charge."

[6] Article 20 provides: "Land development and reclamation fund means fund collected from land use for non-agricultural construction for development and reclamation of cultivated land."

[7] Pang Lu. 2010. "Legislative Idea on Soil Pollution Control". Legal System and Society (3): pp. 24–5.

Control Law; and PRC Solid Waste Law and is also touched on by relevant administrative regulations of State Council as well as local rules, local statutes and departmental regulations. As for control of all kinds of sources of soil pollution, there are also provisions for most of them by special laws and regulations. For example, there are specific laws about how to control air and toxic and harmful substances in the water as the main source of soil pollution and solid waste and radioactive waste and other pollution sources. And there are also special regulations and rules on the use or disposal of pesticides, fertilizers, hazardous chemicals and municipal solid waste. In addition, there is a rudimentary legal system on soil pollution control by monitoring and evaluation of the soil situation and the control and restoration of polluted soil and the legal liability for such pollution. These regulations play an important and active role in actual soil pollution control.

However, if soil pollution becomes increasingly serious, the present applicable laws cannot completely meet the requirements of control. The principal problem is the lack of a guideline for special legislation on soil pollution, which has made relevant regulations on soil pollution control uncoordinated. Soil, air and water are the three elements of the human environment and almost all pollution will enter the soil one way or another. Obviously, soil pollution control needs to be approached in a holistic, comprehensive, legal manner, it cannot meet the necessary requirements if it relies on sporadic and scattered regulations. However, that is the current situation with the existing laws and regulations. The various laws and regulations mentioned above usually contain one or two relevant articles. Furthermore, under current legislation there exist situations where a pertinent basic soil pollution control system is absent, for example, soil pollution area gradation, soil pollution control planning, soil pollution liability identification, born of cost of soil pollution remediation and so on. The lack of these basic systems mean that soil pollution control cannot be carried out efficiently.

5.3.2 The Intended Purpose will be Hard to Achieve if There is Only Reliance on Amendments to Existing Legislation

The current situation is that soil pollution is becoming ever more severe and, as identified above, existing legislation is not adapted to the actual need for control. It is almost impossible to achieve the required purpose successfully by making amendments and supplements to existing relevant laws and regulations; instead it is necessary to enact special laws and regulations on soil pollution control. The reasons are as follows: first, the fundamental problem at present is the lack of a basic or principal legal system: amending and supplementing existing laws and regulations can only provide temporary solutions. But making a new special law could offer a permanent cure. Second, it is hard to include a legislative plan modifying many existing laws and regulations merely on the grounds of meeting the needs of soil pollution control. Third, although modification and revision might work, the process can be slow and will not meet an urgent demand because too many laws and regulations need to be modified or revised. Finally, it is not economic from the angle of the legislation cost. It is suggested here that special legislation would solve the problems by concentrating resources and fundamentally solving the problems.

5.3.3 Special Legislation on Soil Pollution Control is Beneficial to Strengthening People's Awareness

Soil pollution control awareness should be a public psychological experience and the evaluation of soil protection and the prevention and control of soil pollution and other phenomena should be viewed under particular historical conditions. It includes people's perspectives and attitudes to soil pollution control and the cognition of the rights and obligations in soil pollution control. For a long time, at the very mention of pollution people first thought of water pollution, air pollution, noise pollution and solid waste pollution; they were relatively unacquainted with soil pollution, heat pollution and light pollution. What were the reasons? Apart from obnoxiousness (invisibility), the long-term accumulation of soil pollution made it hard to perceive or feel; but another more important reason may have been lack of a special law like the PRC Air Pollution Prevention and Control Law and PRC Solid Waste Law. Because there was no relevant law, people did not know that there were stipulations about protecting the soil and preventing and controlling soil pollution systematically, or that they had their rights and obligations relating to control. If a law on soil pollution control is enacted, it will not only strengthen the legitimate means of controlling soil pollution in our country, but could also enhance people's consciousness of the control. Also the purpose of enhancing people's awareness is to bring their attention to it and then ask them to obey and follow the provisions of preventing and controlling soil pollution. This is also one of the basic purposes of enacting a special legislation.

5.3.4 Further Improvement of Relevant Concrete Laws and Regulations

The pertinence of soil pollution legislation needs further definition. Soil pollution has characteristics including invisibility, lag, cumulation, irreversibility and resistance to treatment. Existing regulations have failed to design systems aimed at the particular characteristics of soil pollution thus reducing the effect of those regulations on pollution control. For example, the effect of controlling soil pollution cannot be achieved by controlling solid waste, sewage and waste gas, because the pollution by these wastes is often intuitional and can be perceived through the senses. However, soil pollution is different and its confirmation is achieved by testing soil quality and its effect on the health of humans and animals. The operability of laws and regulations on soil pollution needs further enhancement. Among the existing regulations relating to its control, some are abstract and not operative enough. For instance, the existing provisions of soil pollution control, only specify "prevent soil pollution", "improve soil" synoptically. However, the provisions do not clearly point out how to protect soil from pollution or how to carry out control, restoration and improvement, which makes it hard to implement these provisions efficiently and specifically. Relevant regulations of soil pollution control need to be improved immediately to adapt to the development of the times. The fact is that some existing regulations on soil pollution control are lagging behind and cannot meet the current requirement of soil pollution control. For example, our country promulgated the Environmental Standard of Soil Quality in 1995. This standard is a technical code with legal character and is an indispensable and essential component of soil pollution control regulations and has decisive significance in confirming soil pollution. However, industry experts generally believe that this standard emphasizes unity too much and does not adapt to the character of soil diversification in our country. At the same time, the critical value of lead provided in the standard is too high and such an amount may already have damaged children's health. In addition, there are too few kinds of organic pollutant in this standard, only BHC and DDT. In fact, the production of the above two kinds of pesticides was stopped in 1983 and the harm caused thereafter is getting lower, but standards of other different pollutants have not been included.

5.4 CONDITIONS AND FEASIBILITY OF SPECIAL LEGISLATION ON SOIL POLLUTION CONTROL

For any legislation, there exists a question of demonstrating its feasibility, because legislation can only be started when the legislative conditions are mature, or relatively mature, or are based on having basic legislative conditions. The feasibility of special soil pollution control means there must be a practical possibility of law-making. There are indications that the conditions for special legislation on soil pollution control have been or could be considered to have been met.[8]

5.4.1 Years of Accumulated Practical Experience of Work

Legislators do not to "make" or "invent" laws, they "state" laws. "Stating" laws is to generalize and summarize a successful experience or some good methods accumulated by long-term social activities under conventional rules, state them through legal form and raise them to legitimate norms to act as a standard of behavior for people behaving similarly in the future. Obviously, legislation cannot be achieved without social life or specific social practice. Although there is no soil pollution control law so far in China, there are practices of such control. The history of the practice of soil pollution control has been present for many years; and in that experience of soil pollution control, some policies, methods or measures have been promulgated. This has all added up to a wealth of experience and has also laid a solid foundation for exceptional legislation on soil pollution control.

5.4.2 China Pays Attention to Legislation on Soil Pollution Control

Considering the severe situation of soil pollution in China, the Environment and Resources Protection Committee of the National People's Congress have, since 1994, turned their attention to legislation. In the meantime, representatives have been proposing bills protecting the rural environment since the Eighth National People's Congress at the second session. As a result, according to representatives' repeated proposals, the Environment and Resources Protection Committee have taken the time to enact Soil Pollution Control Law having studied the environmental and resource legislation plan of National People's Congress. The Decision on Implementing Outlook of Scientific Development and Protecting Environment of State Council of China (No. [2005] 39) promulgated in December 2005 also clearly states: "We should take time to draw up a draft of laws and regulations related to soil pollution." The National Environmental Protection Rules Construction Plan of the Eleventh Five-Year Plan promulgated by National Environment Protection Bureau in November 2005 explicitly brought Law on Soil Pollution Control into the legislation plan of Eleventh Five-Year Plan. These are all appropriate

---

[8] Wang Shuyi. 2008. "Several Thoughts about Enacting Law on Soil Pollution Control". *Wuhan City of China: Law Review* (3): pp. 75–77.

supporting conditions of enacting the Law on Soil Pollution Control of People's Republic of China.

5.4.3 China Has Accumulated Some Experience of Legislation on Soil Pollution Control

Although laws and regulations at present related to soil pollution control are not specifically or directly made for such control, and are scattered through different laws and regulations, they center on soil pollution control in terms of content. Decisions on soil pollution control made by some legislators are also fulfilled through many investigations, studies, analyses and demonstrations; these are the legislators' confirmed summaries and generalizations on soil pollution control through human practice. Therefore, although there are some problems (like being relatively scattered and not systematic, lacking relative principles and strong pertinence as well as not being easy to operate) in these applicable laws and regulations, they are still very significant towards making the present Law on Prevention and Control of Soil Pollution of the PRC. In the meantime, local legislation on soil pollution control has also been extremely active in recent years; and in spite of the fact that most of local legislation is rough and general, it provides a variety of legislative forms and has its own appeals. These can all provide a useful reference for legislation of soil pollution control on the national level. Taking Suggestions on Implementation of Medium-and Low-yielding Farmland Transformation and Construction of Hangzhou in 2002–06, enacted by the Agricultural Bureau and communicated by the government of Hangzhou City, as an example, it put forward a concept of "the soil obstacle factor". Despite the fact that there is no precise definition of "soil obstacle factors" in this normative document, and it is uncertain whether or not the concept is scientific, it provides a new idea for such legislation in our country. Taking another instance, the Zhejiang Regulation of Prevention and Control of Environmental Pollution by Solid Waste provided for implementation of an environmental risk evaluation and restoration system on polluted soil, and made specific provisions for soil environment risk assessment, range of soil restoration, implementation procedures, responsible personnel and forms of liability. Although these rules are a little unrefined, they provide specific system designs and valuable experience for establishing environmental risk evaluation and a restoration system of polluted soil that could be incorporated in further federal soil pollution control legislation.

5.4.4 The Ongoing National Investigation Creates Conditions for Special Legislation

The objective basis of enacting soil pollution control law is to build on the actual situation. Since the Peoples Republic of China was founded, we have carried out two national soil surveys in the end of 1950s and 1970s. They were both geared towards agricultural production and their main purpose was to examine soil fertility, not to reveal soil pollution. To really be familiar with the present soil quality situation in our country, central finance arranged special funds for soil quality situation investigation through a unique fund of national lands and resources investigation in 1999. From 1999 to 2005, central finance arranged a total of RMB 230,000,000 as a special fund, which achieved a substantive result. In early 2005, central finance set up a special fund for the federal soil situation investigation and pollution prevention and arranged an initial fund of RMB 20,000,000. In 2006 central finance even set aside RMB 130,000,000 as special fund. In July 2006, National Environment Protection Bureau and Ministry of Land and Resources jointly raised RMB 1,000, 000,000 to carry out a national soil pollution situation investigation. The relevant investigation report of the soil pollution situation will be promulgated in succession with development of a nationwide soil pollution situation investigation, and will provide a rare scientific basis for soil pollution control legislation.

5.4.5 Overseas Relevant Legislation can be a Reference

Overseas soil pollution control legislation started in 1970s and entered an active period after 1990s. So far, many countries such as the U.S., Netherlands, U.K., Germany, Japan and Korea have already enacted and promulgated special laws or regulations on soil pollution control. The U.S. enacted its Resource Conservation and Recovery Act to regulate, among other things, the land disposal of sod and hazardous waste in 1976, and its so-called "Superfund" legislation to clean up polluted soils in 1980. The Netherlands was the first state in Europe to have specific legislation on soil protection, with clean up regulations dating from 1983, after the public became aware of toxic sites in the country. In 1987 the Soil Protection Act was adopted to protect the functions of the soil through conservation and restoration and to regulate pollution sources. Both laws require the establishment of soil quality standards. In 1991 the state adopted a voluntary system to clean up polluted soils on operating industrial sites. Other laws concerning waste disposal, chemical wastes, nuisance, pesticides and nature conservation help protect the soil as well.[9] At the same time international society has also paid attention to soil pollution control. In November 2006, the Soil Law Expert Panel Environmental Law Committee of IUCN drafted the Soil Protection Protocol (and sustainable use) (Draft). In the meantime, many other international organizations are also promoting international soil protection legislation. It can be said that after decades of accumulating experience, constant maturity and perfection and experience through its legislation and modifications there is much that can be meaningfully referred to for soil pollution control legislation in our country.

5.5 PATTERN AND BASIC ORIENTATION OF SPECIAL LEGISLATION

5.5.1 The Existing Form of Special Law Should be Law

The existing form of modern Chinese law is constitutional law, administrative rule, military statute, local statute, autonomous statute, law and regulation of the SEZs and international treaties acceded to by China and others. The existing form of special law on soil pollution control should be law[10] is one kind of expressive form of the above. Law is usually used to regulate or adjust some aspects of a problem or relationship that is fundamental to, or comprehensive in, national and social life, or to adjust some aspect of an important and basic regulation or system in federal, social and civic life. The problem or social relation it regulates or adjusts is often important and comprehensive; its legal validity is only lower than the constitution but higher than clerical rule, local statute and departmental regulation. It is the basis for making other expressive forms of laws. Therefore, considering that soil pollution control involves agricultural products, food, people's health and national ecology and security of additional aspects, the important role that soil pollution control and the work on it plays in development of social economy in our country, Law on Prevention and Control of Soil Pollution of People's Republic of China is recommended as the name and it should be orientated as "law".

---

[9] Dinah Shelton, Alexandre Kiss. 2005. *Judicial handbook on Environmental Law*. United Nations Environment Programme: p. 88.

[10] Cao Baohe. 2012. "Thoughts about Legislation on Soil Pollution Control". *Kunming City of China: Panorama Weekly* (35): p. 8.

5.5.2 Law on Soil Pollution Control Belongs to General Laws

According to relevant regulation of the constitution, laws in our country can be divided into basic laws and other laws. Basic laws adjust significant social relations and solve problems in national, social and civic life and criminal law, civil law, procedural law, marriage law and others belong to the basic law. The basic law is made by National People's Congress. Other social relations and problems of certain aspects are adjusted and solved by other laws which are also called non-basic laws or general laws. Compared with basic laws, the range of the regulative object of other laws is a little narrower and often limited to a certain aspect or field and made by Standing Committee of National People's Congress. What the Law on Prevention and Control of Soil Pollution of the PRC plans to adjust is the social relations produced in domestic soil pollution control. These social relations are of the same kind and in the same field and are both national and comprehensive. And the basic purpose of making a Law on Prevention and Control of Soil Pollution of the PRC is to provide unified most basic or important legal rules for national soil pollution control, it thus has the characteristic of the content of national universal laws, and should, therefore, be classified as national customary law.

5.5.3 Law on Soil Pollution Control is a "Basic Law" in the Field of Soil Pollution Control

Basic law is also called "lead law" or "leading law", and it means the main or most important law in the field of soil pollution control. As the basic law in a field, it adjusts the most important or main social relation in this field and provides the most basic legal norms or systems for adjustment of other relations. As the basic law in the field of soil pollution and prevention, Law on Prevention and Control of Soil Pollution of the PRC provides unified legal principles and systems, which are the most basic legal evidence of soil pollution control and it provides concrete basis for further regulations with lesser legal effect.

5.5.4 Law on Soil Pollution Control is an Important Part of China's Legal System of Environmental Law

The relationship between Law on Prevention and Control of Soil Pollution of the PRC and the existing PRC Environmental Protection Law is that of "son law" and "parent law". The former is "son law" and the latter is "parent law". The PRC Environmental Protection Law should be viewed as one of the legislative bases when drafting a Law on Prevention and Control of Soil Pollution of the PRC.

The legal system of environmental law in China is made up of a number of sub-legal branches. These sub-legal branches are often divided into three further groups of sub-legal branch; one is made up of sub-legal branch of pollution prevention called "pollution prevention law" which mainly includes PRC Water Pollution Prevention and Control of Law, PRC Air Pollution Prevention and Control Law, PRC Noise Pollution Prevention and Control Law, PRC Solid Waste Law, PRC Radioactive Pollution Prevention and Control Law and so on; another is made up of sub-legal branch of exploiting, using, protecting and managing resources called the "law of natural resources, which mainly includes PRC Forest Law; PRC Grassland Law; PRC Mineral Resources Law; and so on; and the third is made up of sub-legal branch of comprehensive environmental protection and resources exploitation and utilization called "ecological security protection law", which mainly includes PRC Environmental Impact Assessment Law, PRC Cleaner Production Promotion Law, PRC Water and Soil Conservation Law and so on. The Law on Prevention and Control of Soil Pollution of the PRC is aimed at preventing soil pollution and protecting soil and ecology safety and also used to adjust principal social relations produced in soil pollution prevention activities. From the view of the purpose of making the law and regulating the objectives, it obviously belongs to the legitimate branch of environmental law and classified in the group of the sub-legal branch of "pollution prevention law."

5.6 BASIC IDEAS OF ENACTING LAW ON SOIL POLLUTION CONTROL OF THE PEOPLE'S REPUBLIC OF CHINA

5.6.1 Basic Orientation of Law on Soil Pollution Control

Any law on soil pollution control in China should be a "basic law", that is it should provide the most important or fundamental or "basic" issues on soil pollution control in its content. First, it should fix the policy of soil pollution control that will be adopted within a certain period of time either at present or in the future. At the same time, it should set up a system for a supervision and management system, primarily the setting up of organizations with divisions of powers and functions. Second, it should define the basic rights and obligations of every subject in soil pollution control and the supervision of such activity. It should provide basic legal principles and systems for soil pollution control and for preventing soil pollution as well as the basic requirements and measures of restoration or remediation of polluted soil. Finally, it also should clearly provide for the settlement of disputes in soil pollution control and for the adverse legal consequences to be undertaken by parties breaking the law. On the structure of content, chapter divisions or settings should either be taken as standard or should reflect social relations to be adjusted or similar and relative issues that require to be solved.

5.6.2 Basic Purpose of Law on Soil Pollution Control

Under the guidance of scientific development and aimed directly at preventing and controlling soil pollution and protecting soil security the law should be designed to protect people's health and to ensure a sustainable use of soil as its basic purpose and, as its final goal, to pursue the harmony between man and soil. It should take the idea of comprehensive soil ecology management as its basic concept and, based on soil pollution control, regulate the control or restoration of polluted soil as its emphasis, using as its foundation the domestic exiting legal norms on control and also taking into account relevant legislation from the international community, other countries and Taiwan. Based on the above, a special law on soil pollution control could be enacted.

5.6.3 Basic Category of Law on Soil Pollution Control

As for the category of legislation on soil pollution control, it mainly involves two aspects: one is the prevention of soil pollution; the other is the control or restoration of polluted soil. From the perspective of the situation and actual requirement of China's soil pollution control, it should regulate from the aspect of prevention and control. "Control" can be highlighted, but "prevention" should not be neglected. The reason that soil pollution in our country is currently grave is, perhaps, related to the public ignorance on the means of prevention of soil pollution. Therefore, soil pollution control legislation at the present stage should take into account both "prevention" and "control". In addition, the prevention of soil pollution cannot merely be understood in its narrowest sense, i.e., the prohibition of emissions that may cause soil pollution. In fact, making a soil pollution control plan, monitoring soil environment quality, investigating soil pollution and assessing soil environmental risk and others all belong to the prevention of soil pollution.

5.6.4 Basic Composition of Law on Soil Pollution Control

This law should not be simply a "codification" and "collection" or "repetition" and "duplication" of existing legal norms or provisions on soil pollution control.[11] It should be a new law enacted under the guidance of prevailing thought on soil pollution control, on the basis of the concept of the whole ecological perspective and on the premise of respecting the discipline of soil pollution control. It should be a summary of policies, measures, methods and other managerial experiences or lessons adopted in years of activity of soil pollution control. Therefore, policies, measures, methods and effective managerial experiences, which have proved successful in practice, should be established as a code of conduct in a legitimate form by enacting a law. Existing rules on soil pollution control in existing laws in China should be adequately considered and absorbed into the making of this law. For example, there have already been several legal norms of soil pollution control in the PRC Land Management Law; PRC Water Pollution Prevention and Control Law; PRC Solid Waste Law; and PRC Air Pollution Prevention and Control Law; and others. In the making of this law, account should be taken of the pertinent rules on soil pollution control of existing laws, but also look beyond them. The law should pay attention to where existing laws and regulations both connect and conflict with each other to avoid contradictions or discrepancies.

5.6.5 Basic Feature of Law on Prevention and Control of Soil Pollution

This law should not be a "proclamation" law, but be a law with strong maneuverability. A law without operability can only be a policy statement indicating some attitude or standpoint but it cannot be carried out. Laws are not used for public worshiping but are used to regulate people's behavior in everyday life. Therefore, any legislation on soil pollution control should emphasize the founding of feasible systems.

---

[11] Zhang Ming. 2010. "Several Issues Which Should Be Paid Attention to in Legislation on Soil Pollution Control in Our Country". *Guangzhou City of China: Cards World* (2): p. 71.

6. Law on prevention of toxic and harmful substances pollution

Hou Jiaru

Toxic and harmful substances refer to those that are used in daily life that pollute the environment and make people and animals toxic, sicken or die. These types of substances are not used in solid waste, for they usually exist as the raw materials of production, production finished goods or necessities people use every day that are useful substances instead of discarded ones. These types of substances can cause environmental pollution with improper management and use that causes dangers to mankind. China has promulgated no comprehensive legislation on the prevention of pollution caused by the chemical substances up to date, however, some regulations that were originally aimed at controlling the chemical substances, provide, to a degree, legal grounds to prevent chemical pollution. The categories of chemical substances are covered by following regulations, namely: (1) rules on the prevention of pollution caused by toxic chemical substances; (2) rules on radioactive substances; and (3) rules on pesticides.

6.1 LEGAL REGULATION ON CONTROLLING AND PREVENTION OF CHEMICAL SUBSTANCE POLLUTION

6.1.1 Legislation Profile on Prevention of Toxic and Harmful Chemical Pollution

'Chemical' means a chemical substance whether by itself or in a mixture or preparation, whether manufactured or obtained from nature and includes such substances used as industrial chemicals and pesticides.[1] 'Toxic chemical' refers to a chemical damaging to the health and

[1] *Provisions on the First Import of Chemicals and the Import and Export of Toxic Chemicals (HUA XUE PIN SHOU CI JIN KOU JI YOU DU HUA XUE PIN JIN CHUKOU HUAN JING GUAN LI GUI DING), Article 4.*

environment through environmental cumulation, bioaccumulation and bio transformation or chemical reaction after entering the environment, or posing serious harm to the human health and posing potential hazard through contact.[2] 'Hazardous chemicals' refer to highly toxic chemicals and other chemicals that are toxic, corrosive, explosive, flammable or combustion-supporting and can harm people, facilities or the environment.[3]

China has been implementing strict management mechanisms on highly toxic and harmful chemical substances. As early as the 1950s, China issued regulations on the management of agricultural medicines. In 1961, the State Council transferred and issued six safety management rules concerning chemical dangerous goods of production, storage, management, use, transportation and fireproofing of chemical dangerous goods. Later in the 1970s, management of chemical dangerous goods in China began to extend to protection instead of being solely limited to safety management and a series of rules, regulations as well as some safety standards and environmental standards on toxic and harmful chemical substances were formulated.

In order to enhance the safety management of hazardous chemicals, guarantee people's safety in life and assets and protect the environment, the State Council issued the Regulations on the Safety Management of Hazardous Chemicals. These regulations carried out overall and specific regulations on safety management in terms of the production, operation, storage, transportation, use of and disposal of hazardous chemicals, etc. by clarifying requirements on environmental protection from several chemicals. The other laws for hazardous chemicals include the Measures for the Administration of Production Licenses for Hazardous Chemicals, the Measures for the Administration of Operating Licenses for Hazardous Chemicals (revised in 2011), the Measures for the Administration of Safe Use Permit for Hazardous Chemicals (new in 2012), the Measures for the Administration of Registration of Hazardous Chemicals (revised in 2011), the Measures for the Administration of Standardization of Management of Hazardous Chemicals (released in August 2011), the Measures for the Registration of Environmental Administration of Hazardous

---

2 *Regulations on Environmental Management of First-time Imported Chemicals and of Import and Export and Dangerous Chemicals, art. 4.*

3 *Rules on Management of Safety of Dangerous Chemicals* (WEI XIAN HUA XUE PIN AN QUAN GUAN LI TIAO LI) as revised, was adopted at the 144th executive meeting of the State Council on February 16, 2011, which is hereby promulgated, and came into force on December 1, 2011, revised on December 7, 2013, art. 4.

chemicals for public consultations (issued by the Ministry of Environmental Protection (MEP) in 2012), etc.

The Bureau, Customhouse, MOFTEC (Ministry of Foreign Trade, Economic Cooperation) released Regulations on Environmental Management of First-time Imported Chemicals and of Import and Export and Dangerous Chemicals; The National Bureau modified these regulations on 8 October 2007 by its Order No. 41. The revised order deleted articles 9, 10 and 11 of the original regulations. The State Council also issued Management Regulations on Precursor Chemical on 26 August 2005,

Moreover, China has promulgated several laws and regulations on medical management, food health, veterinary drug management, agricultural drug management and controlled chemical management and so on that also make specialized regulations on the management of such chemicals as medical, veterinary and agricultural drugs, food additives, cosmetics and chemicals used in the monitoring of chemical military raw materials and so on. The PRC Environmental Protection Law, PRC Water Pollution Prevention and Control Law, PRC Air Pollution Prevention and Control Law, PRC Marine Environmental Protection Law, PRC Solid Waste Law and other laws and regulations also have rules on preventing toxic and harmful chemicals from polluting the environment. It is a pity that China has not yet formulated a specialized law in enhancing safety controlling on toxic and harmful chemicals.

6.1.2 Principles on Prevention and Treatment of Chemical Prevention

6.1.2.1 Principle of overall management and key controlling

Various chemical substances can cause real or potential dangers to physical health and to the environment. Therefore, all natural or artificially made chemical elements, as well as their compounds and finished goods, must be subject to overall environmental management. The overall environmental management of chemical substances is not to carry out a strict control of all chemical substances without distinguishing their features but to implement category control for reasonable management in accordance with the features of the chemical substances and any ensuing substances and dangerous chemicals. For example, to carry out registration management on all chemical substances to master their production, their condition of use flow; to implement the management of information on normal chemicals; to list chemical substances that could cause serious harm to health and the environment and to demand that the state adopt active mandatory measures for intervention, including prohibiting and strictly limiting the mandatory measures.

6.1.2.2 Principle of whole process management and controlling

The most optimized manner of preventing pollutions of toxic and harmful chemicals is to reduce the production and use of chemicals that might cause pollution or to grant proper placement of these chemicals before they enter the environment. The whole process and each link of the production, management, use, storage, transportation, disposal and discarding of toxic and harmful chemicals may cause pollutions, so their environmental management must be brought to bear on each link so that whole process monitoring is implemented.

Article II in the Rules on Management of Safety of Dangerous Chemicals provides: 'The production, operation, storage, transportation and use of dangerous chemicals as well as the disposal of dangerous chemicals within the boundary of the People's Republic of China must observe laws and regulations concerning other administrative rules related with safety production of this rule and the state.' Article III in Regulations on Preventing Facilities Containing PCB and Its Wastes from Polluting Environment provides: 'this rule is applied to the use of electrical facilities with PCB and collection, storage, transportation, processing, disposal, pollution management and import and export activities of wastes and garbage containing PCB'. Article 5 provides: 'Management organ and individuals who owns electric facilities of PCB and PCBs shall carry out whole-process controlling on PCB pollutions'.

6.1.2.3 Principle of controlling risks

To control the real and potential ecological risks possessed by toxic and harmless chemical substances, the core of pollution prevention is to implement risk controlling, reduce and control the release of toxic and harmless chemicals into the environment and to try to reduce and/or decrease the number of chemical incidents. The key to implementing environmental risk management is to control the safety requirements of toxic and harmful chemicals and incident risks. Article 31 in Environmental Management Methods of New Chemical Substances provides:

> routine declaratory certification holders and corresponding processing holders shall adopt one or many of the following measures on risk controlling in accordance with regulations in registration certification: a) to carry out education on risks and prevention of new chemicals; … certification holders of dangerous new chemical substances (including new chemical substances under key environmental crisis) and processing users should observe the currently existing laws and relevant administrative rules such as the Regulations on the Safety Management of Hazardous Chemicals.

6.1.2.4 Principle combining pollutant prevention with safety management and quality management

The occurrences of toxic and harmful chemical pollution are mostly related to inadequate management or to insufficient and/or improper safety measures, although some are due to the qualities of the chemicals. Enhancing the safety and quality management of chemicals can effectively help to reduce the occurrence of chemical pollution, therefore, pollution prevention and environmental management of such chemicals must be combined with safety and quality management. The fundamental requirements for pollution prevention and environmental management, such as reliance on safety and quality and 'safety as the priority' should be taken as part of the measures; in safety and quality management of toxic and harmful chemicals, the requirement of environmental protection should be part of the safeguards while environmental factors must be taken as among the necessary contents for the sake of safety. Rules on Management of Safety of Dangerous Chemicals sets 'protection of environment' as one of the requirements that also regulate specific requirements and measures on environmental protection.

6.1.3 Basis System for Prevention of Toxic and Harmful Elements

6.1.3.1 Production and management license system

China adopts a system whereby the production of toxic and harmful chemicals must make a request for examination before production. An enterprise that manufactures dangerous chemical substances is required to obtain the approval on examination by people's government at provincial level or above. An enterprise that manufactures highly dangerous chemical substances is required to obtain the approval of provincial people's government. The unit and individual that processes polychlorinated biphenyl power device shall apply for registration to the local administration department of environment protection. Enterprises at the level of country, town and streets are prevented from manufacturing dangerous chemical substances.

The country carries out restrictive controls on new construction, reconstruction and expanded construction of enterprises for manufacturing highly dangerous chemical substances. An enterprise that carries out new construction, reconstruction or expanded construction shall be subject to the approval process according to relevant regulations. And an enterprise that operates hazardous chemical substances is required to be qualified under conditions specified by the Rules on Management of Safety of Dangerous Chemicals. With respect to the circulation of dangerous chemical substances, the relevant regulations shall be complied with. China prohibits the production and management of dangerous chemical substances without a license.

6.1.3.2 Measures and systems on safety protection and pollution prevention

Enterprises concerned in the production, storage and utilization of toxic chemicals, on the basis of their type and property, shall be equipped with corresponding security protection facilities and tools with such functions as ventilation, anti-explosion, decompression, fireproofing, lighting protection, detection, alarming, automatic interlock, cooling, moisture proof and static elimination, etc. Containers filled with dangerous chemicals must be inspected before and after utilization to prevent fire, explosion and poisoning, etc. It is required to build special storage yards or storage rooms for dangerous substances to store dangerous chemical substances.

The transportation, loading and unloading of toxic chemicals shall be carried out according to regulations and requirements relating to the national management of dangerous goods transport and based on the type and property of the transported dangerous toxic chemicals. At same time, corresponding safety protection and pollution prevention measures for crash, sluggish and leakage, etc. shall be taken; with respect to the dangerous chemicals whose properties are incompatible, the shipping of them shall not violate regulations on restricted and mixed shipping; mixing shipping of goods and passengers or the utilization of vehicles for passengers is prohibited where toxic chemicals are being shipped. In cases of rule violation, the consignor may not consign for shipment and the transportation department may not accept the consignment.

It is forbidden to construct new production projects and facilities for loading, unloading and storage in the areas that require special protection such as natural preservation areas, landscapes of famous scenery and areas where the source of drinking water is to be protected. And it is further prohibited to store toxic chemicals in holes, fractures and caverns in permeable layers or abandoned mine craters. In case of an oil pollution accident on ship, or in the sea or a river, a chemical oil dispersant is required to be used, it is necessary to obtain the approval of the relevant supervision department and the usage amount is strictly controlled.

6.1.3.3 Import and export management system

China adopts a system of listing toxic and harmful chemicals for import and export. The State Environmental Protection Administration (SEPA) will work out the list of toxic and harmful chemicals prohibited or strictly limited in China and take strict measures to control the toxic and harmful elements in the list.[4]

With respect to the first time a chemical is imported, it is necessary to submit a registration application of environmental management for first import to SEPA and provide information and samples as required. SEPA will grant registration or temporary registration to the chemical that conforms to the regulations and requirements of China's environmental management, and issue a registration certificate or temporary registration certificate. The chemicals that do not obtain a document of registration environment administration licensing cannot be imported.[5]

With respect to chemicals listed in Directory of Toxic Chemicals Prohibited or Strictly Limited in China, a registration application for environment management of toxic chemicals import requires to be submitted to SEPA. Meanwhile, a registration certificate and releasing notice shall be obtained. With respect to chemicals listed in planned export directory, it is necessary to submit a registration application for environment management of export to SEPA. After SEPA hears the application, it will notify the administration department of the export country to issue a registration certificate for environment management of toxic chemical export with export permission to the chemicals it has agreed may be imported.[6]

6.1.3.4 Supervision and management system on chemicals

Chemicals are divided into four types in China: the first type refers to chemicals that can serve as chemical weapons; the second type refers to chemicals that can serve as precursor for manufacturing chemical weapons; the third type refers to chemicals that can serve as main raw material for manufacturing chemical weapons; and the fourth refers to particular organic chemicals except explosives and pure hydrocarbon compounds. The country will carry out supervision and management on these four chemicals in the form of a publishing directory, and separately and strictly execute rules on examination, production and utilization.

The approval of authority for chemical industry of the state council is required for manufacturing the chemical of the first type, which may be manufactured only in an appointed small-scale facility. With respect to production of specified organic chemicals that have phosphorus, sulfur and fluorous of the supervised chemicals of the second, the third and the

---

[4] Regulations on Environmental Management of First-time Imported Chemicals and of Import and Export and Dangerous Chemicals, arts 3, 5 and 6.

[5] Ibid., arts 9 and 10.

[6] Ibid., arts 12 and 13.

fourth types, a special license system is adopted. The utilization of supervised chemicals of the first type is required approval of the authority for chemical industry of the state council. The utilization of supervised chemicals of the second type is required examination and approval of the authority for chemical industry of provincial people's government. In addition, the country conducts strict controls on the import of supervised chemicals of the first type and stipulates that the supervised chemical of the first type shall not be imported for any purpose except scientific research, medical treatment, drug-making or defense.

6.1.3.5 Emergency response and final treatment system for pollution accident

Every country pays special attention to eliminating accidental pollution by toxic and harmful chemicals and for taking emergency rescue measures following such an accident. In 1988, United Nations Environment Program put forward the 'regional emergency accident awareness and preparation scheme' ('namely Apeier Scheme') to improve the awareness of governments, enterprises and the public on preventing and processing accidental pollution and to strengthening the responses to accidents with the cooperation of the whole society. Many countries pay much attention to this scheme and China also made an active response to it, by successively formulated laws and regulations and by definitely specifying the emergency rescue of accidental pollution by toxic and harmful chemicals, which will be organized, coordinated and implemented by local people's government. The emergency rescue measures include facilities used for controlling, reducing and eliminating pollution, such as the controlling of pathways, food, water sources and the evacuation of personnel, the removal of food and decontamination for polluted areas, as well as the rescue, decontamination, transfer of, and medical treatment for, polluted personnel.[7]

6.1.4 Safety Supervision and Management Mechanism of Chemical Substances

Article 6 of the Rules on Management of Safety of Dangerous Chemicals sets specific regulations on safety supervision and management mechanism of chemical substances. Major departments responsible for production,

---

[7] Rules on Management of Safety of Dangerous Chemicals, arts 66, 67, 68, 69, 70, 71, 72, 73, 74.

operation, storage, transportation, use and disposal of waste dangerous chemicals are mainly contained in the economic trade comprehensive management department under the State Council as well as the economic trade management department of people's government on provincial level, autonomous and municipality directly under the Central Government, public security department, quality check-up department, environmental protection department, railway, civil aviation department, health administrative department, commercial administrative management departments, post department.

These departments carry out separate management functions according to their own duties. The duties of each department are respectively: the State Council and economic trade comprehensive management departments are responsible for safety supervision and the management of dangerous chemicals and for the production, storage, establishment of warehousing companies, review on expansion and re-establishment, packaging of dangerous chemicals, review of professional production companies of containers (including jars used for transportation) and issuing fixed-point business licenses for dangerous goods, certification of domestic dangerous chemicals and organization and coordination of incidents and emergency rescue of dangerous chemicals, etc. The public security departments are responsible for public safety management of dangerous chemicals, issuing purchasing certificates for toxic chemicals and purchasing permits and reviewing transportation certification for toxic chemicals, etc. Quality monitoring departments are responsible for issuing production permits and quality supervision of dangerous chemicals, packages and containers. The environmental protection departments are responsible for the supervision and management of disposing of discarded chemicals, surveying pollution and ecological destruction events of dangerous chemicals; on-the-spot emergency monitoring of toxic chemical events and the rating of imported dangerous chemicals, etc. Railway, civil aviation and traffic departments are responsible for safety management and supervision check-ups on transportation organs and tools for dangerous chemicals. The commercial administrative management departments allow approval and certificates of relevant departments in evaluating and issuing business licenses for production, operation, warehousing and transportation organs, supervising the marketing operation activities of dangerous chemicals. The post department is responsible for supervision and check-up on posted dangerous chemicals.[8]

---

[8] Ibid., art. 6.

6.1.5 Completion of Legislation of Prevention and Treatment of Pollution of Chemical Substances

Compared with legislation on other aspects of pollutions, the legislation on prevention and treatment of chemical pollution was a late starter. Therefore, the legal system for the prevention and treatment on chemical pollution is not yet completed while its management mechanism and measures do not satisfy the needs of pollution controlling that leave much room to be perfected and completed. At present, an urgent need is to formulate a comprehensive Law on Prevention and Treatment on Toxic and Harmful Chemical Pollution that should address prime answers as follows:

1. To clearly limit the scope of adjustment. The definition of chemical substance is expansive, so if no clear limiting scope in legislation is set, it could cause much overlapping and repetition over many of the existing laws and regulations. In order to avoid this, we need to clarify and limit the scope of the legislation by a method regulating the use in the abstract while, at the same time, removing some of the more obsolete laws on chemicals. According to the current legislation and management mechanism in China, drugs, kaif, civil explosive substance, cosmetics and veterinary drugs could be excluded because they are to be adjusted by other specialized legislations.
2. To regulate principals of chemical pollution controlling. In the prevention and treatment law of chemical substance, principles of prevention, whole-process controlling, cleaned production and public participation on controlling of chemical pollution should be clarified.
3. To build an effective supervision management mechanism. China has implemented the method of multiple-department management in its management of chemical substances, thus, the administrative management mechanism of safety management, the management on auditing chemicals, the management of dangerous wastes, agricultural management, food health and drug management have not been structured and/or integrated, in particular the environmental management of chemical substance is weak in terms of institutional construction and management institutions. In order to carry out an overall systematic control on chemical pollution, a management mechanism of unified supervision and management combining responsibilities with duties is required.

6.2 LEGAL REGULATION ON PREVENTION & TREATMENT OF RADIOACTIVE CONTAMINATION POLLUTION

6.2.1 Legislation Profile on Prevention and Treatment of Radioactive Contamination Pollution

Radioactive pollution refers to the radioactive substance or rays caused by human activities on the surface of, or inside, the material, human bodies, sites or environmental media, which exceed the national standards.[9] The objective controlled by legislation on the prevention and treatment of radioactive contamination pollution is artificial radioactive radiation and its substance, as well as activities done by personnel engaged in radioactive activities.

In terms of the legal control on radioactive substances, China formulated the Safety Supervision and Management Rule on Civil Nuclear Facilities[10] in 1986, the Management Rule on Nuclear Materials[11] in 1987, the Radiation Entrenching Rule on Radioisotope and Radioactive Facilities[12] in 1989 and the Emergency Management Rule on Nuclear Plants Accidents[13] in 1993.

In 1987, the former State Environmental Protection Bureau issued the Management Methods on Radioactive Wastes in Cities[14] that sets regulations on industries with radioactive waste and emission sources, agriculture, medicals, scientific research, education and behaviors using radioisotope and radio technology technologies. In 1990, the former Environmental Protection Bureau formulated Management Methods on

---

[9] PRC Radioactive Pollution Prevention and Control Law, 2003, art. 62.

[10] PRC Safety Supervision and Management Rule on Civil Nuclear Facilities (MIN YONG HE SHE SHI AN QUAN JIAN DU GUAN LI TIAO LI), issued by the State Council on October 29, 1986.

[11] Management Rule on Nuclear Materials (HE CAI LIAO GUAN LI TIAO LI), issued by the State Council on June 15, 1987.

[12] Radiation Entrenching Rule on Radioisotope and Radioactive Facilities-(FANG SHE XING TONG WEI SU YU SHE XIAN ZHUANG ZHI FANG SHE FANG HU TIAO LI), issued by the State Council on August 31, 1989.

[13] Emergency Management Rule on Nuclear Plants Nuclear Accidents (HE DIAN CHANG HE SHI GU YING JI GUAN LI TIAO LI), issued by the State Council on August 4, 1993.

[14] Management Methods on Radioactive Wastes in Cities (CHENG SHI FANG SHE XING FEI WU GUAN LI BAN FA), the former State Environmental Protection Bureau, issued on July 16, 1987.

Radioactive Environment[15] for the purpose of carrying out the control and management of nuclear facilities, the application of radioisotope and utilization of associated radioactive minerals that might cause harm to the environment, evaluating environmental influence of relevant radioactive projects, charges of emission certificates and pollution discharging, emergency response to nuclear events, the management of radioactive wastes in cities as well as regulations on the mediation of civil disputes caused by radioactive pollution.

In addition, such governmental departments as the health department, public security department and national nuclear safety bureau and so on also have specific regulations on radioactive food health, an emergency of nuclear medication, medical radioactivity, radioactive substances for aviation transportation as well as management of importing radioactive substances, etc. China has also formulated some national standards on radioactive protection such as the Fundamental Standards on Radioactive Health Prevention (GB4792-84) and the Regulations on Radiation Protection in Nuclear Stations (GB 6249-198), etc.

In order to prevent and treat radioactive pollution, protect the environment, guarantee physical health and promote development and peaceful use of nuclear technology, the Standing Committee of the National People's Congress formulated the PRC Radioactive Pollution Prevention and Control Law[16] in 2003, which is applied to prevent radioactive pollution occurring in the course of site selection, construction, operation, retiring of nuclear facilities, development and utilization of nuclear technology, (uranium) thorium mines and associated radioactive mines within the domain and other regimented sea area of the People's Republic of China.

Further legislative development concurs with the advance of China's nuclear technology and industry. The State Council promulgated the Regulations on the Safety and Protection of Radioisotopes and Radiation Devices[17] in 2005, in which specific obligations are clearly laid down

---

[15] Management Methods on Radioactive Environment (FANG SHE XING HUAN JING GUAN LI BAN FA), the former State Environmental Protection Bureau, issued on June 22, 1990.

[16] PRC Radioactive Pollution Prevention and Control Law (FANG SHE XING WU RAN FANG ZHI FA), formulated by the Standing Committee of the National People's Congress on June 28, 2003.

[17] Regulation on the Safety and Protection of Radioisotopes and Radiation Devices (FANG SHE XING TONG WEI SU YU SHE XIAN ZHUANG ZHI AN QUAN YU FANG HU TIAO LI), issud by the State Council on December 1, 2005.

that the production, sale and use of radioisotopes and radiation devices as well as the transfer, import and export of radioisotopes within the territory of China should be strictly administrated. A licensed system of management and risk control was designed and applied in these regulations in a similar vein to many of the environmental regulations that went before.

The State Council has also touched on the question of nuclear safety and radioactive contamination. The Regulations on the Administration of Transport Safety of Radioactive Articles[18] were promulgated and released in 2009. This time the emphasis was approached from the perspective of transport safety. These regulations are applicable to the transport of radioactive articles and the design and manufacturing of transport containers for radioactive articles and other relevant activities.[19] These regulations mark the pivotal mechanism introduced into the regulation – a category-based division system where radioactive articles are divided into three major categories, upon which different administrative intensities and levels are applied respectively.[20]

The State Council promulgated the Regulations on the Safety Management of Radioactive Waste[21] in 2011. The regulations finished the last-stage administration and management mechanism on the nuclear industry. Activities pertaining to processing, storage and disposal of radioactive waste and the supervision and management thereof are covered by the regulations.

6.2.2 Regulation on Mechanism of Prevention Radioactive Pollution

6.2.2.1 Mechanism on evaluating environmental influence

Articles 18 and 20 of the PRC Radioactive Pollution Prevention and Control Law sets regulations on address, construction price, operation and out-of-service stage that should implement the mechanism for evaluations on the environmental impacts; Article 29 regulates production, sales, use of radioisotopes, accelerators, accelerators for neutron

---

[18] Regulation on the Administration of Transport Safety of Radioactive Articles (FANG SHE XING WU PIN JIAO TONG AN QUAN GUAN LI TIAO LI), issued by the State Council on Semptember 7, 2009.

[19] Regulations on the Administration of Transport Safety of Radioactive Articles, art. 2.

[20] Ibid., art. 3.

[21] Regulations on the Safety Management of Radioactive Waste (FANG SHE XING FEI WU AN QUAN GUAN LI TIAO L), issued by the State Council on November 30, 2011.

production and units of radial facilities containing emission sources formulating evaluation files on environmental impacts and requires a report to the administrative principal department on environmental protection for verification and approval; Article 38 sets out certain regulations on the development and exploration of uranium (thorium) mineral or on environmental influences formulated on closing the mineral.

6.2.2.2 Regulation on aptitude and qualification management mechanism

Article 14 of the PRC Radioactive Pollution Prevention and Control Law provides: 'The country shall implement strict aptitude management mechanism on professional staffs engaging in prevention and treatment of radioactive pollution and shall implement management mechanism on administrative aptitudes on checkup on radioactive pollutions.' This regulation on the implementation of aptitude management on professional staff engaging in the prevention and treatment of radioactive pollution is because of the high degree of danger and social sensitiveness that is directly related to the public interest. Moreover, as is the same with review on prevention and treatment of other pollutions, the data obtained will serve for prevention and treatment of environmental pollution. Therefore, a series of management regulations must be formulated for the staff to observe so that the activities and accuracy of the monitored data can be scientifically ensured.

6.2.2.3 Set-up of obligation of danger masks and caution explanations

Radioactive substances and facilities should be set up with clearly seen radioactive identifications and Chinese warning signs. Fields used to produce, sell, use, store or pipe up radioactive substances and facilities as well as the tools for transporting radioactive substances and tools containing radioactive tools should have obvious radioactive symbols.[22]

The Fundamental Standards on Safety of Ionizing Radiation Protection and Radiation Source (GB 18871-2002) has set out clear regulations on identification, warning signs of radioactive substances and their set-up requirements. Relevant departments should strictly follow the aforesaid standards for manufacturing and set-up so that the public can have clarification on everything.

22 PRC Radioactive Pollution Prevention and Control Law, art. 16.

6.2.2.4 Implementation of 'dual-track approach monitoring mechanism'

On the one hand, organs generating pollution such as the facility operation and the exploitation and use of uranium (thorium) mineral and so on should automatically implement routine inspections for the pollutants emitted and for the impact brought about on the surrounding environment and should regularly report their monitoring results to the administrative principal department on environmental protection of the province, automatic region and automatic city;[23] the operational organ on nuclear facilities should review varieties, density of radioactive elements contained in the surrounding environment of nuclear facilities as well as the total volume of radionuclide emitted from nuclear facilities and should regularly report the review results to the administrative principal departments on environmental protection under the people's government in the province, automatic region and automatic city as well as the administrative principal department on environmental protection under the State Council.[24]

On the other hand, the administrative principal department on environmental protection under the State Council should join other relevant departments under the State Council in organizing the environmental monitoring network and implement monitoring management on radioactive pollutants.[25] The administrative principal department on environmental protection under the State Council is liable for supervising the review on important nuclear facilities in nuclear power plants and shall carry out monitoring on the effluence of other nuclear facilities in accordance with what is needed.[26]

Moreover, the law also regulates mechanism and measures such as the existing censorship,[27] prevention and treatment responsibility mechanism[28] and controlling standards for products and materials,[29] etc.

---

23 Ibid., art. 12.
24 Ibid.,art. 24.
25 Ibid., art. 10.
26 Ibid., art. 24.
27 Ibid., art. 11.
28 Ibid., arts 12, 33.
29 Ibid., arts 17, 22.

6.2.3 Supervisory Mechanism of Radioactive Pollution Prevention

The administrative principal department on environmental protection under the State Council implements the unified supervision and management on the prevention and treatment of radioactive pollution countrywide. Administrative departments on health and other relevant departments under the State Council follow duties and responsibilities regulated by the State Council in implementing supervision and management on the prevention and treatment of radioactive pollution according to law.[30] According to relevant regulations of this law, 'unified supervision responsibilities' in the State Environmental Protection General Bureau would include: formulating and joining administrative principal departments on standardization under the State Council in issuing standards on prevention and treatment of radioactivity;[31] joining other relevant departments under the State Council in organizing the environmental monitoring network to implement review management on radioactive pollution;[32] joining other relevant departments under the State Council in carrying out supervised review on prevention and treatment of radioactive pollution exploited and used for nuclear facilities and uranium (thorium) minerals;[33] being responsible for examination and approval of environmental evaluation files of operation organs of nuclear facilities;[34] and use of nuclear technologies and organs exploiting and using uranium (thorium) minerals.[35]

'Other relevant departments' refers to public security, the State Commission of Science and Technology for National Defense Industry and the transportation department. 'Following duties regulated by the State Council' refers to observance of duties regulated in the Safety Permission Management Methods on Radioisotope and Radioactive Facilities, the Safety Monitoring Safety Rule on Civil Nuclear Facilities, the Emergency Management Rule on Incidents in Nuclear Stations and the Management Rule on Supervision of Civil Nuclear Safety Facilities, and so on, issued by the State Council. For example, the aforesaid statutes regulate that the State Commission of Science and Technology for National Defense Industry is responsible for the management of nuclear facilities and the uranium (thorium) mineral industry as well as the emergency management on nuclear incidents; the department of health is

30 Ibid., art. 8.
31 Ibid., art. 9.
32 Ibid., art. 10.
33 Ibid., art. 11.
34 Ibid., art. 18
35 Ibid., art. 44.

responsible for issuing certificates by use of medium radioactive source of the technology; the public security department is responsible for safety prevention; while the transportation department is responsible for transportation management of radioactive substances; monitoring departments on nuclear safety under the State Council would implement supervision on designing, manufacturing, installation and non-destructive testing activities of civil nuclear safety facilities.

6.2.4 Issues Concerning Implementation of PRC Radioactive Pollution Prevention and Control Law

PRC Radioactive Pollution Prevention and Control Law launched in 2003 helps complete the legal blanket on the supervision and management of radioactive substances for the legal system in our country. But for its implementation the scope of this law is limited in the main specifically to the construction of nuclear facilities, the development of nuclear substances for operations, the issue of nuclear technology and to addressing issues on nuclear waste, it has little direct relationship to the public and has a restricted scope of supervision targets, so at present, the issues for the implementation of this law are not obvious. However, we cannot hold that China has been precise in terms of legal mechanism on the prevention and treatment of radioactive pollution. With economic development and an expansion of the countries utilizing nuclear technologies, such issues should be gradually expanding, so our laws should be progressing and completed step by step.

At present, there are no specialized regulations concerning the inspection and punishment for importing overproof scrap metals in our national law; although we face such new conditions, other than solutions by means of diplomacy. It should be a top priority to formulate relevant management methods on inspection and punishment of overproof scrap metals on radiation, and to further perfect the legal regulation mechanism in the field and make practical efforts to block up the entry of 'ocean garbage' including toxic scraps and so on from outside sources.

6.3 LEGISLATION ON PREVENTION AND TREATMENT OF PESTICIDE POLLUTION

6.3.1 Legislative Profile

Pesticide refers to any substance or mixture of substances chemically synthesized or originating from biological and other natural substances and the formulations made from these substances that are used for preventing, destroying or controlling diseases, pests, weeds and other harmful organisms inimical to agriculture and forestry and for regulating the growth of plants and insects.[36] Pesticide pollution refers to the phenomenon that environmental pollution resulted from the production, transport, sale, storage or utilization of chemical pesticide affects the balance of ecosystem and causes acute or chronic toxicity of people, animals and plants.

Pesticides can cause enormous dangers to living and ecological environments. Therefore, strengthening the recognition of pesticide pollution and taking scientific management measures for prevention and treatment are necessary requirements on utilization of pesticide. China has always attached importance to the management of pesticide. As far back as the 1950s, relevant departments of the State Council promulgated several regulations on the safe management of pesticides, which related to the prevention of pesticide toxicity and the safe management of pesticide's quality, production and utilization, such as the Joint Notification on Strict Prevention of Pesticide Toxicity (in 1956), the Instruction to Safety Operation of '1605' and '1059' Pesticide (Trial) (in 1957) and the Regulations on Strengthening Safety Management of Pesticide (Trial) (in 1959) etc. Since the 1970s, China further strengthened the legislation in this respect. The Standard for Safety Application of Pesticide (Trial) was formulated in 1979. The Regulations on Safety Application of Pesticide, Regulations on Pesticide Registration, and the Temporary Provisions on Test Method of Pesticide Toxicity were jointly issued by relevant departments in 1982. And in 1984, the Standard for Safety Application of Pesticide and Guideline for Reasonable Application of Pesticide etc. were separately issued. In recent decades, China has paid more and more attention to prevention of pesticide pollution. In 1966, five departments including the Ministry of Agriculture, the State Environmental Protection Administration and the State Administration for Industry and Commerce jointly issue a notice strictly preventing utilization of highly toxic and high-persistent pesticides in vegetable production. In order to further strengthen the supervision and management for the production, operation and utilization of pesticides, to guarantee pesticide quality and protect agriculture and forestry production and the ecological environment, the State Council issued the Regulations on Pesticide Administration with the 216th order on May 8, 1996. There are also provisions on the prevention of pesticide pollution in laws and

[36] Regulations on the Control of Pesticides (2001 revision), art. 2.

regulations on the environment such as PRC Agriculture Law[37] and Law of Agriculture Technology Transfer.[38] In addition, except for the direct management for utilization of pesticide, relevant departments of China have taken measures to encourage research and production of low-toxic and low-persistent pesticide, to advocate utilization of bio-pesticide and the comprehensive prevention of pesticide and to develop the establishment of ecological agriculture, as well as promoting pollution-free agricultural products such as green food, organic (natural) food and green vegetables, etc.

6.3.2 Principles on Prevention and Management of Pesticide Pollution

6.3.2.1 Principles on pesticide management

In accordance with the Regulations on the Control of Pesticides, the main principles on pesticide management in China are:[39]

(1) Safety. This refers to the safety of not only human and animals, but also beneficial organisms, crops and the ecological environment. Therefore, it requires the implementation of safe anti-chemicals during the production and use of pesticide; furthermore, the pesticide should be low in both toxicity and residua, that is to say, high-toxic for human and livestock, so that it is easy to be transferred into non-toxic substances that are residually short term.
(2) Efficiency. Efficiency refers to the effectiveness on prevention and management of diseases, pests and grass virus. Several types of pesticide, such as 1605, 3911, 1059 spectrum pesticide are efficient not only in eradicating viruses, but also in removing pests. These types of pesticide can no longer be promoted. Good pesticide is targeted, that will not harm the 'innocent' and 'friendly'.
(3) Economy. Refers to the reducing of chemical costs which keep pesticide prices within farmer's level of consumption; meanwhile, pesticides should not be over-used nor wasted, except scientifically and rationally. Pesticide should be used in the most reasonable way.

---

37 PRC Agriculture Law (ZHONG HUA REN MIN GONG HE GUO NONG YE FA), formulated by the Standing Committee of the National's People's Congress on July 2, 1993.

38 PRC Law of Agriculture Technology Transfer (ZHONG HUA REN MIN GONG HE GUO NONG YE JI SHU TUI GUANG FA), passed on July 2, 1993, revised on August 31, 2012.

39 Regulations on the Control of Pesticides (2001 revision), art. 4.

6.3.2.2 Regulation on pesticide registration

In China, a pesticide registration system is employed. The production (including the original drug production, preparation, processing and packing) of pesticides and imported pesticides must be registered.[40] The registration target includes: all types of pesticides produced domestically; production of pesticides that have been registered; and imported pesticides from foreign companies. The process of registration consists of three stages: field trial stage, provisional stage of registration; and formal registration stage. Pesticides in the first stage are prohibited from sale; pesticides which are used for field experiments, demonstrations and mock marketing need to obtain a temporary registration certificate; before the production and sales of the formal circulation as commodities, pesticides should be obtain the registration certificate.[41]

The Pesticide Registration Certificate and Temporary Pesticide Registration Certificate should provide the expiration date. A renewal is needed by the end of the expiration date; otherwise, it is prohibited to produce or sell any more. If there is any change in dosage form, range or method of use, a further application to register is needed.[42]

While applying for pesticide registration, the developer, producer of pesticide and foreign companies which export pesticides to China should provide pesticide samples to related Agricultural Administrative Departments. Furthermore, they should provide information on chemistry, toxicology, efficacy, residue, environmental impact, labels and so on about the pesticide according to the relative regulations of pesticide registration requirements.[43]

The formal application material should first be reviewed and signed with their opinions by Departments of Agriculture, Chemical Industry, Health, Environmental Protection and National Supply and Marketing Cooperatives within State Council. After that, pesticide registration review members will assess the product chemistry, toxicology, efficacy, residues, and environmental impact of the pesticide. The State Council Administrative Department of Agriculture will issue the eligible pesticide registration certificate according to assessment of pesticide registration review members.[44]

---

[40] Ibid., art. 6.
[41] Ibid., art. 7.
[42] Ibid., art. 7.
[43] Ibid., art. 8.
[44] Ibid., art. 9.

6.3.2.3 Regulation on pesticide production

Pesticide production must comply with the national policies of the pesticide industry. The establishment of pesticide production enterprises (including joint ventures or the establishment of branch and non-pesticide production enterprises setting up a pesticide production workshop) must meet the following conditions:

(1) They have technical personnel and skilled workers compatible with their production of pesticide workers compatible with their production of pesticides.
(2) They have the pesticide plant, production facilities and the sanitary conditions suitable to their production of pesticides.
(3) They have facilities in line with the state labour safety and hygiene standards, and corresponding systems of labour safety and health management.
(4) They have product quality standards and product quality assurance systems.
(5) The pesticides produced should obtain legal registration.
(6) They have pollution control facilities and measures to meet the requirements of the State Environmental Protection, and the discharge of pollutants does not exceed the emission standards prescribed by the countries and regions.[45]

Enterprises, which meet the above conditions and are approved by the administrative departments for the chemical industry of the provinces, autonomous regions and municipalities directly under the central government, should seek the approval of the chemical industry of the State Council administrative department. However, if the requirements of the enterprise are set up and audit or approval authority stipulates other laws, they can be in accordance with the regulations. After the approval, the pesticide production enterprise can apply to the industry and commerce administration authorities for a business license.[46]

The state implements the pesticide production license system. Enterprises producing pesticides of national standards or industry standards should obtain the environmental permit for pesticide production; if national standards or industry standards are not yet available but enterprise standards exist, the production of pesticides shall, upon the examination and approval by the departments for licensing administration of

---

45 Ibid., art. 13.
46 Ibid.

industrial products of provinces, autonomous regions and municipalities directly under the Central Government, be reported to the administrative department of chemical industry of the State Council for approval, and be issued with the approval document for pesticide production.[47]

Pesticide production enterprises should be in accordance with the pesticide product quality standards and the technical regulations for production. The production records must be complete and accurate; the product packaging must be in accordance with the provisions of the stipulating content labels or the specifications must be attached; before leaving the factory pesticide products should be subject to quality inspection in accordance with the product quality inspection certificate; products that do not meet quality standards should not be manufactured.[48]

6.3.2.4 Legal provisions on pesticide management

Units which can work with pesticides include: agricultural production material business units of the supply and marketing cooperatives; plant protection stations; soil and fertilizer stations; agriculture and forestry promotion agencies; forest pest and disease control agencies; pesticide manufacturers and other business units stipulated by the State Council. Manufacturers producing pesticides containing dangerous chemicals must abide by the relevant regulations of the state to apply for administrative license for management environment.[49]

Pesticide manufacturers are required meet the conditions stipulated in Article 18 of the Regulations on Pesticide Administration and relevant laws and administrative regulations. Before operating pesticides, they should apply to the Administrative Department for Industry and Commerce for a business license, if they fail, for whatever reason to obtain it, they are barred form operating. Those who operate pesticides without a business license are ordered to stop their operations and have the illegal income confiscated and a fine imposed.

As to the purchase of pesticides, pesticide products should not only be consistent with the product label or instructions and product quality certificate, but also meet the quality inspection. Pesticides without registration, production environment administrative license or production approval document, product quality certification of product quality standards and which have failed inspection of standards will not be available

[47] Ibid., art. 14.
[48] Ibid., arts 16, 17.
[49] Ibid., art. 18.

for acquisition or selling.[50] The warehousing system is established and implemented for the storage of pesticides to ensure the quality and safety of the pesticide products.[51]

Pesticide manufacturers shall ensure the quality of pesticides. Pesticide products should be consistent with the product label or instructions and product quality certificate. Pesticide manufacturers shall explain to purchasing units and individuals the usage, method of use, dosage, first aid measures and precautions.[52]

Pesticide products past the product quality guarantee period can be sold within the prescribed period after the inspection and approval of the provincial pesticide certification agencies; however, the description of obsolete pesticides should be specified, and the use and dosage be contained.[53]

6.3.2.5 Legal provisions on the use of pesticides

Agricultural administrative departments, at or above the county level, should organize the promotion of safe and efficient pesticides; provide active training to improve the level of farmers' pesticide application technology; and make a pest and disease forecast according to the plant protection policy of 'prevention first, comprehensive prevention and control'.[54] These departments should also strengthen the guidance on the safe and rational use of pesticides and formulate plans for adapting the use of pesticides according to the occurrence of the region's agricultural diseases, pests and weeds, rodents, thereby improving their control by slowing diseases, insects, grass, mice resistant with a rational scheme of the use of pesticides.[55]

Use of pesticides shall comply with the pesticide antivirus procedures. There is a need for correct dispensing, application, good waste disposal and security work to prevent pesticide pollution and pesticide poisoning incidents.[56] The use of pesticides must comply with the provisions of safety and rational use of the relevant national regulations in accordance with the prescribed dose, the number of drugs, medication and safety intervals of spraying to prevent pollution of agricultural and sideline products. Highly toxic pesticides may not be used for health pest control

---

50 Ibid., art. 20.
51 Ibid., art. 21.
52 Ibid., art. 22.
53 Ibid., art. 23.
54 Ibid., art. 24.
55 Ibid., art. 25.
56 Ibid., art. 26.

and shall not be used for vegetables, fruits, tea and medicinal herbs.[57] The use of pesticides should be noted to protect the environment, beneficial organisms and rare species. The use of pesticides to poison fish, shrimp, birds or beasts is prohibited.[58] Forestry, food and health administrative departments shall strengthen the guidance of the safe and rational use of pesticides on forestry, grain storage and health.[59]

6.3.2.6 Other provisions on pesticide management

No unit or individual can manufacture pesticides without environment administrative licensing of pesticide production or an approval document for pesticide product; and no unit or individual can manufacture, operate, import or utilize pesticides that have failed to obtain the registration certificate for pesticide or temporary registration certificate for pesticide. Importing of pesticides must comply with relevant rules of the country; an agent of the owner of the cargo has to show a Chinese registration certificate for pesticides or a temporary registration certificate to the customs.[60]

It is not permitted to manufacture, operate and utilize pesticides of poor quality. Pesticides of poor quality refer to pesticides that have failed to conform to the quality standard, have lost utilization effectiveness or been mixed with harmful components that will result in phytotoxicity and so on.

Manufacturing, operating or utilizing fake pesticides is prohibited. 'Fake' pesticides refers to: material that pretends to be a pesticide; or a pesticide that is passed off as a different pesticide; or the type and name of effective components included is inconsistent with type and name of the effective components shown on the product label or instruction.[61]

It is also illegal to utilize pesticides where there is no label attached to the packaging or where the attached label is incomplete and/or unclear.[62] With respect to pesticide without registration, publishing, playing, setting and pasting of advertisements on it are prohibited. In cases where the registered pesticide is found to have caused serious harm to the safety of agriculture, forestry, persons, animals or the ecological environment, the administration department for agriculture of the State Council, after discussion with the pesticide registration review committee, will publish

57 Ibid., art. 27.
58 Ibid., art. 28.
59 Ibid., art. 29.
60 Ibid., art. 30.
61 Ibid., art. 31.
62 Ibid., art. 33.

a restriction on utilization or revoke the registration. No unit or individual can manufacture, operate or utilize pesticides that are strictly prohibited from production or where the registration has been repealed by the country.[63]

Relevant departments of people's government of the level above the country shall be responsible for the inspection of residual quantities of pesticides in agricultural and sideline products. It is forbidden to sell agricultural and sideline products with overproof pesticides. The treatment of fake pesticides, pesticides of bad quality, out of date, scrapped pesticides, forbidden pesticides, scrapped packaging for pesticides and other waste with pesticides shall be conducted in strict accordance with relevant provisions of environment protection laws and regulations to prevent environment pollution.[64]

6.3.3 Provisions on Supervision and Management Mechanism of Pesticide

The administration department for agriculture of the State Council is responsible for registration and supervision management of pesticide. The administration department for agriculture of government of province, autonomous region and municipality directly under the central government shall be in charge of pesticide registration and supervision management for pesticide in their administrative region. The administration department for agriculture of people's government of country and people's government of city and autonomous district in community is responsible for supervision and management for pesticide in their administration region. Other relevant departments of the people's government of the level above the country level shall take the responsibilities involved in supervision management for pesticide within the scope of their official duty.[65]

63 Ibid., arts 33, 34, 35, 36.
64 Ibid., arts 37, 38, 39.
65 Ibid., art. 5.

7. Law on prevention and control of environmental pollution by solid wastes

Hou Jiaru

7.1 INTRODUCTION

The generation of solid waste is closely related to the production life of human beings. According to paragraph 1 of Article 88 in the PRC Solid Waste Law,[1] solid wastes refer to solid and semi-solid substances that pollute the environment generating from production construction, daily life and other activities. Wastes can be categorized into industrial solid waste, agricultural solid wastes and urban living wastes in line with different resources of solid wastes. In accordance with the danger features and extent, solid wastes would be generally typed into solid wastes and dangerous (harmful) solid wastes.

Waste solids feature characteristics of large quantities, many varieties, extensive production sources, transportable and cross-boundary transfer and the dual features of polluting the environment and availability. Moreover, apart from their danger to the environment and their slow and long-term latency, pollutant dangers are hard to remove. In recent years the gradual upgrading of production amounts, emission volumes and pile-up volumes of solid waste have caused serious environmental pollution and environmental loss. Large quantities of re-usable solid wastes are not utilized and the recovery rate of re-usable resources accounts for only 30 percent of the world's advanced level and values for renewable resources that are not recovered reach 30–35 billion Yuan.

[1] ZHONG HUA RENMIN GONG HE GUO GU TI FEI WU WU RAN HUAN JING FANG ZHI FA (中华人民共和国固体废物污染防治法), adopted at the 16th Meeting of the Standing Committee of the Eighth National People's Congress on October 30, 1995, revised at the 13th Session of the Standing Committee of the Tenth National People's Congress of the People's Republic of China on December 29, 2004; and revised for the second time in accordance with the Decision of Standing Committee of the National People's Congress on Amending the Cultural Relics Protection Law of the People's Republic of China and Other Eleven Laws as adopted at the Third Session of the Standing Committee of the Twelfth National People's Congress on June 29, 2013.

Among the dangers of solid waste pollution are:

(1) Solid waste stack will occupy and pollute the land
Industrial solid waste has low utilization. Most of it is simply stacked or stuffed into containers or randomly abandoned, which not only occupies farmland but also changes the land nature and soil quality due to the poisonous substance in the extravasate of solid waste, with lengthy consequences. Currently, polluted farmland covers up to 100 thousand square meters, causing an annual grain reduction of up to more than 10 million tons.
(2) Solid waste will pollute the water body
The solid waste in water will pollute the water quality. It will directly influence and endanger the existence of aquatic organisms and use of water resources. The particles and dust in the solid waste will also pollute the atmosphere.
(3) Mismanagement of solid waste will threaten human health
In particular, the consequence of some dangerous solid waste is more severe in that it may cause instant pollution and a continuously potential threat. Dangers caused by solid waste pollution on the environment have become inevitable, so to adopt the means of legislation to effectively address the pollution dangers caused by wasted substances has become an issue of certain reality and mission.

7.2 LEGISLATION ON ENVIRONMENTAL POLLUTIONS CAUSED BY SOLID WASTES

The PRC Environmental Protection Law[2] launched and issued on December 26, 1989 has clarified treatment of environmental pollution of solid wastes into its scope for adjustment. Following this, the mechanism construction of prevention on solid wastes has been gradually improved and perfected so that a pollution prevention mechanism system featuring

---

[2] ZHONG HUA REN MIN GONG HE GUO HUAN JING BAO HU FA (中华人民共和国环境保护法), adopted at the 11th Meeting of the Standing Committee of the Seventh National People's Congress on December 26, 1989, promulgated by Order No. 22 of the President of the People's Republic of China on December 26, 1989 and effective on the date of promulgation; and revised in accordance with the Decision of Standing Committee of the National People's Congress at the E Session of the Standing Committee of the Twelfth National People's Congress on April 24, 2014 and effective on January 1, 2015.

extensive coverage scope, strong operability and gradually reasonable and regulated structure has been formed.

The main source of law in the area is the PRC Solid Waste Law, passed October 30, 1995, and revised December 29, 2004 and June 29, 2013.

In order to enhance the management of urban appearance and the environmental health of the city and to create a clean and beautiful working and living environment in the city, the State Council issued Regulation on the Rules on Urban Appearance and Environmental Health[3] in 1992. Based on this, the Ministry of Construction and the Ministry of Environmental Prevention and other departments issued a series of industrial standards and technological rules such as the Administrative Measures for Urban Living Garbage,[4] the Standard for Pollution Control on the Municipal Solid Waste Incineration[5] and the Standard for Pollution Control on the Landfill Site for Domestic Waste,[6] etc.

In order to enhance environmental management on waste import and to prevent the waste import from polluting the environment, the State Environmental Protection Administration, the Ministry of Foreign Trade and Economic Cooperation, the General Administration of Customs, the State Administration for Industry and Commerce, and the State Administration for Import and Export Commodity Inspection jointly issued Supplementary Regulations Concerning Temporary Regulations on Environmental Protection of Wastes in Importing[7] in 1996. The State Entry

---

[3] CHENG SHI SHI RONG HE HUAN JING WEI SHENG GUAN LI TIAO LI (城市市容和环境卫生管理条例), promulgated on June 28, 1992 and came into force as of August 1, 2007.

[4] CHENG SHI SHENG HUO LA JI GUAN LI BAN FA (城市生活垃圾管理办法), adopted at the 123rd Utive meeting of the Ministry of Construction on April 10, 2007, are hereby promulgated and came into force as of July 1, 2007.

[5] SHENG HUO LA JI WU RAN KONG ZHI BIAO ZHUN (生活垃圾焚烧污染控制标准), promulgated in 2000 and revised in 2001 and 2014.

[6] SHENG HUO LA JI CHANG TIAN MAI WU RAN KONG ZHI BIAO ZHUN (生活垃圾填场埋污染控制标准), first released in 1997 and revised in 2008.

[7] GUAN YU FEI WU JIN KOU HUAN JING GUAN LI ZAN XING GUI DING DE BU CHONG GUI DING (关于废物进口环境保护管理暂行规定的补充规定), promulgated on March 1, 1996 by the National Environmental Protection Agency, the General Administration of Customs, the Ministry of Foreign Trade and Economic Cooperation, the State Administration for Industry

and Exit Inspection and Quarantine Bureau issued Management Methods Approved by Inspection Agencies Before Shipping of Raw Materials of Imported Wastes[8] in 1999. The operation of a series of policies and measures guarantee the supervision and management of waste import rules to observe and significantly display the effects of rules and policies of preventing solid waste pollutions.

In order to enhance management and supervision on hazardous wastes and to protect the environmental safety, in the State Environmental Protection Administration of China (SEPA) has formulated a series of standards of National Catalogue of Hazardous Wastes,[9] Pollution control standard for hazardous wastes incineration[10] and Standard for Pollution Control on Hazardous Waste Storage,[11] etc.

In order to guarantee the safety of drinking water and ensure people's health, the State Environmental Protection Administration of China (SEPA) issued the Regulations on Prevention and Management of Pollution on Drinking Water Preservation Area.[12] In order to regulate the disposal of bottom wastes in reservoirs in the Three Gorges and prevent the environmental pollution after the project was impounded, the State Environmental Protection Administration of China (SEPA) and TGP Project Construction Commission under the State Council jointly issued Technical Standard of Solid Waste Cleaning for Reservoir Bed of the Three Gorges on Yangtze River.[13]

Moreover, relevant regulations in other laws and regulations in China also serve as necessary backup for single legislation of preventing solid waste pollution that is an important content in laws and mechanism of

---

and Commerce, the State Administration for Import and Export Commodity Inspection and came into effect as of April 1, 1996.

[8] JIN KOU FEI WU YUAN LIAO ZHUANG YUN QIAN JIAN YAN JI GOU REN KE GUAN LI BAN FA (进口废物原料装运前检验机构认可管理办法), promulgated on November 22, 1999 and effective on January 1, 2000.

[9] GUO JIA WEI XIAN FEI WU MING LU (国家危险废物名录), promulgated on January 4, 1998 and revised June 6, 2008.

[10] WEI XIAN FEI WU FEN SHAO WU RAN KONG ZHI BIAO ZHUN (危险废物焚烧污染控制标准), first promulgated in 1999 and revised in 2002.

[11] WEI XIAN FEI WU CUN CHU WU RAN KONG ZHI BIAO ZHUN (危险废物储存污染控制标准), promulgated on December 28, 2001 and effective July 1, 2002.

[12] YIN YONG SHUI SHUI YUAN BAO HU QU WU RAN FANG ZHI GUAN LI GUI DING (用水水源保护区污染防治管理规定), promulgated on July 10, 1989 and revised December 22, 2010.

[13] CHANG JIANG SAN XIA SHUI KU KU DI GU TI FEI WU QING LI JI SHU GUI FAN (长江三峡水库库底固体废物清理技术规范), promulgated on June 13, 2005 and effective on the date of promulgation.

preventing pollution of solid wastes, such as the Law of the PRC on the Prevention and Treatment of Infectious Diseases;[14] the PRC Marine Environment Protection Law; the PRC Air Pollution Prevention and Control Law; and the PRC Water Pollution Prevention and Control Law, etc.

7.3 LEGAL PRINCIPLES FOR PREVENTING ENVIRONMENTAL POLLUTION BY SOLID WASTES

7.3.1 3-R Principle

The 'Tri-R principle' refers to reduction, recycling and hazard-free treatment of solid wastes. Reduction refers to no more or less generation of solid wastes; recycling refers carrying out comprehensive use of solid wastes through recovery, processing, recycled use and exchange, and so on, to transfer them into second-time raw materials or renewable resources; hazard-free treatment means carrying out various treatments and means of disposal on solid wastes so that they can enter the environment free of dangers. The full and reasonable use of solid wastes has comprised the key contents of recycled economic construction that is both a helpful route to remitting the resource crisis and is an inventive and economic arrangement for preventing pollution by solid wastes.

The legal basis for this rule is the third article in the PRC Solid Waste Law that provides: 'The State shall, in preventing and controlling environmental pollution by solid waste, implement the principles of reducing the discharge of solid waste, fully and rationally utilizing solid waste, and making it hazardless through treatment.'

The 3-R Principle on solid wastes treatments is embodied in the following legal mechanisms, first, it should adopt some economic and technical measures which benefit the comprehensive utilization of solid waste, to fully recycle and reasonably use the solid waste. Second, it should encourage and support the concentrated measures to deal with solid waste in order to protect the environment and facilitate the

---

14 ZHONG HUA REN MIN GONG HE GUO CHUAN RAN BING FANG ZHI FA (中华人民共和国传染病防治法), adopted at the 6th Meeting of the Standing Committee of the Seventh National People's Congress on February 21, 1989, revised at the eleventh session of the Standing Committee of the Tenth National People's Congress of the People's Republic of China on August 28, 2004.

prevention of solid waste pollution. Third, it should organize and draw up the urban and rural construction, land use, region exploitation and industry development, and plan how to completely reduce the danger and production of solid waste so as to fully use and safely handle the solid waste. Fourth, it should encourage companies or individuals to buy and use recycled products. Fifth, it should reinforce the education of solid waste environment pollution prevention, and promote a way of living that is good for environmental protection. The companies, public institutions and residents should undertake the legal responsibility to prevent their solid waste.

The 3-R Principle is an effective rule that is universally applicable for all countries to prevent solid waste environmental pollution while making laws. Practicing this rule can prevent pollution, improve the environment, and save and reasonably utilize the resources. In this way, solid waste becomes beneficial.

7.3.2 Principle of Whole-Process Control on Solid Wastes

Production, collection, storage, transportation and use of solid wastes have the potential to cause pollution of the environment, therefore, to ensure the valid prevention of the hazard, the one-stop controlling and management of the whole process from production, collection, storage, transportation and use to disposal has to be regulated for pertinent controlling and management. The legal basis of this principle are the Articles 16 and 17 in the PRC Solid Waste Law as 'organs and individuals causing solid wastes shall adopt corresponding measures to prevent or reduce environmental pollution of solid wastes'; 'organs and individuals responsible for collecting, storage, transportation, use and disposal of solid wastes shall adopt measures to prevent environmental pollution as against scattering, drainage, filtration or others who shall not topple over, pile up, abandon or involuntarily discharge solid wastes'. The core of this principle is to adopt corresponding standard requirements in each link in accordance with different features of different wastes so as to realize and reach the whole-process standard.

(1) Source control process
First, the design and manufacture of the products and packaging should comply with the specified production standards of the State. The State Standardization Administration has formulated relevant standards to prevent packages from the polluting environment. Second, the State encourages scientific research, production unit research, easily recyclable production, and production of membrane

covering and commercial packages which are easy to degrade in the environment.

(2) Solid waste production process
The companies or individuals who create solid waste should adopt measures to prevent or reduce the environmental pollution of solid waste.

(3) Solid waste discharge process
First, the companies and individuals who collect, store, deliver, utilize and handle the solid waste must adopt prevention measures to prevent scattering, washing away, leakage and others that may pollute the environment. Without authorization, they should not pour, pile up, abandon or leave solid waste. Second, any company or individual is prohibited from pouring or piling up the solid waste in the places such as rivers, lakes, canals, channels, reservoirs or other places specified by law, such as bottomlands and bank slopes below the highest water level.

(4) Solid waste recycling process
First, the companies that produce sell and import the products and packages in the list of compulsory recycling must recycle the products and packages based on the relevant rules of the State. Second, the companies and individuals that use agricultural membranes should adopt the recycled measures to prevent or reduce its pollution of the environment. Third, those who take up the livestock cultivation should rely on the relevant rules to collect, store, use and handle the livestock excrements, avoiding the environmental pollution.

(5) Solid waste solving process
First, it is necessary to reinforce the management and maintenance of those facilities and places engaging in collecting, storing, delivering and disposing of solid waste to ensure their regular function. Second, in nature reserves, landscape reserves, drinking water source reserves, basic farmland reserves and the like, it is prohibited from constructing places to store the solid waste or landfill yard for household garbage. Third, burning of straw outdoors is forbidden in places where many people, airports, transportation main lines are situated or other places specified by the government. Fourth, disassembling, using and disposing of waste electric appliances and vehicles should comply with the relevant law and regulation, and some measures taken to avoid environmental pollution.

(6) Solid waste transferring process
First, to transfer the solid waste out to a province, autonomous area, or directly governed city region for storage and disposal an application should be summited to the relevant Environmental Protection Department of the People's Government (EPDPG). Only when the accepted places EPDPG has agreed: can the transferring places EPDG authorize the transfer. For solid waste from outside PRC borders it is prohibited to pour, pile up or dispose inside the border. Third, solid waste that cannot be used as raw material or used in a safe way should not be imported. The solid waste that can be used as raw material is restrictedly imported and managed as automatically approved importation category. The imported solid waste must be in accordance with the national environmental protection standard and pass the tests of the Quality Supervision, Inspection and Quarantine Department.

7.3.3 Principle of Centralized Treatment of Solid Wastes

The centralized treatment of solid wastes has three main principles. First, to encourage enterprises and business organs to use, collect and have disposal facilities for solid wastes that would open the surplus prevention capacities to others to ensure use, storage and disposal of solid wastes and guarantee use, storage and disposal facilities. Secondly, centralized collection and disposal methods in the region and suggestions on professional and special facilities for use, collection and disposal of solid wastes to centralize solid waste scattering in each pollution sources following certain requirements and conditions for use, storage and disposal; thirdly, to promote 'wastes swap': i.e., wastes in one production process can become features for raw materials in another production process so that transportation of materials between producers and users of wastes can be realized via swap and changing waste into resources with economic benefits.

The government encourages and supports measures for concentrated disposal of solid wastes conducive to environmental protection. Encouraging, supporting and enhancing self-prevention in companies and business enterprises, improves the efficiency of addressing pollution and sets up regional and professional facilities for concentrated disposal so as to save investment, reduce disposal fees and improve treatment levels. Paragraph 3 in Article 3 under PRC Solid Waste Law clarifies that: 'The State encourages and supports adoption of measures for centralized treatment of solid waste in favor of environmental protection.' Article 54 regulates the specific implementation of concentrated disposal of solid wastes as:

administrative department for environmental protection under the State Council shall join the economic comprehensive macro controlling department under the State Council in organizing and formulating the construction planning of field and facilities for concentrated disposal of hazardous wastes before reporting to the State Council for implementation. Local government above the county level shall organize and construct facilities and fields for concentrated facilities of hazardous wastes in line with the construction planning for disposal facilities and construction of hazardous wastes.

7.3.4 Principle of Classified Management for Solid Wastes

The extensive characteristics of sources of solid wastes, management and the control on implementation of solid wastes also concerns almost all administrative organs, so the different management methods of separation and category are adopted for different conditions. According to the category of solid wastes and their extent of danger to the environment, the solid wastes are divided into three categories in the PRC Solid Waste Law, such as industrial solid wastes, urban house refuse and hazardous wastes. In Chapter 3 of the PRC Solid Waste Law, all contents are categorized into three clauses: general regulations, prevention of environmental pollution of solid wastes and prevention of urban house refuse from polluting the environment. In Chapter 4, there are particular regulations on prevention and treatment of environmental pollution of hazardous wastes. The industrial solid wastes and urban house refuse are part of general management measures while the hazardous waste is subject to special management measures.

(1) Industrial solid wastes. Industrial solid waste means solid waste discharged from production activities of industries, transportation, etc.[15]

The supervision and management of industrial solid wastes pollution are mainly under the charge of the environmental protection agencies. The means by which industrial solid wastes pollution is prevented are as follows: specifically a blacklist, pollution craft and equipment elimination system; the industrial solid waste notification register; the law of industrial solid waste storage, facilities, locations construction and management. Companies that create industrial solid waste should construct storage, disposal facilities, and locations to deal with the unrecyclable industrial wastes based on the rules. To store the metallurgical slag, chemical slag, burned

---

15 PRC Solid Waste Law, art. 88.

coal slag, ettle, gangue and other industrial solid wastes in the outdoor, special storage facilities and locations should be constructed. The construction of industrial waste storage disposal facilities and locations should be in accordance with the environmental protection standard stipulated by the State Council Environment Protection Administration Department.

(2) Urban house refuse. Urban house refuse means solid waste discharged from urban everyday life or from services provided to urban everyday life as well as the solid waste that is regarded as urban house refuse under laws and administrative rules and regulations.[16]

PRC Solid Waste Law provides the following regulations for household garbage: regulations for setting out locations to pour and pile up garbage; regulations for garbage that needs to be subject to removal, separate collection and harmless disposal; regulations for using clean energy and delivering clean vegetables to urban areas; regulations for environmental sanitary package and management; along with regulations for architectural garbage pollution.

(3) Hazardous waste. Hazardous waste means waste that is dangerous and is included in the national list of hazardous wastes or identified as such according to the criteria and methods of identification for hazardous waste as prescribed by the State.[17]

Hazardous wastes are among those in the national hazardous waste list or the solid wastes that are dangerous based on the stipulated National Hazardous Waste Identification Standard and Methods. The dangers are mainly ones of explosion, inflammability, oxidibility, poison, causticity and infectivity: random disposal of which will cause severe danger to the environment. Hence, more strict management measures are adopted to prevent hazardous waste pollution.

Apart from the general stipulations, the following special stipulations also require to be executed: (1) fill in the national hazardous wastes list; (2) set out the hazardous waste identification sign; (3) dispose of the hazardous waste intensively; (4) formulate the special relevant legal obligation for the creator, manager, and transferor of hazardous waste; (5) other regulations.

---

16 Ibid.

17 Ibid.

7.3.5 Principle of Developing and Applying Environmental Protection Technology

Solid wastes originate from production and living practice of mankind that shows the gradual improvement of conquering and reforming the nature. Solid wastes can, to a certain degree, be partially dispelled through the degradation and self-cleaning capacities of nature, but the speed of recovery back to the original level of the natural environment cannot satisfy the normal demands of mankind on the environment and in ecological health. Therefore, the most fundamental method to prevent environmental pollution of solid wastes is to improve the scientific and technological progress of relevant realms.

Many articles of the PRC Solid Waste Law reflect the principle of such a scientific guarantee. For example, Article 6: 'The State shall encourage and support scientific research, technological development and the dissemination of advanced prevention and control technologies as well as of scientific knowledge in the field of prevention and control of environmental pollution by solid wastes.' and Article 19: 'The State encourages scientific research and production institutions to do research on and manufacture plastic-sheet covering and packages of commodities that are easy to be recycled or treated, or easy to be degraded in the environment', etc.

7.4 SUPERVISION MECHANISM FOR PREVENTION AND TREATMENT OF SOLID WASTE POLLUTION

To implement the supervision of the prevention and treatment of solid waste pollution, an essential demand on the departments of the government is to obtain reliable data and to carry out scientific decisions that are specific practices of governmental institutions in the performance of their public posts. After much long-term exploration, China has formed a batch of relatively mature supervision management mechanisms.

7.4.1 Environmental Information Disclosure

Information disclosure is the legal system to guarantee and realize the citizens' right to know. Here the right to know means that the individual and organization have the right to know and obtain the archive materials and other information from the administrative organizations.

The mechanism for information disclosure refers to regularly issuing reports on the varieties; production volume; disposal status; and so on, of solid wastes. Paragraph 1 of Article 12 in the PRC Solid Waste Law provides: 'Administrative department on environmental protection under the State Council has established the monitoring mechanism for environmental pollution by solid wastes for formulating unified monitoring regulations and join relevant departments in organizing the monitoring network.' The environmental protection agencies in people's governments in big and medium cities should regularly issue the varieties, production volume and disposal status of solid wastes and join environmental protection conducive for supervision by the masses so as to promote the realization of environmental interests.

7.4.2 Monitoring Environmental Pollution by Solid Wastes

Environmental monitoring is a scientific means to evaluate the environment. It follows the procedures and methods of the relevant technical standards, applying the technologies of physics, chemistry, biology and remote sensing, etc., to inspect, test and evaluate the environmental pollution factors and any environmental changes that may affect the ecological system. As early as on July 21, 1983, the then department for environmental protection in urban and rural construction followed the PRC Environmental Protection Law (for Trial Implementation) and approved and issued Rules for National Environment Monitoring[18] that clarified the mission of environmental monitoring as: to carry out often-time monitoring on various elements of the environment and to grasp and evaluate the environmental quality status and development tendency; to carry out surveillance monitoring on pollutions emitted by relevant organs and to provide accurate and reliable monitoring data and materials for the governmental departments to implement each item of environmental regulations and standards and overall carry out environmental management; to carry out research on environmental check-up technologies and to promote the development of environmental monitoring technologies.

In order to reinforce the operation mechanism of the environmental monitoring network; enhance management on monitoring data materials; ensure the high-efficient transition of data information; provide various

[18] QUAN GUO HUAN JING JIAN CE TIAO LI (全国环境监测管理条例), promulgated on July 21, 1983 and effective on the date of promulgation.

timely reports on environmental monitoring; and provide effective services for the environmental management, the former State Environmental Protection Department issued the National Environmental Monitoring Report Mechanism (trial)[19] on February 21, 1991 and the National Environmental Monitoring Report Mechanism[20] on November 17, 1996 in line with the Rules for National Environment Monitoring that set up the mechanism for environmental monitoring brief paper, the mechanism of environmental monitoring quarterly paper, the mechanism of environmental quality reporting letter, the mechanism of environmental supervision yearbook and the mechanism of data and materials management.

In order to enhance the authoritative reflection of the effect of the operation of these mechanisms, paragraph 2 of Article 12 in the PRC Solid Waste Law regulates: 'Administrative departments on environmental protection under the State Council has set up the mechanism for monitoring solid waste pollution to formulate unified monitoring regulations and to organize monitoring network with relevant departments'. In 2002, in order to improve the disposal level of urban house refuse, quicken hazard-free disposal process of garbage and promote the regulation and standardization of construction and management of garbage disposal construction, the former Environmental Protection Head Bureau carried out environmental monitoring and issued information on the disposal of garbage in the city and emission conditions of treatment facilities in 47 key cities for environmental protection that would reveal that the monitoring of solid wastes pollution had entered a path of smooth operation featuring characteristics of regulation, network and in actual time.

7.4.3 Environmental Impact Assessment

Environmental Impact Assessment (EIA) refers to analysis, prediction and assessments carried out on the environment caused by the implementation of planned and constructed projects that is a mechanism for putting forward strategies and measures to prevent or reduce negative environmental impacts using follow-up monitoring methods and mechanism. Based upon the Law of the PRC on Environmental impact assessment, China has established a legal framework for EIA.

---

[19] QUAN GUO HUAN JING JIAN CE BAO GAO ZHI DU(SHI XING) (全国环境监测报告制度), promulgated on February, 21, 1991 and expired on November 17, 1996.

[20] HUAN JING JIAN CE BAO GAO ZHI DU (环境监测报告制度), promulgated on November 17, 1996 effective on the date of promulgation.

Following Article 13 in the PRC Solid Waste Law as 'to set up project causing solid wastes and to build projects to storage, use and dispose solid wastes must be evaluated on the environmental impacts following the law and observe regulations on the environmental protection management of relevant construction project' that, for the first time, integrates the construction project to prevent solid waste pollution such as storage and disposal of solid wastes into the scope within which environmental impacts must be carried out. According to the regulations in the Directory of Classification Management of Environmental Impact Assessment for Construction Projects,[21] storage and disposal of solid wastes includes landfill of solid wastes, concentrated sewage disposal, garbage from electricity generating, solid waste burning and disposal of urban fecal matter, etc; secondly, on approving the reporting letter of environmental impacts, to formulate the feasibility research report or to design the tasking letter as the premise conditions. Should the official documents on the reporting letter of environmental impact following the law not be obtained, procedures for examination and approval on the feasibility of the project cannot be launched. If the relevant approval procedures on the feasibility of the construction project are obtained in advance, these accreditation procedures shall not be legally binding.

7.4.4 'Tri-Simultaneities'

The 'Tri-simultaneities' is the earliest environmental management system in China. It was created by China based on the experience of the Chinese socialism system construction. It is an effective environmental management system with Chinese characteristics. In 1979, PRC Environmental Protection Law (for Trial Implementation) confirmed the 'Three Simultaneities' by law. Article 6 stipulated:

> when renovating, altering or expanding constructions, the report of influence on environment must be submitted and approved by the environmental protection department and other connected departments before the design begins. Amongst the facilities for preventing pollution and other public harm should be designed, constructed and put into use together with the principle part of the project; and all discharge of dangerous substance must comply with the stipulated standard of the country.

---

[21] JIAN SHE XIANG MU HUAN JING YING XIANG PING JIA FEN LEI GUAN LI MING LU (建设项目环境影响评价分类管理名录), promulgated on August 15, 2008 and effective October 1, 2008.

The PRC Environmental Protection Law (2014) has concluded the experience of 'Tri-simultaneities' mechanism and stipulated in Article 26 that:

> the measures of pollution prevention in the construction project should be designed, constructed and put into use together with the principle part of the project. The measure of pollution prevention must be put into use after previous report of environment influence has passed the inspection of environmental protection administrative department.

As a legal mechanism to prevent environmental pollution initially made by China, it fully reflects the development concept of a coordinated operation between economic construction and environmental protection; therefore, it is further reinforced in legislation for prevention and treatment of solid waste pollution and becomes an important monitoring mechanism for solid waste pollution. Article 14 in the PRC Solid Waste Law provides:

> the evaluation documents on the environmental influence of the construction project need to determine prevention measures for solid waste pollution that must be designed, constructed and put into use simultaneously with main project. The construction project can be put into use or production after the facilities for prevention solid waste pollution are approved as qualified by the administrative department on the environmental protection. The acceptance of prevention facilities for solid waste pollution should be carried out the same time with that of the main body project.

7.4.5 Undertaking Treatment within a Prescribed Limit of Time

Undertaking treatment within a prescribed limit of time mechanism targets the companies that have been involved in heavy pollution. The legislative institutions make decisions to require them to dispose of the pollution source within a time limit to reach the specified disposal demand. It is a preparatory measure before imposing major punishment on the companies that exceed the standard and cause heavy pollution. The environmental law in the country sets out the deadline disposal mechanism and confers the right on the People's Government, which originates from the files of environmental protection by the central PRC 1978 and the 1979 PRC Environmental Protection Law (for Trial Implementation). At that time, China has just begun to emphasize the environmental protection issue. For most companies, the ability to prevent pollution was weak and they did not possess the capacity to keep discharge limits within the national standard. Meanwhile, at that time, the urban companies were mainly state owned. There was an explicit relationship of subjection between government and companies. Hence, based on this subjection, the government could demand that companies causing heavy pollution undertake treatment within a prescribed limit of time, and demand that the companies stop producing because they failed to meet the disposal requirement within the stipulated time.

After 20 years' effort, the capacity of domestic companies to prevent pollution has increased a lot, and most companies now reach the stipulated contamination discharge standard through their own efforts. However, with the development of a market economy, the companies are no longer subordinated to the government; rather, they are the main bodies independently undertaking civil liability. More importantly, in the execution of environmental protection law, the marked problem is that the companies that have been involved in long-term heavy pollution by discharge and have caused severe pollution as a consequence can refuse to correct their problem, while the environmental protection administrative department cannot correct it because of limits to their power. The status between power and responsibility is out of joint and must change with the environmental protection department being granted the decisive power over deadlines for disposal. The PRC Solid Waste Law has made significant reforms to this. According to the Article 81 of the legislation, violating this regulation by causing heavy environmental pollution of solid waste will be disposed of by the people's government above county level, based on the jurisdiction of the State Council's deadline disposal; those who fail to complete the overdue disposal will be disposed by the people's government of corresponding level who will decide whether to stop or close their business. Undoubtedly, this major reform measure will greatly facilitate our environmental protection wok.

7.4.6 On-spot Checkups

The mechanism of On-spot Checkups is the legislative regulation for pollution discharging companies, which is exercised under the jurisdiction of the environmental protection administrative department or other departments with the legal right to exercise the environment supervision right. Its purpose lies in checking or urging the pollution discharging companies to fulfill the legislative requirement of environmental protection. On-spot Checkups can quickly discover infringements and thereof adopt relevant measures. According to the rules and regulations in the PRC Air Pollution Prevention and Control Law and PRC Water Pollution Prevention and Control Law, the environmental protection agencies with the legal right to exercise environment supervision power in the people's government above county level, have the right to do on-site inspection of their governed pollution discharge companies. But they have the responsibility to keep the secrets of the companies' technical and business. The checkup companies should genuinely reflect the status and provide the necessary materials. If they refuse to receive checkups or resort to deception, they must undertake the relevant legal liability.

In order to fully evaluate the economic proceeds, environmental proceeds and social benefits of prevention of solid waste pollution, it is of utmost necessity to carry out On-spot Checkups on the guarantee conditions and capacities of construction status, operation status as well as organs that prevent and treat pollution. To this end, Article 15 in the PRC Solid Waste Law regulates:

> administrative department on environmental protection above the county's level and other monitoring departments on prevention and treatment of solid wastes have rights to carry out on-spot check-up on relevant organs within their domain scope and related with prevention and treatment of solid waste pollution. Organs to be checked up should reflect the conditions truthfully and provide necessary materials. Organs to carry out the check-up should keep technologies and business classified for organs to be checked up. On carry out on-spot checkup, check-up organs can adopt on-spot supervision, sampling collection, survey or copy of materials related with prevention and treatment of solid waste pollution. On carrying out on-spot check-up, the inspectors should show their license.

7.4.7 Extended Producers Responsibilities

As for the concept of extended responsibilities of producers, the Organisation for Economic Co-operation and Development (OECD) illustrated a complete approach in its *Extended Producer Responsibility Framework Report* in 1998, but its definition of responsibilities is too wide in range. Later, in the 2001 *EPR: Government Work Guidance*, the concept of the mechanism of the extended responsibilities of producers has been perfected. Its definition is: as an environmental policy the responsibilities (of substance and/or finance) of producers to their products has been extended to the waste disposal after the product's life cycle. It has two correlated characteristics. First, it transfers all or part of the waste disposal responsibility on municipal governments to the products' producers. Second, it encourages the producers to take account of environmental influences when designing products.

The mechanism of extended responsibilities of producers requires producers to undertake full or part of the responsibilities to environmental pollution once the product is to be disposed of. That is, the producers should not only undertake the responsibilities of environment pollution during production but also the responsibilities of recycling or disposing of the used packing materials. This mechanism has now deepened and been extended to the rule: 'polluters pay'. For the convenience of recycling, producers will take the initiative to use packing designs that consume fewer materials and are easy to recycle.

The Cleaner Production Promotion Law of the PRC pointed out restrictive requirements on the design and recycling of packing materials but with ineffective result. Seen from the status quo of China, setting out a cleaner production law was in fact a preliminarily construct of the mechanism of extended responsibilities of producers. But it was still not perfect; the relevant departments were lacking in cooperation and the relevant control methods were not in place.

Therefore, the revised law has added the requirement for extended responsibilities of producers. Article 3 of the new PRC Solid Waste Law stipulates that the country should adopt the economic, technical policy and measures related to solid waste recycle activities to fully use and recycle the solid waste. Article 18 stipulates that:

> the design and produce of packing materials should comply with the relevant national regulations on cleaner production. The State Council Standardization Administrative Department should make out relevant standards based on the country's economic, technical conditions, solid waste environmental pollution prevention status and products' technical requirement, avoiding the pollution caused by over package. The companies producing, selling, or importing the products and packing materials in the list of compulsory recycling legally should recycle them following the country's relevant regulations.

Article 19 stipulates: 'the country encourages scientific research, production unit research, easy recycle production, and production of membrane covering and commercial package which are easy to degrade in the environment'. In addition, in the legislative responsibility in Chapter 5, it has stipulated the legislative responsibilities if the solid waste environment pollution prevention department fails to fulfill its supervision responsibilities and producers fail to fulfill their extended responsibilities. Obviously, the newly-revised PRC Solid Waste Law has become the new highlight of this law amendment by constructing the law mechanism to realize extended responsibilities of producers via three levels: national compulsory management; companies' self-discipline; and society involvement.

The mechanism of extended responsibilities of procedures demands that producers assume partial or all responsibilities of environmental management of products after invalidation, that is to say, producers should not only assume responsibilities on environmental pollution during the production process but also need to assume responsibilities for recovery, utilization or disposal of products after discarding as useless or used packages. This mechanism is the intensification and extension of the 'polluters pay principle'. Article 18 in the PRC Solid Waste Law regulates:

> designing and manufacturing of products and packaged substances should observe regulations on cleaned products of the country. Standardized administrative departments under the State Council should follow the national economic and technological conditions, status of prevention and treatment of solid waste pollution as well as technological requirements of products to organize and formulate relevant standards so as to prevent environmental pollution caused by excessive package. Companies with production, sales and import of products and packages within the mandatory recovery list must follow relevant regulations to carry out recovery on the product and package.

To build the extended responsibility mechanism of producers can help reduce the production volume of solid waste and reduce its dangers, which can effectively solve the issues of responsibility, separation of production, consumption and disposal of wastes and thus better promote the development of a recycled economy.

7.4.8 Management Mechanism on Environmental Pollution by Solid Wastes

Article 10 in the PRC Solid Waste Law clarifies the definition on management mechanism to prevent solid wastes from polluting the environment as:

> Administrative department for environmental protection under the State Council has carried out unified supervision and management on the prevention and treatment of environmental pollution of solid wastes. Relevant department in the State Council shall be liable for the supervision management work for prevention of environmental pollution by solid wastes within their own duty scope.

The administrative department on environmental protection on local people's governments above the county's level shall carry out unified supervision and management on the implementation of prevention and treatment of environmental pollution of solid wastes in their own administrative regions. Relevant departments in local people's government above the county's level shall be liable for the supervision and management work of environmental pollution of solid wastes within their own duty scope. Administrative department on construction under the State council as well as administrative departments on environment under local people's governments above the county's level shall be liable for the supervision and management of garbage clearing, collection, storage, transportation and disposal.

Overall, management on solid wastes in China can be categorized as two departments in a crosswise direction: the administrative department on environmental protection that is responsible for the prevention and treatment of environmental pollution of solid wastes; and the administrative department on construction that is responsible for management, clearing and disposal of garbage.

In a lengthways direction, it can be divided into two levels:

- State level: the state department of environmental protection is responsible for prevention and supervision management of prevention and treatment of environmental pollution of solid wastes countrywide and for formulating relevant rules and policies, formulating standards and regulations on controlling environmental pollution of solid wastes and planning to prevent pollution, set up mechanisms for checking out environmental pollution and detection networks and organizing inspections as well as participating in the approval and check-up of big construction projects. The department of construction in the country is responsible for management of the environmental health industry countrywide, formulating policies, rules and planning; formulating technical standards and regulations; research and development, education training and information; and monitoring on the urban appearance.
- Local level: the main responsibilities of local environmental protection bureau are: to calculate indicators for disposals of solid wastes each year and to carry out evaluation on the environmental influence on the garbage disposal schemes; to be liable for controlling and managing of urban garbage pollution; and to join approval for big construction projects. Provincial management departments and municipal environmental health management departments are liable for environmental health in the local cities such as cleaning, collecting, transportation, collection and disposal of garbage; recovery, use and disposal of garbage; monitoring on urban appearance; technical training; and urban garbage disposal planning and project application.

7.5 CHALLENGES OF LEGISLATION ON SOLID WASTE IN CHINA AND IMPROVEMENT

7.5.1 Increasing Disposal and Treatment of Electronic Garbage

With economic development, such electronic garbage as computers, telephones, semi-conductors and so on have caused a serious and growing pollution issue on the environment with some places even becoming garbage villages. Heavy metals contained in e-garbage may not be removed on a long-term basis because it causes pollution on the environment. Article 37 in the PRC Solid Waste Law provides: 'Dismantling, use and disposal of wasted electronic products and machinery ships should observe regulations in relevant laws and regulations and environmental pollution should be prevented by measures adopted.' This regulation concerns disposal of e-garbage, but the regulation is too general with weak operability and the relevant laws and regulations to be consulted are too few, so the regulation of this article is, in essence, in vain. Therefore, it is suggested that this article is reconstituted with its operability enhanced.

7.5.2 Completed Relevant Legal Responsibilities

Article 20 in the PRC Solid Waste Law concerning disposal of solid wastes in rural area regulates: 'It is prohibited that straw is burned in the outdoors in areas with concentrated population, surrounding the airport, near the main traffic trunk and those regulated by the local people's government.' This article integrates solid wastes into the adjustment scope in the PRC Solid Waste Law and is, without doubt, a big progress in legislation. However, in the corresponding legal responsibilities, such responsibilities can hardly be traced in the whole legal system. In terms of law, legal regulated behaviors comprise model and law. Legal results compose an inevitable composition in laws and regulations, otherwise, rules and regulations forfeit completeness and will not be considered as rules and regulations, if they do not display inspiration or punishment functions they lose seriousness and the authority of law. Therefore, it is suggested that an article concerning the legal effects of prohibition on burning of straw in Article 71 be added in the law. Moreover, in the information disclosure mechanism regulated in Article 12, the legal responsibilities of administrative departments on environmental protection that fail to issue information at regularly set intervals are lacking and that should be added as the part of legal responsibility in revising the law.

7.5.3 Introducing Mass Litigation

Other than emergency pollutant events, solid waste usually evolves in a long-term process that features long-term potentiality and hysteresis with the dangers only being demonstrated a few years later. Once the pollutant hazards have been caused, they cannot easily be removed with delays and difficulties attendant on their being degraded. Environmental infringement is a particular behavior of violation and there must be a right to sue related to a direct stake, that is to say, the subject able to institute a civil appeal must be the party infringed in terms of individual or property interests by others. Mass litigation, as a typical lawsuit format for expanding just claims, provides a key means for protecting the environment. Paragraph 3 of Article 84 of the PRC Solid Waste Law provides: 'when mediation fails to come out right, the party involved can institute a litigation from the people's court or the party involved can directly institute a litigation to the people's court'. This regulation clearly defines that the subjects who can put forward civil litigation must be the parties involved. But with the features of solid waste pollution and with the parties involved lacking relevant knowledge, the parties involved who institute litigation can obviously go against the interests of parties who have suffered. If the aptitude of suitors can be expanded and the concept of 'group litigation' be introduced, it will not only benefit the maintenance of interests for parties who have suffered but, at the same time, involve more and more public forces to join the environmental protection so as to insist that polluters prevent and treat pollution.

7.5.4 Weak Management Measures on Hazardous Wastes

Hazardous wastes feature characteristics of explosiveness, inflammability, toxicity, corrosivity or communicative illnesses, and so on, they exert huge dangers to the environment if they are merely tossed aside anywhere. Article 53 in the PRC Solid Waste Law demands that organs that produce hazardous wastes organize management planning on them; Article 54 demands that relevant departments organize and formulate construction planning of facilities and fields for concentrated disposal of hazardous wastes and local people's government above the county's level organize the building of concentrated disposal facilities according to law; Paragraph 2, Article 58 regulates the storage duration of hazardous wastes; and Article 65 regulates fees of out-of-service of facilities and fields used for concentrated disposal of hazardous wastes. These regulations help make the management of hazardous wastes more regulated, but one tiny drawback is that legal responsibilities fail to be bound with corresponding articles when the relevant management departments encounter negative acts towards the aforesaid clauses and paragraphs. These measures regulated by law are not persuasive they need to be supplemented with corresponding articles on legal responsibilities.

8. Climate change and energy law

Jiang Xiaoyi

8.1 CHINA'S NATIONAL CIRCUMSTANCES WITH REGARD TO CLIMATE CHANGE AND ENERGY[1]

Global warming has been described as one of the greatest challenges of the twenty-first century.[2] China plays an indispensible role in global warming mitigation in that it is the largest developing country and has become the greatest greenhouse gas (GHG) emitter in the world. Therefore, China's position on climate change and energy issues, to some extent, influences the progress of global warming mitigation. According to the IPCC Report, global warning may have different influences on different countries and regions. In China's case, on the one hand, the climate has also experienced noticeable changes over the past 100 years;[3] but on the other hand, China has its own national circumstances with regard to climate change and energy.

8.1.1 Physical Features

China is vulnerable to the impacts of sea-level rise as a result of global warming, because it has a long continental coastline and most of its relatively developed cities, including Shanghai, are along the continental coastline. China, located in eastern Asia on the western shores of the

---

[1] This part is adapted from Xiaoyi Jiang, *Legal Issues for Implementing the Clean Development Mechanism in China*, (Springer: Berlin), 2012.

[2] A consensus has been reached from a scientific, political, economic or legal perspective. See, eg, Kevin Watkins et al, *Human Development Report of 2007/08: Fighting climate change: Human solidarity in a divided world,* United Nations Development Programme (UNDP) Report (2007). http://hdr.undp.org/en/reports/global/hdr2007-2008/ (last accessed 3 February 2014), and Carolyn Fry, *The Impact of Climate Change: The World's Greatest Challenge in the Twenty-first Century* (2009).

[3] National Development and Reform Commission, People's Republic of China, China's National Climate Change Programme (2007) 4, *available at* http://www.ccchina.gov.cn/WebSite/CCChina/UpFile/File188.pdf (last accessed 3 February 2014).

Pacific Ocean, is the third largest country in the world by area, with 8.6 million square kilometers in total. China's coasts are on the East China Sea, Korea Bay, Yellow Sea, and South China Sea. The country has a continental coastline extending over 18,000 kilometers and an adjacent sea area of 4.73 million square kilometers.[4]

8.1.2 Population

China is facing the challenge of reducing employment pressure caused by a large population and increasing urbanization. China has the largest population in the world: in 2005, the population of its mainland was 1.31 billion, accounting for 20.4 per cent of the world's population.[5] Along with industrialization, an urbanization movement is taking place in China: the urban population accounted for only 26.4 per cent in 1990, and increased to 43 per cent in 2005.[6] However, China is still at a low level of urbanization, with 750 million people living in rural areas, and an urban population accounting for 43 per cent of the national population, lower than the world average.[7] Consequently, large population and urbanization movements bring about huge employment pressure for China, with annually more than 10 million new workers in urban areas.[8]

8.1.3 Economic Development

The priority for China at this stage is reducing poverty and developing its economy goals that demand more energy and will inevitably lead to increased carbon emissions. China's economy has been developing rapidly since the Reform and Opening Up Policy,[9] which was proposed by Xiaoping Deng in 1978. Its annual per capita gross domestic product (GDP) growth rate has remained approximately 10 per cent in the consecutive eight years during the period of 2003–08.[10] Moreover, it is

---

[4] Ibid., 15.

[5] Ibid.

[6] Ibid.

[7] The data was issued in 2001. *See* Chinese Cities and Provinces Information and Links, A China Information Base, *available at* http://www.chinatoday.com/city/a.htm (last accessed 3 February 2014).

[8] *Supra* note 3, at 15.

[9] The economy has changed from a centrally planned system that is under a rigid political control to a more market-oriented economy that has a rapidly growing private sector and is a major player in the global economy.

[10] See *Chinability*, available at: http://www.chinability.com/GDP.htm (last accessed 3 February 2014).

predicted that the high growth momentum will remain in the 21st century.[11]

Although great economic changes have taken place, China is currently at a relatively low level of economic development. In 2005, the GDP of China was about US $1,714 (based on the exchange rate of the same year), only about one-quarter of the world average.[12]

Remarkable disparity in economic development exists among the different regions of China. In 2005, the per capita GDP of the eastern areas was US $2,877, while that of the western areas was US $1,136, only 38.5 per cent of the former. Especially, Shanghai in the eastern areas is experiencing fast economic development: according to international standards on statistics, the per capita GDP in Shanghai in 2006 was over US $7,000.[13]

The income disparity between rural and urban residents is also great. In 2005, the per capita disposable income of urban residents was US $1,281, while that of the rural residents was only US $397, equivalent to 31.0 per cent of the former.[14] Furthermore, poverty eradication is still a huge challenge for China. By the end of 2005, the poverty-stricken people in China's rural areas numbered 23.65 million, with the per capita annual pure income less than 683 Chinese Yuan (less than US $100).[15]

8.1.4 Climatic Conditions

China has relatively harsh climactic conditions, and thus, inhabitants use more energy to maintain a relatively comfortable room temperature. The climate of China is extremely diverse, with tropical areas in the South and subarctic areas in the North, owing to China's extensive territory and complex topography. The northern zone (containing Beijing) has summer daytime temperatures of more than 30 degrees Celsius and winters of arctic severity, with the lowest temperature of minus 30 degrees Celsius in northernmost Heilongjiang Province. The central zone (containing Shanghai) has a temperate continental climate, with very hot summers and cold winters. There are also the famous Three Ovens Cities along the Yangtze River in summer: Chongqing, Wuhan, and Nanjing. The summer temperature in these cities may reach up to 40 degrees Celsius. The

---

11 Ibid.

12 *Supra* note 3, at 16.

13 This is according to the news conference held by the Information Office of Shanghai Municipal Government on February 7, 2007.

14 *Supra* note 3, at 16.

15 Ibid.

southern zone (containing Guangzhou) has a subtropical climate, with very hot summers and mild winters.

Moreover, most parts of China have a continental monsoon climate, with more drastic seasonal temperature variations. As a result, the temperature in China in the winter is 5–18 degrees Celsius lower than that in other areas on the same latitude, such as North America and Western Europe.[16]

8.1.5 Air Quality

Air pollution in China is serious, and more efforts are needed to improve air quality. Although the trend of worsening air quality in the cities of China has slowed, the overall pollution level is still high.[17] According to the *2006 China Environmental Quality Communique*, 62.4 per cent of the monitored cities have met the national air quality standard of Grade II, and 37.6 per cent are worse than Grade II. Fifty-one cities had air quality worse than Grade III, accounting for 8.1 per cent of the total monitored cities.[18]

Air pollution also brings about acid rain.[19] China is one of the countries in the world suffering from severe acid rain contamination, which brings many hazards to the environment, affects the standard of living, and is even harmful to human health. Central, South, Southwest, and East China are the regions with serious acid rain impacts.

8.1.6 Energy Demand

As China astonishes the world with its rapid economic development, energy problems emerge as to how it will fuel its future economic growth: as it will certainly need more energy.

First, China needs more electricity to promote industries and maintain its living standards. More electricity and raw materials are needed as secondary industries still dominate. Furthermore, as the people's living

---

16 *See* General Information of the People's Republic of China (PRC), A China Information Base, *available at* http://www.chinatoday.com/general/a.htm (last accessed 3 February 2014).

17 Ministry of Environmental Protection of the People's Republic of China, China Environmental Quality Communiques 1996–2008 8 (July 2008), *available at* http://jcs.mep.gov.cn/hjzl/zkgb/ (last accessed 3 February 2014).

18 Ibid.

19 Acid rain is caused mainly by SO_2 and NOx from burning coal and oil.

conditions increasingly improve, and urbanization speeds up, more electricity is needed to fulfill people's living standards.

In addition, China's transportation sector is developing rapidly. In the early 1980s, it was very rare to have a private car in China. This situation has changed. With the development of China's economy, the middle class is emerging and growing. Thus, rising incomes make private cars more affordable to the middle class. According to the report of China National Statistics Bureau, by 2001, China had 7.71 million private cars, a number which may mushroom to 140 million by 2020.[20] Under this scenario, transportation fuel consumption would incur a massive increase in demand for energy.

According to World Energy Outlook 2007, China's energy demand is expected to more than double by 2030, with coal expected to fuel about one-half of the increase.[21] Per capita energy use, however, is low compared to international standards. It is equivalent to about one-half of the world average and only 10 per cent of the per capita energy use in the US.[22]

8.1.7 Energy Supply

Coal dominates the energy supply in China. In 2009, coal was 67 per cent of China's total energy supply, while the share of renewable and waste energy accounts for 13 per cent of the total energy supply.[23]

Furthermore, low-energy efficiency and high-energy intensity in China, which are measured by the ratio of energy consumption to GDP, may even compound the energy problems. During 1977–97 China's energy intensity declined about 60 per cent.[24] However, until 2002, China's

---

[20] See 'China to Have 140 Million Cars by 2020', *China Daily* (Beijing), 5 September 2004.

[21] Nobuo Tanaka, World Energy Outlook 2007: China and India Insights Energy Statistics (Nov. 9, 2007), *available at* http://www.iea.org/textbase/speech/2007/Tanaka/weo_beijing.pdf (last accessed 3 February 2014).

[22] 'China Human Development Report 2002' (Stockholm Environment Institute and United Nations Development Programme, 2002) 55 http://www.undp.org.cn/downloads/nhdr/nhdr2002.pdf (last accessed 3 February 2014).

[23] International Energy Agency (IEA), IEA Energy Statistics (Aug. 10, 2008), http://www.iea.org/textbase/stats/pdf_graphs/CNTPESPI.pdf (last accessed 3 February 2014).

[24] William Chandler et al. 'Climate change mitigation in developing countries: Brazil, China, India, Mexico, South Africa, and Turkey' (Prepared for Pew Centre on Global Climate Change, 2002) 13 http://www.pewclimate.org/docUploads/dev_mitigation.pdf (last accessed 3 February 2014).

percentage increase in energy consumption was lower in relative terms than its economic growth rate, which indicates efficiency began to gain. Still, the energy efficiency is relatively low by an international comparison of energy consumption per unit of GDP. The ratio in 2005 was 0.91, which is 2.4 times higher than the global average, 4.9 times higher than in EU countries, and 8.7 times higher than in Japan.[25]

8.1.8 Carbon Emissions

Coal-dominated energy demand thus leads to increased carbon emissions. China has already overtaken the US as the world's largest GHG emitter.[26] In addition, China's energy-related CO_2 emissions are expected to double by 2030.[27]

Despite increasing emissions, China's historical and per capita carbon emissions are relatively low. In accordance with the study carried out by the World Resource Institute, cumulative emissions in China accounted for 8.33 per cent of the world total emissions during the period 1950–2002, and the cumulative CO_2 emissions per capita were 61.7 tons over the same period, ranking 92nd in the world.[28] Even viewed earlier and against the background of cumulative emissions during 1850–2002, China only had a share of 7.6 per cent while the United States had 28.3 per cent and the EU-25 had 26.5 per cent.[29] In addition, statistics from the International Energy Agency indicate that per capita CO_2 emissions from fossil fuel combustion were 3.65 tons in 2004 in China, which was below the world average and equivalent to one-third of the level in

---

[25] Jing Fu, 'Energy Law Aims at Power Conservation', *China Daily* (Beijing), 2 July 2006, 2.

[26] See, e.g., 'Chinese CO_2 Emissions in Perspective' (Netherlands Environmental Assessment Agency 2007), 'the surging power demand from China's rapidly expanding economy caused CO_2 emissions to rise by 9 per cent in 2006 … that increase, coupled with a slight United States decline meant that China's emissions for the year surpassed those of the US by 8 per cent.'

[27] China's Energy-Related CO_2 Emissions © OECD/IEA – 2007, http://www.iea.org/work/2008/asean_training/Emoto.pdf (last accessed 3 February 2014).

[28] Baumert, T. Herzog and J. Pershing, 'Navigating the Numbers: Greenhouse Gas Data and International Climate Policy' (World Resources Institute, Washington DC 2005) 13, http://www.worldresourcesforum.org/files/navigating_numbersper cent20-per cent20baumertpercent202005_0.pdf (last accessed 3 February 2014).

[29] Ibid., 14.

Organisation for Economic Co-operation and Development (OECD) countries.[30]

8.1.9 International Pressure

China is under considerable international pressure to take measures to combat global warming. As a developing country, China is not subject to binding emission cut target in the first Kyoto period before 2012. However, owing to such a significant role in reducing emissions, China has become a focus in the UN post-2012 negotiations as well as other arenas where key countries can meet to discuss global warming mitigation. Furthermore, as a major developing country, China set up a model for other developing countries with regard to commit to reducing carbon emissions.

The following conclusions can be drawn from the above-analyzed national circumstances with regard to climate change and energy: first, China is likely to suffer severely from climate change if it does not take any immediate measures to reduce emissions. Second, large energy demand to fuel economic development as well as the dominance of coal in energy supply bring about a large share of global emissions, putting China under considerable pressure to reduce carbon emissions. Third, China is facing a real challenge in reducing emissions without undermining its economic development due to lack of clean technology and knowhow.

8.2 CLIMATE CHANGE POLICY AND LAW

The international community has been working together to minimizing the effect of climate change through the conclusion of the 1992 United Nations Framework Convention on Climate Change (UNFCCC) and its innovative 1997 Kyoto Protocol. China has begun to pay official attention to climate change issues since ratifying the UNFCCC in 1992. With the increasing international concerns about climate change, China's positions have also changed throughout the two decades. In order to fulfill its climate change responsibilities and to reach the reduction goals on

---

[30] See Statistics and Balance, International Energy Agency http://www.iea.org/stats/index.asp (last accessed 3 February 2014). Organization for Economic and Cooperation Development (OECD) countries consists of most of the developing countries.

different phases, China has released various national policies and political documents that aim to promote sustainable development and to address climate change issues. According to the different characteristics of its positions, the development of China's climate change policy and law can be divided into the following three phases (see Table 8.1).

8.2.1 Phase 1: 1992–2005 China's Sustainable Development Strategy and Plan

The UN Conference on Environmental and Development (UNCED) was held in 1992.[31] The conference expressed new thinking about the sustainable development of human society, and called for each nation to develop and put into effect their individual national strategies and plans to promote sustainable development.[32] In this scenario, based on its national circumstances, China unveiled its own Agenda 21 in 1994, which was the first national blueprint for sustainable development.

At the same time, China ratified the UNFCCC in 1992. Under the UNFCCC, China is required to develop national inventories of anthropogenic emissions by sources and removals by sink of all GHGs and launch national strategies for climate change mitigation and adaptation to expected impact. China would also take climate change into account in their relevant social, economic, and environmental policies; cooperate in scientific, technical, and educational matters; and promote technology transfer, sustainable management, education, public awareness, and the exchange of information related to climate change.[33]

Against this background, the main task during this period was sustainable development. As a developing country, China was not under great international pressure to reduce GHG. Climate change was considered as an environmental problem and was put into sustainable development strategy and plan.

---

[31] The United Nations Conference on Environment and Development, also known as the Earth Summit, was a major United Nations conference held in Rio de Janeiro from 3–14 June 1992. The UNCED resulted in the following documents: Rio Declaration on Environment and Development; Agenda 21; Convention on Biological Diversity, Forest Principles and Framework Convention on Climate Change (UNFCCC).

[32] See UN Conference on Environment and Development, United Nations, http://www.un.org/geninfo/bp/envirp2.html (last accessed 3 February 2014).

[33] Ibid.

Table 8.1 Phases of development of China's climate change policy and law

Phase	Period	Event	Climate change policy and law	Main characteristic
1	1992–2005	The UN Conference on Environmental and Development was held in 1992. China ratified the UNFCCC in 1992.	*China's Agenda 21* in 1994 The 9th FYP (1996–2000) in 1996 The 10th FYP (2001–05) in 2001	Climate change was considered an environmental problem and was put into sustainable development strategy and plan.
2	2005–09	Kyoto Protocol entered into force in 2005.	*National Assessment Report on Climate Change 2006* *China's National Climate Change Program 2007* *China's Policies and Actions for Addressing Climate Change 2008* *China's Policies and Actions for Addressing Climate Change 2009* *Measures for the Operation and Management of CDM Projects in China in 2005*	China wanted to get more involved in international climate regime and fulfill its reduction responsibilities as a developing country.
3	2009–	Copenhagen Climate Summit was held in 2009.	The draft of *Climate Change Addressing Law 2014* The 12th FYP (2011–15) *China's Policies and Actions for Addressing Climate Change (Annually)* *Measures for the Administration of the Clean Development Mechanism Fund 2010* *Measures for the Operation and Management of CDM Projects in China (Revised) 2011* *Interim Measures for the Management of Voluntary Greenhouse Gases Emission Reduction Trading in China 2012* *Interim Measures for the Management of Pilot Carbon Emissions Trading 2014*	Climate change issues have been put at the top of agenda of the Chinese Government. China takes various measures to address climate change issues.

China's Agenda 21 – White Paper on China's Population, Environment, and Development in the 21st Century was completed in May 1994. China's Agenda 21 explicitly expresses China's determination to take the path of sustainable development through the coordination of population, economy, society, natural resources, and the environment. With regard to climate change, *China Agenda 21* states that:

> China wishes to bring the emission of GHGs under control, reduce the growth rate of carbon dioxide emissions, study measures for reducing emissions of methane and nitrous oxide, maintain, strengthen greenhouse gas sinks and constructs climate change monitoring, forecasting and service systems.[34]

In order to control GHGs, a national program would be formulated, including afforestation and energy development plans and targets for emission levels.[35] Emphasis was also placed on research of the identification of GHGs, the impact of GHGs and countermeasures and methods for reducing GHGs.[36] Improvement of energy efficiency and development of renewable energy resources through increasing public awareness, accelerating technological advances and international cooperation were also the significant activities for controlling GHGs.[37] In addition, market mechanisms and financial, taxation and economic legislation that can be effectively used for promoting GHGs reduction were mentioned in China's Agenda 21.[38]

Obviously, China was just at its initial stage of controlling GHGs, and thus the specific climate change policies and actions were not stipulated in detail in China's Agenda 21. Nonetheless, many policies in the agenda concerning economic development and local environmental protection clearly match the UNFCCC's objective to addressing climate change, such as sustainable energy development, clean technology development, and action on forest issues.[39]

Subsequently, China has strengthened the sustainable development and climate change mitigation through integrating its Agenda 21 into concrete

---

[34] China's Agenda 21 1994, Ch. 18(31), available at http://www.acca21.org.cn/english/index.html (last accessed 3 February 2014).

[35] Ibid., Ch. 18(32).

[36] Ibid., Ch. 18(33).

[37] Ibid., Ch. 18(34)(35).

[38] Ibid., Ch. 4.

[39] Institute for Global Environmental Strategies and Chinese Renewable Energy Industries Association (ed), *CDM Country Guide for China* (First edition ed, 2005) 101 http://cdm.ccchina.gov.cn/UpFile/File626.PDF (last accessed 4 February 2014).

successive national development plans. 'Five-Year Plan' (FYP) is a major component of China's national economic plans, mainly functioning to make plans for major national construction programs, productivity distribution and major ratios in national economy, and set objectives of and make directions for national economic development in the long term.[40]

In March 1996, the 9th FYP (1996–2000) and the 2010 Long-Term Program for National Economic and Social Development of the People's Republic of China was approved. At that time, China was at a crucial phase of deepening economic restructure and opening up to the outside world. Against this background, the main objective of the 9th FYP was to promote the stable, rapid and healthy development of national economy.[41] Guided by the China's Agenda 21, sustainable development was set as an important guideline and strategic objective of China's social and economic development.

The 10th FYP (2001–2005) and National Development Strategy for 2015 were issued in March 2001, where sustainable development was again the major focus. China recognized its position as the second largest emitter, following the US, and thus environmental issues were emphasized.[42] Ten objectives were established in order to promote the sustainable development and improve environmental quality in China. Among them, controlling CO_2 emissions and optimizing energy restructure were major energy and environment strategies. It was required to reduce energy consumption by improving energy efficiency and utilizing renewable energy. In addition, forest coverage was raised to 18.2 per cent of national territory and the amount of major pollutants was reduced by 10 per cent from the 2000 level.[43]

The 9th FYP for National Economic and Social Development (2006–10) fully demonstrated the urgency to solve environmental and energy

---

[40] See Introduction to Five-Year Plans, http://www.china.org.cn/95e/95-english1/1.htm (last accessed 4 February 2014).

[41] See Report on the Outline of the Ninth Five-Year Plan (1996–2000) for National Economic and Social Development and the Long-range Objectives to the Year 2010 http://www.china.org.cn/95e/95-english1/2.htm (last accessed 4 February 2014).

[42] 'New Five-Year Plan Gives Priority to Environmental Protection', *People's Daily*, Beijing, 13 March, 2001 http://english.people.com.cn/200103/13/eng20010313_64836.html (last accessed 4 February 2014).

[43] *China's New Five-Year Plan Gives Priority to Environment* (2001) China Council for International Cooperation and Environment http://www.harbour.sfu.ca/dlam/newsletters/0103.html (last accessed 4 February 2014).

issues, which have posed a great threat to national economic development.[44] Facing this situation, China should develop a circular economy and saving society with a view to promoting sustainable development. In addition, the clear targets concerning GHG emissions were set. Energy consumption (per unit of GDP) would be reduced by 20 per cent over five years from 2005 level, the amount of pollutants would be reduced by 10 per cent from 2005 level, and forest coverage would be raised to 20 per cent of the national territory.[45]

To sum up, China began to attach great importance to environmental issues through bringing sustainable development thinking into general national strategies and plans. The regulations concerning climate change and energy development in these strategies and plans provide an overall guideline to reducing GHG emissions.

8.2.2 Phase 2: 2005–09 China More Involved in International Climate Change Regime

The Kyoto Protocol entered into force in 2005. According to the Kyoto Protocol, industrialized countries are assigned legal binding reduction targets for GHG emissions by an average of 5.2 per cent during the first commitment period 2008–12 below 1990 levels while developing countries, whose paramount task at present is economic development and ridding themselves of poverty, are free of emission obligations during this period. On the one hand, China was free of reduction obligations during this period. On the other hand, as a major GHG emitter and developing country, it was expected to play an important role in combating global warming and to take on more reduction responsibilities in the post-2012 period.

In addition, in order to assist with the massive reductions of GHG emissions necessary to arrest the processes of climate change, three 'financial mechanisms' – Joint Implementation (JI), the Clean Development Mechanism (CDM) and Emissions Trading (ET) – have been devised under the Protocol. As the only one among the three Kyoto mechanisms open to Contracting Parties classified as industrialized countries and developing countries, the CDM allows industrialized countries to achieve a portion of the required emission reductions through providing financial assistance or clean technology transfer in emission

---

[44] See China's Eleventh-Five Year Plan (2006–10), Ch 6 http://en.ndrc.gov.cn/hot/t20060529_71334.htm (last accessed 4 February 2014).

[45] Ibid.

abatement projects undertaken in countries without emission targets, while the latter may define the conditions in which these projects take place.

In this scenario, China wanted to fulfill its reduction responsibilities as a developing country, and thus promulgated a series of specific policies and blueprints to deal with climate change. On the other hand, under the international reduction pressure, China constantly demonstrated its positions on reduction targets. Moreover, China also wanted to get more involved in the international climate regime. China saw the potential benefits the CDM would bring and made regulations to manage and operate the CDM projects.

In order to effectively fulfill the obligations under the UNFCCC and the Kyoto Protocol and portray a picture of how China would be affected by a changing climate, China's first National Assessment Report on Climate Change 2006[46] was formulated and released jointly by 12 government departments in 2006.

This report reviews the fact and impact of climate change on China and projects the trend of climate change in the twenty-first century on the basis of scientific research outcomes on climate change. Also, it assesses the potential impact of international climate change regulations on China's ecological, environmental, economic and social development and thus puts forward the relevant position, principles and policies on addressing global warming. The report is divided into three parts: Climate change in China and the Future Trend; Climate Change Impacts and Adaptation; and Integrated Evaluation on Policies of China Responding to Climate Change. The main conclusions indicated in the report are that climate change is happening in China; the temperature will continue to increase and dominantly, the adverse impact of climate change has been observed in China. In light of this report, China realized the urgency to actively address climate change and that it should be done through technological innovation and decision-making.

The authoritative and comprehensive report does not only demonstrate China's determination to address climate change, but also provides scientific evidence for making policies on promoting economic and social sustainable development in China.

As mandated under the UNFCCC and on the scientific basis of National Assessment Report on Climate Change 2006, the State Council

---

[46] China's *National Assessment Report on Climate Change* (I) & (II) http://www.climatechange.cn/EN/abstract/abstract8379.shtml# (last accessed 4 February 2014).

hereby formulated and released China's National Climate Change Program 2007[47] in 2007, which is presented as a 'basic outline' guiding China's efforts to cope with climate change.

The program outlines objectives, basic principles, key areas of actions, as well as policies and measures to address climate change for the period up to 2008. It is a national strategy for climate change mitigation and adaptation to expected impacts, which would not only play a positive role in addressing climate change in China, but would also make a new contribution to the international community.

In addition, China annually releases the China's Policies and Actions for Addressing Climate Change to demonstrate its efforts and contributions to addressing climate change. China's Policies and Actions for Addressing Climate Change 2008 (White Paper)[48] was released in October 2008. It systematically introduced the achievements of addressing climate change in China and carrying out the national strategies. In addition, *China's Policies and Actions for Addressing Climate Change* 2009 (White Paper) was released in November 2009. China concludes in the paper that it is clearly aware of the challenges brought about by climate change while advancing its modernization and urbanization, and it will take into account its basic national conditions and development stage, unswervingly adhere to the path of sustainable development, and make greater contributions to the cause of addressing global climate change.

CDM is a project-based carbon emissions trading scheme open to developing and developed countries. Early in the year of 2004, the 'Interim Measures for Operation and Management of Clean Development Mechanism Projects in China' had been released with a view to providing a legal basis to guide the implementation of CDM projects in China. The CDM Measures[49] replaced the former ones and were issued on 12

---

[47] National Development and Reform Commission, the People's Republic of China, *China's National Climate Change Programme* (2007) en.ndrc.gov.cn/newsrelease/P020070604561191006823.pdf (last accessed 4 February 2014).

[48] *China's Policies and Actions for Addressing Climate Change 2008* (Information Office of the State Council of the People's Republic of China) http://www.gov.cn/english/2008-10/29/content_1134544.htm (last accessed 4 February 2014).

[49] *Measures for the Operation and Management of CDM Projects in China 2005* (promulgated by the Ministry of Foreign Affairs, Ministry of Science and Technology, Ministry of Finance and State Development and Reform Commission, Order No. 37, Oct. 12, 2005, effective Oct. 12, 2005), *available at:* http://cdm.ccchina.gov.cn/english/NewsInfo.asp?NewsId=905 (last accessed 4 February 2014).

October 2005. They stipulate competent CDM institutions, legal requirements for CDM projects, key entities involved, legal steps in developing CDM projects, etc.

8.2.3 Phase 3: 2009– Climate Change Issues Top of Agenda

The first Kyoto period expired in 2012 and the international community held a series of conferences to discuss the climate change combat actions. However, the prospect of international climate regime is still uncertain. In spite of that, China has become one of the focuses of climate negotiations; although it will be under considerable pressure to reduce carbon emissions without undermining its economic development. Facing this situation, China set the following goals to control the emissions of GHGs until 2020 before the Copenhagen Climate Summit as China's contribution to the international efforts addressing climate change:

- lower CO_2 emissions per unit of GDP by 40–45 per cent by 2020 compared to 2005;
- increase the share of non-fossil fuels in primary energy consumption to around 15 per cent by 2020; and
- increase forest coverage by 40 million hectares and forest stock volume by 1.3 billion cubic meters by 2020 from 2005.

Therefore, after the year of 2009, climate change issues have been put at the top of agenda of the Chinese Government. Nowadays, China takes various measures to address climate change issues.

Currently, the Chinese Government is working on its 12th FYP for National Economic and Social Development, which was endorsed by the National People's Congress (NPC) on 14 March 2008. Faced with severe pollution, a predicted surge in urbanization and a struggle to ensure adequate energy supplies to fuel its rapid growth, China has outlined plans to reduce carbon emissions in the latest five-year economic plan and announced several new carbon and energy targets from 2010 levels, namely[50]:

- increase the proportion of non-fossil fuels in energy consumption to 8.4 per cent by 2015;

---

[50] See key targets of China's 12th five-year plan, English.new.cn. March 5 2011, http://news.xinhuanet.com/english2010/china/2011-03/05/c_13762230.htm (last accessed 4 February 2014).

- reduce energy consumption per unit of gross domestic product (GDP) by 16 per cent from 2010 levels by 2015; and
- reduce carbon dioxide emissions per unit of GDP by 17 per cent from 2010 levels by 2015.

The Working Strategy on Controlling GHG Emissions under the 12th FYP was released by the National Development and Reform Commission (NDRC) subsequently in 2009 with a view to realizing the reduction goal under the plan.

In addition, having adopted market mechanisms throughout its economy, China is now embracing carbon trading and is exploring provincial and/or city-based trading schemes. It is the first time it has included a commitment to gradually introducing market mechanisms to control carbon pollution. The 12th FYP refers to establishing low-carbon product standards, improving the statistical accounting systems for GHG emissions and the 'step-by-step establishment of carbon emission trading markets'.

The carbon market derives from the three market-based mechanisms under the Kyoto Protocol. Since the first CDM project in China in June 2005, China has dominated the global carbon market through participating in CDM projects and become the largest beneficiary. Already today, CDM projects launched in China have been responsible for approximately 60 per cent of the total carbon credits produced under the scheme.[51] In order to deal with various problems surrounding the CDM, the CDM Measures were revised in June 2011.

The major change of the revised CDM Measures is that the legal responsibilities of related participants are highlighted. Besides a provision of 'the implementation of CDM projects shall be ensured to be transparent and efficient and the responsibilities and obligations of each participants in the project shall be clarified'[52] in the Chapter of General Provisions, a new Chapter of Legal Responsibility is also added. The new chapter explicitly stipulates the circumstances under which, and the types of penalties for which, the CDM related participants will be punished. Moreover, the application procedure is refined with the eligible companies divided into state-owned and other companies. The state-owned companies submit their applications to the NDRC directly while other

---

[51] See CDM Statistics: CERs Issued by Host Party, UNFCCC http://cdm.unfccc.int/Statistics/Issuance/CERsIssuedByHostPartyPieChart.html (last accessed 4 February 2014).

[52] *Measures for Operation and Management of CDM projects in China 2011* (PRC), art 5.

companies submit their applications to the Provincial Development and Reform Commission (PDRC). The other major change of the revised CDM Measures is the provision regarding revenue from the transfer of Certified Emission Reduction (CERs). As mentioned previously, the regulation on ownership issue of emission reduction resource is deleted; the allocation ratio is also revised. The detailed regulations on collecting and using of the revenue are specified to be the Measures for the Administration of the Clean Development Mechanism Fund[53] in the revised CDM Measures.

In addition, emissions trading establishes a system of emission rights trading whereby one party might directly purchase from another party some of its rights to emit GHGs. Emissions trading schemes (ETS) may be established as climate policy instruments at the national level and the regional level. Voluntary Emissions Reduction (VER) Trading Schemes of CO_2 have already been trailed, providing much experience. China launched a carbon emission trading system led by the China Beijing Environmental Exchange, the Shanghai Environment Energy Exchange and the Tianjin Climate Exchange, which were all set up in 2009.[54] The public trading of carbon emission credit on the exchanges could help China gain its pricing rights in the global carbon emissions market. But these exchanges served as platforms for individual small-scale deals.[55] It was expected that the situation could be changed when the Chinese Government issued the Interim Measures for the Management of Voluntary Greenhouse Gases Emission Reduction Trading in China (hereinafter the VER Measures)[56] in June 2012 after two years' preparations.

The VER Measures are enacted to deal with the problem that VER trading lacks a standardized and uniformed management system through clarifying many key issues, including trading products, trading venues,

---

[53] *Measures for the Administration of the Clean Development Mechanism Fund 2010* (PRC), available at http://www.gov.cn/flfg/2010-10/21/content_1727534.htm (last accessed 4 February 2014).

[54] See, Shai Oster, 'China Expand Markets for Carbon Trading', *The Wall Street Journal* (The US), 11 November 2008, A11.

[55] *Tianjin Climate Exchange Launch Carbon Contract* (2009) China Tells, available at http://blog.chinatells.com/2009/09/1976 (last accessed 4 February 2013).

[56] *Interim Measures for the Management of Voluntary Greenhouse Gases Emission Reduction Trading in China 2012* (PRC), available at http://thecleanrevolution.org/_assets/files/Interim-Regulation-of-Voluntary-Greenhouse-Gases-Emission-Trading-in-China(1).pdf (last accessed 4 February 2013).

new methodology, application procedures and accreditation procedures of qualifications of the verification and validation organizations. The VER Measures also provide working measures for the management of verification and validation system to improve the performance of the verification and validation organizations and the qualification of their staff. In addition, the Measures clearly stipulate that the China Certified Emission Reduction (CCER) can be used to offset allowances under the prospective Cap-and-trade program, building a linkage to the existing pilot schemes.

Although the release of the VER Measures cannot solve all the problems in VER trading, it lays a legal foundation for the operation of emissions trading by clarifying some fundamentals of the carbon market. In the meanwhile, it also provides a preparatory and adaptation period for companies.

With the support of the 12th FYP, NDRC of China has approved a mandatory 'Cap-and-trade' emissions trading pilot scheme in seven provincial regions by 2013 and will expand it nationally in 2015 in an effort to encourage carbon emission reductions. The municipalities and provinces given the green light include Beijing, Tianjin, Shanghai, Chongqing, Shenzhen, Hubei and Guangdong. As the pilot schemes were proposed, seven pilot municipalities and provinces began to design the ETS within their respective administrative areas. However, due to the differences in previous experience in carbon trading, industrial structure, economic development and capacity development on climate change, the actual progress varies between regions. To date, all the seven pilot provincial regions have completed their respective ETS designs and are putting their schemes into operation. Moreover, they have all issued Interim Measures for the Management of Carbon Emissions Trading to provide a legal basis for their schemes.

Currently, China is considering introducing a nation-wide emissions trading scheme in its next five-year plan, covering the period from 2016. However, making cap-and-trade a reality in China will be challenging. Schemes are intended to be launched in 2013 and the key issues, including the future design of the scheme, timetable for implementation, obstacles and challenges remaining and perspectives for a nation-wide emissions trading scheme, are still under discussion. The future success or failure of the emissions trading scheme in China will have major implications on the future of carbon trading globally.

Although the Chinese Government has released a series of policies to deal with climate change, there is no existing climate change legislation. However, there are many discussions in the field of academia on the topic of whether it is necessary and possible for China to draft a specific climate change law. The discussions can be grouped into four opinions. The first one thinks China should draft a specific law addressing climate change;[57] the second proposes that it is difficult for China to formulate a specific law for addressing climate change and that instead climate change should be brought in as a chapter in the energy law when drafting the Energy Law;[58] the third thinks China should mitigate and adapt to climate change through revising the existing laws and regulations;[59] the last one suggests that global warming and regional climate change mitigation should be brought into the PRC Air Pollution Prevention and Control Law.[60]

Given the significance of climate change mitigation and carbon emissions reduction, China plans to draw up new laws and regulations to provide a legal basis for combating climate change. China's top legislative body approved its first climate change resolution in August 2009 and announced plans to draw up a new law to combat global warming. A draft called on the government to take further measures to control GHG emissions and accelerate efforts to tackle the challenge of global warming. In addition, the draft resolution says that 'the role of science and technology in leading and supporting the fight against climate change should be given fully play'.[61] Up to the date of 21 July 2014, the draft of

---

[57] Dahe Qin, *Perfecting Legal System and Addressing Climate Change*, [trans of: 秦大河：《完善法律制度，应对气候变化》，载《光明日报》], 20 April, 2009; Hongchun Zhou, *Practical Meaning of Developing a Low Carbon Economy in China and Political Suggestions,* [trans of 周宏春：《中国发展低碳经济的现实意义及政策建议》，载《中国经济时报》, 28 December, 2009.

[58] China Legal Science Association on Energy Law: *Accelerating the Legislation of the Energy Law Addressing Climate Change* [trans of: 中国法学会能源法研究会：《加快〈能源法〉立法，应对气候变化座谈会》], available at: http://www.energylaw.org.cn/html/news/2009/12/18/20091218143577705.html (last accessed 4 February 2014).

[59] Mingde Cao, *Addressing Climate Change from a Legal Perspective*, [trans of: 曹明德：《气候变化的法律应对》，载《政法论坛》], 2009(7); Ying Yang and Zuiyue Liu, *Shortcomings of the Legislation of Climate Change and Its Countermeasures* [trans of: 杨兴、刘最跃：《我国气候变化立法的缺 陷及其对策分析》，载《时代法学》], 2006(2).

[60] The Ministry of Environmental Protection: *PRC Air Pollution Prevention and Control Law (The Draft of Revision),* [trans of: 中华人民共和国环境保护部：《中华人民共和国大气污染防治法》（修订草案送审稿）第六章].

[61] 'Legislators to Deliberate Draft on Climate Change', *China Daily* (Beijing), 25 August 2009 http://www.chinadaily.com.cn/china/2009-08/25/content_8614750.htm (last accessed 4 February 2014).

Climate Change Addressing Law had been completed, but the details of its content has not been officially made public.

In conclusion, China has not only brought sustainable development and GHG emission reduction into national strategies and plans, but has also launched climate-specific programs. More particularly, China has found itself with a growing obligation to cut its mounting emissions of GHG since 2007, thus accelerating its steps to curb climate change. All these regulatory documents and the climate change law mentioned above may serve as the policy and legal guarantee to further enhance China's capabilities for addressing climate change.

8.3 ENERGY LEGAL SYSTEM

As mentioned earlier, China's carbon emissions is closely connected to its sizeable energy demand and the dominance of coal in its energy supply, putting China under considerable pressure to make reductions. Under these circumstances, besides climate change policies, China's attempts to address CO_2 emissions have predominantly focused on legislation in areas such as energy efficiency, the feed-in tariff under its renewables law, other specific laws for energy-related industries, or promoting a low-carbon economy.

8.3.1 Energy Efficiency and Renewable Energy

The main legislation for energy efficiency is the PRC Energy Conservation Law 1997,[62] which was enacted by the NPC Standing Committee in November 1997. The law was revised in October 2007 and entered into force in April 2008 as the former energy conservation law no longer met China's development need of transiting the focus of economic development from energy and resources consumption to energy saving. For this reason, the PRC Energy Conservation Law 1997 was revised to secure a strong legal framework for building an energy-saving society.

The revised law consists of seven chapters. The main content is about the administration of energy conservation, rational use of energy and energy conservation from the general aspect, industrial energy aspect, construction energy aspect, transport energy aspect, energy conservation by public institutions aspect and by key energy consuming entities

[62] *PRC Energy Conservation Law 1997*, last revised in 2007, http://www.lawinfochina.com/display.aspx?lib=law&id=6467 (last accessed 4 February 2014).

aspect, technological progress in energy conservation, incentive measures and legal liabilities.

The outstanding achievement of the new law lies in adopting many effective measures and regulations to decrease energy consumption in China, which are as follows:

- Energy conservation has been set as a basic national policy of China.[63]
- In order to effectively promote energy conservation, the energy conservation target responsibility system and the energy conservation examination system should be implemented.[64]
- The energy conservation evaluation and review system to fixed investment projects should be implemented.[65]
- The indoor temperature control system shall be implemented to public buildings using air-conditioning heating and refrigeration and urban power conservation management should be enhanced with a view to strengthening construction energy conservation.[66]
- The public transport, non-vehicles and the utilization of clean fuels are encouraged.[67]
- The management of the major energy consuming industries[68] is emphasized.[69]

---

63 Ibid., art 4: 'Energy conservation constitutes a long-term strategic policy in the nation's economic development'.

64 Ibid., art 6: 'The State takes the completion of energy conservation targets as an item to assess and evaluate the performance of the local people's government and the persons in charge thereof'.

65 Ibid., art 15: 'With respect to the projects inconsistent with compulsory energy conservation standards, the competent examination and approval department shall not approve or verify ...'.

66 Ibid., arts 37–40.

67 Ibid,, s 4.

68 The key energy consuming industries fall into two categories: the industries with over ten thousand tons of energy consumption volumes per year and the industries with five thousand to ten thousand tons of energy consumption volumes per year specific by the competent departments. They often include electric power, iron and steel, non-ferrous metals, building materials, oil processing, chemical, coal and other industries.

69 See *PRC Energy Conservation Law 1997*, last revised in 2007, art 49: 'The major energy consuming industries should make annual reports concerning energy consumption last year to the energy conservation administrative department'.

- The Chinese Government places an emphasis on energy conservation technological development and propels enterprises to carry out energy conservation technological transformation.[70]
- China would implement energy conservation favourable tax policies, would guide financial institutions to raise the credit supports for energy-saving projects and would adopt energy-saving favourable price policies.[71]

In February 2005, the NPC Standing Committee adopted the PRC Renewable Energy Law 2005,[72] confirming the role of renewable energy in China's national energy strategy and promoting the development and utilization of renewable energy.

The law is divided into eight chapters. Chapter 1 is a general introduction to the objectives and application of this law. The law explicated stated that: 'the government encourages economic entities of all ownerships to participate in the development and utilization of renewable energy and protects legal rights and interests of the developer and uses of renewable energy on the basis of law'.[73] In addition, the energy authority of the State Council is the competent department for the management of renewable energy at the national level and energy authorities of local people's governments above the county level within their own jurisdiction.

Chapter 2 is concerned with the resource survey and development plan. Medium- and long-term targets of the total volume for the development and utilization of renewable energy at national level and local level should be set on the basis of the result of renewable energy. Meanwhile, national and local renewable energy development and utilization plans are to be prepared.

Chapter 3 focuses on industry guidance and technology support, setting out the responsibilities of the government in guiding the renewable energy industries and highlighting the importance of scientific and technical research.

Chapter 4 formulates the details concerning promotion and application of grid-connected renewable power generation, biological fuel and energy crops, solar energy and the renewable energy in rural areas.

---

70 Ibid., arts 60–66.

71 Ibid., art 76.

72 *PRC Renewable Energy Law 2005*, http://martinot.info/China_RE_Law_Beijing_Review.pdf (last accessed 4 February 2014).

73 Ibid., art 4, para 2.

Chapter 5 stipulates price management and fee sharing of renewable energy power. Differentiated pricing and public cost sharing (realized by a grid cost-sharing system) systems are set up, whereby all citizens are required to share the extra costs associated with developing renewable energy.

Chapters 6 and 7 state economic incentives and legal responsibilities, which would encourage the entire society, particularly companies, to develop and use renewable energy, as well as financially penalizing companies and individuals that do not meet the obligations set out for them by the law. In order to support the development of renewable energy, a renewable energy development fund was established through a preferential loan with a financial interest subsidy to certain renewable energy projects by financial institutions and tax befits to certain projects are granted.

To sum up, the PRC Renewable Energy Law 2005 provides a legal guarantee for supporting renewable energy development and utilization in China through protecting legal interests and rights of companies, removing barriers to the development of the renewable energy market, setting up a financial guarantee system and creating a social atmosphere conductive to renewable energy.

8.3.2 Energy-related Industries

As mentioned earlier, the massive energy demand in China derives from power generation. The Electricity Law 1995,[74] adopted in 1995 and entered into force in 1996, is the fundamental law in electrical legislation in China. The law has made a contribution to promoting the power industry in China. However, with the development of a market economy and reform in China, this law, which features administrative monopolization on the management of power, has hardly been able to meet the economic and social development in China. Based on that, the amendment to the Electricity Law 1995 has already been brought into national law-making plans.

---

[74] *PRC Electricity Law 1995*, http://www.chinahotelsreservation.com/china_law/Electricity_Law_china_law_of_the1143.html (last accessed 4 February 2014).

In addition, PRC Coal Industry Law 1996[75] was issued with a view to rationally developing, utilizing and protecting the coal resources, standardizing the production and marketing of coal, and promoting and ensuring the development of the coal industry,[76] the environmental aspect and sustainability aspect are not emphasized under the PRC Coal Industry Law. Also, the PRC Mineral Resources Law, which was passed in 1986 and was revised in 1996 with a view to developing the mining industry, to promoting the exploration, development, utilization and protection of mineral resources and to ensuring the present and long-term requirements of the socialist modernization. The law was enacted to regulate the mining industry without highlighting the environmental benefits, let alone climate change and energy issues.

With regard to methane recovery and utilization, there are no special provisions in the legislation in place to promote that in China, but several measures have been issued at a national level as well as a local level to accelerate the use of methane, especially in rural areas. China has released the Emission Standard of Coalbed Methane/Coal Mine Gas (on trial)[77] in order to enhance the management of GHG emissions and global warming mitigation.

8.3.3 A Low-carbon Economy

According to the report made at the 16th National Congress of the Communist Party of China in 2002, with a view to dealing with the environmental degradation caused by an unclean industrialization model, China shall lay out a new industrialization model as its only pathway to protect the environment without undermining high-speed economic growth.[78] Such industrialization features high-technology products, good economic returns, low levels of natural resources consumption and environmental pollution and efficient deployment of manpower.[79] Hence, as for climate change, the new industrialization model may also assist the

---

75 *PRC Coal Industry Law* last revised in 2011, http://www.lawinfochina.com/display.aspx?lib=law&id=1034 (last accessed 4 February 2014).

76 Ibid., art 1.

77 *Emission Standard of Coalbed Methane/Coal Mine Gas (on trial) 2008* (General Administration of Quality Supervision, Inspection, and Quarantine of the Environmental Protection Ministry of the People's Republic of China) www.ep.net.cn/cgi-bin/dbbz/doc.cgi?id=1067 (last accessed 4 February 2014).

78 See 'The Circular Economy in China', Cleaner Product in China http://www.chinacp.org.cn/eng/cppolicystrategy/circular_economy.html (last accessed 4 February 2014).

79 See ibid.

reduction of carbon emissions through applying advanced technologies and decreasing energy consumption, thus promoting the shift to a low-carbon economy.

Against this background, China promulgated the PRC Cleaner Production Promotion Law 2002[80] and the PRC Circular Economy Promotion Law 2008,[81] which are supposed to provide a significant legal guarantee for supporting a new industrialization model in China.

The PRC Cleaner Production Promotion Law 2002, approved by the Standing Committee of the NPC, China's top legislative body, in June 2002 and entering into effect in January 2003, is the first specific legislation targeting at preventing pollution. Since then, management of the promotion and implementation of cleaner production[82] is on the way to becoming legislation.

The law consists of six chapters and 42 articles. Chapter 1 covers general provisions, outlining the definition, objective, scope and other basic information about the cleaner production. Chapter 2 defines the Chinese Government's responsibilities to realizing cleaner production. Chapter 3 focuses on the requirements of enterprises or individuals to implement cleaner production. Chapter 4 is concerned with the inducement measures to encourage the cleaner production while Chapter 5 states the legal liability. Chapter 6 is a supplementary article about when it comes into effect.

The China NPC is preparing to issue a specific law with the aim of increasing resource utilization rate, protecting and improving environment and realizing sustainable development through promoting the circular economy in China.

After the proposal of a new industrialization model, the circular economy was introduced into China and started to flourish. Circular

---

[80] *PRC Cleaner Production Promotion Law* 2002, http://www.chinacp.com/EN/PolicyDetail.aspx?id=39. (last accessed 4 February 2014).

[81] *PRC Circular Economy Promotion Law* 2008, http://www.chinaenvironmentallaw.com/wp-content/uploads/2008/09/circular-economy-law-cn-en-final.pdf (last accessed 4 February 2014).

[82] Cleaner production in this legislation means the:

> continuous application of measures for design improvement, utilization of clean energy and raw materials, the implementation of advanced processes, technologies and equipment, improvement of management and comprehensive utilization of resources to reduce pollution at source, enhance the rates of resource utilization efficiency, reduce or avoid pollution generation and discharge in the course of production, provision of services and product use, so as to decrease harm to the health of human beings and the environment.

economy is a new economic development model which is believed to be capable of becoming environmentally friendly to economic development by making a full and efficient use of resources and energies and minimizing waste discharge through the technological innovation of the traditional industries, thus fundamentally eliminating the sharp conflict between the environment and development that has previously existed. Compared to the traditional economy, circular economy is an eco-efficient economy with '3 Rs' principle – Reduce, Reuse, and Recycle. Under the circular economy, one facility's waste, including energy, water, materials – as well as information – may be reused by another facility's input. By working together, the whole society obtains a larger collective benefit, with low resources input, high utilization rate and low emissions.[83] Therefore, the development based on a circular economy is essential for China to establish a new industrialized model and ultimately realize sustainable development.

In spite of the significance of circular economy in China, a lack of theoretical framework and practical tools could be an impediment to its effective application. To countering this, the Chinese Government started to draft the PRC Circular Economy Promotion Law in December 2005, and the PRC Circular Economy Promotion Law 2008 was ultimately approved.

Overall, the Cleaner Production Promotion Law 2002 and the Circular Economy Promotion Law 2008 could create a favourable legal environment for saving energy and reducing emissions. Clean production is the first step to reach the ultimate goal of circular economy. Only by developing the circular economy, can it be possible for China to realize the shift to a low-carbon economy.

8.3.4 Existing Problems in the Energy Legal System

Against the background of global warming, the existing energy legal system has more and more outstanding deficiencies to assist in carbon emissions reduction. The major existing problems in energy legal system are as follows:

First, the energy legal system is incomplete. Due to the fact that the complicated international climate change regime poses new challenges to China's energy and economic development, China lacks a basic energy

---

[83] Jianyu Zhang, 'Approaching Circular Economy', *China Daily* (Beijing), 1 October 2004 http://www.chinadaily.com.cn/english/doc/2004-10/01/content_379348.htm (last accessed 4 February 2014).

law that reflects the energy strategy and policy orientation and coordinates ties between energy and energy-related activities comprehensively.

The basic energy law is indispensible in China, because it may provide more systematic and comprehensive norms of specific conduct in certain areas. The Law on Legislation of the PRC 2000 stipulates that: 'State legislative power shall be exercised by the National People's Congress and its Standing Committee. The National People's Congress enacts and amends basic laws and the Standing Committee of the NPC enacts and amends laws other than those that shall be enacted by the NPC.'[84] In this respect, the basic law has more binding effect than specific laws.

In addition, China now has five specific energy laws, covering the coal, mineral resources, electric power, energy conservation and renewable energy sectors with a view to promoting energy efficiency and the development of renewable energy.[85] However, based on both the international and domestic circumstances, these laws fail to meet the requirements to cope with climate change in the long term. The large energy demand and energy security are critical issues for China, which demands more effective regulations on energy utilization and management behaviour. Against this background, specific laws concerning energy cannot be effective or powerful enough to address energy issues. Similarly, the existing specific energy laws cannot provide adequate legislative support for climate change mitigation. There is still a lack of specific laws for petroleum, gas, nuclear and other energy resources.

Second, the legislative ideas and techniques of the energy legal system lag behind current social development and requirements. The legislative objectives of these laws are mostly set from an economic perspective rather than an environmental perspective; and in this regard, the existing energy legal system can hardly assist in fulfilling the reduction targets.

Third, the existing specific laws have relatively low applicability. Many provisions are too generous and lack certainty and adequacy: the accountability system of offenders, especially, remains weak and the individual specific laws lack harmony and coordination.

---

[84] *Legislation Law of the People's Republic of China 2000* (PRC), art 7, http://www.gov.cn/english/laws/2005-08/20/content_29724.htm (last accessed 4 February 2014).

[85] These laws include *Electricity Law of the People's Republic of China 1996, PRC Energy Conservation Law 1997, PRC Renewable Energy Law 2005, PRC Coal Industry Law 1996* and *PRC Mineral Resources Law 1986.*

8.4 INSTITUTIONAL FRAMEWORK OF CLIMATE CHANGE AND ENERGY

The Chinese Government has formed an institutional framework addressing climate change, which can be divided into institutional framework of general climate change issues and institutional framework of energy management.

As early as 1990, the Coordination Group was established under the Environmental Protection Committee of the State Council at that time to face the challenges presented by climate change. An office of the committee was set up as the State Meteorological Administration. In 1998, central government organizations were streamlined, and National Coordination Committee on Climate Change (NCCCC) was set up. It was a cross-ministries body under the State Council and was responsible for deliberation and coordination on climate-related policy issues and activities and negotiations with foreign parties. For several years, it provided guidance to central government departments and local governments addressing climate change issues; it was updated in October 2003, and presently compromises 17 ministries and agencies.[86] The Office of the NCCCC is situated in the Department of Regional Economy of NDRC and is responsible for routine work of the Committee.

In order to strengthen the leadership on addressing climate change and reducing GHGs, the State Council decided to establish an enlarged body – the National Leading Group to Address Climate Change and Reduce GHGs under the directorship of the Chinese Premier. The Leading Group is responsible for deliberating and determining key national strategies, guidelines and measures on climate change, as well as coordinating and resolving key issues relating to climate change. The office, whose capacity is enhanced compared with that of the NCCCC, is set up within the NDRC.

Thus, the NCCCC and the Leading Group at central government level may strengthen coordination and cooperation between relevant ministries and departments of the State Council and ensure they fulfill their

---

[86] These ministries and agencies include the National Development and Reform Commission (NDRC), the Ministry of Foreign Affairs, the Ministry of Science and Technology, China Meteorological Administration, Environmental Protection Ministry, Ministry of Finance, Ministry of Commerce, Ministry of Agriculture, Ministry of Construction, Ministry of Communications, Ministry of Water Resources, State Forestry Administration, Chinese Academy of Science, State Ocean Administration, Civil Aviation Administration, National Bureau of Statistics and the Ministry of Land of Resources.

responsibilities concerning climate change. With regard to the regional administration system, it is required that the local governments at different local levels should enhance the organization and leadership on local responses to climate change, and formulate and implement local climate change programmes as a matter of priority.[87] This is because the risks from the future impact of climate change will vary between and within different regions in China. Only if actions are made at the local level to address climate change, therefore, will it be possible for these policies and strategies to have a real effect in the coming years.

Raising energy efficiency and promoting renewable energy utilization are key points to addressing climate change. The institutional arrangements for energy management have undergone several reforms since the new People's Republic of China was founded in 1948. Nevertheless, there is no specific energy management institution in China. Instead, the power of energy management is scattered throughout different ministries and departments.

The National Energy Commission was set up in 1980, followed by the Energy Ministry set up in 1988 and the Coal Ministry in 1993. After the Coal Ministry was revoked in 1998, the power of energy management in China began to be scattered among different ministries and departments. The Bureau of Energy under the NDRC was established in April 2003. It is responsible for studying energy development and utilization both at home and abroad, putting forward the relevant strategies, plans and major policies for energy development, administering energy utilization in China and formulating policy measures for energy conservation and renewable energy development.[88] Furthermore, the National Energy Leading Group, set up in June 2005, is headed by the Premier with the main task of conducting research on major energy development and utilization policies, strategies and programmes. The Office of the National Energy Leading Group is set within the NDRC, responsible for undertaking the day-to-day work of the Leading Group.

Besides the Bureau of Energy and the National Energy Leading Group, the other ministries and agencies concerning the energy management are NDRC, Environmental Protection Ministry, the Ministry of Land and

---

87 National Development and Reform Commission, the People's Republic of China, *China's National Climate Change Programme* (2007) 56, www.ccchina.gov.cn/WebSite/CCChina/UpFile/File188.pdf (last accessed 4 February 2014).

88 *Main Functions of Departments of the NDRC*, National Development and Reform Commission http://en.ndrc.gov.cn/mfod/t20050519_0901.htm (last accessed 4 February 2014).

Resources, the Ministry of Water Resources, Ministry of Science and Technology, State Electricity Regulatory Commission, State-owned Assets Supervision and Administration Commission, etc. Among these organizations, the NDRC is responsible for formulating energy policies and deciding energy prices; State-owned Assets Supervision and Administration Commission takes charge of managing the assets and high-level personnel of state-owned energy corporations; and the Ministry of Land and Resources is the main department to manage the development of hidden resources.

In conclusion, on the one hand, many departments are involved in the energy management, not only indicating the importance of energy issues, but also ensuring the inter-supervision; on the other hand, the lack of a unified standard for energy management system is likely to bring about low work efficiency and conflicts between different policies, regulations and institutions.

Currently, China considers climate change issues as a matter of priority. The Chinese Government has adopted a series of legal, economic, administrative and technological measures to address climate change. With regard to management institutions of climate change in China, the relatively high level of specific climate change institution – NCCCC – demonstrates the significance of climate change issues in China. In addition, the local governments at different levels have the responsibility of enhancing the organization and leadership on local responses to climate change, illustrating the essential role of local efforts in combating climate change.

Furthermore, the legislation concerning the development of a circular economy and energy efficiency, utilization and development play crucial roles in supporting the effective enforcement of climate change policies and laws in China. China has not only formed a relatively complete energy legislative framework, but has also set up many fixed energy conservation and development targets. Although there is no specific and high-level energy management institution in China, which has impeded the energy development, the Chinese Government is making efforts to deepen the reform of energy management and decision systems.[89] A more powerful and effective energy management institution system is set to be established.

---

[89] See Information Office of the State Council of the People's Republic of China, *China's Energy Conditions and Policies* (2007) http://en.ndrc.gov.cn/policyrelease/P020071227502260511798.pdf (last accessed 4 February 2014).

8.5 CONCLUSION AND SUGGESTIONS: MEETING A CHALLENGE OF CLIMATE CHANGE[90]

The only way for China to meet the challenge of climate change is to develop a low-carbon economy. Decoupling the growth of carbon emissions from economic development is challenging but achievable in China.[91] The effectiveness of a governance system in general may influence the effective global warming mitigation, but an effective governance system requires instruments for policy coordination, rule of law, and the realization of established goals.

8.5.1 Taking Immediate Action to Address Climate Change

It is necessary for China to attach great importance, and take immediate action, to address climate change issues. First, scientific evidence has confirmed that climate change would have an irreversible adverse impact on China. Second, China, with surging economic development and therefore a major emitter, has been under great international pressure to reduce its carbon emissions. In addition, China must pay serious attention to the *Stern Review Report*,[92] which was released in 2006 and is the most comprehensive review ever carried out on the economics of climate change. It states that if countries do not act and spend money on averting climate change now the world will face a depression worse than that of the 1930s.[93] China is no exception: although China's economy is developing at an incomparable rate in, this economic advance is at the expense of environmental interests. In these circumstances, if China does not take immediate action to address climate change, it will spend even more money having to compensate for the adverse impacts of climate change in the future.

---

[90] This part is adapted from Xiaoyi Jiang, *Legal Issues for Implementing the Clean Development Mechanism in China*, (Springer: Berlin), 2012.

[91] *China can Achieve Low Carbon Growth* (2009) Economic & Social Research Council http://www.esrc.ac.uk/ESRCInfoCentre/PO/releases/2009/april/china.aspx (last accessed 4 February 2014).

[92] Nicholas Stern, *Stern Review on the Economics of Climate Change* (British Government, 2006), http://webarchive.nationalarchives.gov.uk/+/http:/www.hm-treasury.gov.uk/independent_reviews/stern_review_economics_climate_change/stern_review_report.cfm (last accessed 4 February 2014).

[93] See Rafael Epstein, 'Stern Report warns of huge costs of climate change', *ABC*, (London), 30 October 2006 http://www.abc.net.au/am/content/2006/s1776326.htm (last accessed 4 February 2014).

Therefore, climate change should be put at the top of the agenda and China should take immediate action to address it. The actions required may include both minimizing its impact and adapting to its inevitability. In addition, the action should not only be taken by the Chinese Government but also the whole society: the general behaviour of Chinese people and their thinking can influence climate change mitigation as China is a populous country. In this regard, the climate change issue in China cannot be solved without public commitment. Finally, the human-induced climate change is a complex system, which cannot be settled by a single solution. Therefore, the Chinese Government should take various measures, including technological measures, legal measures as well as financial measures, to combat climate change.

8.5.2 Making Appropriate Climate Change Policy

Proactive climate change policy

China has made a series of climate change-related policies although the government has refused to consider a fixed cap on emissions. However, the problem of its current strategy on climate change is that the strategy is short-term, temporary, and transitional. There is no long-term vision and no future targets yet and also there is no clear, long-term negotiation plan.

Based on the above and in light of the lasting impact of climate change, China should have its own solutions to climate change, which have to be sustainable in both economic and environmental terms. It is necessary to get a consensus within China of long-term strategy of climate change first and then clearly define targets and a roadmap of priority actions.

Coordinated climate change policy

In addition, due to the complexity and diversified impact of climate change, the Chinese Government should develop a coordinated strategy for climate change. First, China should coordinate economic development with emissions reduction. The maintenance of economic growth is a key to the ability to develop and implement effective policies to minimize the impact of climate change, and to adapt to its inevitability. To achieve this, China should adhere to industrial development with the basic goal of saving energy and reducing emissions. Meanwhile, technological, environmental and social aspects should also be fully considered when developing these strategies.

Second, China should coordinate and integrate its energy efficiency policy within its climate change policy. It has been confirmed that climate change is prominently caused by increases of human-induced carbon emissions. In this regard, the climate change issue is closely related to energy utilization. Therefore, improving energy efficiency is a key factor in addressing climate change.

Third, the Chinese Government should provide guidance to local governments, the corporate sector as well as individual citizens as to how daily behaviour could be integrated with climate change policy in order to address these issues in a systemic way.

Finally, the climate change policy should also contain both domestic efforts and international negotiation and cooperation. Climate change is a universal problem, which cannot be solved by any single country. Therefore, China, on the one hand, should make both domestic efforts to reduce carbon emissions, and, on the other, actively participate in international climate change policy regimes and make use of international cooperation. In this regard, both the domestic efforts and international cooperation should be coordinated into its climate change policy.

8.5.3 Setting-up Clear Reduction Targets

In order to effectively implement the climate change policy, the Chinese Government should set up clear carbon emission reduction targets and an appropriate regulatory regime to ensure compliance and accountability.

First, the Chinese Government should make a long-term carbon emission reduction target. The overall long-term target should be divided into several short-term targets at particular stages. Meanwhile, the whole target can also be divided into several targets and distributed to the local governments and related coal power plants.

Second, in order to achieve the reduction targets, a clear accountability system should be established. The local governments at different levels should assume more local autonomy over climate change issues. China has proposed a new promotion system under which local officials' careers will be judged by their performance in meeting clean development and energy efficiency targets rather than merely by economic performance. Thus, the focal point is ensuring that this system will be strictly enforced. In addition, energy-related companies should also take on reduction responsibility according to their reduction targets and the contracts of responsibility should be signed and enforced. The entrepreneurs should integrate climate change into their risk management strategies and manage their targets through adjusting production; correspondingly, the government should provide supporting policies to reward or punish the companies.

8.5.4 Adjusting the Existing Legal System

As mentioned earlier, a specific law for addressing climate change based on China's national circumstances is expected to play a significant role in the climate regime in future. Therefore, drafting a complete and favourable specific law for addressing climate change is a great challenge to China. It is both significant and necessary to enact a basic and comprehensive law with a high legal level to deal with the dilemma of reducing carbon emissions without undermining economic development. The basic energy law is expected: (1) to provide a legal basis for the formulation and amendment of the specific laws concerning energy; (2) to assist in solving the conflicts between the different specific energy laws and the specific laws in other areas; and (3) to effectively safeguard the implementation of energy strategies and programs in China. In addition, the specific energy laws are of deficiencies, and thus revisions are needed to meet the demand of climate change mitigation.

9. Land management law

Tou Xiaodong

Land is one of the most important assets of human beings. A famous saying about the role of labor in wealth creation by William Petty known as the father of political economy that "labor is the father of wealth and land is the mother of wealth" illustrates the importance of land. From the biological aspect, most of the food consumption and more than 95 percent of the protein of human beings so far are taken from the land, and more than 80 percent of the calories and more than 75 percent of the protein are from the food provided by cultivated land. Throughout the entire course of human history, battles over land resources have never ceased: the tribal wars in primitive societies, the strife between countries in the slave society, the strong waves of peasant uprisings in the feudal society, the enclosure movements during the period of Industrial Revolution and the frequent land revolutions and reforms of all countries in modern society are all related to land resources. All the examples of the battles illustrate that the land resource is the survival basis of human beings and the most basic material condition of national survival and development of each country. With the economic development and population growth of the world, the scarcity of land resources is increasingly becoming the focus of world concern, so that its legal protection and regulation has become one of the issues to which legislatures and jurists in all countries have been paying increasing attention.

9.1 OUTLINE OF LAND RESOURCE

9.1.1 Definition of Land Resource

As an important resource element in ecosystems, land is the survival foundation not only of human beings, but also of all living things on the earth. Because of its critical importance, scholars of various fields and legislations of various countries have defined the concept of land resource from different points of view.

9.1.1.1 Ecological definition

From the ecological point of view, land is defined in general ecology as follows:

> Land is a solid structure, and it is an independent nature synthesis consists of many kinds of nature factors such as climate, landforms, rocks, soil, biology and hydrology. Land changes dynamically because of the influence of the changes of climatic and hydrological factors and the changes of land characters caused by long-term human production activities.[1]

As is seen from the definition, besides the basic nature of land, the ecological description of land focuses on the change in land caused by environmental changes and human activities, namely the systematicness of land recourse. This definition can thus remind us of the idea that the change in land resources will in turn affect the surrounding environment and the foundation of human existence, the very reason why we need to study its legislative protection.

9.1.1.2 Technetronic definition

From the perspective of technological science, land is defined in *China Agricultural Encyclopedia: Volume of Agricultural Economy* as "the natural synthesis composed of soil, topography, geology, hydrology, climate, vegetation and other natural elements. It is an indispensable substance for human's survival and social production; it is also the most decisive object in rural production relations." And it argues that:

> As a living space, land is [an] untransferable condition for human survival, and as standing room and working space of workers, land is [a] necessary condition of reproduction. People can obtain material and energy from the land, what's more, people can receive material and energy from the universe with it. Only when humans' labor combines with the nature forces of land, can human beings take production activities and create material wealth.[2]

This argument can be considered to be a description of the usefulness of land to human beings, namely a description of the resource attribute of land.

---

[1] Sun Ruyong. 1993. *General Ecology*. Beijing City of China: Higher Education Press: p. 223.

[2] The editorial board of Agricultural Encyclopedia of China. 1991. *China Agricultural Encyclopedia. Volume of Agricultural Economy*. Beijing City of China: China Agriculture Press: pp. 350–352.

9.1.1.3 Economic definition

From an economic perspective, land was defined by Richard T. Ely, an American land economist as follows: "The word of land used by economists refers to nature forces of all kinds or natural resources, including not only the surface of the Earth, but also all the material above ground and below ground."[3] In 1972, Food and Agriculture Organization (FAO) of the United Nations held a meeting of international experts meeting on land evaluation in Wageningen of Netherlands. In the conference document (Background Document for Expert Consultation on Land Evaluation for Rural Purposes), the concept of land was specially defined as follows:

> Land is the geographically specific area of the earth's surface and the atmosphere, the soil and underlying geology, the topography, the hydrology and the plant vertically above and below this area. It also includes the various results of human activities in the past and present within this area as well as the significant influence on the present and future uses of the land by human beings exerted by animal populations within this area.

9.1.1.4 Juristic definition

From a legal point of view, "land" is defined in *English-Chinese Dictionary of Anglo-American Law* as follows:

> In the general sense, the term "land" refers to the earth's surface, but in the legal sense it includes everything above and below the earth's surface, even including the air, liquid and buildings. As a legal concept, land is a three-dimensional area consisting of the earth's surface, the space above and below the surface, as well as everything growing on or permanently affixed to it.[4]

In *Black's Law Dictionary*, the legal meaning of land is defined as: "land is an immovable and indestructible three-dimensional area consisting of a portion of the earth's surface, the space above and below the surface, and everything growing on or permanently affixed to it."[5]

---

[3] Richard T. Ely, Edward W. Morehouse. 2003. *Elements of Land Economics*. Beijing City of China: The Commercial Press: p. 10.

[4] Xue Bo. 2003. *English-Chinese Dictionary of Anglo-American Law*. Beijing City of China: Law Press: p. 777.

[5] Bryan A. Garner. 2004. *Black's Law Dictionary*. Eagan: West Group: p. 892.

9.1.1.5 Legislative definition

In general, the legislative definitions of land vary from country to country due to the difference of their intentions. In the narrow sense, land is the terrestrial section of the earth's surface. In the broad sense, land is a natural synthesis that consists of many interactional natural elements such as landforms, rocks, soil, vegetation and water. The PRC Land Management Law provides that land refers to all the land within the management scope of all the administrative areas of the PRC, and that it is classified by end-use into three categories, namely, land for agriculture, land for construction and unused land. According to the provisions on land rights in relevant laws, land resources in China only refer to the terrestrial section of the earth's surface, the waters and vegetation on it are not included in the category, the mineral resources under it and the environmental elements are excluded from the category as well. In China, land is one kind of environmental element existing independently with water and mineral resources and forests. Therefore, the meaning of land in China is the narrowest.

9.1.2 Natural Characteristics of Land Resource

There is an inevitable and close logical relationship between the important position of land resource in the world political and economic system and its own characteristics. In sum, the natural characteristics of land resources mainly consist of the following aspects:

9.1.2.1 Finiteness

The finiteness of land resource means that the area of land in the world is substantially fixed, and that humans have no ability to significantly change its area by virtue of our current ability to transform nature. According to economic theory, scarcity is one of the two elements of resources. "Scarcity means a state that goods are always finite compared with the demand for them." There exists an essential connection between the fact that land has been classified as a resource and the fact that the area of global land is finite. The earth is known as a "blue planet", because 71 percent of the earth's surface is covered by oceans while the remaining 29 percent of it is its terrestrial section with less than 30 percent of this terrestrial section able to be exploited by humans.[6] In recent years, the area of land has been constantly reduced because of

---

[6] Fu Zhiheng. 2008. Study on land resources protection and law systems associated with land (a thesis for master's degree of East China University of Political Science and Law): p. 3.

environment problems such as desertification: soil erosion resulting from inadequate protection of land resources. The finiteness of land resources not only means that the total area of land in the world is finite, but also that in the same period of history, the areas of all types of land such as woodland, farmland and urban construction land is relatively finite, and an area increase of one type of land will inevitably result in an area decrease of other types. With the rapid growth of population and the tremendous development of productive forces, human society has entered an historic period when land resources all over the world have developed at a high pace, and the finiteness of land resources is been becoming more and more obvious.

9.1.2.2 Systematicness

Systematicness of land resource means that land resources is a key component of the land ecosystem. Land is a comprehensive concept, and it is a natural synthesis which consists of a lot of the earth's surface and all the natural elements on it including physiognomy, climate, hydrology, soil, vegetation, etc. Land is constantly under the influence of human activities. Land is neither the simple combination of these natural elements, nor is it the synonym of soil. No single natural element such as soil and physiognomy is taken as the principal element of land. All the natural elements interact with each other and mutually restrict each other. From the perspective of ecology and environment, any change of land ecosystem will have much effect on the surrounding environment.

9.1.2.3 Spatiality

Spatiality of land means that the utilization of land resource includes not only the utilization of animals, plants and the space above the surface, but also the utilization of soil, rocks and minerals below the surface as well as the utilization of the carrying capacity of the earth's surface. Spatiality of land resources also means that the location of land is relatively fixed. A land resource remains above the same location on the earth's surface, and its location is almost fixed, unless it has undergone geological changes over a long period of time. What is more important is that spatiality of land resources implies the more irreplaceable nature, namely physical carrying capacity. We often say that the survival and development of human beings need "space", but without the carrying capacity of land resources, biological evolution and human civilization will be a castle in the air, and the survival and development of human beings completely impossible.

9.1.3 Legal Characteristics of Land Resource

9.1.3.1 Characteristics in public law

Social relations associated with land resources are objects of protection in public law. Because of the special natural characteristics mentioned above, there are many social relations related to land resources that will eventually involve the politics, economics and the environmental protection of a country, and the survival and development of its human beings. So social relations regulated by legal provisions on land resources are of fundamental interests to states, society and individual citizens. Therefore, laws, throughout history, have protected land resources as a special kind of property. We can understand the special status of land resource when we read the provisions of our own country's constitution. First of all, Article 6 of the PRC Constitution provides that the basis of the socialist economic system of the PRC is socialist public ownership of the means of production, namely, ownership by the whole people and collective ownership by the working people. Land ownership is the fundamental component of economic system, and the two kinds of land ownership in our country are also the embodiment of socialist public ownership provided by our constitution. Secondly, Article 9 of the PRC Constitution provides for the ownership of other natural resources such as mineral resources, waters, forests, mountains, grassland, unreclaimed land and beaches, but Article 10 especially provides for the ownership of land. Provisions of our country's criminal law also indicate the special status of land resource. In the Criminal Law of the People's Republic of China, there are four kinds of crimes directly related to the protection of land resources, and they are provided not only in section 6 "Crime of undermining protection of environment or resources" of Chapter VI "Crime of disrupting the order of social management", but also in section 8 "Crime of disturbing market order" of Chapter III "Crime of Disrupting the order of socialist market economy" as well as in Chapter IX "Crime of dereliction of duty". The Criminal Law protects land resource from many aspects such as land ecological environment, rights to land resources, transfer of land rights and state administrative authority over land resources.

9.1.3.2 Characteristics in private law

Land is a special object of real right. In terms of civil legislation related to land, Real Right Law of the People's Republic of China reiterates the ownership system of land resources prescribed in the PRC Constitution. In nomology, "ownership" is a concept in private law, and it is a jus in re propria. But according to the constitution and correlated laws, the ownership of land shall not be transferred or disposed freely. So the ownership of land resource is not directly subject to private laws. But as a subordinate right of ownership of land resource, use right to land is a jus in re aliena and it can be transferred and circulated. So the right of use of land resources is directly subject to private laws. The separation of the ownership of land resources and the right of use to land resources is peculiar, and it differs from the property right to ordinary real estates in our country. So, to some extent, land resource is a kind of special object of real right.

9.1.4 Land Resource in China

9.1.4.1 Total quantity and average quantity per capita

In our country land resource is abundant in total quantity. Our country has 9,600,000 square kilometers of land which accounts for about one-fifteenth of the total land area of world, and the land area of our country is the third biggest in the world. But the average quantity per capita is relatively smaller than those of many other countries. The population of our country is the largest in the world, approximately 1.3 billion, so the average land area per capita of our country is only one-third that of the world average. The average cultivated land per capita of our country especially is less than those in other countries. The average cultivated land per capita is less than 1.4 mu which equates to one-third of that of the world average, one-seventeenth of that of Canada and one-eighth of that of America.[7]

9.1.4.2 Land types and land quality

Generally speaking, there are various types of land in our country, but there is less level land than mountainous land, and the proportion of cultivated land is small. Land types are complex and diverse because of the many different terrains and climates. In a north–south direction, the land stretches for 5,500 kilometers across five climate zones including the tropic zone, sub-tropical zone, warm temperate zone, temperate zone and cold temperate zone. In an east–west direction, it stretches for 5,200 kilometers and from coast to inland its moisture transits from humid to sub-humid, semi-arid to arid. With respect to topography, the land changes from the eastern plain where the average elevation is below 50 meters to Qinghai-Tibet Plateau whose average elevation is over 4,000 meters. But the land

---

[7] See the website of On Land Quality of China, available at http://www.tudizy.com/ (last visited June 8, 2014)

resources that constitute our country manifest their own distinguishing characteristics: there is more mountainous land than level land, and the proportion of low-quality, difficult-to-use land is large, any reserves of cultivated land, especially, are in short supply. China is a mountainous country, and the area of mountainous land, including hills and plateau, is approximately 6,337,000 square kilometers which account for 66 percent of the whole territory of the country: a significant part of mountainous land is difficult to use. Nearly 27 percent of the whole territory cannot be used for farming, forestry, animal husbandry or fishing, since the desert accounts for 7.4 percent, the Gobi accounts for 5.9 percent, the rocky mountain accounts for 4.8 percent, the cold desert accounts for 1.6 percent, the glacier and the permanent snow account for 0.5 percent meanwhile the land which has been occupied by settlement and for road traffic accounts for 7 percent. The cultivated land, which is crucial to agricultural production, only accounts for about 10 percent of the whole territory. In addition, little of the available wasteland of China is appropriate for farming, less than 2 percent of that of the world. What is more, since most of the wasteland appropriate for farming is distributed in remote mountainous areas and is barren it is difficult to reclaim and develop.

9.1.4.3 Land distribution and land utilization

The distribution of land resources in dimension is quite uneven. First, the distribution of land resource of any concrete type is irregular. For example, the cultivated land resource, which is quite finite, is located mainly in the plains area of the east monsoon region, but most of grassland resources are in the east of the Inner Mongolian Plateau. Secondly, the average quantity per capita of land resource is also unevenly located. The development and utilization of land resources is a long-term historical process. Due to the complexity of natural conditions and the particularity of the development process of each region, the land utilization in China is convoluted. For example, in the vast Northeast Plain, the Han people use cultivated land mainly to plant minor cereals such as sorghum and corn, while the Korean people use their cultivated land mainly for rice planting. Farmers in Shandong Province are experienced in planting peanuts, but farmers in Henan and Hubei are more skilled in planting sesame. Under similar natural conditions, certain areas of Taihu Basin, Pearl River Delta and Sichuan Basin have become national silkworm breeding centers.[8]

[8] See the website of On Land Quality of China, available at http://www.tudizy.com/ (last visited June 8, 2014)

9.2 CHALLENGES IN LAND RESOURCE PROTECTION IN CHINA

With the development of industrialization and urbanization, land resource protection in China will face many challenges. The main challenges are as follows:

9.2.1 Land Ecosystem Deterioration

The development and utilization of land resources has resulted in increasingly serious ecological environmental problems. Of all the elements of the global ecological environment, the deterioration of land is the most serious, and the whole world is confronted with land ecological environment problems such as desertification, soil erosion and fertility decline because of excessive deforestation and excessive land utilization. Nowadays, the land ecological environment is faced with the situation where the scope of deterioration is expanding, the degree of deterioration is becoming aggravated and the hazard of deterioration is being exacerbated: it is characterized by the phenomena of soil erosion and salinization are intensifying, grassland and forests are degrading, wetland is shrinking, and biodiversity is reducing. In our country, the area of desertified land already amounts to 1.74 million square kilometers accounting for 18.13 percent of the whole territory, and it results in annual direct economic loss of more than 50 billion yuan (RMB); the area of soil erosion is already up to 3.67 million square kilometers accounting for 37.08 percent of the whole territory, and the area of soil erosion which should be controlled has already reached more than 2 million square kilometers; the area of salinization amounts to about 900,000 square kilometers accounting for 9.38 percent of the whole territory; the speed of desertification is much higher than that of desertification control, and the area of desertification is still expanding by 2,469 square kilometers a year.[9]

---

[9] Huang Yiguang, Pang Youlin. 2001. 'Sustainable land use and its realization'. *Journal of Anhui Agriculture University* (Social Science Edition) (4): pp. 9–12.

9.2.2 Land Waste

The structural imbalance of land use threatens the economical use of land resources. With rapid economic development, the scale of urban construction and productive construction has been expanding unceasingly, and the urbanization and industrialization result in a growth in demand for construction land. The proportion of land concerned with industry, commerce and residences is irrational but there is also an unreasonable land use structure within industry. Since land use structure is unsound, the limited land resource cannot be effectively allocated, waste is, therefore, becoming serious.

9.2.3 Reduction and Degradation of Cultivated Land

On one hand, soil erosion, secondary salinization and desertification because of ecological environment change and natural disaster has resulted in the reduction and degradation of cultivated land. On the other hand, because a lot of development and construction plans are not scientific, cultivated land occupation by non-agricultural construction in the process of urbanization results in the permanent loss of cultivated land. Soil erosion is an important reason why the cultivated land has sharply reduced and degraded. Secondary salinization and gleization because of unreasonable irrigation is another reason; so too is desertification. Because of irrational reclamation, excessive firewood gathering and grazing, vegetation destruction, change of water sources and movement of sand dunes, the desertification in our country has been expanding for the past three decades. Nowadays, the area of desert and desertified land has risen to 1.689 million square kilometers accounting for 17.6 percent of the whole territory, it is 34.4 percent larger than that in the early days of new China.[10] Obviously, soil erosion, secondary salinization and desertification as well as the permanent loss of cultivated land resulting from urbanization have brought direct or indirect impacts on the productive capacity of cultivated land.

9.2.4 Land Pollution

Environmental pollution and irrigation with sewage has resulted in land pollution. The sources of land pollution are mainly from industry,

---

[10] Teng Xuesong. 2011. 'Study on problems in land resource protection in our country and countermeasures against them'. *Haerbing City of China: Heilongjiang Science and Technology Information* (5): p. 118.

households, agriculture and transportation. In industry, a lot of pollutants are discharged into rivers, farmland or irrigation systems along with industrial wastewater, waste gases and solid waste, and they have polluted, directly or indirectly, a large amount of land. In recent years, the boom of township enterprises has resulted in serious land pollution due to the characteristics of township enterprises as follows: wide distribution and lack of capital and technology. Meanwhile, in the farming process, application of fertilizers and pesticides has also, directly or indirectly, polluted the land. In addition, mining and unreasonable accumulation of tailings have resulted, directly or indirectly, in land pollution.

9.3 LEGISLATION ON LAND RESOURCE PROTECTION IN CHINA

9.3.1 Legal System of Protection and Management

The PRC Constitution provides for some essential problems relating to land, such as the scope of state-owned land and collective land, land expropriation and the transference of the land use rights in Article 9 and Article 10, and it confirms the framework of public ownership of land and that of land use right transference. The Real Right Law of the PRC concretely provides for state ownership of land, and collective ownership of land as well as the registration and circulation system of land use rights. The PRC Land Management Law and the Regulations for Implementation of Land Management Law make stipulations to land utilization planning, land usage control and cultivated land protection from the point of view of the comprehensive utilization of land resources, which are the main legal documents on land management in China. Meanwhile, other national and local legislation provides for land protection. First, much national legislation especially over land such as the PRC Soil and Water Conservation Law; Regulations for Land Reclamation; Rules on Management of Nature Reserve Land; Regulations for Fundamental Farmland Protection; Measures for Investigation and Punishment of Illegal Land Use Cases; Interim Regulations of the PRC Concerning the Assignment and Transfer of the Right to the Use of the State-owned Land in the Urban Areas; Interim Provisions on the Examination and Approval of the Assignment of the Right to the Use of the State-owned Land; and Interim Measures for the Allocation of Land Use Rights provide for land protection. Secondly, much local legislation especially over land such as Interim Regulations of Beijing City Concerning the

Implementation of Assignment; and Transfer of the Right to the Use of the State-owned Land in the Urban Areas Interim Measures of Shanghai for state-owned land lease also provide for land protection. Besides these, there are articles and provisions relevant to land protection in many other national legislations such as the PRC Environmental Protection; the Law of the PRC on Management of the Urban Real Estate; the PRC Forest Law; the PRC Grassland Law; the PRC Mineral Resources Law; the PRC Agriculture Law; General Principles of the Civil Law of the PRC; and Criminal Law of the PRC. All of the laws mentioned above constitute an operational system of legal rules on land resource protection and management, and they are the most direct legal bases of land management across our country.

In addition to the legal rules mentioned above, some related judicial interpretations by the Supreme People's Court such as the Approval by the Supreme People's Court on How to Apply Article 13 of the PRC Land Management Law and Article 14 of the PRC Forest Law and the Guidelines of the Supreme People's Court on Further Promoting Judicial Work of Real Estate Dispute Cases under Current Situation solve some difficult problems in the process of the implementation of related laws. These judicial interpretations have played a significant role in perfecting the legal system for land resource protection and management.

9.3.2 Legal System on Land Survey and Land Statistics

Article 27, Article 28 and Article 29 of the PRC Land Management Law provide for a land survey system and land statistical system as follows: The land resources investigation system should be established. The land administrative departments of the people's governments at and above the county level shall carry out land surveys together with related departments at the same level. Landowners or users should provide good cooperation and necessary data and materials required. Land administrative departments of the people's government at and above the county level shall, together with related departments at the same level, grade the land according to the results of the surveys, their planned uses and the unified standards formulated by the State. The State establishes the land statistical system. Land administrative departments of the people's governments at and above the county level shall, together with the statistical departments at the same level, formulate plans for statistical surveys and compile statistics about land according to law and regularly issue statistical data about the land. Landowners and users shall provide related materials and it is strictly forbidden to provide false and concealed materials or refuse to provide or delay the delivery of materials. The statistical materials about the land areas issued by land administrative departments and statistical departments serve as the basis for people's governments at all levels in compiling the general plans for the utilization of land. The State shall establish the national land management information system to conduct dynamic monitoring of the utilization of land.

9.3.3 Legal System on Land Utilization Planning and Land Usage Control

Chapter 3 of the PRC Land Management Law provides for land utilization planning system as follows: People's governments at all levels shall compile general plans for land use in accordance with the national economic and social development program, the requirements of national land consolidation and resources and environmental protection, land supply capacity and the requirements of various construction projects. General plans for land use at a lower level shall be compiled according to the general plans for the utilization of land at the next higher level. The total amount of land for construction uses in the general plans of land use compiled by local people's governments at all levels shall not exceed the controlled targets set in the general plans for land use at the next higher level and the total amount of cultivated land should not be lower than the controlled targets set in the general plans for land use at the next higher level. In mapping out the general plans for land use, the provinces, autonomous regions and municipalities shall ensure than the total amount of cultivated land under their jurisdiction shall not be reduced.

Article 4 of the PRC Land Management Law provides for land usages control system as follows: The State is to place a strict control on the usages of land. The State shall compile general plans to set usages of land including those of farm or construction used or unused. A strict control is to be placed on turning land for farm use to that for construction use, to control the total amount of land for construction use and exercise a special protection on cultivated land. Land should be used strictly in line with the purposes of land use defined in the general plan for the utilization of the land whether by units or individuals.

9.3.4 Legal System on Soil Erosion Control and Land Quality Preservation

Much of the national and local legislations such as the PRC Soil and Water Conservation Law provide for soil erosion control system as follows: The soil and water conservation shall follow the guiding line of "prevention focused, protection first, comprehensive planning, integrated management, reality based, appropriate priority, reasonable management, and outcome-oriented". The people's governments at or above the county level shall strengthen centralized leadership for soil and water conservation, include the soil and water conservation in their planning for economic and social development of the same level, and arrange dedicated funding for the tasks defined in the soil and water conservation planning and organize the implementation. The State implements the target-based responsibility system and assessment, awarding and punishment system for the local people's governments at all levels in the key areas for prevention and management of soil and water erosion. The competent water resources department of the State Council is responsible for the soil and water conservation nationwide. The competent water resources department of a local people's government at or above the county level is responsible for the soil and water conservation within its administrative area. The competent water resources department of a people's government at or above the county level prepares the soil and water conservation planning together with relevant departments of the same level, and organizes the implementation after reporting the drafted planning to the people's government or a department authorized by the government and obtaining approval.

Many national and local legislations provides for the land quality preservation system. For example, the PRC Environmental Protection Law provides for it as follows: The people's governments at various levels shall provide better protection for the agricultural environment by preventing and controlling soil pollution, the desertification and alkalization of land, the impoverishment of soil, the deterioration of land into marshes, earth subsidence, the damage of vegetation, soil erosion, the drying up of sources of water, the extinction of species and the occurrence and development of other ecological imbalances, by extending the scale of a comprehensive prevention and control of plant diseases and insect pests, and by promoting a rational application of chemical fertilizers, pesticides and plant growth hormone.

The PRC Land Management Law provides for it as follows: People's governments at all levels shall adopt measures to maintain and protect irrigation and drainage facilities, ameliorate the soil to raise fertility and prevent desertification, salinization, water loss and soil erosion and pollution.

9.3.5 Legal System on Land Reclamation

Some national and local laws and regulations provide for land reclamation system. For example, Article 42 of the PRC Land Management Law provides for it as follows: Whereas land is damaged due to digging, cave-in and occupation, the units or individuals occupying the land should be responsible for reclamation according to the relevant provisions of the State; for lack of ability of reclamation or for failure to meet the required reclamation, land reclamation fees shall be paid, for use in land reclamation.

Regulations for land reclamation provide for land reclamation system as follows: For the land which is destroyed and deserted in such production activities as mining of mineral resources, baking blue bricks and tiles and coal-fired electricity generation, corresponding measures should be taken to restore it to the state that it can be utilized according to the principle of "who damage, who reclaim". The units or individuals who have the missions of land reclamation shall fulfill their reclamation tasks. For the destroyed land due to productive construction, it can be reclaimed by units or individuals themselves, or the reclamation tasks can be contracted out to other qualified units or individuals. The waste of companies nearby should be made full use of for land reclamation. To both sides who reclaim land with waste and who dump waste in appointed land reclamation areas, the party with the waste and the party with the land reclamation area shall not charge any fees to each other. The units or individuals who are obligated to reclaim land should be responsible for reclaiming the state-owned land used by other units or collective land un-expropriated by the state. The state encourages production and construction entities to use the reclaimed land in preference to others. When land reclaimed is used for farming, forestry, husbandry, fishing and sideline, agricultural tax on it can be derated in accordance with the state provisions; when it is used for capital construction, preferential policies can be enjoyed according to the state provisions.

9.3.6 Legal System on Cultivated Land Protection

Many national and local legislations provide for cultivated land protection systems. For example, the PRC Land Management Law provides for it as follows: To cherish and give a rational use to the land as well as to give a true protection to the cultivated land are seen as a basic principle of land use in the country. A strict control is placed on the turning of land for farm use to that for construction use, to control the total amount of land for construction use and exercise special protection over cultivated land. The state fosters the system of compensation for cultivated land being occupied. In the cases of occupying cultivated land for non-agricultural construction, the units occupying the cultivated land should be responsible for reclaiming the same amount of farmland as that occupied. Where units that occupy cultivated land are not able to meet the conditions of reclamation of land or the land reclaimed is not up to requirements, the units concerned should pay the land reclamation fees prescribed by provinces, autonomous regions and municipalities for reclaiming land for cultivation. The people's governments of all provinces, autonomous regions and municipalities shall formulate plans for reclamation of cultivated land, ensure that units which occupy cultivated land reclaim land as planned or organize the land reclamation according to the plan and examine and accept the land reclaimed. Where occupation of land for construction purposes involves the conversion of agricultural land into such land, the examination and approval procedures in this regard are required. The requisition of basic farmland and land exceeding 35 hectares outside the basic farmland must be approved by the State Council. Land should be used sparingly for non-agricultural construction purposes. Where wasteland can be used, no cultivated land should be occupied; where poor land can be used, no good land should be occupied. It is forbidden to build kilns, graves or houses on cultivated land or to dig sand, collect stones, mine or carry away soil away from it. Occupying basic farmland to develop horticulture or dig ponds to breed fish is forbidden. No unit or individual is allowed to let the land lie idle or go wasted. Where cultivated land, that has been occupied and approved for non-agricultural construction but construction has not commenced within one year, it should be cultivated by the unit or individual that originally cultivated the land or cultivated by units occupying the land. Where construction work fails to start for over one year, a land idling fee shall be paid according to the provisions by various provinces, autonomous region and municipalities. Where construction work fails to start for two successive years, the people's governments at and above the county level shall revoke the right of use for the land with the approval of the original organ that granted the approval. Where the land used to be owned by peasant collectives, it should be turned over to the original rural collective economic organizations for re-cultivation. Where a unit or individual that has contracted for land operation has given up cultivation and allowed the land to go wasted for two successive years, the original contracting-out party shall terminate the contract and recover the land contracted out for cultivation.

9.3.7 Legal System on Basic Farmland Protection

Much national and local legislation provides for basic farmland protection system. For example, the Regulations on the Protection of Basic Farmland provides: the State fosters the system of protecting the basic farmland. With regard to the protection of basic farmland, the policy of overall planning, rational use, a combination of use and maintenance, and strict management shall be carried out. The protected areas of basic farmland shall be demarcated in general plans for land utilization at the county level and the township (town) level. The following cultivated land shall be demarcated as basic farmland protected areas and subject to stringent controls according to the general plans for the utilization of land: cultivated land in the grain, cotton and oil-bearing crops production bases approved by the land administrative department of the State Council or the local people's governments at and above the county level; cultivated land with good water conservancy and water and soil conservation facilities; medium- and low-yielding farmland where the execution of an amelioration plan is in progress or that is transformable; vegetable production bases; and experimental plots for research and teaching. Once a protected area of basic farmland is designated, no unit or individual can alter or occupy the farmland within it without authorization. When selecting sites for important national construction projects related to energy, communications and water conservancy, etc., and there is no way to avoid occupying cultivated land in protected areas of basic farmland, an application for approval must be submitted to the State Council in accordance with the procedures and authorities of examination and approval stipulated in the PRC Land Management Law. Units and individuals are prohibited from allowing cultivated land to lie idle or wasting land in protected areas of basic farmland in any other ways. Where a cultivated land in protected areas of basic farmland that has been occupied for non-agricultural construction upon approval of the State Council is not used for over one year after the approval and is still cultivable and yieldable, it shall be cultivated by the unit or individual that originally cultivated the land, or cultivated by the units occupying the land. Where construction work fails to start for over one year after the approval, the land idling fee shall be paid according to the provisions by various provinces, autonomous regions or municipalities. Where construction work fails to start for two consecutive years, the people's government at and above the county level shall revoke the use right of the land with the approval of the original organ of approval. Where a unit or individual that has contracted for land operation has given up cultivation and allowed the land to go to waste for two consecutive years, the original contracting-out party shall terminate the contract and withdraw the land contracted out.

10. Ocean and freshwater resources conservation law

Chang Hong

10.1 OCEAN CONSERVATION

10.1.1 Introduction

The ocean plays a significant role for mankind. The development of human civilization has, however, resulted in dwindling ocean resources. In China, following the adoption of the open door policy in 1978, the economy grew extremely fast: but the cost of that economic growth was the deterioration of natural resources. Ocean conservation, therefore, has become a necessity for China to deal with.

China ratified the United Nations Convention on the Law of the Sea (UNCLOS) in 1996 and has also established a legal regime for the ocean conservation. This includes the PRC Marine Environmental Protection Law;[1] the PRC Islands Protection Law;[2] the Sea Areas Use Management Law;[3] the PRC Fisheries Law;[4] the PRC Wild Animal Protection Law;[5] and subordinate regulations and rules (such as the Regulation on Management of the Foreign-related Marine Scientific Research[6]). The following section provides an overview of Chinese legislation on ocean conservation.

---

[1] PRC Marine Environmental Protection Law, State Council of P. R. China Gazette, 2 (2000), 5–13.

[2] PRC Islands Protection Law, Standing Committee of National People's Congress Gazette, 1 (2010), 20–25.

[3] Sea Areas Use Management Law of P. R. China, Standing Committee of National People's Congress Gazette, 7 (2001), 570–574.

[4] PRC Fisheries Law, Standing Committee of National People's Congress Gazette, 6 (2004), 548-552.

[5] PRC Protection of Wildlife Law, Standing Committee of National People's Congress Gazette, 6 (2004), 543–546.

[6] Regulation on Management of the Foreign-related Marine Scientific Research, State Council of P. R. China Gazette, 18 (1996), 694–697.

10.1.2 Legislation

10.1.2.1 Marine Environmental Protection Law

The PRC Marine Environment Protection Law (MEPL) was first adopted in 1982 and then revised in 1999. Chapter II of 1999 MEPL is about the supervision and administration of the marine environment. The competent State administrative department in charge of marine affairs, in conjunction with relevant departments of the State Council and the provincial governments in the coastal areas, must work out a national marine functional zoning scheme and submit it to the State Council for approval.[7] The coastal local governments shall, in accordance with the national and local marine functional zoning scheme, make use of the sea areas in a scientific and rational way.[8] The State shall draw up, in accordance with the marine functional zoning scheme, national marine environment protection plans and regional marine environment protection plans in key sea areas.[9] Governments at provincial level in the coastal areas adjacent to key sea areas and their marine environment supervision and administration departments may set up regional marine environment protection cooperation bodies for the implementation of regional marine environment protection plans, the prevention and control of marine environment pollution and marine ecological conservation in key sea areas.[10]

The revised 1999 MEPL is applied to China's internal waters, territorial seas, contiguous zone, exclusive economic zones, continental shelf and other marine areas which are under China's jurisdiction. This revised MEPL added two chapters which are respectively: "Marine environmental supervision and management" and "Marine ecological protection". Other than that, the old Chapter III, which was entitled "Prevention of pollution damage to the marine environment by marine oil exploration and exploitation", was substituted by the new Chapter VI "Prevention and control of pollution damage to the marine environment by marine construction projects". Additionally, the provisions relating to legal liabilities had increased enormously from four to 22.

The revised 1999 MEPL had paid special attention to the issue of implementation of international conventions or treaties. Article 97 of

---

7 MEPL 1999, art. 6.

8 Ibid.

9 Ibid., art. 7. In 2002, the State Oceanic Administration published the National Marine Functional Zoning, 30 sea areas in Bohai Sea, Yellow Sea, East China Sea and South China Sea are listed as key sea areas.

10 Ibid.

1999 MEPL has emphasized that: "If an international treaty regarding environment protection concluded or acceded to by the People's Republic of China contains provisions differing from those contained in this law, the provisions of the international treaty shall apply, unless the provisions are ones which the People's Republic of China has announced reservations."

10.1.2.2 Islands Protection Law

China promulgated the PRC Islands Protection Law (IPL) in 2009. This Law is formulated in order to protect the ecosystems of islands and their surrounding waters, and to promote sustainable economic and social development.[11] In the meantime, it also protects the maritime rights and interests of the state.[12]

The state council and the coastal local governments at all levels shall include the protection and rational development and utilization of islands in their national economic and social development plans, take effective measures to strengthen the protection and administration of islands and prevent the ecosystems of islands and their surrounding waters from being damaged.[13] The State is the authorized owner of uninhabited islands.[14] The State Council and the coastal local people's governments at all levels shall take measures to protect the natural resources, natural landscapes, and historical and cultural relics of islands.[15] It is prohibited to excavate or destroy coral and coral reefs. It is also prohibited to fell mangroves in the surrounding waters of islands.[16] The state shall protect island vegetation, promote the conservation of freshwater resources and support the construction of engineering facilities on inhabited islands for freshwater storage, desalination and introduction of freshwater from outside the islands.[17]

Island protection has huge relevance to the protection of a state's maritime rights and interests. In order to better protect China's, IPL emphasizes special protection to the islands which would facilitate national defense and those islands that constitute territorial base points.[18] It should also establish an inspection mechanism that could protect

---

[11] IPL, art 1.
[12] Ibid.
[13] Ibid., art. 3.
[14] Ibid., art. 4.
[15] Ibid., art. 16.
[16] Ibid.
[17] Ibid., art. 17.
[18] Jiwen Chang, *Environmental Protection*, 2009, Vol. 22, pp. 31–3.

marine natural resources and the marine environment as well as national sovereignty. But this is not currently stipulated in the IPL.[19] With respect to IPL implementation, it is important to coordinate with other laws or regulations.[20]

10.1.2.3 Conservation of marine living resources

With respect to the conservation of marine living resources, the Fisheries Law plays a leading role. The Fisheries Law was first adopted in 1986 and subsequently revised in 2000 and 2004.

The 2004 Fisheries Law was formulated for the purpose of enhancing the protection, increasing, developing and reasonably utilizing fishery resources, developing aquiculture, boosting fishery production and protecting the lawful rights and interests of fishery workers.[21] The state shall arrange continental-river and inshore fishing pursuant to the fishable amount of the fishery resources.[22] It is stipulated that the state shall determine the total allowable catch of the fishery resources and implements a fishing quota system in conformity with the principle that the fishing amount shall be lower than the growth amount of the fishery resources.[23] The fishery administration department of the State Council is responsible for organizing the investigation and evaluation of fishery resources, and providing the scientific basis for the implementation of the fishing quota system.[24] The total amount of the fishing quota for internal waters, territorial seas, exclusive economic zones and other sea areas under China's jurisdiction shall be determined by the fishery administration department of the State Council, and shall be distributed to local government level after it is submitted to and approved by the State Council.[25] In case the fishing amount exceeds the quota set by the upper level administration, the government must reduce its fishing quota the following year.[26]

According to the 2004 PRC Fisheries Law, a fishing license system is applied to the fishing industry. For the large-scale dragnet and purse-net operations in the ocean and the fishing activities in the common fishing areas determined by the agreement concluded between the People's

---

19 Ibid.
20 Ibid.
21 PRC Fisheries Law 2004, art. 1.
22 Ibid., art. 21.
23 Ibid., art. 22.
24 Ibid.
25 Ibid.
26 Ibid.

Republic of China (PRC) and other relevant countries or on the high seas, the license shall be approved and issued by the fishery administration department of the State Council.[27] The fishing license for other operations shall be approved and issued by the fishery administration department of the local government.[28] Fishing license for sea areas under other countries' jurisdiction must be approved by the fishery administration department of the State Council, and must observe relevant treaties and agreements concluded or acceded to by the PRC and the laws of relevant countries.[29]

With respect to the protection of fishing resources, fishery administration departments of the local government shall work out overall plans and take measures to increase fishery resources in the fishery waters under their jurisdiction.[30] The fishery administration department may collect fees from companies and individuals profiting by fishing in such waters and devote the collected money to the growth and protection of fishery resources.[31] The state shall protect the aquatic germplasm resources and their surviving environment, and establish protected areas where the aquatic germplasm resources with high economic, heredity and breeding value can increase and breed.[32] No entity or individual shall be engaged in fishing activities in the protected areas for the aquatic germplasm resources without the approval of the fishery administration department of the State Council.[33]

Several bans are set for the protection of fishery resources. It is not permitted to fish in prohibited fishing areas or within the prohibited fishing periods. Moreover, there is a ban on selling an illegal fishing catch from the prohibited fishing areas or during the prohibited fishing periods.[34] Methods of destroying fishery resources, such as killing fish by explosions, with poison or with electricity, are also banned.[35] Fishing with nets smaller than the standard set by the government is not allowed;[36] nor is catching the aquatic animal fry with important

---

27 Ibid., art. 23.
28 Ibid.
29 Ibid.
30 Ibid., art. 28.
31 Ibid.
32 Ibid., art. 29.
33 Ibid.
34 Ibid., art. 30.
35 Ibid.
36 Ibid.

economic value.[37] With respect to underwater explosions, exploration and construction that may have a serious impact on fishery resources, the construction entities shall consult in advance with the fishery administration department and take measures to prevent or minimize the damage to fishery resources.[38] In cases where any damage to fishery resources occurs therefrom, the government shall order the responsible party to bear the compensation.[39]

Other than the 2004 PRC Fisheries Law, the 1999 MEPL Chapter III has touched on the conservation of marine living resources as well. It is provided that the State Council and local governments shall adopt effective measures to protect typical and representative marine ecosystems such as mangroves, coral reefs, coastal wetlands, islands, bays, estuaries and important fishery waters.[40] Sea areas where rare and endangered marine species are naturally and densely distributed, marine natural/historical relics and natural landscapes with great scientific and cultural significance should be protected as well.[41] For marine ecosystems with important economic and social values that have already been damaged, efforts must be made to restore them.[42] The State Council and coastal governments at provincial level shall, in accordance with the need for marine ecosystem conservation, establish marine nature reserves.[43] The establishment of national marine nature reserves shall be subject to the State Council for approval.[44] Areas with special geographic conditions, ecosystems, living or non-living resources could be identified as marine nature reserves; special management shall be implemented in those areas by adopting effective protection measures.[45] Exploration and exploitation of marine resources shall be rationally distributed in accordance with national marine functional zoning scheme and shall not cause damages to marine ecological environment.[46] The state shall encourage the development of ecological fisheries, promote multiform production methods and improve marine ecological conditions.[47] Environmental

---

[37] Ibid., art. 31.
[38] Ibid., art. 35.
[39] Ibid.
[40] MEPL 1999, art. 20.
[41] Ibid.
[42] Ibid.
[43] Ibid., art. 21.
[44] Ibid.
[45] Ibid., art. 23.
[46] Ibid., art. 24.
[47] Ibid., art. 28, para.1.

impact assessments shall be conducted before the approval of new construction, reconstruction and extension of aquaculture base.[48] Aquaculture shall determine breeding density in a scientific way, rationally feeding and applying manure and accurately using medicines, so as to prevent marine pollution.[49] The exploitation of resources of islands and surrounding sea areas shall adopt strict ecological protection measures. Meanwhile, islands topography, shore and beach, vegetation and ecological environment of the surrounding sea areas must not be damaged.[50]

Moreover, the PRC Wild Animal Protection Law (WAPL), which was adopted in 2004, has shed some light on the conservation of marine living resources. In Chapter I, it is mentioned that the wildlife protected under this law refers to rare or near extinction species of both terrestrial and aquatic wildlife.[51] As regards the protection of the species of aquatic wildlife which are not rare or near extinction, the Fisheries Law will be applied. The fishery administration under the State Council is responsible for the nationwide administration of aquatic wildlife.[52] The fishery administration under local government shall be responsible for the administration of aquatic wildlife in their respective areas.[53] The wildlife under special state protection consists of two categories: first-class protection and second-class protection.[54] The revised lists of wildlife under special state protection are drawn up by the department of wildlife administration under the State Council and announced after being submitted to and approved by the State Council.[55] In major areas where wildlife lives and breeds, nature reserves should be designated.[56] The departments of wildlife administration at various levels monitor the impact of the environment on wildlife; if harm is being caused, these departments conduct investigations and deal with the matter jointly with other relevant departments.[57] If a construction project causes adverse effects to the survival of wildlife under special state or local protection, the construction unit must submit an environmental impact report.[58] The

---

48 Ibid., para. 2.
49 Ibid., para. 3.
50 Ibid., art. 26.
51 WAPL 2004, art. 2.
52 Ibid., art. 7.
53 Ibid.
54 Ibid., art. 9.
55 Ibid.
56 Ibid., art. 10.
57 Ibid., art. 11.
58 Ibid., art. 12.

department of environmental protection shall, in examining and approving the report, seek the opinion of the department of wildlife administration at the same level.[59] If natural disasters present threats to wildlife under special state or local protection, the local governments shall take timely measures to rescue them.[60] The departments of wildlife administration shall regularly carry out surveys of wildlife resources and keep records of them.[61]

10.1.2.4 Foreign-related marine activities legislation

The Regulation on Management of the Foreign-related Marine Scientific Research was adopted in 1996. This regulation is formulated for the purposes of strengthening the administration of foreign-related maritime scientific research conducted in the sea areas under China's jurisdiction. It promotes the exchanges and cooperation in maritime scientific research between China and foreign countries as well as safeguarding the national security and maritime rights and interests.[62]

Marine scientific research has only relatively recently become an area of concern to the international community as well as for international law and national laws. Several factors account for this development.[63] The most important one undoubtedly is the successful results achieved by conducting marine scientific research. Other factors like, growing awareness by developing coastal states of the importance of marine scientific research and the expanding scale of marine scientific research, also account for increasing regulation for marine scientific research.[64]

The United Nations Convention on the Law of the Sea has devoted all of Part XIII to marine scientific research. However, there are certain inconsistencies between China's regulation and UNCLOS. According to China's regulation, when there is a discrepancy between UNCLOS and China's regulation, UNCLOS prevails. Despite this, the provisions in China's regulation are far from certain and there should be a supplementary rule to clarify the issue.[65]

---

[59] Ibid.

[60] Ibid., art. 13.

[61] Ibid., art. 15.

[62] Regulations on Management of the Foreign-related Marine Scientific Research, 1996, art. 1.

[63] See A.H.A. Soons, *Marine Scientific Research and the Law of the Sea* (The Hague, 1982), at 1.

[64] Ibid., at 2.

[65] See Zou Keyuan, 'Governing Marine Scientific Research in China', in *Ocean Development and International Law*, 2003, 34:1, 1–27, at 16.

Marine scientific research in disputed waters is also a crucial problem, especially for China, which is located in the South China Sea community. China and Japan have had a dispute over a Chinese research vessel conducting marine scientific research in the East China Sea: Japan accused China of violating Japan's sovereignty and maritime interests; China argued that there was no clear boundary delimitation between the two countries in the area.[66] However, the two countries finally agreed to establish a framework for mutual notification of marine scientific research operations to be conducted in the disputed sea areas of the East China Sea.[67]

In terms of ocean conservation, only one article of the regulations may have relevance. Article 8 stipulates that the introduction of harmful substances into the marine environment is prohibited. Furthermore, exploration or operation by use of explosives without authorization in conducting foreign-related maritime scientific research is not allowed.

In the Rules on Governing the Laying of Submarine Cables and Pipelines, which was adopted in 1989,[68] Article 6 mentions that the owners of submarine cables and pipelines shall submit a report about the impact of the cable and pipeline laying construction project on the marine resources and environment. The 1992 Implementing Rules on Governing the Laying of Submarine Cables and Pipelines[69] includes more provisions regarding ocean conservation. Besides the aforementioned environmental impact report, a feasibility study report of sewage discharge project is also required.[70] It also further amplifies that the marine resources and environmental impact reports should include: (1) the status of marine resources and the environment of the waters where the submarine pipeline will be passing through; (2) a comprehensive evaluation on the marine resources and ecological environmental impact to the surrounding waters during the construction session and of the period it becomes operational, and the resolutions of the above-mentioned impact; and (3) a marine resources and environmental impact assessment of any construction accident and the contingency planning.[71] As for abandoned submarine cables and pipelines, they

---

66 Ibid., at 18.

67 Ibid.

68 Rules on Governing the Laying of Submarine Cables and Pipelines, State Council of P. R. China Gazette, 3 (1989), 110–12.

69 Decree of the State Oceanic Administration, No. 3, 26 August 1992.

70 Implementing Rules on Governing the Laying of Submarine Cables and Pipelines 1992, art. 5.

71 Ibid., art. 9.

should be properly handled and may not pose a threat or impede the normal exploitation of marine resources activities.[72]

10.1.2.5 Marine protected areas

Last but not least, marine protected areas (MPAs) are an effective management tool that can contribute to improving the health, integrity and productivity of marine ecosystems and help advance the integrated ocean management.[73] This is provided by Article 23 of the 1999 MEPL:

> Areas with special geographic conditions, ecosystems, living or non-living resources and areas which call for special need in marine development may establish marine special reserves, and special management shall be implemented by adopting effective protection measures and scientific development methods.

The State Oceanic Administration (SOA) issued the Rules on the Management of Special Marine Reserves in 2010.[74] It is stressed that the state shall scientifically designate the MPA in the consideration of the whole marine conservation picture and manage them in an integrated way.[75] The state should also take the conservation as priority and in the meantime exercise the exploitation moderately.[76] The SOA shall, in cooperation with the coastal governments at provincial level and other relevant departments of the State Council, formulate the planning of MPAs and guide the designate and management of the MPAs at local level.[77]

As regards to the establishment of MPAs, in accordance with the geographic location, the status of marine resources and environment, current exploitation situation and socio-economic development needs, MPAs can be divided into special geographical conditions protected areas, marine ecological protected areas, marine resources protected areas, and marine parks.[78] The state shall establish special MPAs due to the significance of the sea areas. The establishment of MPAs should be subject to the assessment committee, which is responsible for the

---

[72] Ibid., art. 14.

[73] Agardy Tundi S. (1997), *Marine Protected Areas and Ocean Conservation*, US: Academic Press, pp. 81–2.

[74] Circular No. 21, 2010, State Oceanic Administration.

[75] Rules on the Management of Special Marine Reserves 2010, art. 4.

[76] Ibid.

[77] Ibid., art. 5.

[78] Ibid., art. 10.

evaluation and argumentation.[79] With respect to the management, it is provided that the local government should establish an administrative department to implement marine ecological exploitation and conservation legislation.[80]

Natural landscapes, historical monuments, rare or endangered marine species and the migratory passage of important marine creatures should be strictly protected.[81] Invasive species should be prevented from entering the MPAs.[82] The signs and facilities that are used to indicate the territorial baseline points shall not be undermined.[83] MPAs can be divided into key protected areas, moderate use areas, ecological and resource recovery areas and reserved zones according to the characteristics and management needs of the ecological environment and resources.[84] In the key protected areas, construction activities that make no contribution to the protection of the sea are strictly prohibited.[85] In the moderate use areas, under the premise of ensuring the safety of marine ecosystems, the appropriate use of marine resources is allowed. Use of resources in an ecological way is encouraged, such as developing eco-tourism and aquaculture industry.[86] In the ecological and resource recovery areas, according to the results of scientific research, restoration measures can be taken to restore the marine ecosystem, resources and habitats.[87] In the reserved zones, human interference is strictly controlled. Any forms of construction activities or other activities that may change the ecological conditions are prohibited.[88] The SOA is responsible for developing contingency plans for the protected area and its surrounding areas.[89] Furthermore, in conjunction with the relevant departments and units, the oceanic administrative department shall take measures to eliminate or mitigate the damage in accordance with the contingency plans.[90] Emergency equipment and facilities should be provided in the MPAs and the inspections and maintenance shall be conducted on a

---

79 Ibid., art. 12.
80 Ibid., art. 18.
81 Ibid., art. 33.
82 Ibid., art. 34
83 Ibid., art. 35.
84 Ibid., art. 31.
85 Ibid., art. 32.
86 Ibid.
87 Ibid.
88 Ibid.
89 Ibid., art. 30.
90 Ibid.

regular basis.[91] They are subject to the approval of the SOA. The construction projects must be in line with the overall planning of MPAs. Environmental impact assessment and the sea area use assessment should be conducted before the approval.[92]

However, MPA site selection is mainly concentrated in coastal areas, and does not reach the remote sea areas. China's far-flung sea areas are mostly designated as Exclusive Economic Zones (EEZ), but they are rich in marine living resources as well as fishery resources and it would, therefore, be more significant and meaningful to establish MPAs there, although how to establish an MPA in a disputed marine area is complicated.[93] Furthermore, marine areas' functions are not clearly defined and the classification of the areas is not practical, resulting in the insufficient protection of the marine areas.[94]

10.2 FRESH WATER RESOURCES CONSERVATION

10.2.1 Introduction

Water is one of the most basic conditions for the survival of human beings and for the health of the planet. The demand for water has increased worldwide either for drinking water or for other purposes associated with modern living standards. However, the distribution of fresh water resources is not even. While in some regions there may be an excess, in others there may be a shortage.[95] Moreover, human activities may have direct or indirect effects on the quality of water supply. Therefore, to ensure that the fresh water resources are used and developed in a sustainable way is a challenge for both governments and local communities. The role performed by law is critical: a sound and well-balanced fresh water resources law should be viewed within the contemporary context. In many cases, existing legislation to manage and conserve the supply of fresh water has come down from the days when

---

91 Ibid.

92 Ibid., art. 38.

93 Li Fengning, 'Implementation and Improvement of China's MPA regime', *Law Science Magazine*, 2003, 3, 75–84, at 76.

94 Ibid.

95 D. Fisher (2009), *The Law and Governance of Water Resources: The Changes of Sustainability*, Cheltenham: Edward Elgar, p. 1.

the resource was considered to be inexhaustible.[96] Nowadays, the philosophies of sustainable development, rational use of resources and environmental protection have outdated old water resources legislation in many countries. This is the case for China.

10.2.2 2002 Water Law

The PRC Water Law was first adopted in 1988 (1988 Water Law). It was revised on 29 August 2002 and the new PRC Water Law entered into force from 1 October 2002 (2002 Water Law).[97] The 2002 PRC Water Law follows some of the principles set out in the 1988 Water Law. First, in order to achieve sustainable development and environmental protection, conservation of resources and boosts to the economy should be achieved in a harmonized way. Secondly, water saving economy and society should be established. Thirdly, unified management and optimal allocation of the water resource is promoted. Fourthly, the basic role of the market should be exerted to the allocation of water resource. Fifthly, the effective law enforcement must be strengthened.[98]

The 2002 PRC Water Law consists of eight chapters. Chapters I, VII and VIII are respectively general provisions, legal liability and supplementary provisions. In accordance with Chapter I, the state shall, with respect to water resources, adopt a system that organizes the administration by watersheds as well as by administrative areas.[99] The department of water administration under the State Council shall be in charge of the unified administration and supervision of water resources of the nation.[100] The watershed authorities, set up by the department of water administration under the State Council, at the important rivers and lakes (hereinafter referred to as the watershed authorities) shall, within their respective jurisdiction, exercise the water resource administration and supervision provided for by laws and regulations and authorized by the department of water administration under the State Council.[101] The departments of water administration in the local governments shall be in

---

[96] Ibid.

[97] PRC Water Law Standing Committee of National People's Congress Gazette, 5 (2002), 21–30.

[98] (2002), 'New Century, New Water Law, New Starting Point', www.envir.gov.cn/info/2002/9/95854.htm, accessed 27 February 2013 (in Chinese).

[99] Water Law 2002, art. 12.

[100] Ibid.

[101] Ibid.

charge of the unified administration and supervision of water resources within their respective administrative areas.[102]

Chapter II stipulates the water resources planning. The significance and legal status of the planning are stressed and it also emphasizes that the planning should be exercised based on both watershed and regional conditions in a unified fashion. The water resources' planning includes both watershed planning and regional planning.[103] Each of them also comprises general planning and specialized planning.[104] Specialized planning normally focuses on a specific purpose, say, flood control, irrigation, navigation, fisheries and so on, while the comprehensive planning is conducted with whole picture in mind.[105]

Chapter III regards water resources' development and utilization. The development and utilization of the water resources should be considered together with the upstream and downstream interests and be subordinated to the flood control arrangement.[106] The development and utilization of water resources shall give priority to satisfy the needs of the urban and rural inhabitants in their domestic use of water. Then it should consider agricultural, industrial and ecological needs for water as well as those of navigation.[107] In case of inter-watershed diversion, an overall plan and a scientific justification must be conducted in order to avoid damage to the ecological environment.[108] The formulation of national economic and social development plans, urban planning, and the layout of major construction projects, shall be compatible with the conditions of the local water resources and the requirements of flood prevention. The scientific justification shall be undertaken as well.[109] In areas where the water sources are insufficient, the development of manufacturing, agricultural and service industries that consume a large amount of water shall be restricted.[110] It is provided that the state shall encourage rain water collection and sea water desalination.[111] The government also encourages the development of hydropower stations. However, the ecological environment must be protected and the need for flood control, water supply,

---

102 Ibid.
103 Ibid., art. 14.
104 Ibid.
105 Ibid.
106 Ibid., art. 20.
107 Ibid., art. 21.
108 Ibid., art. 22.
109 Ibid., art. 23.
110 Ibid.
111 Ibid., art. 24.

irrigation, navigation and fisheries should be taken into account.[112] When the permanent dams or sluice gates are built on rivers that are migrating channels for aquatic creatures, or are navigable or suitable for bamboo and log rafting, the construction entity must simultaneously build facilities for the passage of fish, ships, bamboo or log rafting.[113] Otherwise, other remedial measures shall be taken after the approval by authorized departments. Regarding the policy of the resettlement of inhabitants due to the construction of water projects, it is stipulated that the state shall appropriately arrange the resettled inhabitants.[114]

Chapter IV is about conservation of water resources. In the formulation of a plan for the development, management and utilization of water resources, the water administration department, the watershed authorities, and other relevant departments shall pay attention to the maintenance of the rational volume of river flow and the rational water level of the lakes, reservoirs, and groundwater as well as the maintenance of the natural purifying capacity of the water.[115] Any water resources exploration, exploitation, protection or other activities should strictly observe the approved water plan, pursuant to Chapter IV.[116] Where a unit or individual acts against the plans and thus causes the lowering of the functions of the rivers or lakes, the over-exploitation of groundwater, the sinking of the land surface or the pollution of water bodies, they shall bear the responsibility of bringing such a phenomenon under control.[117] As for the water functional zoning system, it is elaborated in Article 32 of Chapter IV. In important rivers or lakes that have been identified by the state, the water administration department under the State Council, in cooperation with the environmental protection department, may delimit the water functional regions according to the watershed planning, water resources protection plans and economic and social development requirements.[118] For trans-provincial rivers and lakes, water functional zones shall be delimited by the water administration departments, the environmental protection departments, and other relevant departments of governments at provincial level.[119] The water functional zoning plan shall be examined by the water administration department, jointly with the

[112] Ibid., art. 26.
[113] Ibid., art. 27.
[114] Ibid., art. 29.
[115] Ibid., art. 30.
[116] Ibid., art. 31.
[117] Ibid.
[118] Ibid., art. 32.
[119] Ibid.

environmental protection department, under the State Council.[120] Water administration departments of local governments at or above the county level, or the watershed authorities, shall monitor the water quality of the water functional zones. Furthermore, they shall determine the pollutant-carrying capacity of those water areas based on water functional zoning requirements for the water quality and the natural purifying capacity of the water. The water administration department may give opinions to the departments of environmental protection on the limitation of the total amount of pollutants that can be discharged into those water areas.[121] Regarding the protection of drinking water resources, drinking water resources conservation districts shall be set up.[122] It is not permitted to build any outlet for discharging sewage into the drinking water resources conservation districts.[123] The establishment, modification or expansion of outlets for discharging sewage into rivers and lakes shall be subject to the approval of the water administration departments or watershed authorities. The environmental protection departments shall be responsible for the examination and approval of the environmental impact reports of those construction projects.[124]

The allocation of water resources and the water saving regulations are provided in Chapter V. In the case of water resources allocation, the middle- and long-term plans for the supply and demand of water resources shall be formulated on the basis of the present water supply and demand situation, the national plan for economic and social development, the watershed plan, and the regional plan.[125] It should also follow the guidance of a few principles, say, coordination of the supply and demand of water resources, achieving comprehensive balance, protection of the ecological environment and implementation of the water saving regulations.[126] Water allocation plans and preliminary plans for water distribution under drought and emergency conditions that cover more than one province, autonomous region or municipality directly under the Central Government shall be worked out by the river basin authorities through consultation with the relevant people's governments of provinces, autonomous regions or municipalities directly under the Central Government, which shall be implemented upon approval by the

[120] Ibid.
[121] Ibid.
[122] Ibid., art. 33.
[123] Ibid., art. 34.
[124] Ibid.
[125] Ibid., art. 44.
[126] Ibid.

State Council or the department authorized by the State Council.[127] In the term of water saving regulations, the state shall apply a system that combines the control of total amount and is managed on a quota basis.[128] For the different industries, the various industrial departments of provincial governments shall set the quota for different industries water use within their respective administrative areas and submit the quota to the water administration and quality supervision and inspection departments at the corresponding level for examination and approval.[129] The approved quota shall be published by local government and registered by the State Council.[130] The development planning department of the local government shall, jointly with the water administration department at the corresponding level, formulate the annual plan for water use on the basis of the water resources available for their respective administration areas, the determined quota for water use, the economic and technical conditions, and the plans for allocation of water.[131] The plan shall control the total amount of the water used annually within their respective administrative areas. In that sense, while the local governments are responsible for controlling the total amount of water used, the various industrial departments of the local governments are responsible for formulating the water use quota of different industries. The entities and individuals that collect water resources directly from rivers, lakes, or underground shall apply for the water collection licensed from the water administration departments or watershed authorities and pay fees in order to obtain the right to collect water.[132] However, collection of a small amount of water for household use, raising livestock shall be excluded from the license system.[133] The State Council shall provide specific measures for the implementation of the water collection license system and the levying of water resource fees.[134] For agriculture, the governments at various levels shall promote the water-saving irrigation mode and water-saving technology, and shall take necessary measures against leakage in agricultural water storage projects and transmission to enhance the efficiency of

---

[127] Ibid., art. 45.
[128] Ibid., art. 47.
[129] Ibid.
[130] Ibid.
[131] Ibid.
[132] Ibid., art. 48.
[133] Ibid.
[134] Ibid.

agricultural water use.[135] For the industry, advanced technology, techniques, and equipment shall be adopted to increase the water circulation and enhance the reusability of water.[136] The state shall gradually eliminate techniques, equipment and products that consume large amounts of water. Specific lists that show backward techniques, equipment and products shall be published by the general economic administration department under the State Council together with the water administration and other relevant departments under the State Council.[137] The producers, sellers, or users in these productions and operations shall, within a specific time limit, stop the production, sale and use of the techniques, equipment and products that are included in the list.[138] With respect to household water use, the government shall take effective measures in light of local conditions to promote water-saving household water appliances, to reduce the leakage and loss in urban water supply pipes and to improve the efficiency of daily water use.[139] It shall strengthen the concentrated disposition of urban sewage to encourage the use of recycling water and to enhance the utilization of recycling water.[140] The government at various levels shall take active measures to improve the conditions of drinking water for urban and rural residents.[141] It is required that construction projects must have a plan for water-saving measures and shall be accompanied by the construction of water-saving facilities.[142] The water-saving facilities shall be designed, constructed and put into use at the same time as that of the principal project.[143] Those using the water supplied by water projects shall pay water fees to the water supply entities according to the provisions of the state.[144] The water price is fixed according to several criteria, such as reasonable profits, high quality and favorable prices.[145]

Chapter VI highlights disputes settlement and the inspection of law enforcement. Any dispute concerning the water issue arising between

---

135 Ibid., art. 50.
136 Ibid., art. 51.
137 Ibid.
138 Ibid.
139 Ibid., art. 52.
140 Ibid.
141 Ibid., art. 54.
142 Ibid., art. 53.
143 Ibid.
144 Ibid., art. 55.
145 Ibid.

different administrative areas shall be handled through consultation.[146] Pending a settlement of the dispute, no party may construct any water project to drain, block, collect, or dam (store) water within a certain area on either side of the common boundary of the administrative areas, and no party may unilaterally alter the existing water situation, unless an agreement is reached between the parties concerned or an approval is granted by the government at the next higher level.[147] Any dispute concerning the water issue between units, between individuals or between units and individuals shall be resolved through consultation. Where a party is unwilling to have the dispute resolved through consultation, or the consultation fails, the party may request the government or the competent department authorized by such a government to mediate the dispute, or may directly institute civil proceedings in the court.[148] Where the mediation by the government or department fails, the parties may institute civil proceedings in the court as well.[149] Pending a settlement of the dispute, no party may alter the existing water situation unilaterally.[150] When handling any dispute concerning water, the government or the competent department authorized by such a government, shall have the power to take temporary measures with which the parties must comply.[151]

When it comes to law enforcement, the water administration department and the watershed authorities shall strengthen the supervision and administration of acts which are violating this law and punish illegal acts according to the law. The water administration departments of the governments and the watershed authorities shall have the right to take following measures when performing the duties of supervision and inspection prescribed by this law: (1) to demand the entity under inspection to provide the relevant documents, licenses and materials; (2) to demand the entity under inspection to make explanations with respect to the issues related to the enforcement of this law; (3) to make investigation on site; and (4) to order the entity under inspection to stop the acts that violate this law and to perform their legal obligations.[152] The relevant entities or individuals must cooperate with the functionaries of

---

146 Ibid., art. 56.
147 Ibid.
148 Ibid., art. 57.
149 Ibid.
150 Ibid.
151 Ibid., art. 58.
152 Ibid., art. 60.

water supervision and inspection.[153] If the government or the water administration department at the next higher level finds the department of water administration at the corresponding level or at the next lower level has violated the law or neglected their duties in supervision and inspection, the wrongful department shall be ordered to correct its acts within a specific time limit.[154]

This 2002 PRC Water Law was meant to effectively protect and make use of water resources to maintain economic society sustainable development. However, the law inappropriately emphasized the governmental administration role by overlooking water rights' regime and any public participation role.[155] A water rights' regime is the precondition and foundation for better management of water resources. Without providing any provisions regarding water rights, the government is still playing the main role in the process of water allocation and acquirement:[156] it should pay more attention to other stakeholders, who, according to the 2002 PRC Water Law, have no opportunity to take part in the decision-making process.[157]

10.3 CONCLUDING REMARKS

It is noted that ocean conservation is subject to several different legislative controls: the challenge is how to effectively coordinate them all. When it comes to the conservation of fresh water resources, the 2002 PRC Water Law plays a lead role. However, the 2008 PRC Water Pollution Prevention and Control Law is also relevant to water conservation. Under Chinese law water pollution prevention and control is separate from water resources conservation. This might need to be changed into a more integrated regime in the future.

---

153 Ibid., art. 61.

154 Ibid., art. 63.

155 See Yao Huie and Xu Kelei, 'Progress and insignificancy of China's New Water Law', in *Journal of The East China University of Politics and Law*, 2003, 3, 45–8, at 48.

156 Ibid.

157 Ibid.

11. Biodiversity conservation law

Yu Wenxuan

Biodiversity refers to "the variability among living organisms from all sources including, inter alia, terrestrial, marine and other aquatic ecosystems and the ecological complexes of which they are part; this includes diversity within species, between species and of ecosystems."[1] China has over 30,000 types of higher plants, and 6,347 kinds of vertebrates, accounting for 10 percent and 14 percent of the world's totals respectively. China also has 599 types of terrestrial ecosystems.[2] The legislation plays an important role in biodiversity conservation in China.

11.1 EXISTING BIODIVERSITY CONSERVATION LEGISLATION IN CHINA

In China, the biodiversity conservation legal system comprises constitutional provisions,[3] biodiversity-related laws,[4] regulations,[5] rules and

---

[1] *The Convention on Biological Diversity*, art. 2.

[2] See the website of Biodiversity Clearing House Mechanism of China, available at http://www.biodiv.gov.cn/dyxxz/200402/t20040226_88574.htm (last visited April 11, 2014).

[3] *The Constitution* provides that the State respects rational utilization of natural resources and the rare animals and plants; forbids any organizations and individuals embezzling or damaging natural resources by any means. These stipulations serve as constitutional provisions for biodiversity conservation and sustainable utilization in China. See *The Constitution,* arts 9 and 26.

[4] Biodiversity-related laws include *PRC Environmental Protection Law 1989, revised in 2014*; *PRC Forest Law 1984, revised in 1998*; *PRC Marine Environmental Protection Law 1982, revised in 1999*; *PRC Agriculture Law 1993, revised in 2013*; *PRC Water Law 1988, revised in 2002*; *PRC Land Management Law 2004*; *PRC Wild Animal Protection Law 1988, revised in 2004*; *PRC Fisheries Law 1986, revised in 2000 and 2004*; *PRC Seed Law 2004, revised in 2013*; *PRC Patent Law 2000*; *PRC Law on Prevention and Control of Desertification 2001*; *PRC Animal Epidemic Prevention Law 2007; PRC Grassland Law 1985, revised in 2002*; *Law on the Entry and Exit Animal and Plant Quarantine, revised 2009*; *PRC Soil and Water Conservation Law 1991, revised*

normative documents.[6] The contents of these biodiversity conservation legislations include the following aspects:

11.1.1 Ecosystem Protection and Conservation

The ecosystem is one of the three main elements of biodiversity. China has taken the following measures to protect and conserve the ecosystem:

(1) Classification and categorization. Ecological function protection zones are classified as headwaters conservation, soil conservation,

---

in 2010; etc. These laws provide legal grounds for biodiversity management from the perspectives of pollution prevention law, ecosystem conservation law and natural resources law. In addition, other laws like *Civil Procedure Law*; *Criminal Procedure Law*; and *Administration Procedure Law* contribute to the biodiversity conservation in China.

[5] China's biodiversity-related regulations are mainly composed of administrative regulations, which include: *Regulations on Aquatic Resources Reproduction Protection 1979*; *Administrative Regulations on Wild Medical Materials Resource 1987*; *Implementation Regulations of Fisheries Law 1987*; *Regulations on Prevention and Control of Forest Diseases and Insect Pests 1989*; *Regulations on City Greening 1992*; *Regulations on Protection of Terrestrial Wild Animals 1992*; *Regulations on Natural Reserves 1994; Regulations on Protection of Aquatic Wild Animals 1993*; *Regulations on Implementation of Water and Soil Conservation Law 1993*; *Regulations on Protection of Traditional Chinese Medicine Varieties 1992*; *Administrative Regulations on Breeding Stock and Poultry 1994*; *Regulations on Wild Plant Protection 1996*; *Regulations on Implementation of Law on Entry and Exit Animal and Plant Quarantine 1996*; *Regulations on New Plant Species Conservation 1997*; *Regulations on Basic Farmland Protection 1998*; *Regulations on Implementation of Forest Law 2000*; *Administrative Regulations on Agricultural GMOs Biosafety 2001*; and *Regulations on Implementation of Patent Law 2010*; etc. These regulations focus on the conservation and protection of ecosystems, species resources and genetic resources. Although some of them are not directly targeted at biodiversity conservation, they play important roles in the biodiversity conservation and sustainable utilization in China.

[6] The rules and normative documents include *Rules on Process and Package of Commercial Crop Seed 2001*; *Rules on Crops Seed Labeling 2001*; *Rules on Evaluation of Major Crop Varieties 2001*; *Regulations on Evaluation of Ecological Function Protection Zones 2002*; *Administrative Regulations on Franchise of Crop Seed 2002*; *Administrative Regulations on Urban Zoo 2004*; *Administrative Regulations on Approving Introduction of of Foreign Terrestrial Wild Animal Species and Quantity 2005*; *Administrative Regulations on Forest Germ Plasm Resources 2007*; *Implementing Regulations on New Plant Varieties Conservation 2007*; etc.

wind-prevention and sand-fixation areas, biodiversity conservation, flood accommodation, etc.[7]

(2) Living environment conservation for wildlife, including establishment of nature reserves in the zones and waters where the key protected wild animals live and are propagated.[8] It also includes the conservation of the living environment of wild plants, e.g. establishment of nature reserves, conservation stations or signs, etc.[9]

(3) Forest ecosystem conservation. This includes restricting lumbering, encouraging afforestation, enlarging the afforestation areas, collecting afforestation fees, forest foundation, etc.[10]

(4) Grasslands ecosystem conservation, including basic grasslands conservation and grasslands nature reserves.[11]

(5) Aquatic ecosystem conservation, including water function zones, drinking water resources conservation, etc.[12]

(6) Water and soil conservation, including afforestation, vegetation and hillside fields conservation, lumbering management, etc.[13]

(7) Marine ecosystem conservation. This mainly includes conservation of four types of marine ecosystems, namely, typical marine ecosystems, areas where the rare and endangered marine organisms are naturally centralized; marine organisms' living areas which are of great economic value, natural marine historical vestiges and landscapes which are of great scientific and cultural value.[14]

11.1.2 Nature Reserves

The nature reserves serve as an import approach to conserving China's biodiversity. Competent administrative departments of nature reserves establish special management institutions with professional staff within the nature reserves.[15] The management tools include the following aspects:

---

[7] Ministry of Environmental Protection, China Science Academy: *National Ecological Function Districts*, July 2008.

[8] PRC Wild Animal Protection Law 1988, revised in 2004, art. 10.

[9] Regulations on Wild Plant Protection, 1996, art. 11.

[10] PRC Forest Law 1984, art. 8.

[11] PRC Grassland Law 1985, revised in 2002, arts 42 and 43.

[12] PRC Water Law 1988, revised in 2002, arts 32 and 33.

[13] PRC Soil and Water Conservation Law 1991, revised in 2010, arts 16, 22, 24 and 37.

[14] PRC Marine Environmental Protection Law 1982, revised in 1999, art. 20.

[15] The Regulations on Nature Reserves 1994, art. 21.

(1) Categorization and classification. China classifies the nature reserves into four levels, namely national, provincial, municipal and county level, and categorizes the reserves into three categories, namely key, buffer and experimental areas. Each reserve will be managed according to the level and the category.[16]
(2) Planning. In China, regulations on nature reserves include national nature reserves development plans and nature reserves construction plans. The former is developed by government, while the latter by management institutions or competent administrative departments of the reserves.[17]
(3) Financial support. The funds necessary for reserve management should be provided by government at county level and above where the reserves are located, while the state gives rational subsidies for national nature reserves.[18]
(4) Limited exploitation and utilization. The specific measures include forbidding lumbering, herding, hunting, fishing, medicine collecting, cultivation, grass burning on waste land, mining, quarrying, dredging, etc. Sightseeing and traveling projects which are not in accordance with the aim of the reserve conservation are strictly forbidden. In the experimental areas of nature reserves, construction of facilities that could pollute the environment and damage the resources or landscape are prohibited.[19]

11.1.3 Utilization of Wild Animals and Plants

The management of wild animal utilization plays an important role in biodiversity conservation. In China, the basic point of the management is the state ownership of the wildlife. The legislation focuses on the protection and sustainable utilization of the wildlife.

(1) Wild animal ownership. While the State has the ownership of wild animal resources, institutions and individuals enjoy the rights of utilizing the wild animal resources,[20] e.g. domestication, propagation, hunting, fishing, etc. These rights should get approval from relevant competent organs.
(2) Wild animal protection. Based on the "Catalogue of Key Protected

---

16 Ibid., art. 18.
17 Ibid., art. 17.
18 Ibid., art. 23.
19 Ibid., arts 26, 29 and 32.
20 PRC Wild Animal Protection Law 1988, revised in 2004, art. 3.

Wild Animals", China protects rare and endangered wild animals and categorizes the protected wild animals into state level and local level, and Class I and Class II. Different measures are adopted accordingly for each type of protected wild animal.[21]

(3) Utilization management. China regulates the wild animal utilization through "utilization permits" and "limited utilization". The utilization permit is mainly presented in forms such as a domestication and propagation permit,[22] a hunting permit, gun-holding permit,[23] fishing permit,[24] import and export certificates,[25] etc. Limited utilization focuses on limited quotas,[26] hunting/fishing zones, hunting/fishing periods,[27] trading activities,[28] transportation and carrying,[29] etc.

According to the Regulations on Wild Plants Protection, the Administrative Ordinance on Breeding Stock and Poultry and the Seed Law, the regulations on wild plants utilization focuses on the following aspects:

(1) Catalogue of Key Protected Wild Plants. China categorizes the key protected wild plants into state level and local level. At state level, those key protected wild plants are further distinguished as Class I and Class II. Different measures will be adopted accordingly for each level and class of protected wild plants.[30]
(2) Utilization management, including collecting permit,[31] restrictive buying and selling,[32] import and export management,[33] resources surveys and filing,[34] etc.
(3) Management of wild plants' living environment. With nature reserves, China prevents projects which may cause negative effects

---

[21] Ibid., art. 9.
[22] Ibid., art. 17.
[23] Ibid., art. 18.
[24] Ibid., art. 16.
[25] Ibid., art. 24.
[26] Ibid., arts 18 and 19.
[27] Ibid., art. 20.
[28] Ibid., art. 22.
[29] Ibid., art. 24.
[30] Regulations on Wild Plant Protection, 1996, art. 10.
[31] Ibid., arts 16 and 17.
[32] Ibid., art. 18.
[33] Ibid., art. 20.
[34] Ibid., art. 15.

on the living environment of important wild plants and takes measures to save them.[35]

11.1.4 Management of Germ Plasm

The competent authorities under the State Council and provincial governments provide special protection for domestic animals and poultry species of special value, especially those which are also rare or on the brink of extinction, through germ plasm resources conservation farms, gene base and testing stations.[36] Governments at county level and above provide support for the survey, evaluation, conservation, breeding and utilization of domestic animals and poultry germ plasm resources.[37] The import and export,[38] breeding and farming,[39] and management[40] of domestic animals and poultry resources are also subject to administrative regulations.

The Seed Law provides that the state protect the germ plasm resources. No institutions and individuals are allowed to possess or destroy the germ plasm resources.[41] The State has the ownership of the germ plasm resources. Any institutions and individuals who provide germ plasm resources for foreign countries must receive prior approval from competent agricultural or forestry authorities under State Council.[42] It is not permitted to collect or cut natural germ plasm which is protected by the state. Whenever it is for special purposes like scientific research, and the collecting and cutting is necessary it should be approved by competent agricultural or forestry authorities under State Council and provincial governments.[43] The Seed Law also regulates the collection, arrangement, appraisal, registration, conservation, interchange, utilization and cataloguing of germ plasm resources, germ plasm resources base, germ plasm resources protection zones and areas, etc.[44] The Administrative Regulations on Forest Germ Plasm Resources (2007) makes regulations on forest germ plasm resources.

---

35 Ibid., arts 9–14.
36 The Administrative Ordinance on Breeding Stock and Poultry 1994, art. 7.
37 Ibid., art. 8.
38 Ibid., art. 9.
39 Ibid., arts 10–14.
40 Ibid., arts 15–22.
41 PRC Seed Law 2004, revised in 2013, art. 8.
42 Ibid., art. 10.
43 Ibid., art. 8.2.
44 Ibid., art. 9.

11.1.5 Management of Traditional Chinese Medicine Species

China has classified the wild medicine materials into three grades.[45] Those who collect materials of Grade II and III should get the permit for medicine collection.[46] The key protected traditional Chinese medicine species should be those listed in the national medicine standards; the species which have been identified by hygiene authorities under State Council as the species complying with provincial, autonomous regions and municipal cities standards can apply for protection.[47]

11.1.6 New Variety Management

In accordance with the Patent Law, animal and plant species cannot be granted a patent.[48] However, new plant species can apply for "species rights" in accordance with the Ordinance on New Plant Species Conservation.[49] Microorganisms are not regarded as animals or plants, and thus can be protected under the Patent Law. The non-biological method for the production of animals and plants can be conferred with a patent right.[50]

11.1.7 Quarantine

The following articles are not allowed to enter China: pathogens, pests and other harmful organisms of animals and plants, animals and plants from epidemic-stricken countries and regions as well as their output and other quarantine articles; corpses of animals and plants; soil. When it is necessary for the entry of the articles mentioned above, a request must be submitted to the competent authorities responsible for animal and plant quarantine for approval.[51] State authorities and customs authorities responsible for the quarantine of animals and plants should implement quarantine and supervision of the entry and exit of animals and plants, and the manufacturing, processing and storage of their output.[52] Other

---

45 The Administrative Ordinance on Wild Chinese Medicine 1987, art. 4.

46 Ibid., art. 9.

47 The Ordinance on Protection of Traditional Chinese Medicine Varieties 1992, art. 5.

48 The Patent Law, art. 25.1.

49 The Ordinance on New Plant Species Conservation 1997, art. 2.

50 The Patent Law, art. 25.2.

51 The Law on the Entry and Exit Animal and Plant Quarantine, revised 2009, art. 5.

52 Ibid., art.7.

relevant rules include application and approval of quarantine certificates,[53] re-quarantine,[54] transition quarantine,[55] as well as their outputs, quarantine of transportation tools,[56] etc.

11.2 CHALLENGES FOR CHINA'S BIODIVERSITY CONSERVATION LEGISLATION

Existing legislation provides an important legal basis for the biodiversity management in China. However, existing legislation needs to be improved in its objectives, legislative integration, legal regimes and legislation progress. These problems have limited the effectiveness of biodiversity management.

11.2.1 Objectives

In China, a civil law country, the objectives of law decide its content and influence its implementation. Without clearly defined objectives, laws or regulations cannot function to protect biodiversity. Existing legislation does not seek to directly protect the three elements of biodiversity – genetic resources, biological species, and ecosystems. Rather, it focuses on economic value rather than ecological value. Most importantly, there is not a specific law or regulation protecting biodiversity regardless of economic interests, which should be significant in the context of Chinese legal framework.

For example, the *Wild Animal Protection Law (2004)* stipulates: "The wild animals as stipulated in this law refer to rare, endangered terrestrial, aquatic wild animals, useful animals or terrestrial wild animals with important economic and scientific research value."[57] Thus, while this law is commonly regarded as a species conservation law, its objective focuses squarely on the importance of species based on their rarity, particularity and economic value, rather than the role that the species might play in the ecosystem based on their quantity, structure and ecosystem functions.[58]

---

[53] Ibid., arts 11, 12, 21, 24 and 30.

[54] Ibid., art. 22.

[55] Ibid., arts 23–27.

[56] Ibid., arts 34–38.

[57] PRC Wild Animal Protection Law (2004), art. 2.

[58] Yang Yuan: *Discussion on perfecting the legal system of animal protection, Territory and Natural Resources Study*, 2003, Vol.1.

In terms of ecological protection, it is stipulated in *Regulations on Nature Reserves (1994)* that the objective is to strengthen the construction and management of nature reserves, absent provisions on biodiversity conservation are included.[59] Obviously, the management of ecological protection is not based on the biodiversity. As a result, among provincial or national 100 nature reserves, 22 percent of them are damaged to different extents because of the development of "ecological tourism", and 11 percent have degenerated. Only 16 percent of them are under the environmental monitoring, and only 20 percent monitor and control the amount of tourism.[60]

Such problems also exist in the legislation for wetlands, which provides well-recognized habitat for many kinds of life forms. The legislation relating to natural resource utilization mainly focuses on economic aspects, paying insufficient attention to the ecological value. The objective of the law is the better development and utilization of wetlands rather than conservation of their ecosystems.[61] The Ramsar Convention[62] emphasizes both conservation and utilization of the wetlands, rather than either of the two extremes. Such a notion is critical to biodiversity conservation for China.[63]

11.2.2 Legislative Integration

A whole set of statutes in China are loosely related to biodiversity conservation, including laws, regulations, rules and normative documents. Yet a special biodiversity law has not yet been developed, and there are not enough essential regulations. No single statute specifically deals with the ecosystem conservation, sustainable utilization of

---

59 Regulation on Nature Reserves 1994, art. 1: "The Regulations are formulated with a view to strengthening the construction and management of nature reserves and to protect the natural environment and resources."

60 Qi Xuerui: Legislation on Conservation and Sustainable Development of Yellow River Wetland, see http://www.studa.net/jingjifa/110621/11211092.html, last visited September 16, 2011.

61 Chen Hongjun: Discussion on conflicts and countermeasures of wetland conservation of China, *Consumption Guidance,* 2006, Vol.11; Liu Xaiochun, Xie Qingxia and Wu Xiaojun: Research on the status and perfection of wetland conservation law of China, *Science Mosaic*, 2006, Vol.12.

62 The Ramsar Convention (formally, the Convention on Wetlands of International Importance, especially as Waterfowl Habitat) is an international treaty for the conservation and sustainable utilization of wetlands. It is named after the city of Ramsar in Iran, where the Convention was signed in 1971.

63 Lin Canling: *International Environment Law*, People Press, 2004, p. 411.

resources, or the protection of genetic resources. Most of biodiversity conservation legislation is presented in the form of rules and normative documents. This situation has negative effects on legislation enforcement: there is no sufficient legal ground for biodiversity conservation. In China, this problem is obvious in some emerging fields, such as biosafety and genetic resources conservation.

The closest relevant legislation to biodiversity conservation and sustainable development in China is the *Regulations on Nature Reserves (1994)*. Its major objective is to strengthen the construction and management of nature reserves,[64] not ecological conservation. According to this Regulation, nature reserves refer to areas, on land, inland water bodies, or marine districts, which represent various types of natural ecological systems, or with a natural concentrated distribution of rare and endangered wild animal or plant species, or where natural traces or other protected objects with special significance are situated, and so delimited out for special protection and administration according to relevant laws.[65] This definition separates the ecological system into different kinds of areas with some "reprehensive" features. But the areas without these features are still parts of biodiversity. These areas have not been given enough emphasis in the Regulation.

In terms of genetic resource protection, statutes have been enacted relating to the management of agricultural crop germ plasm resources,[66] wild plant resources,[67] new plant varieties,[68] poultry animal germ plasm resources,[69] wild animal resources[70] and traditional Chinese medicine varieties.[71] However, there are no specialized laws or regulations for marine biological genetic resource management, microbiological genetic

---

64 The Regulation on Nature Reserves 1994, art. 1.

65 Ibid., art. 2.

66 For example, The Rules on Process and Package of Commercial Crop Seeds, 2001: Rules on Crops Seed Labeling, 2001: Provisions on Evaluation of Major Crop Varieties, 2001: Administrative Regulations on Franchise of Crop Seed, 2002; etc.

67 For example, The Regulation on Wild Plant Protection, 1996, etc.

68 For example, The Implementing Regulations on New Plant Varieties Conservation, 2007, etc.

69 For example, The Administrative Ordinance on Breeding Stock and Poultry, 1994, etc.

70 The Regulation on Protection of Terrestrial Wild Animals, 1992; Regulation on Nature Reserves, 1994; Regulation on Protection of Aquatic Wild Animals, 1993, etc.

71 For example, The Ordinance on Protection of Traditional Chinese Medicine Varieties, 1992, etc.

resource management, flower genetic resource management, biological genetic resource access or benefit sharing. In terms of new biological varieties protection, China has stipulated protection of new plant varieties, but not of new animal or microbiological varieties. In terms of ecological protection, wetlands are closely connected to many relevant environmental factors, therefore the legislation on wetlands should not relate only to one or other of certain environmental factors, but should apply to all relevant environmental factors. In China, although the concept of "wetlands" is referred to in some laws, most only put particular emphasis on the conservation and utilization of a specific type of resource, such as water, farmland, wild animals, etc. Comprehensive laws such as the Environmental Protection Law or the Land Management Law also mainly emphasize the administration of the atmosphere, soil, water quality or pollution, in addition to farmland. Lack of special legislation often results in negative impact on biodiversity protection. In 2000, Monsanto proposed 64 patent applications on soybeans with the "marker gene" relating to high productivity, an invention based on soybeans illegally obtained from China.[72] These applications were approved by some countries with the result that any use of the soybeans with that marker gene must be paid a patent royalty. China had no special legislation dealing with bio-piracy at that time and could not take effective measures. Until 2008, the newly revised Patent Law made some stipulations on genetic resources,[73] but still did not directly relate to benefit sharing; in such a situation, China could not benefit from Monsanto's patents.

Existing legislation inadequately focuses on biodiversity conservation, and, even when it does, it does not provide for adequate administrative management. For example, according to the Regulation on Nature Reserves, both forestry and environmental protection administrations have authority over nature reserves management. However, their functions are not defined clearly. The Regulation provides:

---

[72] Pang Ruifeng: Infringe rights of Monsanto while planting Chinese soybean? Monsanto to monopoly high productivity soybeans in China, see *Southern Weekday*, October 25, 2001.

[73] Article 5.2 of The Patent Law provides: "No patent will be granted for an invention based on genetic resources if the access or utilization of the said genetic resources is in violation of any law or administrative regulation." Article 26.5 provides: "For an invention based on genetic resources, the applicant shall state the direct source and the original source of the genetic resources in the application documents. If the applicant is not able to state the original source, it or he shall state the reasons."

> The competent department of environmental protection administration under the State Council is responsible for the integrated management of the nature reserves throughout the country. The competent departments of forestry, agriculture, geology and mineral resources, water conservancy, and marine affairs and other departments concerned are responsible for relevant nature reserves under their jurisdiction.[74]

Here the "integrated management" function of environmental protection administration and the function of other departments are not clearly defined. Sometimes, environmental protection administration can barely enter some nature reserves for inspection purposes, because the nature reserves are usually operated by the local forestry administration, which are sometimes unwilling to undergo inspection by the environmental protection administration.

11.2.3 Legal Regimes

Some of the legal regimes of the existing biodiversity conservation legislation in China should be improved. The legal rights to the biodiversity, especially the genetic resources and traditional knowledge of the state, the indigenous people and local communities, are not clearly stipulated. The participation by the public should be given more emphasis, and environment impact assessments (EIA) and strategic environmental assessments (SEA) should play more positive roles. There is not enough financial support and there are few incentives to encourage biodiversity conservation, and the liability articles in some laws and regulations do not provide firm enough legal bases to address the violation.

11.2.3.1 Rights protection

The "rights" here refer to the interests of individuals, communities, businesses, institutions, local governments and the state, and how they relate to the access and utilization of biodiversity. There are a number of problems in terms of legal rights in existing biodiversity conservation legislation. Regarding species and genetic resources, the Wild Animal Protection Law, provides for the state ownership of wild animal resources,[75] and the state ownership of their genetic resources can be implied by relevant provisions. But in the Regulations on the Protection

---

[74] The Regulation on Nature Reserves 1994, art. 8.

[75] Wild Animal Protection Law 1988, art. 3, "Wild animal resources shall be owned by the state."

of Wild Plants, the ownership of wild plant resources and microbiological resources is not clearly stipulated, which is one of the main reasons for the loss of genetic resourses. For this reason, when an Australian company Redlands Nursery[76] applied in 1995 for the rights of a breeder based on *Homalomena Occulta,* a medical plant originating from China, and the application was approved by the Australian authorites in 1998, China could not take any effective legal measures.

The existing legislation does not pay sufficient emphasis to genetic resources access and benefit sharing. Due to the absence of enforceable stipulations on the accessing of genetic resources, China loses a large amount of biological genetic resources. Without a benefit-sharing mechanism, benefits can be acquired by private companies, including international companies, while the interests of the state and indigenous residents cannot be protected. The Monsanto case mentioned above illustrates this problem: the approved the patents application, based on the soybeans illegally obtained from China, resulted in indigenous people being deprived of their share of the benefit from the genetic resources derived from China.

Furthermore, sufficient attention is not paid to the rights of indigenous people, especially over their traditional knowledge. "Traditional knowledge" is defined as the "knowledge, innovations and practices of indigenous and local communities embodying traditional lifestyles relevant for the conservation and sustainable use of biological diversity".[77] The access and the benefit sharing of biological genetic resources are closely connected with the interests of indigenous people. Although the protection of traditional knowledge is gaining more and more attention and the relevant competent authorities are also beginning to take actions,[78] the practice still faces some difficulties due to the lack of clearly defined legal rights.

11.2.3.2 Public participation

Public participation can address the biodiversity issue in several areas: assembling existing knowledge on the approximately 2 million species known to science; conducting inventories and monitoring to provide real-time data on the occurrence of organisms; and discovering and

---

76 See http://www.redlandsnursery.com.au/, last visited May 3, 2011.

77 The Convention on Biological Diversity, art. 8(j).

78 Ministry of Environmental Protection is now drafting The Administrative Ordnance on Access and Benefit Sharing of Biological Genetic Resources.

describing new species.[79] In the Asia-Pacific region, many local communities have been directly responsible for the protection of the existing resources and the maintenance of delicate ecosystems and their flora and fauna. In the Philippines, there is a provision in the Constitution wherein the State shall encourage non-governmental community based or sectorial organizations that promote the welfare of the nation.[80] Since biodiversity conservation involves many aspects and is related to the interests of several stakeholders, it is crucial that there are clear stipulations on public participation. Public participation is regarded as one of the basic principles in China.[81] Traditionally, the biodiversity conservation in China has been mainly driven by the government, but confined by funds and human resources, it is difficult for the administrative departments to effectively accomplish the objectives of biodiversity conservation. Public participation, therefore, will be very important in efforts to resolve this problem. There are only general provisions on public participation in the Law on Prevention and Control of Desertification[82] and other related legislations and the approaches for public participation,

---

[79] Cynthia Parr, 'Addressing biodiversity issues through public participation', see www.tmsp.umd.edu/.../EOL%20TMSP%20Position%20Paper%20csp.docx, last visited September 14, 2011.

[80] Lourdes E Tolentino, 'Public participation in Philippine Biodiversity Conservation', see http://enviroscope.iges.or.jp/modules/envirolib/upload/1504/attach/ir98-2-5.pdf, last visited September 14, 2011.

[81] The Environmental Protection Law, art. 6: "All units and individuals shall have the obligation to protect the environment." The Law on Environmental Impacts Assessment, art. 5: "The state encourages relevant entities, experts and the general public to participate in the appraisal of the environmental impacts in appropriate ways." Article 21 provides:

> Unless it is provided by the state that it is necessary to keep confidential, for the construction projects which may impose significant environmental impacts and for which it is necessary to work out a report of environmental impacts, the construction entity shall, before submitting the construction project for examination and approval, seek the opinions of relevant entities, experts and the general public by holding demonstration meetings, hearings or by any other means.

[82] The Law on Prevention and Control of Desertification 2001, art. 3: "The following principles shall be observed in preventing and controlling desertification: ... (6) to combine government support with local self-reliance, combine organization by the government with participation by people from all walks of life, and encourage units and individuals to contract for prevention and control of desertification; ..."

as well as the remedial measures when the right is infringed, are not defined. Meanwhile, there are no incentive measures in existing legislation, which does not favor participation, and makes it difficult to bring the whole society into desertification prevention.[83]

11.2.3.3 Incentives

China's biodiversity conservation mainly depends on government finance and international funds, which are obviously not enough to resolve the problems of biodiversity destruction. Taking the support by the Global Environment Facility (GEF) in China in recent years as an example, the largest proportion of the financial support is on climate changes and energy, accounting for 60 percent of the total, while biodiversity accounts only for 13 percent, much lower than the international level, since internationally the support for biodiversity conservation projects are almost equal to the projects in other fields.[84] In such a situation, some incentive measures should be taken to raise more funds for biodiversity conservation.

11.2.3.4 Liabilities

Chinese laws and regulations typically lack liability clauses: if there are any, their enforceability is frequently weak. In the field of biodiversity conservation, penalty provisions have been included in relevant laws and regulations, such as for the smuggling of wild animals and plants and other relevant products, as well as for the forging and trading of approval documents, import and export licenses (certificates) or markings. However, most of the provisions are general, without specific standards, making implementation by administrative and judicial organs difficult. Some quantified standards are proposed in Supreme People's Court's Interpretations on the Trial of Criminal Cases of Smuggling, and Interpretations on the Trial of Criminal Cases of Damaging Wild Animal Resources, but some are simply too impractical to be adjudicated.[85] It follows, that when legal obligations cannot be carried out and at the same

---

[83] GEF/UNDP China National Environment Convention Performance Capability Self-assessment Office, Report on self-assessment of China's capability of performing international environment convention, *Environment Science Press*, 2006, p. 141.

[84] Xia Yingzhe, 'China-GEF: National plan and international cooperation on biodiversity', Thesis for Sino-EU Biodiversity Strategy Seminar, Oct, 2006.

[85] Wan Ziming: *Research on operation mechanism of CITES and countermeasures for convention performance of* China, Master's thesis of Northeast Forestry University, 2002.

time violators cannot be punished, the implementation of statutes will be negatively affected.

11.3 RECOMMENDATIONS FOR IMPROVING BIODIVERSITY CONSERVATION LEGISLATION

The problems with objectives, the legal system, legal regimes and lagging legislation progress challenge the biodiversity conservation and rational utilization in China. The existing legislation focuses more on economic value than biodiversity. There is not a specific statute dealing with biodiversity, which is very important to protect the biodiversity conservation legal system in China, which, as a civil law country, should provide enough legal bases for biodiversity conservation. As to the legal regimes, the protection of the rights of the state, indigenous peoples and local communities, which are related to genetic resources and traditional knowledge, need to be improved; nor have public participation, incentive measures or environmental impacts played their roles in biodiversity conservation and, further, liability articles need to be clarified in some of the laws and regulations. In this part, suggestions are proposed to resolve these problems: the problems relating to implementation will be discussed from the aspect of the legislative process, enforceability and effectiveness.

11.3.1 Objectives: Clear Definition

Biodiversity conservation legislation should avoid both extreme protectionism and extreme utilitarianism. Extreme protectionism causes the loss of internal motivation and sometimes conflicts with the rights and interests of some indigenous residents; while extreme utilitarianism definitely poses a threat to biosafety and biodiversity. Based on this notion, the objectives of biodiversity conservation legislation should comprise three elements: effective protection, sustainable utilization, and promotion of social and economic development. "Effective protection" means providing sufficient a legal basis for the protection of the three aspects of biodiversity, requiring the legislation to put "protection" top in the hierarchy of objectives, when the utilization of biodiversity appears to conflict with "protection". "Sustainable utilization" means a pattern of biodiversity use, aiming to meet human needs while preserving the biodiversity so that these needs can be met not only in the present, but also for generations to come. "Promoting social and economic development" means the provision of an ecological basis for social and economic progress, based on the effective protection and sustainable use of biodiversity. All these objectives should be achieved through an integrated legal framework, specific legal regimes and effective implementation.

11.3.2 Legal System: An Integrated Framework

An integrated legal framework is critical to biodiversity conservation and sustainable utilization. The "integrated legal framework" means a rounded statute system, comprising all the necessary elements needed for biodiversity protection and sustainable utilization. An integrated biodiversity legal framework should be composed of a special comprehensive law as well as regulations or rules to protect the three elements of biodiversity. The specific law and regulations on genetic resources management and biosafety should be formulated as soon as possible, and some existing legislation should be revised to meet the requirements of biodiversity conservation.

11.3.2.1 Comprehensive legislation

Comprehensive biodiversity conservation legislation should provide basic grounds for both biodiversity conservation and initialization and the further legislation at a lower level. It would be preferable if the comprehensive legislation could be enacted as a law, because this has the highest legal validity in the legal hierarchy in China. In this law, first, the objectives should be clearly defined as effective protection, sustainable utilization, and promoting social and economic development. Secondly, this law should emphasize the protection measures, especially those measures protecting the ecological system as a whole, the genetic resources and related traditional knowledge, including in situ conservation and ex situ conservation. Thirdly, the utilization of biodiversity should be on a sustainable basis, ensuring the reasonable quality and quantity of biodiversity, but especially without destroying the ecological system on which biodiversity relies. Fourthly, public participation should be encouraged in this law, providing incentive measures for the whole society to support biodiversity conservation.

11.3.2.2 Special legislation

After the national law on biodiversity conservation and sustainable utilization is formulated, the next most urgent step is to promulgate the special regulations on biological genetic resource and biosafety. These regulations are aimed at implementing the national statute. According to the Legislation Law of China, the regulation should be formulated and issued by the State Council. The biological genetic resource legislation should focus on access and benefit sharing of the genetic resources, and traditional knowledge related to genetic resources should also be included. The regulation, or its implementing rules, should regulate all kinds of genetic resources, especially those ignored currently, such as marine biological genetic resources, flower genetic resources and micro-biological genetic resources. For the regulation on biosafety, the main contents should include the stipulations on contained research, environmental release, commercialization, trans-boundary movement, emergency, legal liability, etc.[86]

11.3.2.3 Amendments

Some existing legislations should be revised. First, genetic resource conservation should be added to the Regulations on Wild Plant Protection. An article should be added to Chapter II of this regulation ("Wild Plant Protection"), providing that the regulations prohibit accessing wild plant genetic resources and relevant traditional knowledge without approval. In Chapter IV ("Legal Liabilities"), the administrative liabilities should include the responsibilities for violating this article. Secondly, the amendments should also be made to include articles for species protection in the Forest Law, Grassland Law, Water Law and the Regulations on Scenic and Historic Areas. These articles should focus on species protection from the view of biodiversity conservation, meaning protection for their ecological functions instead of economic functions. Thirdly, the Regulations on Nature Reserves should be re-formulated as law,[87] providing biodiversity protection as one of the objectives and adding the stipulations about biodiversity protection in this law.

11.3.3 Legal Regimes: More Specific and Detailed

Further legislation should provide more specific and detailed legal regimes, especially the protection of rights to genetic resources and benefit sharing, public participation and incentives to biodiversity conservation, and the legal liabilities.

---

86 Yu Wenxuan, *Studies on Biosafety Legislation*, Tsinghua University Press, pp. 277–94.

87 The existing special statue related to nature reserves is regulation, i.e. The Regulations on Nature Reserves. In China, laws are promulgated by NPC or its standing committee, while regulations are promulgated by the State Council.

11.3.3.1 Rights protection

Further legislation should put more emphasis on the rights of individuals to use and conserve biodiversity. The most urgent step is to clearly define the rights to genetic resourses, especially those of indigenous residents. The rights related to genetic resources include access and benefit sharing, including the rights on the traditional knowledge related to these genetic resourses. The special legislation on genetic resourses should at least provide the management of the different purposes of genetic resources access, the subjects who can access and share the benefits of genetic resources, the contract on genetic resourses access and benefit sharing, the application and approval process, monetary and non-monetary benefits,[88] and the guidance of access and benefit sharing, etc. The Nagoya Protocol on Access to Genetic Resources and the Fair and Equitable Sharing of Benefits Arising from Their Utilization provides some requirements and guidelines in these aspects.

---

[88] According to the Annex of The Protocol on Access to Genetic Resources and the Fair and Equitable Sharing of Benefits Arising from Their Utilization, monetary benefits may include, but not be limited to: (a) access fees/fee per sample collected or otherwise acquired; (b) up-front payments; (c) milestone payments; (d) payment of royalties; (e) license fees in case of commercialization; (f) special fees to be paid to trust funds supporting conservation and sustainable use of biodiversity; (g) salaries and preferential terms where mutually agreed; (h) research funding; (i) joint ventures; and (j) joint ownership of relevant intellectual property rights. Non-monetary benefits may include, but not be limited to: (a) sharing of research and development results; (b) collaboration, cooperation and contribution in scientific research and development programs; (c) participation in product development; (d) collaboration, cooperation and contribution in education and training; (e) admittance to ex situ facilities of genetic resources and to databases; (f) transfer to the provider of the genetic resources of knowledge and technology under fair and most favorable terms; (g) strengthening capacities for technology transfer; (h) institutional capacity-building; (i) human and material resources to strengthen the capacities for the administration and enforcement of access regulations; (j) training related to genetic resources with the full participation of countries providing genetic resources, and where possible, in such countries; (k) access to scientific information relevant to conservation and sustainable use of biological diversity; (l) contributions to the local economy; (m) research directed towards priority needs, such as health and food security, taking into account domestic uses of genetic resources in the party providing genetic resources; (n) institutional and professional relationships that can arise from an access and benefit-sharing agreement and subsequent collaborative activities; (o) food and livelihood security benefits; (p) social recognition; and (q) joint ownership of relevant intellectual property rights.

11.3.3.2 Participation and incentives

Public participation was proposed in Resolution on Carrying out Scientific Development Strategy and Reinforcing Environmental Protection (2006), which showed that China had started to place more emphasis on public participation in ecological conservation. However, there is still a long way to go to set up an effective public participation institution. Further biodiversity conservation legislation should make stipulations on the approaches and procedures for public participation, for example: to organize public hearings for important decisions and policies that may affect biodiversity prior to decision-making and project construction, and then to provide timely relevant information; to encourage environmental NGOs to participate in biodiversity conservation; to promote public participation in the biodiversity-related legislative process; to push forward public interest suits in civil actions; etc. These provisions should be clearly written in the proposed specific biodiversity law and nature reserves law. In the meantime, further legislation should encourage the whole of society to promote biodiversity conservation by providing incentives. Such incentive measures should include, but not be limited to, preferential policies and tax reductions. For instance, the project relating to biodiversity conservation should enjoy income tax reduction over a certain period, say three years from when the project is established. The government can also provide subsidies to biodiversity protection activities of NGOs, which will benefit the biodiversity conservation greatly.

11.3.3.3 Liabilities

The legal liability cannot be completed only within the framework of biodiversity conservation legislation. In China, such biodiversity conservation legislation as exists, seldom imposes a negative effect on violators; so any improvement to the legal liability may have a long way to go. Ultimately, the stipulation on destroying the biodiversity should be included in further Criminal Law amendments; this stipulation could be added in Chapter VI "Crimes of Obstructing the Administration of Public Order" – "Crimes of Undermining Protection of Environmental Resource" of the existing Criminal Law of 1997. Meanwhile, a specific Environmental Damage Compensation Law could significantly improve the enforceability of the stipulations of biodiversity violation.[89] In this specific law, neglect in biodiversity management or accessing genetic

---

[89] Some NPC representatives have proposed formulating an "Environmental Damage Compensation Law". See http://www.chinacourt.org/html/article/2010 03/10/398593.shtml, last visited May 5, 2011.

resources without approval, etc, should be stipulated clearly. Where the provisions of The Tort Liability Law and The General Principles of the Civil Law can apply,[90] this law should make general stipulations, such as to applicable types and criterion of liability.

---

[90] Articles 65–68 of The Tort Liability Law and art. 124 of The General Principles of the Civil Law.

12. Forest resources law

Zhang Shijun

12.1 OVERVIEW OF FOREST RESOURCES AND ITS LEGISLATION

12.1.1 A Brief Introduction to Forest Resources

As an ecosystem, "forest" refers to trees of intensive growth and other plant communities dominated by woody plants, including woodland, trees and other woodland plants and animals in the woodland habitat, etc. Forest resource is an umbrella term for national or regional forest areas, tree species and timber volumes, etc. It is composed of forests, but is not completely the same as forests. Forests protected by laws in China refer to forest resources: according to the Regulations on the Implementation of PRC Forest Law, bamboo forests should be regarded as part of the forest; as should woods that include trees and bamboo; and forestland that includes arboreal lands with a canopy density over 0.2.

The definition of the concept of "Forest Resources" is the starting point for the "Forest Law"; it is related to the definition of the scope of protection and the spiritual guidance set out by the PRC Forest Law.[1] The "PRC Forest Law" and "Regulations on the Implementation of PRC Forest Law" are specific laws and regulations to control forestlands and woods, but these laws and regulations cause many problems with the basic concept of woods, forestlands, forests, and forest resources.[2] The relationship between the concept of forest, forest resources, forestland, and woods is not clear and is often muddled. In order to solve these problems, it is necessary to reconstruct the four concepts identified in the "Forest Law". There are two main ways to solve the problem with the concepts: one is to expand the meaning of "forest" in the law with

[1] Gao Lihong, Liu xianhui, Research on the legal conflict of the concept of "Forest Resources" and its solutions, *Jiangxi Social Sciences*, 2012(7), p153.

[2] Zhang Ping, Legal Analysis on the Reform of China's Collective Forest Property Rights System, *Hebei Law Science*, 2009(12), p146.

reference to the experiences of foreign legislations. The other is to adopt the concept of "forest land and woods" instead of "forest".[3]

The features of forests are as follows: first, their production cycle is long. It takes several years, or even decades, for trees to grow into useful timber. Unfortunately, forests are very vulnerable to natural disasters and human activities. Secondly, forests can be utilized sustainably. As regenerative resources, forests can grow continuously and with proper felling and timely care can be exploited sustainably. Thirdly, they are multifunctional. As an important environment element, forests not only help conserve water and soil, and make air cleaner, but can also function as habitats for animals.

According to their ecological characters, forests can be categorized as equatorial rain forests, monsoon forests, subtropical broad-leaved evergreen forests, temperate broad-leaved deciduous forests, mid-temperate theropencedrymion or subfrigid coniferous forests and so on. In line with the Forest Law of the People's Republic of China, forests are divided into five categories based on their different usage:

- Shelter forests: forests, woods and clusters of bushes with the main aim of protection, including water source conservation forests, water and soil conservation forests, shelter forests against wind and for fixing sand, shelter forests for farmland and cattle farms, forests for embankment protection and shelter belts for highways.
- Timber forests: forests and woods with timber production as the main aim, including bamboo groves to produce bamboo materials.
- Economic forests: woods with the production of fruits, edible oils, drinks, flavorings, industrial raw materials and medicinal materials as the main aim.
- Fuel forests: woods with the production of fuel as the main aim.
- Special-purpose forests: forests and woods with national defense, environmental protection and scientific experiments as the main aims, including national defense forests, experimental forests, mother tree forests, environmental protection forests, ornamental forests, woods at ancient and historical sites, revolutionary memorial places and forests in nature reserves.

Classified by purpose of use, such classification methods in the PRC Forest Law are typically accorded to the value of the forest to human

---

[3] Du Guo-ming, Reform of the basic concepts in Forest Law, *Hebei Law Science,* 2012(8), p. 87.

beings. But if insufficient consideration is given to the ecological value of a forest, enormous damage can easily be caused to the natural forest especially if a natural forest with high ecological value is reclassified as a timber forest. As an example, the natural forests of the upper Yangtze River were erroneously classified as timber, resulting in natural forests being cut down. From the perspective of ecological construction, in accordance with their ecological value, forests should be divided into natural forests, second-growth forests and plantations and their protection and use be dependant on the circumstances.[4]

As an important ecosystem and natural resource on earth, forests have various functions. Protecting forests is of great significance for environmental protection, economic development and scientific research.

(1) Water and soil preservation, wind sheltering and sand fixation. Forests can conserve water and preserve soil. It has been measured that the average rainfall will not become surface runoff if the forest belt reaches 80 meters – water flows will be conserved to be groundwater runoff. Through the prevention of surface runoff, forests can prevent or reduce the loss of soil in the forest areas and nearby places. They can also protect land in areas near forests, lakes, rivers and lower reaches. By retaining water, they can protect lower reaches from flood and drought. With flourishing root systems, forests can prevent soil from moving. Trees thick with leaves can stop storms and protect soil from wind erosion, thus checking the wind and fixing the shifting sand.

(2) Climate control and air cleaning. With large areas of leaves, forest trees can reduce the direct rays of sunlight and slow down changes of temperature so that the temperature differences both within the same day and between different seasons becomes relatively small. At the same time, trees absorb water from soil and release it to the atmosphere through transpiration. As a result, air gets more moisture and the precipitation is increasing.

    By absorbing carbon dioxide and releasing oxygen in the process of photosynthesis, forests are regarded as "green factories" producing oxygen. They can also prevent dust and reduce the content of smoke and heavy metal in the air. For instance, one hectare of pines can prevent 35 tons of dust annually.

---

4 Zhang Xiaoqiang, Comparative study on forestry legislation law between United States of America and China and its benefit to the amendment of Chinese Forest Law, *World Forestry Research*, 2005(4), p. 67.

Furthermore, the branches and leaves of forests help reduce, prevent and change the noise intensity, helping to maintain a quiet atmosphere as a "living noise silencer". It is estimated that forests with a width of 40 meters can reduce noise by 10 to 15 decibels.

(3) Nurturing creatures and maintaining species. The forest ecosystem is a complex structure, sheltering various species, and providing a wealth of hidden food and a good habitat coupled with an excellent climate and being less subject to human disturbance. It serves as a stable functioning and higly bio-productive ecological system, a paradise for all kinds of wild fauna and flora, and a bio-genetic treasury.

(4) Supplying forest products. One of the direct functions of forests is to provide forest products, including construction materials, cross-ties and even firewood for cooking and warming.

(5) Landscaping and life improvement. As a symbol of life, green helps people relieve their exhaustion, forget about troubles and boost confidence. People are keen to enjoy their natural beauty and they delight in forests as an antidote to the nervous rhythm of life and poor urban environment. Forests provide irreplaceable places and opportunities for people to have a break, enjoy themselves and recuperate. Abundant forest resources reflect not only national wealth but also national prosperity and social civilization.

12.1.2 Problems of Forest Resources Protection in China

With a vast territory and copious natural conditions, China is blessed with diverse tree species and forest types. This abundance in forest resources is widely recognized throughout the world. Among over 20,000 kinds of woody plants in the world, more than 7,000 can be found in China, including over 2,800 kinds of arbor trees. Of 30 genuses of larch firs and cypresses, 26 of them, nearly 200 kinds, are located in China. The variety of broad-leaved trees in China is as large as 260 genuses, more than 2,000 kinds. There are some endemic species in China, including ginkgo, met sequoia, Chinese cypress, cedar, golden larch, Taiwan larch, Fujian cypress, Chinese dove tree, Encomia ulmoides, camplotheca acuminata, spicebush and mountain leechee.

However, China's forest resources confront many problems mainly due to their over-exploitation and over-utilization, but also because for a long time little attention was paid to their preservation and protection.

First, the forest coverage and the forest resources per capita are low, far below the world average level. According to the seventh national forest resources inventory, forests in China cover an area of 195,452,200 hectares, with a 20.36 percent coverage rate, only two-thirds of the world average level and ranking 139th globally. The forest area per capita is 0.145 hectares, less than a quarter of the world average level. The forest storage per capita is 10.51 cubic meters, one-seventh of the average level in the world.

Secondly, the distribution of the forests is very uneven, forming a barrier for their environmental effects. The natural forests are mainly located in high cold border areas in north-east and south-east China. Forest resources are scarce in the west of Inner Mongolia, in the densely populated and well-developed areas in northern China, the Central Plains and the lower reaches of the Yangtze River and the Yellow River. The forest coverage rate is even lower than 1 percent in some regions and the disproportion of forest distribution intensifies the deterioration of ecological environment in most areas of China.

Thirdly, forest resources have suffered severe destruction. The forest consumption in some provinces exceeds the quota distributed by the State Council. Thanks to the strict management of forestry authorities, the over-deforestation momentum has been reduced to some extent, and the enforcement of the limited deforestation has been improved. Nevertheless, over-deforestation has never been completely prevented and the large consumption offsets the growth of forests, making it difficult for the total forest coverage rate to increase.

The consequences of too few forest resources is all too apparent: the shortage in timber and forest by-products, the reduction of precious animals and plants, the destruction of ecosystems, the declining quality of the environment, water and soil erosion, silting rivers, lakes and reservoirs and increasing natural disasters like floods, droughts and mud-rock flows. As a result, ecological problems are still among the most prominent problems that restrict China's sustainable development; ecologic products are still in the greatest shortage; and the ecological gap is still one of the major gaps between China and developed countries.

12.2 HISTORICAL DEVELOPMENT OF FOREST LAW

Forests used to play a significant central role in land ecosystems, with 45 percent coverage of the earth. Unfortunately, due to fast growing populations and intensified human activities, forests, especially primitive and tropical rainforests, have suffered serious destruction. The rapid reduction of these areas has had a negative influence on the global climate and biodiversity. Therefore, protecting forest resources has become one of the top and most urgent tasks for governments throughout the world. Most countries have enacted laws to protect forest resources, and the 1992 United Nations Conference on Environment and Development (UNCED) published the 'Declaration of Principles on Forest Issues' to promote the management, preservation and sustainable development of forests, so as to keep the diversity and complementary functions and usages.

The legislation on the protection of forest resources in China dates back as far as the Western Zhou Dynasty, when there was a ban on cutting down trees. However, forest protection legislation in a modern sense began only after the Xinhai Revolution (1911), the ROC Government issued Forest Laws in 1914 and 1932 respectively. Legislation on forest protection has developed rapidly since China's reform and opening up. On February 23, 1979, the sixth meeting of the Fifth National People's Congress Standing Committee adopted the Forest Law (for Trial Implementation). In the same year, the "Resolution on Tree-planting Day" was adopted by the National People's Congress (NPC), setting March 12 of each year as China's Tree-planting Day. Since then, China has successively formulated and promulgated a number of forest resource protection laws, regulations and rules, such as The Emergency Notice on Resolutely Stopping the Deforestation of Forests (1980), The Implementation Rules of the Nationwide Voluntary Tree-planting Campaign (1982) and the Management Rules of Deforestation and Reforestation (1987).

The formal *PRC* Forest Law was passed at the NPC in 1984, followed by The Implementation of Forest Law in 1986. The 1984 Forest Law was revised in 1998, highlighting the role of forests in the protection of ecological environment. Two years later, the State Council issued the Regulations on the Implementation of PRC Forest Law to elaborate details in terms of implementing provisions of the Forest Law. In addition to these efforts at the national level, local level legislation has also developed vigorously, forming a legal system for forestry protection.

12.3 FUNDAMENTAL PRINCIPLES OF THE FOREST LAW

The Forest Law revised in 1998 is the major law in China to protect forests, which stipulates "the policy of universal forest protection, afforestation, combination of felling and cultivation and sustainable exploitation, on the basis of afforestation." This law has significant provisions on the licensing of state-owned major forest zones, the right to use forestland, the circulation and requisition of forest woods, the management of requisition of forestlands, the compensation of forests' ecological effects, the tasks of forestry public security organs, the exportation of precious woods and the legal responsibilities involved. Those provisions are able to cater for the requirements of market economy.

12.3.1 Protecting the Ownership and Right of Use According to the Law

The term "Forest Right" was not the creation of the legal theory, it does not exist in the system of traditional civil property rights and cannot be found in the extraterritorial relevant legal systems. "Forest Right" was developed by law enforcement personnel at the grass-roots level and affirmed in state policy, its connotation and denotation were not completely and definitely defined by any law in the country.[5] At present, China uses the word 'the ownership of forest resources' in the forest legislation.

Identifying ownership is the starting point to conducting forest-associated actions. According to Article 3 of the Forest Law, "the ownership and right of use of legally registered forest, forest wood and forestlands shall be protected by law. Any unit or individual shall not infringe."

According to the Forest Law there are three types of forest ownership: state ownership, collective ownership, and personal ownership. Natural resources laws made provisions for state ownership, such as, "the ownership of water resources exercised by the State Department on behalf of the State" (art. 3 of Water Law), "public ownership, the ownership of State-owned land exercised by the State Department on behalf of the State" (art. 2 of the Land Management Law), "mineral resources belong to the state, the ownership of mineral resources exercised by the State Department on behalf of the State" (art. 3 of the Mineral Resources Law), "the ownership of state-owned grasslands exercised by the State Department on behalf of the State" (art. 9 of the Mineral Resources Law), "sea area belong to the state, the ownership of sea area exercised by the State Department on behalf of the State" (art. 3 of the Sea Area Utilization Management Law). However, we cannot find the provisions like "the ownership of state-owned forest exercised by the State Department on behalf of the State" in Forest Law, and the right to possess, use, dispose and make earnings from state-owned nature

[5] Liu Xianhui, Research status and reflection on Forest Law science: Based on the analysis of CSSCI Legal Papers, *Journal of Shanghai University of Political Science & Law*, 2014(3), p. 59.

resources are exercised by the State Council and local governments respectively which is in contradiction to other nature resources law.[6] In addition, too many restrictions on the collective ownership of forests and trees personal ownership in Forest Law, resulted in the market mechanisms and economic instruments failing to protect the forest resources.

Although there is no consensus on the concept of forest rights in academia, most scholars expressed concern on the potential ecological risk in the current forest tenure reform and transference. Some scholars believe that the forest tenure reform will stimulate the enthusiasm of farmers in forest management, but it is very likely to lead to short-sighted actions by individual farmers pursuing economic benefits and thereby endangering the whole forestry ecological security. Meanwhile, due to the "the inadequacies of ecological compensation under the classification management lead to the loss of ecological forest, forest denudation caused ecological worries and biodiversity conservation is facing serious challenges", China has to depend on "the regulation of modern procedures for public interest and physical sense."[7]

12.3.2 Providing Financial Support for Forestry

Forest resources are one of the fundamental conditions of sustainable development. However, because forestry features long market cycles, low rate of investment returns and notable social and ecological effects but relatively weak market competitiveness, it is of crucial significance for the government to provide financial support for the forestry. Article 8 of Forest Law reflects the principle of national financial support for forestry, namely, establishing the system of forestry funds, measures on encouraging investment, and policies about taxation remission.

12.3.3 Sustainable Utilization Based on Forestry Cultivation and Management

According to Article 5 of the Forest Law, "Forestry development applies the policy of universal forest protection, positive afforestation, combination of felling and cultivation and sustainable exploitation, on the basis of afforestation." It considers afforestation, forest cultivation and forest protection as the most fundamental work in the forestry development.

---

6 Cai Shouqiu, Several problems of the Amendment of the Forest Act of the PRC, *Modern Law Seienee*, 2004(5), p. 54.

7 Zhao Huiyu, Ecological risk and countermeasure strategies of China's Forest Rights reform, *Legal Science*, 2009(12), pp. 129–37.

Logging forests on the condition of protection, it ensures the sustainable exploitation of forest resources by following the natural law of ecological succession.

12.4 MAIN CONTENTS OF THE FOREST LAW

Based on aforementioned principles, legal institutions are designed and arranged in Chinese legislation to distribute responsibilities, set management rules and articulate legal procedures with regard to forestry protection. The following legal institutions will be demonstrated and analyzed, according to the Forest Law.

12.4.1 Forest Rights

12.4.1.1 The ownership of forest resources

Forest rights, the ownership of forests, refers to the rights of the subjects to occupy, utilize, gain profit from and dispose of forests, forest trees and forestlands. There are four different categories: state ownership, collective ownership, unit or group ownership and individual ownership. Forest resources belong to the whole people, or the state, excluding those specifically belonging to collective ownership. Forest trees planted by state-owned units are managed by those units and the profits are distributed according to state regulations. Forest trees cultivated by collective units belong to those units. Trees planted by rural residents in front of or behind houses, on household plots or on private hilly land belong to those individuals. If collectives or individuals contract for afforestation on barren mountains and uncultivated lands suitable for forests, the trees planted belong to the collectives or individuals.

According to the Forest Law, measures to protect forest ownership mainly include ownership confirmation, returning illegal possessions, removal of obstacles and compensation for loss. Article 3 of the Forest Law stipulates that:

> For the forests, trees and woodlands owned by the state and the collective and the trees and woodlands owned by private individuals, the people's government above the county level shall register and record them, issue certificates and confirm the ownership and the right to use. The State Council may authorize the competent forestry authorities under the State Council to register and record the forests, trees and woodlands in key forest districts determined by the State Council to be owned by the state, issue certificates and inform relevant local people's governments.

12.4.1.2 The forestlands usufruct and forest trees transference

According to Article 15 of the Forest Law, the right of use for the following forests, trees and woodlands can be transferred according to the law. It can also, according to the law, be priced and converted into shares or used as conditions for equity or cooperative joint ventures for forestation and operation of trees. However, woodlands shall not be converted into non-woodlands.

(1) timber stands, economic forests and firewood forests;
(2) the woodland right of use for timber stands, economic forests and firewood forests;
(3) the woodland right of use for cutting banks and the burns of timber stands, economic forests and firewood forests;
(4) the right to use other forests, trees and other woodlands stipulated by the State Council.

This provision plays a significant role in optimizing the distribution of production factors, vitalizing forest resources assets and promoting the development of forestry. Meanwhile, the prohibition of turning forestlands into non-forest lands can prevent the loss of forest resources in disguised form.

12.4.1.3 Dispute resolution mechanism on forest ownership

As a type of civil dispute over property rights, disputes on mountain forest ownership occurs between parties about the ownership and the right of the use of forests, forest trees and forestlands.

According to Article 30 of the Administrative Reconsideration Law, if an individual, legal person or any other organization considers that a specific administrative action of an administrative agency has infringed upon his or its ownership and right to use natural resources acquired legitimately, he or it shall first apply for administrative reconsideration. Here, natural resources include land, mineral resources, rivers, forests, mountains, grasslands, unreclaimed land, beaches and maritime water. If he or it refuses to accept the decision of the administrative reconsideration, he or it could bring litigation. Furthermore, Article 37 of the Administrative Procedural Law; Article 1 and Article 7 of the Opinions of the Supreme People's Court on Issues of Administrative Procedural Law (Trial); and Article 17 of the Forest Law have similar provisions on ownership dispute resolution. They all stipulate that administrative reconsideration is the mandatory procedure of administrative litigation. The procedure comes in a chronological order: administrative adjudication, administrative reconsideration and administrative litigation.

Article 17 of the Forest Law states: "Before the dispute regarding the ownership of trees and woodlands is resolved, no party shall cut trees in dispute." Article 5 of the Methods of Resolving the Disputes on the Ownership of Forest Trees and Forestlands (the 10th rule of the Forestry Department) provides that: "Before the dispute regarding the ownership of trees and woodlands is resolved, no units or individuals shall fell trees in dispute or undertake construction activities on forestlands in dispute."

12.4.2 Institution on Forest Protection

According to Article 8 of the Forest Law, the state carries out the following protective measures with respect to forest resources:

(1) to impose a quota on forest cutting and encourage forest planting in order to expand the area of forest coverage;
(2) to offer economic support or long-term loans to the collectives and private individuals who plant and cultivate forests according to relevant stipulations of the central and local people's governments;
(3) to advocate comprehensive utilization and saving on the use of timber and encourage the development and utilization of timber substitutes;
(4) to collect forest cultivation levies that shall be used exclusively for forest planning and cultivation purposes;
(5) to ensure that coal and paper sectors shall apportion out of their output of coal, pulp and paper a certain amount of funds which shall be used exclusively for the nurturing of mine timber and timber for paper making;
(6) to establish the forestry fund system.

The State shall establish the forestry ecological efficiency compensation fund, which is to be used for the building, cultivation and management of protected forests with ecological efficiency and the forest resources and trees with special uses. The forestry ecological efficiency compensation fund shall be used exclusively for its designated purpose and shall not be used for any other purpose. The specific methods will be formulated by the State Council.

12.4.3 Forest Felling License and Restriction

According to the Forest Law and the Regulations on the Implementation of PRC Forest Law, logging forests and woods shall comply with the following provisions:

(1) For mature timber stands, the approaches of selection cutting, clear cutting and shelter wood cutting shall be applied respectively in light of different situations. Clear cutting shall be put under strict controls and the reforestation shall be completed in the same or next year of the cutting.
(2) Among the protected forests and forests with special uses, the national defense forest, the parent stand, the environmental protection forest and the scenic beauty forest cutting is only permitted for cultivation and reforestation purposes.
(3) Among the forests with special uses, the trees on sites of historic interest and revolutionary commemoration and the forest in the natural protection area cutting is forbidden.
(4) Annual deforestation is strictly controlled. Annual quotas for cutting are to be proposed according to the principle of proper management and sustainable exploitation, and submitted to the State Council for approval.

    In compliance with the principle that the consumption of timber shall be lower than the growth, the State imposes strict controls over the volume of annual forest cutting. In the formulation of the annual cutting quotas, the state-owned enterprise, institution, farmland, factory or mine shall be calculated as a unit for state-owned forests and trees, and the county as a unit for collectively used forests and trees and privately owned trees. The competent forestry authorities at the provincial, autonomous region and directly administered municipality shall compile a summary sheet, which shall be submitted to the State Council for approval after the examination of the people's government at the same level. The state formulates a unified annual timber production plan that should not exceed the approved annual cutting quota. The scope of mandatory administration shall be stipulated by the State Council.
(5) Before units or individuals are permitted to cut down trees, they are required to apply for a cutting license and conduct the cutting according to the provisions of that license; this does not cover cutting by rural citizens of isolated trees in their private farm plots and surrounding their houses. The authorities in charge of examining and issuing cutting licenses shall not issue the cutting licenses in excess of the annual cutting quota. To transport timber out of forest districts, it is necessary to present the transport documentation issued by the competent forestry authorities, with the exception of timber uniformly allocated and transferred by the State.
(6) Land reclamation at the expense of deforestation, rock quarrying, sand quarrying, soil extracting and other activities at the expense of

deforestation is forbidden. Firewood cutting and grazing is also forbidden in seedling forests and special use forests.

12.4.4 Sealing off for Cultivation and the Institution of Natural Preservation Zones

Sealing off mountainous areas for reforestation is an approach to regenerate forests by the use of banning orders in designated areas. It targets those open forests which have a natural renewal ability, barren mountains, uncultivated lands and young forestlands unsuitable for the growth of forests and in need of improvements in forestlands. Local governments shall decide the areas for sealing off and the periods on which this should occur based on their own contexts. In the designated areas, activities including cultivating wasteland, chopping firewood and grazing are prohibited or restricted.

In order to protect special forest ecosystem and precious and rare wild plants and animals, the Forest Law provides that:

> The competent forestry authorities under the State Council and the people's government at the provincial, autonomous region or directly administered municipality level shall delimit natural protection areas to strengthen protection and administration in typical forest ecology areas in different natural terrain, forest districts where previous animals and plants grow and breed, natural tropical rain forest districts and other natural forest districts with special protection value.

12.4.5 Afforestation

Afforestation is one of the basic approaches for expanding forest resources, increasing forest coverage rates and improving the ecological environment. The Forest Law provides specific provisions on this issue.

(1) Formulating afforestation plans. The target of national forest coverage rate is 30 percent. Local governments at or above the county level should determine their owns goals of forest coverage rate. For mountainous areas, the coverage rate is over 70 percent, while hilly areas and plain areas are over 40 percent and 10 percent respectively.

(2) Organizing tree-planting activities. Tree planting and forest protection are duties to be performed by every citizen. Males between the ages of 11 and 60 and females between 11 and 55, except the disabled, should undertake the obligation of tree planting. Everyone shall plant three to five trees every year or undertake alternative

tasks of preparing soil, growing seedlings, planting, managing and protecting them according to corresponding quantity of work. The Forest Law also provides a system for the responsibilities of tree planting. The government at various levels should organize all the citizens to plant trees to accomplish the tasks designated by the plans. Competent forestry departments and other competent departments should organize afforestation on barren mountains and uncultivated land owned by the state. Collective economic organizations should organize afforestation on land owned by the collective. The competent units concerned should organize afforestation activities according to local conditions on both sides of railroads, highways, rivers and around lakes and reservoirs. The afforestation is in the charge of respective units in industrial and mining areas, lands for organizations and schools, troop camping areas, farms, grazing lands and fishing grounds. The collective or individuals can contract for afforestation on barren mountains and uncultivated lands owned by the state or collective.

12.4.6 Forest Fire Prevention

Forest fires are a major disaster in damaging forest resources. Consequently, the Forest Law requires that local governments at all levels should take serious measures both to prevent and extinguish forest fires, these include:

(1) specifying forest fire prevention periods and banning the use of fires in forest regions during this period; fires may only be used as a necessity and only under extraordinary circumstances, and even then must be approved by the county government or its authorized agency;
(2) installing fire prevention facilities in forest regions;
(3) in cases of fire, immediately organizing local army units, civilians and the relevant departments to help extinguish the fire;
(4) with respect to those who are injured, disabled or sacrificed in the process of fire fighting, the fire fighter's unit or the local government shall offer medical treatment or a pension.

As well as the above, the Regulations on Forest Fire Prevention also establishes the responsibility system of administrative leaders in fire prevention, the organization of a system of forest fire prevention, and the investigation and statistical systems of forest fires.

12.4.7 Prevention and Control of Forest Insect Pests

Forest plant diseases and insect pests are another of the important reasons for a reduction of forest areas, production capacities and environmental effectiveness. Consequently, the Forest Law requires that the competent departments of forestry at all levels are to be responsible for the organization of the work of prevention and control of forest plant diseases and insect pests. These departments are to be responsible for stipulating the quarantine range of forest tree seedlings; delimit the epidemic area and the protection area; and conduct quarantine of forest tree seedlings. The Regulations on Forest Pest Prevention also state the following controlling measures:

(1) establishing and improving institutions in charge of the prevention and control of forest plant diseases and insect pests;
(2) quarantining tree seeds and seedlings from abroad and prohibiting quarantined organisms from being introduced either from outside China's borders or being spread domestically;
(3) designating quarantine regions and protection zones to prevent quarantined organisms from spreading;
(4) strengthening the protection of various beneficial creatures in forests, and reproducing and nurturing them in a planned way to realize biological prevention and control;
(5) establishing and improving the system of monitoring and prediction of forest diseases and insect pests;
(6) introducing measures to prevent and control forest diseases and insect pests in the light of actual requirements;
(7) implementing the reporting system against the emergence of forest plant diseases and insect pests;
(8) rewarding people with notable achievements in the prevention and control of forest plant diseases and insect pests; and punishing those who fail to fulfill their duties or obligations of preventing and controlling.

12.4.8 Forestry Fund and Forest Ecological Benefit Compensation Fund

The forestry fund is a special fund established by the state for the development of forestry. Its main sources include national investment in forestry, financial allocation, expenses for growing saplings withdrawn by forestry departments according to regulations, funds for renewal and improvement, and donation from units or individuals for forestry development. It is mainly used for the renewal of cutover lands and the expenses of afforestation, forest cultivation and forest protection in barren mountains and uncultivated lands. The central and local forestry authorities manage the forestry fund according to their authorization. The fund can only be used for a fixed purpose; the annual balance is allowed to be rolled over for use in the following year.

The forest ecological benefit compensation fund is established specially for shelter forests and special-purpose forests. As these forests mainly serve to conserve water and soil, regulate the climate and beautify the environment, they cannot be bought or sold. The investment in afforestation and forestry cultivation cannot make profits and or receive compensation either. To guarantee reproduction, Article 8 of the *Forest Law* stipulates that:

> The State shall establish the forestry ecological benefit compensation fund, which shall be used for the building, cultivation and management of protection forests with ecological benefit and the forest resources and trees with special uses. The forestry ecological benefit compensation fund shall be used exclusively for its designated purpose and shall not be used for any other purpose. The State Council shall formulate the specific methods about its utilization.

In addition to aforementioned funds, forest vegetation recovery expenses are also collected to ensure any reduction in forestry resources is compensated. Prospecting, mining and various construction projects may not occupy or should occupy as little forestry land as possible. In case of necessary occupancy or expropriation of forestlands, upon examination and approval of the competent forestry authorities under the government above the county level, the examination and approval formalities for land needed for construction shall be reviewed in line with relevant land administration laws and administrative regulations. The land-use organization shall pay forest vegetation recovery fees in line with the relevant provisions of the State Council.

The forest vegetation recovery fees are to be used for designated purposes. The competent forestry authorities shall use them, according to relevant stipulations, for afforestation and the recovery of forest vegetation. The area of afforestation shall not be smaller than the area of forest vegetation reduced as a result of forestlands occupied or expropriated.

The competent forestry authorities at a higher level shall periodically urge and inspect the counterparts at a lower level in the organization of afforestation and recovery of forest vegetation.

No organization or private individual shall divert the forest vegetation recovery fees. The competent auditing authorities of the people's government above the county level shall strengthen their supervision of the situation in connection with the use of the forest vegetation recovery fees.

12.4.9 Prohibition and Restriction of the Export of Precious Woods

According to Article 38 of the Forest Law, the State forbids or restricts the export of precious trees and their products and derivatives. The list of such precious trees and the annual export quantitative restrictions are to be formulated by the competent forestry authorities under the State Council together with relevant authorities under the State Council and submitted to the State Council for approval.

To export the precious trees or their products and derivatives, restricted according to the provisions of the above paragraph, it is imperative to review the examination of the competent forestry authorities under the government at the provincial, autonomous region or directly administered municipality where the exporter is located. After that, approval from the competent forestry authorities under the State Council must be obtained. The customs will only release the goods upon the presentation of the approval documentation from the competent forestry authorities under the State Council.

Where the imported and/or exported trees or their products and derivatives fall into the category of endangered species, the import and export of which is restricted by the international covenants that China has acceded to, it is mandatory to file an application with the national administrative authorities in charge for a certificate of import and export permission. The customs will only release the goods upon the presentation of the import and export certificate.

12.4.10 Forest Public Security System

The state sets up forest public security authorities to maintain social public security in forest zones, protect forest resources and impose administrative penalties upon illegal activities like illegal and indiscriminative logging. According to Article 18 of the Forest Law, the forest public security authorities, established in line with the relevant provisions of the state, are responsible for the maintenance of social security and protecting the forest resources within their jurisdiction. They also could exercise administrative punishment rights on behalf of the competent forestry authorities under the State Council within their scope of the mandate.

12.5 LEGAL LIABILITIES

All activities relating to forest resources utilization and management, including forest cultivation, planting, felling and exploitation, shall be undertaken according to the laws. Any illegal activities and/or crime of damaging forest resources or interrupting the order of forestry production, operation and management shall be liable for legal responsibility.

The Forest Law stipulates three different types of liabilities for offenders: civil liability, administrative liability and criminal liability.

12.5.1 Civil Liability

Whoever engages in illegal felling of forest or other trees, in violation of the provisions of this law, or who engages in reclamation, quarrying, sand gathering, earth gathering, seed collection, resin collection or other activities resulting in the destruction of forests and woods, or who cuts firewood or grazes cattle in young forest lands or special-purpose forests resulting in the destruction of forests and woods shall compensate for the losses incurred in accordance with law and shall be ordered by the competent forestry department to plant from one to several times the number of trees destroyed. The way to "compensate for the losses incurred in accordance with law" is actually seeking damages in accordance with the civil law on compensation: the party bears civil liability.

12.5.2 Administrative Liability

The administrative liability in the Forest Law mainly applies to government personnel who are not meeting their responsibilities as designated by the law:

(1) the person in charge and other personnel who are directly responsible and who issue timber-felling permits beyond the approved annual felling quotas, or who issue timber-felling permits, timber-transport permits, export approval documents or import or export permits beyond authority;
(2) the personnel directly responsible if any timber-felling unit or individual fail to fulfill the renewal afforestation tasks pursuant to provisions;
(3) functionaries of the competent departments of forestry engaging in forest resources protection and forestry supervision and administration and functionaries concerned of other state organs who abuse

power, neglect their duty and indulge in self-seeking misconduct, activities that do not actually constitute a crime, etc.

The Forest Law also provides a special way to undertake administrative liability – the subject of liability can be an order by the competent forestry department to replant trees. For instance: "the offender shall be ordered by the competent forestry department to replant ten times the number of trees piratically felled," "whoever engages in indiscriminative felling of forests or other trees, shall be ordered by the competent forestry department to plant five times the number of trees indiscriminately felled" (art. 39):

> Whoever, in violation of the provisions of this law, engages in reclamation, quarrying, sand gathering, earth gathering, seed collection, resin collection and other activities resulting in the destruction of forests and woods shall compensate for the losses incurred according to law; the offender shall be ordered by the competent forestry department to stop the illegal acts, to plant more than 100 percent and less than three times the number of the trees destroyed (art. 44, para.1);
>
> Whoever, in violation of the provisions of this law, cuts firewood or grazes cattle in young forest lands or special-purpose forests resulting in the destruction of forests and woods shall compensate for the losses incurred according to law; the offender shall be ordered by the competent forestry department to stop the illegal acts and plant more than 100 percent and less than three times the number of the trees destroyed (art. 44, para. 2).

The Forest Law further provides that: "If the offender refuses to plant trees or fails to conform to relevant state provisions in planting trees, the competent forestry department shall do it on his/her behalf, and the expenses required shall be paid by the offender" (art. 44, para.3).

12.5.3 Criminal Liability

(1) Whoever sets forests on fire shall be investigated for criminal liability according to Article 144 of the Criminal Law. Whoever negligently allows forestland to catch fire shall be investigated for criminal liability according to Paragraph 2, Article 115 of the Criminal Law.

(2) Whoever engages in falsifying, buying and selling of timber felling permits, timber transport permits, export approval documents and import or export permits in violation of the provisions of this law where the case constitutes a crime shall be investigated for criminal liability according to Paragraph 1, Article 280 of the Criminal Law.

(3) Whoever illegally fells or destroys rare and precious trees in violation of the provisions of this law where the case constitutes a crime shall be investigated for criminal liability according to Article 344 of the Criminal Law.
(4) Whoever piratically fells or indiscriminately fells forest or other trees or illegally purchases timber that he/she clearly knows was piratically felled or indiscriminately felled in forest regions where the case constitutes a crime shall be investigated for criminal liability according to Article 345 of the Criminal Law.
(5) Functionaries of the competent departments of forestry engaging in forest resources protection and forestry supervision and administration and functionaries concerned of other state organs who abuse power, neglect duty and indulge in self-seeking where the case constitutes a crime shall be investigated for criminal liability according to Article 397 of the Criminal Law.
(6) Whoever issues timber felling permits beyond the approved annual felling quotas, or issues timber felling permits, timber transport permits, export approval documents or import or export permits beyond their authority in violation of the provisions of the law where the case constitutes a crime shall be investigated for criminal liability according to Article 207 or Article 397 of the Criminal Law.

For criminal liability of forest resources, academic controversy surrounds the identification of deforestation and illegal felling of trees and its accountability. Research has focused on the object of a crime and the forms of bearing its liability, some scholars argue that the social relationship upset by the crime of illegal felling of trees in current legal provisions is merely the normal development of forest resources and forestry production under the protection of law, but "neglects the forest ecological value", therefore, full consideration should be given to the "Forest is a complex system that provides many ecological benefits" when sentencing.[8] China's criminal law emphasizes the protection of traditional property legal interests, and ignores the protection of "environmental law benefits." Independent environmental legal interest should be one of the protection objectives. It seems that the environment criminal law should protect dual legal interests, but in reality, too much

8 Huang Xia, Tang Shuang-e, Dang Bang-jun, Analyzing the protection of Criminal Law in Forest Resources – Speculating upon the extent of offence against society of the crime of felling trees unlawfully, *Modern Law Science*, 2003(4), pp. 119–22.

attention is paid to protecting property and consequential personal injury. In fact, damages to the "Environment" (and resources) itself are not a basis of conviction and sentencing.[9]

[9] Zhang Shijun, Cao Wei, Analysis of the juridical person offence against the Environment Resource Protection, *Hebei Law Science*, 2004(7), p. 32.

13. Mineral resources law

Zhang Shijun

13.1 INTRODUCTION TO MINERAL RESOURCES

13.1.1 Concept of Mineral Resources

In the natural sciences, minerals generally refer to rocks and minerals of economic value that exist in the earth's surface or crust. Mineral resources is a reference to rocks and minerals extant in the earth's surface or crust that can be used in production and daily life. They include various metal ores in solid, liquid or gaseous state, non-metallic minerals and energy minerals, such as iron ore, copper ore, bauxite ore, phosphate, oil, oil shale, natural gas, etc.

In light of the Rules for the Implementation of the PRC Mineral Resources Law (1996), mineral resources refer to the natural resources with value for utilization, which are formed through geologic functions and exist under solid, liquid or gaseous state. These include not only the substances which can be explored and exploited under the current technical and economic conditions, but also those with potential value to be explored and exploited in the future. Due to the fact that the use of mineral resources depends greatly on their classification, they are mainly classified according to various elements and minerals. Mineral resources are divided into four categories according to the Rules for Implementation of the Mineral Resources Law, namely: energy minerals (including coal, oil, natural gas, uranium, etc), metal minerals (such as gold, silver and copper), non-metallic minerals (such as crystal and mineral salt) and water and gaseous minerals (including groundwater, mineral water, carbon dioxide, etc).

13.1.2 The Features of Mineral Resources

Before analyzing regulations on mineral resources protection, it is necessary to study the inherent features of which the legislation is based on. Unlike forestry resources, they are not renewable, thereby, making effective management more crucial.

13.1.2.1 Non-renewable

Mineral resources are formed under ground in a geological process over a lengthy geological age. The formation of each deposit needs a very long span compared with short human history, which indicates that they are non-renewable in the context of human society.

13.1.2.2 Finite

The mineral resources on the earth are finite. The quantity exploited by humans equals the amount by which they be reduced. They cannot be supplemented.

13.1.2.3 Unequal spatial distribution

Mineral resources are formed under certain geological conditions, which are as diverse as the different regions; as a result, their distribution is extremely uneven in the crust.

The unique features of mineral resources described above determines that how they are used, protected and managed fairly has become, and will continue to be, an urgent task for human society.

13.1.3 The Status Quo and Problems of Mineral Resources in China

China is one of the few countries in the world with an abundant and full range of mineral resources. The proven reserves of mineral resources in China account for about 12 percent of those in the world, ranking China third for such reserves. Geologists have already discovered 171 kinds of minerals in China of which 155 have been verified. Both the proven resources and that of over 20 other kinds of minerals has established China as one of the leaders in the world.

Yet, compared with other countries, there are also some disadvantages to this great variety of mineral resources. Some of the minerals have only lean ores and few have rich ones. For example, the average grade of iron ore is only 33.5 percent. Besides, there are many paragenetic minerals and multi-composition ores with few single ores. What is worse, they are not evenly distributed and their geological conditions are very complicated to exploit. For instance, 74 percent of China's coal is located in Shanxi, Shan'xi, Inner Mongolia and Xinjiang, while 70 percent of phosphate is discovered in Yunnan, Guizhou, Sichuan and Hubei. Additionally, the average possession of mineral resources possession is less than half of the rest of the world. For example, the average possession of petroleum resources is only 11 percent of the world's average level, and natural gas is less than 5 percent, fossil resources, are only 58 percent, Lowering China's ranking to 53rd.

All the disadvantages presented here pose serious difficulties for the exploitation, utilization and protection of China's mineral resources. Given the demand of economic development in the long run, mineral resources in China are, actually, not very rich. Therefore, only a development path of resource conservation could keep China's economy sustainable and healthy with the harmony of her population, energy and environment. Unfortunately, there are many problems in exploring, exploiting and protecting mineral resources in China at present.

13.1.3.1 Serious waste and damage in the course of exploration and exploitation

Because of the outmoded mining technology as well as a backward management philosophy, China's mining industry is prevalent with an extensive mining method. As a result, the exploitation effectiveness is extremely low. This can be reflected in the following three aspects:

(1) The recycle rate in the mines of the whole state is generally very low. There is a serious waste of mineral resources in places where reserves have been proven. At present, the total recycle rate of mineral resources in China is only 30 percent, lower than the world average by 20 percentage points. The comprehensive exploitation of paragenetic and associated ores account for only one-third of the total, and the recycle rate of mineral resources is less than 20 percent.
(2) The mineral resources are not widely used. The comprehensive utilization level is very low, leading to the great loss of many precious and useful ingredients. When they cannot be recycled and exploited comprehensively, it not only causes serious energy waste, but also environment pollution owing to the loss of the chemical components. China's total energy utilization rate is only 30 percent, with that of iron ore resources at 36 percent and non-ferrous metal resources at 20 percent. Only 20 percent of the comprehensive rate of mines reach 70 percent.
(3) Predatory exploitation is rampant, such as unauthorized mining and mining disproportionally, resulting in serious damages of mineral resources.

13.1.3.2 Environmental pollution and destruction in the course of exploration and exploitation

Environmental consideration is generally absent in mining planning and management. As a consequence, there are environment problems caused by sewer drainage as well as those caused by mining. The former mainly includes water bursting in mines, surface collapses at karst water-filled mines, salt water intrusion in coastal mines, the depletion of water resources, debris flow, collapses in the pits and earthquakes. The latter refers to slope instability caused by open-pit mining of mineral resources, which result in landslides and slumps, mine heat damage and mine earthquakes, etc.

13.1.3.3 Land occupation of mineral residues and related water and soil pollution

Mining waste piling up may occupy a vast area of land (including coal ore, rocks stripped in open-pit mining and tailings); some of these residues even have the danger of self-ignition and causing landslides. Additionally, mining waste water (including mine drainage, ore-dressing waste water, waste water produced by the piling up of the ore and residues and other industrial and sanitary waste water in the mine area), if discharged without proper treatment, can pollute surface water, underground water, and soil and crops to various degrees. Acid pit water from some coal mines and poly metal zones sulfur causes not only serious environmental pollution, but also corrosion of mine machinery and concrete structures, it even affects people's health. What is more, there are also serious environmental problems when utilizing mineral resources, such as the terrible air pollution caused by soot and sulfur dioxide from coal burning.

13.2 DEVELOPMENT OF LEGISLATION ON THE MINERAL RESOURCES PROTECTION IN CHINA

The Provisional Regulations on the Mining Industry of the People's Republic of China were promulgated as early as 1951. It mainly stipulated rules of managing the old mining areas and exploring new ones, after clarifying the responsibility of those exploration entities. By the end of 1965, the State Council drew up Temporary Rules of the Protection of Mineral Resources, especially for mineral resources protection and rational utilization.[1] After the 1970s, China promulgated and implemented the Environmental Protection Law (for Trial Implementation); the Water Pollution Control Act and some other laws concerning

[1] Wu Xingnan, Sun Yuehong, Natural Resources Law, *Chinese Environment Science Press*, 2004, p. 289.

mineral resources protection and the prevention of mining pollution and groundwater pollution.

In 1986, the PRC Mineral Resources Law was drafted and issued, clarifying the state's ownership of mineral resources. It also stipulated the exploitation right, the registration system of exploration right, as well as the compensated exploitation system of the mineral resources. Based on the Mineral Resources Law, the State Council and its competent departments promulgated many successive relevant regulations, including the Interim Procedures of the Reconnaissance and Registration of Mineral Resources; the Interim Rules for Mining Registration of Mining Enterprises Owned by the State (revised in 1990); the Interim Procedures of Mineral Resources Supervision and Administration; the Interim Procedures of the Registration of Oil; and Natural Gas Reconnaissance and Exploitation.

In 1994, the Rules on the Implementation of the Mineral Resources Law; the Regulations on the Compensation Fee of Mineral Resources; and the Regulations on the Coal Production Licenses were enacted. In 1996, the state revised the Mineral Resources Law to reform the management system of mining rights. It established the legal institutions that exploration right and exploitation right can be bought and transferred according to the law. The jurisdiction for approving mineral resource exploitation and issuing licenses were also redefined in this law. The legal institution that the owner of the exploration right has the priority to exploit in exploration areas strengthened the exclusiveness of exploration and exploitation rights and protected the legitimate rights of mine owners effectively. In the same year, the PRC Coal Industry Law was issued and put into effect.

Mineral resources law is a general term for all kinds of laws and regulations that regulate the various social relations among the state, mine owners, relevant organizations and citizens in the process of mineral resources exploration, exploitation and protection.

13.3 FUNDAMENTAL PRINCIPLES OF MINERAL RESOURCES LAW

Legal principles are fundamental rules with which entities must comply while planning, managing, developing, utilizing and protecting mineral resources. They prescribe highly unspecific actions to outline regulatory objectives and values where those regulated are left free to devise their own systems for serving these principles.[2]

13.3.1 Principle of State Ownership of Mineral Resources

According to the Article IX of the Constitution: minerals, water, forests, mountains, grasslands, wastelands, beaches and other natural resources are owned by the state, that is, all the people. Article 3 of Mineral Resources Law stipulates that:

> Mineral resources belong to the State. The right of State ownership of mineral resources is exercised by the State Council. State ownership of mineral resources, either near the earth's surface or underground, shall not change with the alteration of ownership or right to the use of the land which the mineral resources are attached to.

This provision clearly articulates the concurrent system between the mineral resources ownership and the land ownership.

Mineral resources ownership, on the one hand, is a special property right. On the other hand, related laws authorize competent government authorities with administrative powers to regulate their management, a very strong public law nature in terms of the utilization, management and relief of state ownership. It shows that China has formed a dualistic private and public legal structure with regard to the state ownership of mineral resources.

The state ownership of mineral resources is approached through the legal authorization of mining rights, namely, the rights of exploration and exploitation, through the supervision and management of mining, as well as the compensated use of mineral resources. The state protects the right of exploration and exploitation from encroachment and maintains the order of production in the mining and exploration areas from interference and disruption.

13.3.2 Principle of Rational Exploitation and Sustainable Development

As non-renewable resources, mineral resources must be developed and utilized according to the principle of sustainable development. The state has the responsibility of developing and utilizing mineral resources

---

[2] J. Black, 'Forms and paradoxes of principle-based Regulation', *Capital Markets Law Journal*, 2008(3).

rationally. According to Article 7 of the Mineral Resources Law, the State should apply the policy of unified planning, rational distribution, comprehensive exploration, rational mining and comprehensive utilization with regard to the exploration and development of mineral resources, to make sure that the mineral resources are explored and exploited properly and the rights of owners are protected. Meanwhile, organizations and individuals are forbidden from occupying or damaging mineral resources illegally. Government at all levels shall strengthen the protection of mineral resources.

13.3.3 Principle of Combining Mineral Resources Development with Environmental Protection

Mineral resources development and utilization is closely related to the environment, because their exploitation is likely to affect the natural environment directly, resulting in environmental pollution and destruction. Not only should mineral resources be protected, but also the surrounding environment should be conserved during the process of exploration and exploitation. The Mineral Resources Law stipulates that whoever develops mineral resources shall comply with the regulations on environmental protection and prevent environment pollution. According to laws and regulations concerning mineral resources, China has established a series of institutions to mitigate any adverse environmental impacts in the process of mineral resources exploration and exploitation.

13.4 MAIN CONTENTS OF THE MINERAL RESOURCES LAW

13.4.1 Property System

The mineral resources property system includes ownership, exploration right and exploitation right.

13.4.1.1 Ownership

With regard to the ownership of mineral resources, civil law countries have adopted an "exploitation right doctrine", while common law countries apply a "land owner doctrine." China implements a single system of state ownership through the State Council, on whose behalf, the Ministry of Land and Natural Resources exercises specific authority. The state ownership of the mineral resources, either on the surface or underground, does not change with the alteration of the land ownership or land use right which the mineral resources are attached to.

The State ownership of mineral resources is the core and foundation of the mineral resources property. It could be reflected by the compensated acquisition of exploration and exploitation rights. Whoever exploits mineral resources shall pay resources tax and tax compensation in accordance with the relevant provisions.

13.4.1.2 Exploration rights

An exploration right is the right to explore for mineral resources within the legally obtained exploration permit. Units and individuals who have obtained an exploration license are the owners of the exploration right. Exploration right not only refers to the right of exploring, but also entitles the holder to a priority in mining. "The exploration licensees have the right to carry out specified exploration activities within the designated exploration area and have the privileged priority to obtain the mining right to the mineral resources in the exploration area." Articles 16 and 17 of Rules on the Implementation of the Mineral Resources Law stipulate the rights and obligations of the exploration right owner. The rights exploration licensees mainly permit the right of exploring and implementing related supporting measures, an adjacent right, a land use right and mining privileges, as well as the priority over new mineral exploration. Licensees must fulfill the following obligations: (a) starting and completing the exploration within the time limit prescribed; (b) reporting to the exploration registration authorities on the situation relating to the start of exploration, etc.; (c) conducting the exploration in accordance with the exploration construction designs; (d) conducting a comprehensive exploration as well as an evaluation of the paragenetic and associated minerals while ascertaining the key minerals; (e) compiling and submitting mineral resources exploration reports; and (f) complying with the relevant laws and regulations. If the exploration licensees, after obtaining the temporary right to use the land, damage the properties of other people during the exploration, they have to make compensation.

13.4.1.3 Exploitation rights

An exploitation right is the right to mine mineral resources and obtain the minerals mined within the mining permit in accordance with the law. Units and individuals, who have obtained mining permit, are the owners of the mining right.

An exploitation right is a property right derived from the ownership of mineral resources. According to the law, the state owns the right to possess, use, dispose and benefit from mineral resources and as the mineral resources are a physical entity, the right can be realized through the transfer of the exploitation right. Furthermore, the function of the mining right is to explore the mineral resources whose proven reserves provide the necessary minerals for the state and society. The purpose of obtaining a mining right is to mine or process the mineral products and to gain profits from the sale of commodities within the areas specified in the mining license.

Article 30 and 31 of the Rules on the Implementation of the Mineral Resources Law provide the rights and obligations of exploitation right owners. Any concessioners enjoy the following rights: (a) conducting the mining activities within the terms and the mining area prescribed by the mining license; (b) selling the mineral products themselves, except for those mineral products which the State Council has proscribed for unified purchase by the designated units; (c) constructing the production and living facilities necessary for the mining operation within the mine area; (d) obtaining the right to use the land necessary for the production and construction in accordance with the law. When exercising their rights as provided, the concessioners must abide by other laws and regulations that require them to obtain approvals or go through other formalities.

The concessioners must fulfill the following obligations: (a) conducting mine construction or mining activities within the term approved; (b) conducting efficient protection, rational mining and the comprehensive utilization of the mineral resources; (c) paying the resources tax and the mineral resources compensation pursuant to law; (d) complying with the state laws and regulations regarding labor safety, water and soil conservation, land reclamation and environmental protection; and (e) being subject to the supervision and management from both the competent departments in charge of geology and mineral resources and the relevant competent departments, and filling out and presenting the mineral reserve forms and mineral resources development and utilization statistics reports according to the relevant provisions.

13.4.1.4 Transfer of exploring and mining rights

Exploration and exploitation rights can be legally transferred, but, in China, the exploration and mining rights are not freely transferable. The Mineral Resources Law provides the conditions of transfer: Article 6 provides:

> The exploration licensees, after fulfilling the specified minimum input to exploration and obtaining approval in accordance with law, may transfer the exploration right to others. A mining enterprise that has obtained the mining right but needs to change the ownership, because of merger, division, forming

> of an equity joint venture or contractual joint venture, sale of its assets, or change of ownership of its assets in other manners, may transfer its mining right to others, subject to approval in accordance with law. Profiteering in exploration right or exploitation right shall be prohibited.

There had been severe limitations on mineral rights in China's mining legislation. The Mineral Resources Law, which was enacted in 1986, prohibited the free transference of the exploration and mining rights in any form. The amendment to the law in 1996 adopted strict limitations, instead of prohibition of exploration and mining rights the exploration and mining rights can only be transferred under the condition of "Corporate merger or discrete, joint venture or cooperation with others, or due to the sale of corporate assets, and other case that changes corporate property rights."

The statutory extent is extremely narrow, even when the right is transferred within the scope of the statutory limitation, government permission must be first be obtained. Meanwhile, the *Mineral Resources Law* still retains provisions like "making a profit by reselling the exploration and mining rights are forbidden" in order to set strict limits on system designs.

However, from the legal perspective, it is inevitable that such limitations not only harm the efficiency of the use of private property rights, but are also contrary to the requirements of market reform in China. Under the conditions of a market economy, the transference of a mineral property right can be the inherent requirement of private property rights and making a profit by reselling it may become the driving force of the development of economy, property rights can maximize their value when owned by a clever man.[3]

From the practical point of view, the owner of prospecting or mining right is unlikely to resell it under normal conditions, unless it is not making a profit. It is expressly prohibited or restricted for market mechanisms to play a role in the transfer process in the exploration and mining rights. Moreover, according to The Regulation On The Transfer Of Mining Rights enacted by the State Department in February 1998 and Provisional Administrative Rules for the Transfer of Mining Rights issued by Ministry of Land on November 2000, there is no provision in the transfer approval process for requiring that profit making should be

3 Kang Ji-tian, Research of China modern mining system – Based on the "Mineral Resources Law" Revised Framework Proposal, *Presentday Law Science*, 2014(1), p. 37.

audited. In practice, this provision has become a tool for unscrupulous officials demanding bribes or looking for excuses.[4]

13.4.2 Mineral Resources Planning

National Mineral Resources Plan, under the guidance of the State Council is long-term planning based on the national economy and social development. It is an overall arrangement formulated by relevant departments in accordance with national legal procedures concerning the exploration, exploitation and utilization of mineral resources during a certain period. The competent department of the State Council in charge of minerals organizes the relevant departments, provinces, autonomous regions and municipalities to formulate the plans and implement them following their approval by the State Council.

The National Mineral Resource Plan should make overall arrangements for the distribution of the mineral resources and provide a reasonable explanation for the approval of the scope and development of mineral resources. It is divided into industry development planning and regional development planning, which are conducted by the relevant departments of the State Council and provinces (including municipalities, and autonomous regions) respectively. Their reports should be submitted to the competent department of the State Council in charge of planning and that of geology and mineral resources for their records.

Based on the overall use of mineral resources planning at the national, provincial, city and country level, there has to be a system in which all kinds of special plans are compatible with each other. The national mineral resources plan includes such specific items as overall planning for resources; geological exploration planning; the planning for the development, utilization and protection of the resources; and the planning of mining eco-environmental protection, etc. At present, the state is carrying out the 2008–15 National Mineral Resources Planning.

13.4.3 The Management System of Mineral Resources Exploration

13.4.3.1 The registration of exploring mineral resources

Anyone who wishes to explore for mineral resources, including certain minerals, must register for application, approval and registration in

---

[4] Hu De-sheng, Research on several fundamental issues in amending the Mineral Resources Law of PRC, *Journal of China University of Geosciences (Social Sciences Edition)*, 2007(6), p. 42.

accordance with the rules of the State Council on the registration and management of mineral resources exploration.

The state conducts a unified block registration system for mineral resources exploration. The department in charge of geology and mineral resources under the State Council is responsible for the registration work regarding exploration of mineral resources. The State Council may authorize other relevant departments to handle the registration work regarding exploration of some specified minerals. The management measures for registering mineral exploration through the block system are formulated by the State Council.

The mineral reserves approving agency under the State Council or mineral reserves approving agencies of provinces, autonomous regions and municipalities directly under the central government, are responsible for examining and approving the exploitation reports to be used for the purpose of mining construction designing, and shall, within the prescribed time limit, give official replies to the units that submitted the reports. Unless it is approved, an exploitation report may not be used as the basis for the purpose of mining construction designing.

Archives of mineral exploration results and statistic data of reserves of various minerals shall be subject to unified management, and shall be collected or compiled for submission to the competent authorities, in accordance with the stipulations by the State Council.

13.4.3.2 Protective measures in the exploring process

Comprehensive survey and assessment of mineral resources In conducting a general survey of mineral resources, while surveying for major minerals, a preliminary comprehensive assessment shall be made of the minerogenetic conditions involving all paragenetic or associated minerals and of the economic perspective of those minerals in the area being surveyed. In prospecting for mineral deposits, a comprehensive assessment of the paragenetic and associated minerals of commercial value within the mining area must be made and their reserves calculated. Any prospecting report without such comprehensive assessment shall not be approved. However, an exception shall be made for those mineral deposits for which the planning department under the State Council has made other stipulations.

The technical installations and safety measures In conducting general surveys and prospecting for specified fragile non-metallic minerals, fluid minerals, combustible, explosive and soluble minerals and minerals containing radioactive elements, the methods prescribed by the relevant departments under the people's governments at or above the provincial level must be used, and necessary technical installations and safety measures must be applied.

13.4.4 Management System of Mineral Resources Exploitation

13.4.4.1 Exploitation license system

All units and individuals that exploit minerals in China's territory and maritime areas must obtain approval in order to acquire a mining license; without it, no exploitation activity is allowed. According to the importance and types of the minerals, the approval, registration and license issuing of mineral resources exploitation is in the charge of the geological and mineral authorities of the central, provincial, city and county level.

Article 16 of the Mineral Resources Law defines the scope of issuing exploitation licenses. Mining for the following mineral resources is to be approved by the department in charge of geology and mineral resources under the State Council; mining licenses for this mining are also issued by the same department:

(1) those mineral resources within a state planned mining area or within those mining areas which are of great value to the national economy;
(2) those mineral resources, not within the above-mentioned areas, but the mineable reserves of which are evaluated as large and desirable in scale;
(3) specified minerals for which protective mining policy is proscribed by the State;
(4) those mineral resources in neighboring seas or other marine areas under China's jurisdiction; and
(5) those mineral resources the State Council otherwise specifies.

The categorization standards of large- and medium-scale mineral reserves shall be formulated by the mineral reserves approving agency under the State Council.

The competent departments authorized by the State Council may conduct examinations and issue mining licenses for such specified minerals as oil, natural gas and radioactive minerals. Mining for minerals that are beyond the proscription of the first and second paragraph of Article 16 and whose reserves are evaluated as medium in scale shall be examined and approved by the departments in charge of geology and mineral resources under the governments of the provinces, autonomous regions and municipalities directly under the central government. The relevant mining licenses shall also be issued by these departments. The management measures governing the mining of mineral resources that are beyond the prescription of the first, second and third paragraph of this article shall be formulated by the Standing Committee of the People's Congress of Provinces, Autonomous Regions and Municipalities directly under the central government. Where the mining has been examined and approved and the relevant mining licenses are issued in compliance with the proscription of the third and fourth paragraph of this article, the departments in charge of geology and mineral resources under the people's governments of the provinces, autonomous regions and municipalities directly under the central government shall collect information regarding such approval and issuance and submit the information to the department in charge of geology and mineral resources under the State Council for record and filing.

13.4.4.2 Collectively-owned mining enterprises and mining individuals

The Mineral Resources Law and the Rules on the Implementation of the Mineral Resources Law clarify the position of the collectively-owned mining enterprises and mining individuals, as well as the mineral types and resources they are allowed to exploit. The state has adopted a policy offering vigorous support, rational planning and proper guidance as well as carrying out administration of collectively-owned mining enterprises and mining individuals. It encourages collectively-owned mining enterprises to mine resources within the areas designated by the State, and permits individuals to mine scattered and dispersed mineral deposits, as well as sand, stone and clay usable only as common building materials, and small amounts of minerals for their own use in daily life. However, individuals may not mine for: minerals that because of the scale of their reserves are more efficiently mined by larger enterprises; specified minerals for which a protective mining policy is prescribed by the state; and other minerals for which individual mining is prohibited by the state. The state shall direct and help collectively owned mining enterprises and mining individuals to continuously raise their technical levels, and to increase their mineral resources utilization rate and economic efficiency. Randomly exploiting or damaging mineral resources is prohibited.

13.4.4.3 The mineral resources compensation fee

Everyone who mines mineral resources must pay the mineral resources compensation fee of the relevant provisions of the State, except as otherwise stipulated by laws or administrative regulations. The compensation fee shall be collected proportionally according to the sales revenue of mineral products. Under the national budget, it should be managed especially for the fixed purpose of mineral resources prospecting. Mining rights owner who meets the standards of laws and regulations could have their compensation fee remitted or reduced. The Chinese Government started levying compensation fees for mineral resources in 1994, which terminated the history of compensation-free mining in China.

However, there are many criticisms on the provisions of compensation fees for mineral resources. The legislative purpose for mineral resources compensation in the Regulations on the Compensation Fees of Mineral Resources is to protect and promote the exploration, protection and rational development of mineral resources; to safeguard national interests in property of mineral resources; to publicize the state ownership of mineral resources. However, the provisions of Article 11 show that these fees that should mainly be used to explore the mineral resources, actually result in the fees becoming a source of local subsidies and fail to uphold the rights of state ownership. Moreover, China has a very low mineral resources compensation rate (0.54 percent), so the compensation cannot reflect the interests of state ownership. People from both academia and practice departments believe that the current tax structure is irrational; there is duplication of collection; a low tax rate; a failure to reflect the scarcity of mineral resources; and failure to play a regulatory role, many of them advocate reform of the tax system. Some of them have argued that the compensation and resource taxes should be abolished and replaced with a royalty, some advocate changing the compensation into a royalty but reserving the resource tax.[5]

13.4.4.4 Dispute resolution

Disputes over the limits of mining areas between different parities are to be settled through consultation; if no agreement is reached through consultation, the relevant local government at or above the county level shall handle the case on the basis of the limits that have been verified and fixed according to law. Disputes over the limits of mining areas that cross provinces, autonomous regions, or municipalities directly under the central government shall be settled by the governments of the relevant provinces, autonomous regions or municipalities directly under the

---

[5] Xie Qingxia, Dai Maohua, A review of the researches on the Mineral Resources Law, *Ecological Economy*, 2011(1), p. 184.

central government through consultation. If no agreement is reached through consultation, the dispute will be settled by the State Council.

13.4.4.5 The regulations on mineral resources exploitation and protection

First, specific mining areas and minerals are to be exploited in a planned way. Mining areas to be mined under the state plan; those which are of great value to the national economy; and specified minerals for which a protective mining policy is prescribed by the State, shall be mined by the State in a planned way. No unit or individual may be permitted to mine them without the approval of the relevant departments under the State Council.

Secondly, comprehensive exploitation should be implemented in the paragenetic and associated minerals with industrial values. While mining major minerals, its paragenetic and associated minerals of commercial value shall be comprehensively mined and utilized in accordance with a unified plan, so as to avoid waste. Effective protective measures shall be adopted to avoid loss and damage to ores that cannot be mined in a comprehensive way or that must be mined simultaneously but which cannot be comprehensively utilized immediately, and also to tailings containing useful components.

Thirdly, rational mining sequences, methods and processes should be followed: in mining mineral resources, mining enterprises must adopt rational mining sequences and methods and undertake a proper ore-dressing technique. The recovery rate and impoverishment rate in mining and the recovery rate in ore dressing of the mining enterprise must meet the design requirements.

Fourthly, in mining mineral resources, it is essential to abide by the state provisions for issues such as labor, safety and hygiene and ensure the necessary conditions to safeguard safety in production. It is also essential to observe the legal provisions on environmental protection to prevent pollution.

13.4.5 Environment Protection System in the Process of Mineral Resources Exploration

Because of the significant influence on the environment posed by the development and utilization of mineral resources, China applies certain environmental protection regulations to reduce environmental pollution and destruction. Among others, some of the most important institutions are a special planning system for ecological and environmental protection; an environmental impact assessment of a construction project; "Three Simultaneous" system; land reclamation systems; and the regulations on protecting scenic spots and cultural monuments, etc.

In order to lay equal stress on development and environment protection and to improve the utilization rate, the state has implemented a special planning system for mining ecological protection. Overall planning and protection shall be carried out for: (a) ecological environment protection in the process of exploration and construction; (b) the "Three Wastes" treatment in the process of exploration and utilization; (c) mine land reclamation and land protection and utilization; (d) the control of environment pollution and ecological damages in mining areas and; (e) monitoring and control of geological disasters. An assessment of environmental impact and "Three Simultaneous" shall be conducted for projects of mineral resources exploration and exploitation. If cultivated land, grassland or forestland is damaged by mining, the relevant mining enterprise shall take measures to utilize the affected land, such as by reclamation, tree and grass planting, as appropriate to the local conditions. That is based on the principle that "anyone who causes destruction to land should make reclamation".

However, especially because of the lack of a powerful environmental restoration system, the current mineral resources laws are working against the protection of mining ecological environment. Some scholars have therefore suggested that China should establish a mining ecological environment restoration system from the perspective of public law. Currently, ecological environment restoration has become an important form of protection of the ecological environment, in some places the construction of related systems has developed enormously in recent years, some places have even issued their local regulations and have obtained a great deal of experience in legislation. Hence, in revising the Mineral Resources Law, concrete regulations should be made on mine ecological environment restoration. On the one hand, administrative authorities should be provided with some public powers, which will enable them to protect the environment, on the other hand, the amendment should including the following aspects: a public participation system; public interest litigation; provisions to encourage autonomy between the parties; and the regulations should provide for more services in mining areas and coordinate the interests of various parties. Meanwhile, for the mining rights holder, the amendment should provide appropriate incentives to improve the safeguard of private rights and to evoke their enthusiasm towards the restoration of mining ecological environments.[6]

[6] Li Xiandong, Yang Cheng, Discussion on some problems concerning the amendments to Mineral Resource Law, *Natural Resource Economics of China*, 2013(4), p. 6.

13.5 LEGAL LIABILITIES

Anyone who violates the laws and regulations of mineral resources shall bear corresponding legal liabilities, mainly administrative or criminal liability. Legal liabilities arise if the following activities are conducted:

13.5.1 Liabilities for Illegal Mining

There are three types of cases associated with illegal mining:

(1) Mining without licenses. If a person, in violation of the provisions of this law, mines without a mining license, enters and mines without authorization in a mining area that is embraced in State plan or a mining area that is of great value to the development of the national economy or mines without authorization specified minerals of which protective mining is prescribed by the State, he shall be ordered to stop mining, compensate for the losses caused, and his mineral products and unlawful proceeds shall be confiscated, and he may also be fined an amount 50 percent less than the value of what he has mined. If he refuses to stop mining and thus causes damage to the mineral resources, the persons who are directly responsible shall be investigated for criminal responsibility in accordance with the provisions of Article 156 of the Criminal Law.

(2) Cross-border mining. If a person mines beyond the approved limits of his mining area, he shall be ordered to return to and mine in his own area and compensate for the losses caused, and the mineral products extracted outside his area and his unlawful proceeds shall be confiscated, and he may also be fined. If he refuses to return to his own mining area and causes damage to the mineral resources, his mining license shall be revoked and the persons directly responsible shall be investigated for criminal responsibility in accordance with the provisions of the Criminal Law.

(3) Destructive mining. If a person, in violation of the provisions of this law, mines mineral resources in a destructive way, he shall be fined and his mining license may be revoked; if serious damage is caused to the mineral resources, the person directly responsible shall be investigated for criminal responsibility in accordance with the provisions of Article 156 of the Criminal Law.

13.5.2 Liabilities for Illegal Transfer of Mineral Resources and Mining Rights

If a person purchases, sells or leases mineral resources or transfers them by other means, his unlawful proceeds shall be confiscated and he shall be fined.

If a person, in violation of the law, profiteers in exploration rights or mining rights, his exploration or mining license shall be revoked and his unlawful proceeds confiscated, and he shall be fined.

13.5.3 Liabilities for Illegal Behavior of Officials

State officials in charge of the supervision and administration of exploration and mining of mineral resources or other relevant state functionaries who commit malpractice for personal gain, abuse their power or neglect their duties, approve exploration and mining of mineral resources or issue exploration or mining licenses, in violation of this law, or who do not stop illegal mining activities and punish illegal miners, shall be investigated for criminal responsibility if the action constitutes a crime; if their acts do not constitute a crime, administrative penalties shall be imposed.

13.5.4 Liabilities for Other Behavior

If a person steals or plunders mineral products or other property of mining enterprises or exploration units, damages mining or exploration facilities, or disrupts order in production and other work in mining areas or areas under exploration, he shall be investigated for criminal responsibility in accordance with relevant provisions of the Criminal Law; if the case is obviously minor, he will be punished in accordance with relevant provisions of the Regulations on Administrative Penalties for Public Security.

14. Protected areas law

Ren Shidan

14.1 INTRODUCTION

In China, the concept of the protected area has both a broad sense and a narrow sense. In the broad sense, protected areas mean the general term of all sorts of natural areas which are specially protected by state laws, including nature reserves, scenic interest areas,[1] forest parks,[2] cultural and natural heritages and so on. In the narrow sense, protected areas, only refer to nature reserves that are:

> such areas, on land, inland water bodies, or marine districts, which represent various types of natural ecological systems, or with a natural concentrated distribution of rare and endangered wild animal or plant species, or where natural traces or other protected objects being of special significance are situated, and so delimited out for special protection and administration according to relevant laws.[3]

The first protected area in the world was the Yellowstone Park of the United States, which was first designated as such in 1872, 142 years ago, while the first protected area in China is Dinghushan Nature Reserve in Guangdong Province, which was established by the Chinese Academy of Sciences (CAS) in 1956. The establishment of protected areas in China started fairly late, but has developed rapidly. By the end of 2012, China has built up nearly 2,632 nature reserves, 963 scenic interest areas, 2,747 forest parks, 213 national wetland parks and 138 geographic parks. Various types of protected areas now cover over 18 percent of the

---

1 According to Article 2 of Regulations on Scenic and Historic Areas (the State Council, 2006), scenic interest areas refers to such areas with viewing, cultural or scientific values, concentrated natural or cultural landscapes and with beautiful surroundings where people can visit or engage in scientific or cultural activities.

2 According to Article 3 of Rules on Management of Forestry Parks (Forest Ministry, 1993), forest parks are zones with beautiful forest-viewing, concentrated natural and humanities landscapes and with a certain scale for people to visit, rest or conduct scientific, cultural or educational activities.

3 The Regulations on Nature Reserves (the State Council, 1994), art. 2.

country. A few very large nature reserves in sparsely populated areas of Tibet, Xinjiang and Qinghai account for about 30 percent of this coverage, while the coverage in other provinces is significantly lower. The coverage of protected areas in the eight westernmost provinces is around 20 percent, and in the rest of China is barely 5 percent.[4]

Compared to the achievements of the construction of protected areas, the legislation in China is relatively backward. Although China has already passed some regulations on protected areas, like the Rules on Management of Forestry Parks (Forest Ministry, 1993); the Regulations on Nature Reserves (the State Council, 1994); and the Regulations on Scenic and Historic Areas (the State Council, 2006) there has been no special law of the country of protected areas administration until now. Without a united law of protected areas, there is no guarantee that protected areas legislation will be systematic, harmonized, hierarchical, and scientific. Whether it is based on the practical needs of environmental protection and ecological construction in China, or on the theoretical foundation of environmental law system institution, it is necessary to enact a comprehensive law covering the construction and administration of all sorts of natural protected areas in China.[5]

The purpose of this chapter is essentially to address the problem that the legislation of protected areas in China is relatively backward, through analyzing the legislative situation and the existing main problems, as well as discussing methods necessary for feasible solution. Starting with a presentation of the current legislation of protected areas in China (section 2), the chapter then focuses on problems relating to current legislation of protected areas (section 3). Finally, the last section (section 4) comes to the conclusion that the most appropriate solution lies in enacting an extensive framework of Protected Area Law of People's Republic of China, and amending or enacting regulations under its guidance to regulate different kinds of protected areas, so as to ensure the all-around protection and administration of protected areas in China.

---

[4] Yan Xie, Song Wang, Peter Schei, *China's Protected Areas*, Tsinghua University Press, 2004, pp. 282–3.

[5] Dianquan Wang, "Discuss the basic theory of legislation of Natural Protected Area Again", *Academic Journal of Zhongzhou*, May, 2007, Vol. 3, p. 94.

14.2 LEGISLATION

The current national legislation of protected areas in China can be roughly divided into two cases: one is about different kinds of special legislation of protected areas administration, which are all administrative regulations and departmental rules, and whose legal force is less than law, such as the Rules on Management of Forestry Parks (Forest Ministry, 1993);[6] the Regulations on Nature Reserves (the State Council, 1994);[7] the Regulations on Scenic and Historic Areas (the State Council, 2006);[8] and so on, the other is legal provisions concerning the protected area in other laws and regulations, such as the 2014 Environmental Protection Law; 1988 Wild Animal Protection Law (revised in 2004); 1984 Forest Law (revised in 1998); 1985 Grassland Law (revised in 2002); 2002 Water Law.[9] Given that nature reserves, scenic interest area

---

[6] The Rules on Management of Forestry Parks was adopted at executive meeting of the Forest Ministry on December 11, 1993 and promulgated by Decree No. 3 of the Forest Ministry of the PRC. The regulation clearly defines systems of planning, protection and management of forest parks.

[7] The Regulations on Nature Reserves was adopted at the 24th Executive Meeting of the State Council on September 2, 1994, promulgated by Decree No. 167 of the State Council on October 9, 1994 and effective as of December 1, 1994. Establishment and management of nature reserves within the territory of the PRC or the other sea areas under the jurisdiction of the PRC must comply with the Regulations. The regulation clearly defines construction conditions, establishment procedures, zoning protection and management systems of nature reserves.

[8] The Regulations on Scenic and Historic Areas were adopted at the 149th Executive Meeting of the State Council on September 6, 2006, promulgated by Decree No. 474 of the State Council on September 9, 2006 and effective as of December 1, 2006. The Regulations clearly define systems of planning, protection and management of scenic interest areas.

[9] The 2014 Environmental Protection Law is the fundamental law in the field of environmental protection, and it is the basis for special laws on environmental protection. Articles 17 and 23 of the law are related to protected areas and natural resource conservation. Article 17 provides:

> The people's governments at various levels shall take measures to protect regions representing various types of natural ecological systems, regions with a natural distribution of rare and endangered wild animals and plants, regions where major sources of water are conserved, geological structures of major scientific and cultural value, famous regions where karst caves and fossil deposits are distributed, traces of glaciers, volcanoes and hot springs, traces of human history, and ancient and precious trees. Damage to the above shall be strictly forbidden.

forest parks are the main types of Chinese protected area system, the following section will focus on legal provisions of these three protected areas.

Article 23 provides: "In urban and rural construction, vegetation, waters and the natural landscape shall be protected and attention paid to the construction of gardens, green land and historic sites and scenic spots in the cities in light of the special features of the local natural environment." Article 8 of the Wild Animal Protection Law (the Standing Committee of the NPC, 1988, revised in 2004): "The State shall protect wildlife and the environment for its survival, and shall prohibit the illegal hunting, catching or destruction of wildlife by any unit or individual." Article 24 of the Forest Law (the Standing Committee of the NPC, 1984, revised in 1998) provides:

> The competent forestry authorities under the State Council and the people's government at the provincial, autonomous region or directly-administered municipality level shall delimit natural protection areas to strengthen protection and administration in typical forest ecology areas in different natural terrain, forest districts where previous animals and plants grow and breed, natural tropical rain forest districts and other natural forest districts with special protection value. The administrative methods for natural protection zones shall be formulated by the competent forestry authorities under the State Council, upon whose approval such methods shall be implemented. Earnest protection should be extended to precious trees outside of the natural protection areas and the plant resources with special value inside the forest districts; without the approval of the competent forestry authorities at the provincial, autonomous region or directly-administered municipality, no cutting and collecting shall take place.

Article 43 of the Grassland Law (the Standing Committee of the NPC, 1985, revised in 2002) provides:

> The competent administrative department for grasslands under the State Council or the people's governments of provinces, autonomous regions or municipalities directly under the Central Government may, in compliance with the relevant regulations on administration of the nature reserves, set up grassland nature reserves in the following areas: (1) typical grasslands; (2) ranges of rare and endangered species of wild animals and plants; and (3) grasslands of important ecological functions and worthy of economic and scientific research.

Article 33 of the Water Law (the Standing Committee of the NPC, 2002) provides:

> The State establishes a protection system for zones of drinking water sources. The people's governments of provinces, autonomous regions or municipalities directly under the Central Government shall define the drying-up of the water sources and pollution of the water bodies, for the purpose of ensuring town and county residents' safety in respect of drinking water.

14.2.1 Legal Provisions of Nature Reserves

14.2.1.1 General legal provisions

A. General requirements of the establishment and administration of nature reserves The state shall practice economic and technological policies and measures favorable to the development of nature reserves, and incorporate the development planning of nature reserves into the national economic and social development plans.[10] The local economic construction, the production activities and everyday life of local residents shall be properly considered when the nature reserves are established and managed.[11] The people's governments at or above the county level shall strengthen leadership for the work concerning nature reserves. All units and individuals shall have an obligation to protect the natural environment and resources within nature reserves and have the right to report on or file charges against units or individuals who have destroyed or seized the nature reserves.[12] The people's governments at various levels shall give awards to units or individuals who have made outstanding contributions to the establishment and management of nature reserves and the related scientific research.[13]

B. Management system of nature reserves The state shall practice a system which combines integrated management with separate departmental management for the management of nature reserves. The competent department of environmental protection administration under the State Council is responsible for the integrated management of the nature reserves throughout the country. The competent departments of forestry, agriculture, geology and mineral resources, water conservancy, and marine affairs and other departments concerned are responsible for relevant nature reserves under their jurisdiction. The people's governments of provinces, autonomous regions and municipalities directly under the central government shall decide, according to the specific condition of the locality, on the establishment and the responsibilities of

---

10 Regulations on Nature Reserves (the State Council, 1994), art. 4.
11 Ibid., art. 5.
12 Ibid., art. 7.
13 Ibid., art. 9.

the administrative departments of nature reserves in the people's governments at or above the county level.[14]

14.2.1.2 Legal provisions on the establishment of nature reserves

A. Conditions on the establishment of nature reserves In the areas which meet one of the following requirements, a nature reserve shall be established:[15]

(i) typical geographic areas with representative natural ecosystems, and those similar areas where the natural eco systems have been damaged to some extent, but can be restored through proper protection;
(ii) areas with a natural concentrated distribution of rare and endangered wild animals or plant species;
(ii) those areas which are of special protection value, such as marine and coastal areas, islands, wetland, internal water bodies, forests, grassland and deserts;
(iv) natural remains which are of scientific or cultural value, such as geological structures, famous karst caves, fossil distribution areas, glaciers, volcanoes, and hot springs;
(v) other natural regions requiring special protection by the approval of the State Council or the people's governments of provinces, autonomous regions or municipalities directly under the central government.

B. The category of nature reserves Nature reserves are divided into national nature reserves and local nature reserves, national nature reserves are those that have distinctive characteristics whether viewed from inside or outside the country; have a major international influence in science; or are of special value for scientific research.[16]

C. The establishment procedure for nature reserves The establishment of a national nature reserve requires an application from the people's government of the province, autonomous region or municipality directly under the central government where the proposed nature reserve is located or by the competent department of nature reserves under the

---

14 Ibid., art. 8.
15 Ibid., art. 10.
16 Ibid., art. 11.

State Council. After the appraisal by the National Nature Reserves Appraisal Committee, the competent department of environmental protection administration under the State Council shall coordinate with relevant department to provide appraisal comments on the application and then submit it to the State Council for approval.

The establishment of a local nature reserve requires an application from the people's government of the county, autonomous county, municipality or autonomous prefecture where the proposed nature reserve is located, or from competent department of nature reserves in the people's government of the relevant province, autonomous region or municipality directly under the central government. After the appraisal by the local nature reserves appraisal committee, the competent department of environmental protection administration in the people's government of the province, autonomous region or municipality directly under the central government shall coordinate with relevant departments to provide appraisal comments on the application and then submit it to the people's government of the province, autonomous region or the municipality directly under the central government for approval, and meanwhile submit it to the competent department of environmental protection administration under the State Council and the relevant competent administrative department of nature reserves under the State Council for the record.

The establishment of a nature reserve involving more than two administrative divisions requires an application from the people's government of relevant regions after their consultation. The application then goes through the same procedures described in the preceding two paragraphs.

The establishment of maritime nature reserves must be approved by the State Council.[17]

D. Sub-area protection of nature reserves Nature reserves may be divided into three parts: the core area, buffer zone and experimental zone. The intact natural ecosystems and the areas where the rare and endangered animals or plants are concentratedly distributed within nature reserves should be included in the core area into which no units or individuals are allowed to enter. Scientific research activities are generally prohibited in the core area except for those approved according to Article 27 of the Regulations. A certain amount of the area surrounding the core area may be designated as the buffer zone, where only scientific

---

17 Ibid., art. 12

observations and other research activities are allowed. The area surrounding the buffer zone may be designated as the experimental zone, which may be entered for various activities such as scientific experiments, educational practices, visits and investigations, tourism, and the domestication and breeding of rare and endangered wild animals or plant species. If the people's government responsible for the approval of the establishment of the nature reserves thinks it necessary, a certain amount of the area surrounding the nature reserve may be designated as the outer protection area.[18]

14.2.1.3 Legal provisions on the management of nature reserves

A. Technical regulations and standards The competent department of environmental protection administration under the State Council shall organize relevant administrative departments of nature reserves under the State Council to formulate national technical regulations and standards for the management of nature reserves. The relevant competent administrative departments of nature reserves under the State Council shall, within the field of divisions of work, formulate the technical regulations on the management of various types of nature reserves, and submit them to the competent department of environmental protection administration under the State Council for the record.[19]

B. Supervision and inspection of the management of nature reserves The competent departments of environmental protection administration in the people's governments at or above the county level have the right to conduct supervision and inspections of the management of all the nature reserves within their administrative division. The relevant competent administrative departments of nature reserves in the people's government at or above the county level have the right to conduct supervision and inspection on the management of the nature reserves they are responsible for. The units subject to inspection shall truthfully report the situation to them and provide them with the necessary information. The inspectors shall keep confidential technological know-how and business secrets of the units inspected.[20]

---

[18] Ibid., art. 18.
[19] Ibid., art. 19.
[20] Ibid., art. 20.

C. Management organization of the management of nature reserves
The competent administrative departments of the nature reserves of the people's governments of provinces, autonomous regions and municipalities directly under the central government or the competent administrative department of nature reserves under the State Council shall be responsible for the management of the national nature reserves. The competent administrative department of nature reserves in the people's governments at or above the county level shall be responsible for the management of the local nature reserves within their administrative divisions. The relevant competent administrative departments of nature reserves shall set up a special administrative agency in each nature reserve and provide specialized technical staff who are to be responsible for the management of the nature reserves.[21]

D. Prohibition and restriction on human activities in nature reserves
Within nature reserves, such activities as felling, grazing, hunting, fishing, gathering medicinal herbs, reclaiming, burning, mining, stone quarrying and sand dredging etc., shall be prohibited unless it is otherwise provided by relevant laws and regulations.[22]

Nobody shall be allowed to enter the core area of nature reserves. Where scientific observations and investigation thereto are necessary for scientific research, the unit concerned shall submit the applications and activity plans to the administrative agency of the nature reserves in advance, and these must be approved by the competent administrative department of nature reserves in the people's government at or above the provincial level. The entrance into the core area of national nature reserves shall be approved by the competent administrative department of nature reserves under the State Council. For residents living in the core area of the nature reserve who are required to move out, the local people's government shall see to the proper settlement for them.[23]

Tourism, production and trading activities are prohibited in the buffer zone of nature reserves. In buffer zone, for non-destructive activities such as scientific research, educational practice and specimen collection for teaching or scientific research, applications and activity plans shall be submitted to the administrative agency of the nature reserves in advance and be approved by the same agency. All units and individuals who participate in such activities described in the preceding paragraph shall

---

21 Ibid., art. 21.
22 Ibid., art. 26.
23 Ibid., art. 27.

submit a copy of the report of the activity result to the administrative agency of the nature reserves.[24]

With respect to the visiting and sightseeing tourist activities in the experimental zone of national nature reserves, the administrative agency of the nature reserves shall put forward the activity program. After it is reviewed by the competent administrative department of nature reserves of the people's government of the province, autonomous region or the municipality directly under the central government, the program shall be submitted to the competent administrative department of nature reserves under the State Council for final approval. With respect to the visiting and sightseeing tourist activities in the experimental zone of local nature reserves, the administrative agency of the nature reserve shall put forward the activity program, and submit it to the competent administrative department of nature reserves of the people's government of the province, autonomous region or the municipality directly under the central government for final approval. Visiting and sightseeing tourist activities in nature reserves must be conducted according to activity program approved. The management of such activities is strictly enforced and all units and individuals who enter nature reserves for visiting or sightseeing tours must submit themselves to the management of the administrative agency of nature reserves. Visiting and sightseeing tourist projects that violate the protection guidelines of nature reserves will be prohibited.[25]

In cases where foreigners wish to enter a local nature reserve, the host unit shall apply in advance for approval by the competent administrative department of nature reserves of the people's government of the province, autonomous region or the municipality directly under the central government. In cases involving national nature reserves, the host unit shall apply for approval by the competent administrative department of nature reserves under the State Council.[26]

No production installations may be built in the core area and buffer zone of nature reserves. In the experimental zone, no production installations that cause environmental pollution or damages the natural resources or landscapes shall be built. Other installations to be built in these areas must not exceed the discharge of pollutants prescribed by national or local discharge standards. If the installations that have been built discharge more pollutants than are specified by the national or local discharge standards in the experimental zone of nature reserves, such

---

24 Ibid., art. 28.
25 Ibid., art. 29.
26 Ibid., art. 31.

pollution shall be eliminated or controlled within a prescribed period of time. Remedial measures must be adopted to correct the damage caused. The projects constructed in the outer protection zone of nature reserves must not affect the environmental quality inside the nature reserves. If the damage has been done, the relevant units will be ordered to eliminate and control the pollution within a prescribed period of time.[27]

14.2.2 Legal Provisions of Scenic Interest Areas

14.2.2.1 Administrative system of scenic interest areas

The competent department of construction under the State Council is responsible for the supervision and administration of scenic interest areas throughout the country. Other departments concerned under the State Council are responsible for the relevant supervision and administration of scenic interest areas according to the division of duties provided by the State Council.

The competent departments of construction under the people's governments of provinces and autonomous regions and the competent departments of scenic interest areas under the people's governments of municipality directly under the central government shall be responsible for the supervision and administration of scenic interest areas throughout the respective administrative regions. Other departments concerned under the people's governments of provinces, autonomous regions or municipality directly under the central government shall be responsible for the relevant supervision and administration of scenic interest areas according to the division of duties provided by rules.[28]

14.2.2.2 Classification and examination of scenic interest areas

Scenic interest areas are divided into national scenic interest areas and local scenic interest areas. Natural and human landscapes, which can reflect important natural changes and historical and cultural development, basically in the natural state or in original appearance, with national representation, may apply for the establishment of national scenic interest areas with national representation, or for the establishment of local scenic interest areas with local representation.[29]

The establishment of a national scenic interest area requires an application from the people's government of province, autonomous

---

[27] Ibid., art. 32.
[28] Ibid., art. 5
[29] Ibid., art. 8.

region or municipality directly under the central government. The competent department of construction under the State Council shall cooperate with the competent department of environmental protection administration, the competent forestry department, the competent cultural department and other relevant departments under the State Council, put forward a review opinion, and then submit it to the State Council for approval and announcement. The establishment of a provincial scenic interest area requires an application from the people's government of county level. The competent department of construction under the people's government of province, autonomous region or municipality directly under the central government shall cooperate with other relevant departments, put forward a review opinion, and then submit it to the people's government of province, autonomous region or municipality directly under the central government for approval and announcement.[30]

14.2.2.3 Planning of scenic interest areas

In order to effectively protect, reasonably construct and scientifically administer: the planning for every scenic interest area must be comprehensive. The planning of scenic interest areas is divided into overall planning and detailed planning.[31]

The overall planning of scenic interest areas should reflect the requirements of the harmonious coexistence between man and nature and the all-round progress of economy and society, assert the principles of protection priority, and strengthen natural characteristics, cultural connotation and local features of scenic resource.[32]

The detailed planning of scenic interest areas determines the site, the layout and scale of construction projects such as infrastructure, tourism or cultural facilities and so on, and make clear the scale and design conditions for construction, according to different requirements of center and other scenic spots. The detailed planning of scenic interest areas should be in accordance with the overall one.[33]

14.2.2.4 Legal provisions on the protection of scenic interest areas

The following activities are not permitted in the scenic interest areas:[34]

---

30 Ibid., art. 10.
31 Ibid., art. 12.
32 Ibid., art. 13.
33 Ibid., art. 15.
34 Ibid., art. 26.

i. activities destroying landscape, vegetation and terrain such as quarrying, mining, reclamation, repairing graves or monuments and so on;
ii. building facilities for storage of explosive, flammable, toxic, radioactive or corrosive goods;
iii. carving on or smearing the scene or facilities;
iv. littering.

It is also forbidden to establish various development zones in scenic interest areas, or to build hotels, guesthouses, training centers, sanatoriums or other constructions irrelevant to the protection of scenic interest resources in the core scenic areas, which violate the planning of scenic interest areas; constructions which already exist, shall be moved out step by step, according to the planning.[35]

14.2.2.5 Legal provisions on the utilization and administration of scenic interest areas

Administrative agencies of scenic interest areas shall protect ethnic folk and their traditional culture, implement healthy and beneficial sightseeing and cultural and recreational activities, and popularize historical, cultural and scientific knowledge, according to the characteristics of scenic interest areas.[36]

Receiving visitors beyond the allowed capacity, or implementing tour activities in the zones without security assurance is prohibited.[37]

Ticket income from scenic interest areas and compensable use fee of scenic interest resources shall be used especially for the protection and administration of scenic interest resources, as well as for the compensation of the loss of the owners and users of property in scenic interest areas.[38]

The administrative agency shall not engage in activities for profit, or authorize administrative functions such as planning, administration, supervision and so on to enterprises or individuals. Staff of the administrative agency may not take part-time jobs in enterprises within scenic interest areas.[39]

---

35 Ibid., art. 27.
36 Ibid., art. 30.
37 Ibid., art. 36(2).
38 Ibid., art. 38(2).
39 Ibid., art. 39.

14.2.3 Legal Provisions on Forest Parks

14.2.3.1 Administrative agencies of forest parks and their duties

The competent forestry departments under the people's government of county level shall be responsible for the administration of forest parks.[40] An administrative agency shall be established according to law, if forest parks are set up in zones of management of state forestry bureaus, state forest farms, state nursery gardens, collective forest farms and other organizations; but if forest parks are set up in the zones of management of state forest farms and state nursery gardens, their management offices are also the administrative agencies of forest parks.[41] The management office is responsible for the planning, construction, operation and management of the forest park. The management office has operational rights, by legislation, over the forests, trees, woodland, wildlife, water scenery, scenic spots and all kinds of facilities within its interest.[42]

14.2.3.2 Establishment and classification of forest parks

Forest parks are divided into national forest parks, provincial forest parks and county (municipal) forest parks, according to the ornamental, cultural and scientific value of the forest and human landscapes, tourist conditions, reputations and so on:[43]

(i) National forest parks. If the forest landscape is especially beautiful and human landscape is fairly concentrated, with high ornamental, cultural and scientific value, a special geographic location, a regional representative, a complete tourist service facility, and an above average reputation, the provincial competent forestry department provides a written application, a feasibility analysis report, charts, pictures and other relevant materials to the forest ministry, who is responsible for approving the establishment of the national forest park.

(ii) Provincial forest parks. If the forest landscape is beautiful and human landscape is relatively concentrated, with fairly high ornamental, cultural and scientific value, a special geographic location, a regional representative in the relevant administrative region, necessary tourist service facilities, and a reasonable reputation, the county (municipal) competent forestry department provides the

---

40 Rules on Management of Forestry Parks (Forest Ministry, 1993), art. 3.

41 Ibid., art. 4.

42 Ibid., art. 5(1).

43 Ibid., arts 6, 7, 8.

written application, the provincial competent forestry department approves the establishment of the provincial forest park and submits it to the Forest ministry for the record.

(iii) County (municipal) forest parks. If the forest landscape is beautiful, with some ornamental, cultural and scientific value and a local representative, the county (municipal) competent forestry department examines and approves the establishment of the county (municipal) forest park, and the provincial competent forestry department submits the relevant materials to the forest ministry for the record.

14.2.3.3 Planning and construction of forest parks

The planning of forest parks is to be undertaken by administrative agencies of forest parks, which may be authorized to authorize national planning design and scientific research organizations with planning and design qualifications.[44] The construction of forest parks shall be implemented on the basis of following the designs initially approved. The investment and construction may be conducted in various different ways, but the relationship of administrative subordination to the administrative agencies of forest parks may not be changed.[45] The construction of facilities should be in accordance with the design of the overall plan. Hotels, guesthouses, nursing homes and other engineering facilities should not be built in the precious scenery, important scenic spots or the core scenic area. Only necessary protective and ancillary facilities can be built.[46]

14.2.3.4 Protection of forest parks

Land reclamation which might cause deforestation, rock quarrying, sand quarrying, soil extracting and any other activities resulting in deforestation are forbidden in the forest parks. Any unit or individual cutting trees must abide by relevant provisions of forestry regulations, business plans and technical codes.[47]

The occupation, expropriation or assignment of forestlands must be approved according to the law.[48]

---

44 Ibid., art. 7(2).
45 Ibid., art. 10.
46 Ibid., art. 11.
47 Ibid., art. 12.
48 Ibid., art. 13.

Administrative agencies must impose all measures linked to afforestation, forest fire prevention, forest pest control and to the protection of woods, forestlands and wildlife resources.[49]

14.2.3.5 Administration of forest parks

The units and individuals who come into forest parks for touring and other activities may be charged for tickets and related costs. All the units, residents and other tourists in forest parks are to protect facilities in the parks and comply with the administration system;[50] administrative agencies of forest parks shall install fireproofing, sanitation, environmental protection, security and other installations and signs in conformity with regulations, and maintain the tour order;[51] the forestry public security organs shall be responsible for the security administration of forest parks.[52]

14.3 PROBLEMS

Through the analysis of section 2, we can see that the protected area legislation in China generally presents a legislative mode of combining categorized departmental legislation and other provisions. The categorized departmental legislation refers to the body of specific regulations, which are based on the categorized classification, and enacted by relevant authorities.[53] Many important existing regulations, such as the Regulations on Nature Reserves and the Regulations on Scenic and Historic Areas of the State Council and the Rules on Management of Forestry Parks of the State Forestry Administration, belong to categorized departmental legislation. What is more, the provisions relevant to the protected area protection in the laws such as the Environmental Protection Law (the Standing Committee of the NPC, 2014); the Wild Animal Protection Law (the Standing Committee of the NPC, 1988, revised in 2004); and the Forest Law (the Standing Committee of the NPC, 1984, revised in 1998) all belong to the legal system of the protected areas of China as well.

---

49 Ibid., art. 17.

50 Ibid., art. 15.

51 Ibid., art. 16.

52 Ibid., art. 18.

53 Benxin Xu, "The comprehensive frame legislative mode of Natural Protected Areas in China", *Social Science of Inner Mongolia*, Nov. 2010, Vol. 31, p. 31.

The legislative mode of combining categorized departmental legislation and other provisions has played an important role in the legal construction surrounding China's protected areas. However, with the development of these protected areas, the defects in the existing legislative mode is becoming increasingly noticeable.

14.3.1 Confused Legal Concepts and Lack of Clarity on Adjustment Objects

The existing laws and regulations in China widely use the concept of "nature reserves". Except for "nature reserves" in the Regulation on Nature Reserves, there are "protection zones of drinking water sources" in the Water Law (the Standing Committee of the NPC, 2002) and "enclosed and forbidden reserves of desertified land" in the Prevention and Control of Desertification (the Standing Committee of the NPC, 2001) which are easily confused because of their similarity.

As to the adjustment objects, there are overlapping parts among different categories of protected areas, such as nature reserves, scenic interest areas, forest parks, and so on. The overlap, as well as the different authorities involved, increases the difficulty of management and protection.

The disunity of the expositions and understandings of the core concepts of the same adjustment object will almost certainly lead either to multiple jurisdictions or to a jurisdiction vacuum, not only meaning that some natural or cultural resources cannot get effective protection from state laws, but also making it hard for administrators to grasp the scope of the object in the work leading to a situation where there is a shortage of laws.

14.3.2 Narrow Adjustment Scope and Lack of Openness in Legislative System

Protected areas in China are categorized on the natural character of the protected object, not by adopting the categories defined by the International Union for Conservation of Nature (IUCN) which are based on administrative objects and methods. Compared to the IUCN's definition and category of "protected area",[54] the category system of protected areas

---

[54] IUCN defines "Protected Area (PA)" as "a clearly defined geographical space, recognized, dedicated and managed, through legal or other effective means, to achieve the long term conservation of nature with associated ecosystem services and cultural values". In 1994, IUCN approved the "International

in China is not compatible with that of IUCN's. According to the Regulation on Nature Reserves (the State Council, 1994), all nature reserves in China should belong to Category I a (Strict Nature Reserves). But many nature reserves essentially belong to Category II (National Parks) in terms of actual management since they play a role in biodiversity conservation while being open to tourists. In the light of international standards or definition, many scenic interest areas in China should not be part of Category II (National Parks), but of Category V (Protected Landscapes/Seascapes), because these areas are basically managed as tour sites without much consideration of biodiversity conservation or ecosystems. Quite a few of forest parks in China do not technically belong to Category V (Protected Landscapes/Seascapes) because of mono-cultural forests. In addition, there are not protected areas that clearly belong to Category IV (Habitat/Species Management Areas) or Category VI (Managed Resource Protected Areas). Obviously, China's legislation has not covered some categories of protected areas like national parks, natural monuments and scenery or seascape protection areas. What is more, there are only three departmental regulations in all China's categories of protected areas at present. The adjustment scope of protected area legislation is too narrow to protect the protected areas as a whole.

14.3.3 Low Legislative Level and Lack of Unity in Legal System

In the China's current protected areas legislation, the Regulation on Nature Reserves and the Regulation on Scenic Interest Areas are administrative regulations, whose legal level and effect are less than law, and so cannot take precedence over other relevant regulations or coordinate with

---

Classification System of Protected Areas" and suggested all countries in the world implement it. According to major management objectives of PAs, IUCN divides PA management into six categories. Category Ia: Strict Nature Reserves, which are managed mainly for science or wilderness protection; Category Ib: Wilderness Areas, which are managed mainly for wilderness protection; Category II: National Parks, which are managed mainly for ecosystem protection and recreation; Category III: Natural Monuments, which are managed mainly for conservation of specific natural features; Category IV: Habitat/Species Management Areas, which are managed mainly for conservation through management intervention; Category V: Protected Landscapes/Seascapes, which are managed for landscape/seascape conservation or recreation; Category VI: Managed Resource Protected Areas, which are managed mainly for the sustainable use of natural resources. See: Dudley, N. (ed.) (2008) Guidelines for Applying Protected Areas Management Categories, IUCN: Gland, Switzerland. pp.8–9.

other departmental laws effectively.[55] The Administrative Measures on Forest Parks is a departmental regulation, whose level is even lower. Given the experience of the construction of protected areas elsewhere in the world, it is obvious that the key to success is that the state enacts formal laws to set out clear provisions on the attributes of protected areas, establishes administrative and supervisory authorities and an environmental policy, and so on. For example, the Basic Law of National Parks of America and the Federal Law of Special Protection of Natural Zones of Russia.

In addition, while unable to lead other relevant departmental regulations, the low legislative level of the Regulation on Nature Reserves leads to conflict on the contents of different types of relevant legislation on nature reserves. For example, as to the procedure of the establishment of a national nature reserve, the Regulation on Nature Reserves provides:

> After the appraisal by the National Nature Reserves Appraisal Committee, the competent department of environmental protection administration under the State Council shall coordinate with relevant department to provide appraisal comments on the application and then submit it to the State Council for approval.[56]

However, the Administrative Measures of the PRC for Nature Reserves for Aquatic Plants and Animals (the Ministry of Agriculture, 2010) provides: "After the appraisal by the appraisal committee, the department of fishery administration under the State Council shall submit it to the State Council by rule for approval."[57] This procedure does not involve the competent department of environmental protection administration under the State Council. The conflict between different levels of effect of regulations influences the unity of legal system tremendously.

14.3.4 Executive-led Legislation and Lack of Priority of Ecological Protection

The current legislation on protected areas in China is drafted by the relevant resources administrative departments. These departments tend to be more concerned about themselves rather than worrying about the overall situation. These separate laws of protected areas cannot form a

---

[55] Yan Ma, "Nature reserves in China current situation and problems", *Environmental Protection*, 2006, Vol. 11(A), pp. 42–46.

[56] The Regulations on Nature Reserves (the State Council, 1994), art. 12(1).

[57] Measures for the Administration of Aquatic Animals and Plants Conservation Areas (Ministry of Agriculture, 2010), Article 8.

unified legal system of protected area protection and administration, but instead turn into instruments to expand their powers and preserve their benefits.[58] Moreover, under the departmental legislative mode, there is still a probability that economic growth is given more credence than natural protection because the reality is that the administration is executive led.

14.4 RECOMMENDATION

Although increasing areas of China have been protected, the loss of biodiversity in protected areas continues. Scholars believe that the most fundamental reason that protected areas in China have failed to get all-around and effective protection is that there is still a lack of a reasonable, clear and flexible legal framework.[59] As the result, it is becoming urgent to enact a comprehensive law covering the construction and management of all kinds of protected areas in China. In fact, NPC Environmental and Resources Committee authorized the department concerned to draft the PRC Nature Reserves Law in 2004, but it is still in process. It is probably because of China's regional differences and the various kinds of natural protection lead to the lack of operability of a comprehensive and united legislation.

14.4.1 Strengthen Comprehensive Legislation, Enact the PRC Protected Area Law

A comprehensive legislative model could solve the poor coordination of departmental legislation; give full consideration to the characteristics of the different natural types; make the principle stipulations about construction and management of protected areas; and coordinate the relationship between all kinds of relevant legislation on protected areas.

It is suggested that the "Protected Area Law of the People's Republic of China" be the name of the law. Although the term "nature reserves" has been widely recognized and used in China, it has become synonymous with the natural ecosystem and rare and endangered species of wild fauna and flora and natural relics because of the definition in the Regulation on Nature Reserves. The universality and containment of

[58] Xianpu Wang, Guofa Cui, *The Construction and Administration of Nature Reserves*. Beijing: Chemical Industry Press, 2003, p. 240.

[59] Yan Xie, Song Wang, Peter Schei, *China's Protected Areas*, Tsinghua University Press, 2004, p. 5.

protected areas influence the legislative intent, adjustment scope and other issues of protected areas in China directly. As the ICUN's concept of the protected area has been widely recognized by the world, this comprehensive law of all kinds of protected areas should be urgently enacted in China so that the country conforms to the general trend of international nature conservation and ecological construction and to meet the needs of international standards. Professor Wang Xi suggests to referring to the IUCN's concept of protected areas and defining the China's protected area as "land and ocean regions, specially delimitated to protected the biodiversity and nature and relevant cultural resources, administrated by laws and other effective means, including all kinds of nature reserves, forest parks, geological parks, scenic interest areas and so on."[60]

The legislative idea and content should follow the natural integrative requirement, pay attention to the relationship of interdependence and interaction between all kinds of protected areas, realize the integrative protection of natural patterns, cultural environment, material forms and ecological functions and put effort into promoting the efficiency of protected areas. The law should reflect the multi-goals and final value pursuit of the protection of protected areas, and reflect the principle of integrated planning, scientific establishment, systematic management, priority protection, strict liability and public participation.[61]

14.4.2 Improve Framework Legislation, Build a Reasonable Category System of Protected Areas

Different kinds of protected areas each have their own characteristics and management objectives, and the same kinds of protected areas in different regions will have differences as well. The legal regulation of protected areas should have a principle direction as well as specific behavior requirements. As this obviously cannot be solely undertaken by a law of protected areas, it is necessary to use other supporting laws and regulations. As the result, it will be necessary to build a reasonable system with categories of protected areas and an improved framework legislation.

---

60 Xi Wang, Yunpeng Qu, "Proposals for the development of a Protected Area Law", in Yan Xie, Song Wang, Peter Schei, *China's Protected Areas*, Tsinghua University Press, 2004, p. 137.

61 Canfa Wang, "Natural reserves need high level legislative protection urgently", *Environmental Protection*, 2011, Vol. 4, p. 26.

14.4.2.1 Use the IUCN Category System as the reference to build the category system of China's protected areas

The IUCN divided protected areas into six categories in its Guidelines for Applying Protected Areas Management Categories in 2008, according to the different main objectives and management methods.[62] The IUCN category system has the following advantages:[63] (a) it helps to reduce confusion of terminology because different countries use different names to refer to protected areas with similar management objectives and thus, it is possible for people to communicate with each other using the "common language" of the category system; (b) it demonstrates the range of objectives that different kinds of protected areas can meet, and represents varying degree of human intervention ranging from a strictly protected area to a sustainable use reserve; (c) it underscores the fact that protected areas belonging to different categories are equally important and no one type is to be superior to the other. Hence, category I (Strict Nature Reserves) should not be seen as more important than category VI (Managed Resource Protected Areas), and the choice should be based on the appropriateness to the particular context and objective; (d) it assists in the design and review of national systems of protected areas, and in the integration of protected areas into the broader landscape/seascape using the full range of management categories; and (e) it enhances communication and understanding; and facilitates international accounting and comparison.

However, in the IUCN category system, some categories lack effectiveness in operation because they are hard to grasp; what is more, instead of copying the IUCN category system completely, most countries in reality improve it according to their own conditions or absorb the idea of the management of it.[64] China could learn much from the successful experience of the countries like Australia and Bulgaria who have brought in the IUCN category system and integrated it with their own conditions. It is thus clear that China should treat the IUCN category system as a reference and guidance, and build the category system of China's protected areas on the basis of the combination of it and China's own conditions and specific legislative objective. (See below Table 14.1.)

---

[62] Benxin Xu, note 53 above, p. 31.

[63] Kishore Rao, "Applying the IUCN Protected Areas Category System in China", in Yan Xie, Song Wang, Peter Schei, *China's Protected Areas*, Tsinghua University Press, 2004, pp. 397–9.

[64] Ke Zhou, Jiaru Zhou, "To Improve the Legislation of the Category System of Natural Reserves in China", *Journal of Capital Normal University* (Social Sciences Edition), 2007(2), p. 62.

Table 14.1 Recommended categories for China's protected area system

Category	Name of each Category	Objectives	Examples	Existing protected area types in China
Ia	Strict Nature Reserve	To preserve habitats, ecosystems and species in as undisturbed a state as possible to maintain genetic resources in a dynamic and evolutionary state, and maintain ecological processes. To permit non-destructive scientific research.	Dinghushan, Foping, Wolong, Xishuangbanna, Nanjin Islands, Changbaishan	National NRs of forest Ecosystem type, including the core zone
Ib	Wilderness Protection Area	To preserve the natural attributes and qualities of a large area of unmodified or slightly modified land/ and or sea, without permanent or significant habitation. To enable local resident people to live at low densities and in balance with the available resources to maintain their lifestyles.	Qiangtang, Kekexili, Anxi Jihan Desert, Wula'ersuosuolin, Menggu Wild Ass	National NRs of prairie and meadow ecosystem or desert ecosystem, including the buffer zone
II	National/ Provincial Park	To protect natural and scenic areas of national or international significance for spiritual, scientific, educational, recreational or tourism purposes. To take into account the needs of the resident local people without adversely affecting the other objectives of management.	Juzhaigou, Huanglong, Fanjingshan, Jinyunshan, Jinfoshan, Gonggashan, Xiguliangshan, Danxiashan, Qinghaihu, Zhumulangmafeng, Yaluzangbu Gorge, Taibaishan, Hanasi, Lushan	NRs of ecosystem, wildlife or natural monument types, including the experimental zone; National SLHSs or Forest parks
III	Natural Monument	To protect specific outstanding or unique natural features for their inherent rarity, representative or aesthetic or culture significance. To provide opportunities for research, education, interpretation and public appreciation. To deliver such benefits to local people as are consistent with the other objectives of management, and ensure that such use is sustainable.	Jixianshangyuan, Dianzixiang, Yitong Volcanos, Shanwang biological fossil, Heyuan dinosaur eggfossil, Wudalianchi, Qinglongshan	NRs of the natural Monument type

Table 14.1 (cont.)

Category	Name of each Category	Objectives	Examples	Existing protected area types in China
IV	Wildlife Sanctuary	To maintain the habitat conditions necessary to protect species, biotic communities or physical features of the environment through specific manipulative management intervention. To deliver such benefits to local people as are consistent with the other objectives of management, and ensure that such use is sustainable.	Datian, Dafeng Milu, Wanglang, Zhuhuan	NRs of the forest ecosystem. wildlife type
V	Protected Landscape/ Seascape	To maintain the harmonious interaction of people and nature through the protection of landscape/seascape and the continuation of traditional land uses and cultural practices. To maintain the diversity of landscape/seascape and habitat, and of associated species and ecosystems. To benefit local communities through the sustainable use of the PA resources and services.	Many current forest parks and ecological function areas. Many "outer zones" of current nature reserves, Xiangshan	NRs of the forest ecosystem type, prairie and meadow ecosystem types, including the outer protection area; SLHSs; Forest parks, Coastal parks, Wetland parks Community PAs
VI	Ecological Reserve/ Managed Resource Area	To manage largely unmodified natural system to ensure long-term protection and maintenance of biodiversity and ecological function, while providing a sustainable flow of goods and services to meet community needs.	Panda corridors, Dongzaigang, Xingkaihu, Ruo' ergai, Poyangh	NRs of all kinds of Ecosystem types, including the experimental zone; Forest Parks, Coastal parks, Wetland parks, Community PAs

Source: Yan Xie, Song Wang and Peter Schei, *China's Protected Areas*, Tsinghua University Press, 2004, pp. 297–298.

14.4.2.2 The framework legislation of the combination of "One Category One Law" and "One Region One Law"

Framework legislation represents an ecosystem-oriented integration of legal systems, using a whole view to treat the ecosystem and the interrelation of it and environmental problems. Framework legislation can adapt to changes in society, in the economy and ecological conditions, providing an extensive and flexible legal framework to solve the problems of environment and resource.[65] As protected areas are very specialized, different laws must be enacted according to different categories, and it is this reliable legislative safeguard that will protect different categories of protected areas effectively.[66] Therefore, not only is there a need to enact the PRC Protected Area Law, but also a need to amend or make management rules for all categories of protected areas to regulate them, within the framework of the Protected Area Law, to ensure every category of protected areas realizes its management objectives, and the framework objectives of "one category one law" and "one region one law".

---

[65] Xi Wang, *Environmental Law*, Beijing: Law Press, 2002, p. 361.

[66] Jiuhua Yu, *The Theory and Practice of the Effective Administration of Natural Reserves*, Xianyang: Northwest Agricultural and Forestry University Press, 2006, p. 136.

15. Environmental liability

Zhao Xiaobo and Zhang Jianwei

15.1 DEFINITIONS AND CATEGORIES

Matters involving environmental liability have been widely recognized in many discussions on environmental issues. However, there is much confusion about the term 'environmental liabilities'. According to China's legal theory, legal liability is primarily defined as one kind of obligation, the implementation of which is guaranteed by the compulsion of law. In the environmental law context, 'environmental liability' refers to obligations based on the principle that a polluting party should pay for either part or the entire damage caused by its activities. Clearly, 'environmental liability' is an umbrella term, it includes three types of environmental liabilities: the civil liability, administrative liability and criminal liability. The violators may potentially face fines, penalties, and jail terms for violations of environmental statutes. In this chapter, these types of liabilities will be briefly defined, and the characters of each form of liability will be studied in both theoretical and practical dimensions.

15.2 ENVIRONMENTAL CIVIL LIABILITIES

Environmental civil liabilities are associated with civil obligations, and refer to the negative results for the breach of civil laws.[1] As a basic civil obligation, civil activities must be in compliance with the law with state

[1] Although China follows the continental legal traditions, there is no Civil Code so far. Instead, rules for adjusting civil issues are prescribed by numerous specific laws and regulations. Among others, three most important laws regarding to civil issues are the《中华人民共和国民法通则》[General Principles of the Civil Law] (People's Republic of China (PRC)) National People's Congress, Order No 37, 12 April 1986;《中华人民共和国侵权责任法》[The Tort Law of the People's Republic of China] (People's Republic of China) National People's Congress, Order No 21, 26 December 2009; and《中华人民共和国物权法》PRC Property Law (promulgated by National People's Congress, Mar. 16, 2007, effective Oct. 1, 2007), Issue No. 14 Serial No. 1229 ST. COUNOL GAZ. May 20, 2007.

policies;[2] in cases where no specific regulation exists social ethics should be applied to maintain state economic plans and proper social economic order.[3] Therefore, the basis of pollution compensation claims lie in various provisions of the civil laws and the Environmental Protection Law. The purpose of environmental civil liabilities is to provide remedies for the victims of environmental damage in a timely manner and to deter potential environmental offenders from conducting environmental pollution, ecological and other damages.

15.2.1 Environmental Civil Liabilities under Civil Laws

Generally speaking, civil liabilities could be arise from breach of contract and from the conduct of other tortious activities. In China, scholars tend to take environmental civil liability as a substitute for environmental tort liability, which arises from personal injuries or damage to properties or potential threats to the rights or interests caused by polluters.

The General Principles of the Civil Law (General Principles hereafter) prescribes that citizens and legal persons who, through their own fault encroach upon state or collective property, or the property or person of others, shall bear civil liability.[4] In addition, Article 124 of the General Principles prescribes that any person who pollutes the environment and causes damage to others in violation of state provisions for environmental protection and the prevention of pollution shall bear civil liability in accordance with the law.[5] Article 90 of the Property Law states that people who hold the rights to use real property may not, in violation of the laws of the state, release air, water, or solid waste.[6] The Tort Law of the People's Republic of China[7] (Tort Law hereafter) was adopted by the Standing Committee of 11th NPC and came into force on 1 July, 2010. Article 65 of the Tort Law defines the environmental tort liability which provides that a polluter should be liable for the environmental pollution he caused. Major civil liabilities the polluter may incur include elimination of the hazard and compensation for damages.

---

2 《中华人民共和国民法通则》[General Principles of the Civil Law] (PRC) National People's Congress, Order No 37, 12 April 1986, art. 6.

3 Ibid., art. 7.

4 Ibid., art 106, para 2.

5 Ibid., art 124.

6 《中华人民共和国物权法》[PRC Property Law] (2007), art 90.

7 《中华人民共和国侵权责任法》[The Tort Law of the People's Republic of China] (2009).

15.2.2 Civil Liabilities under Environmental Laws

As the most important specific environmental legislation in China, the 2014 Environmental Protection Law sets up statutory foundations for the environmental civil liability as well. It prescribes in Article 64 that: 'Those who caused environmental pollution and ecological damages, should bear tortious liabilities according to the relevant provisions of *Tort Law* of P.R.C.'[8] At the same time, a number of other specialized environmental protection laws and regulations on air, water, solid waste and relevant issues also contain provisions concerning environmental civil liabilities.[9] For instance, the Water Pollution Law provides that an entity or individual damaged by water pollution is entitled to claim the elimination of the hazard and compensation for the damages against the polluter.

15.2.3 Liability Standards

The term 'liability standard' refers to rules for environmental civil liability distribution. It has been widely recognized that the environmental liability regime should adopt special doctrines. Among others, the strict liability is the most significant doctrine applied in cases involving environmental pollution damage worldwide. Under this doctrine, the violation of law or the subjective fault of the polluter is ignored as a fact of causality; this doctrine has been provided by civil and environmental laws in China. Provisions under the General Principles[10] and a number of environmental laws and regulations reflect the strict liability doctrine.

---

8 《中华人民共和国环境保护法》 [Environmental Protection Law], (PRC) National People's Congress, Order No 9, 24 April, 2014 (came into force from 1 January, 2015) art. 64.

9 See, e.g.,《中华人民共和国海洋环境保护法[Marine Environmental Protection Law] (PRC) National People's Congress, Order No 26, 1 April 2000, arts 32–40;《中华人民共和国水污染防治法》[PRC Water Pollution Prevention and Control Law] (PRC) National People's Congress, Order No 87, 1 June 2008, art. 46; 《中华人民共和国大气污染防治法》[Air Pollution Prevention and Control Law (2000 revision)], art. 46; 《中华人民共和国水土保持法》[PRC Soil and Water Conservation Law] (PRC) National People's Congress, Order No 39, 1 March 2011, arts 32–42; 《中华人民共和国固体废物污染环境 防治法》[PRC Solid Waste Law] (PRC) National People's Congress, Order No 31, 1 April 2005, arts 53–64; 《中华人民共和国放射性污染防治法》[PRC Radioactive Pollution Prevention Law] (promulgated by the President), (PRC) National People's Congress, Order No 6, 1 October 2003, arts 42–45.

10 《中华人民共和国民法通则》[General Principles of the Civil Law], art. 106, para. 3.

Based on those provisions, courts may make decisions about cases involving pollution and civil compensation for losses caused by pollution.

As a milestone of environmental liabilities, the Tort Law establishes three important civil liability standards for environmental claims.

(1) *Polluter Pay Principle (PPP).* Article 65 of the Tort Law confirms the Polluter Pay Principle (PPP) as a general principle. Where any harm is caused by environmental pollution, the polluter shall assume the tortious liability.[11]
(2) *Strict liability.* Article 65 of the Tort Law establishes a general principle for a polluter's liability: The polluter shall bear tortious liability without regard to fault (strict liability) if damage is caused by environmental pollution. To challenge such liability, the company or individual responsible for damaging pollution bears the burden of proving that it is entitled to an exemption from or mitigation of liability under the law, or that there is no relationship between his conduct and the environmental pollution that caused the damage.[12]
(3) *Joint liability.* Where damage is caused by pollution attributable to a third party, the victim may seek compensation from either the polluter or the third party. The polluter, after paying compensation, shall be entitled to be reimbursed by the third party.[13] If there were two or more companies or individuals responsible for causing pollution, the proportion of damages for which each party is liable shall be determined according to the type of pollutants, the volume of emissions and other factors.[14]

Although the Article 65 introduced the concept of polluter, it offered no legislative definition for it. Normally speaking, 'polluter' is a broad concept that covers natural persons, legal persons and organizations who cause environmental pollution, such as serious environmental degradation of physical, chemical, or biological functions, or any combination of such functions. According to the Tort Law, 'damage' refers to infringements to victims' civil rights and interests caused by the polluters.[15] It includes

---

11 《中华人民共和国侵权责任法》[The Tort Law of the People's Republic of China], art. 65.

12 Ibid.

13 Ibid., art. 68.

14 Ibid., art. 67.

15 Ibid., art. 2, para. 2.

substantial damage, threat of substantial damage, and substantial hindrance. Damages to the life, health, ownership of a person or legal person, pure economic losses, mental distress are typical of substantial damages.

15.2.4 Statutory Claims

The protection of citizen's health and lawful property rights is the main objective of China's civil law.[16] This objective, together with other commonly recognized civil law principles, is embedded in China's civil law and in the relevant provisions of its environmental statutes. In China, almost all environmental statutes contain provisions concerning the protection of personal and property rights and interests to the extent these are infringed by pollution. Based on those provisions, citizens and organizations have the legal right to bring a lawsuit against polluters.[17]

Generally speaking, there are two types of civil statutory claims: life or health related claims and property related claims. The first type mainly refers to physical injuries. But in some cases, mental distress is also a trigger for compensation. Article 22 of the Tort Law provides that the damage of infringement which causes serious mental distress may also be compensable. For example, people who suffer mental distress caused by noise pollution are able to claim compensation based on the tort liability. The second type of claims is similar to private nuisance liabilities under the common law system, which refer to a legal action redress harm arising from the use of one's property. For example, Article 83 of the General Principles provides a private nuisance action that could be used by adjacent property users in the event of harm to the enjoyment of their property caused by the actions of a neighbouring discharger. Actual damages and/or emotional damages, which are akin to pain and suffering, are two imperative conditions for a compensable damage.[18]

---

[16] Citizen's lawful civil rights and interests of are protected by law, no organization or individual may infringe upon them. 《中华人民共和国民法通则》 [General Principles of the Civil Law], art. 5; see also art. 98.

[17] Citizen's lawful property is protected by law and no organization or individual may appropriate, encroach upon, destroy or illegally seal up, distrain, freeze or confiscate the property of others. 《中华人民共和国民法通则》 [General Principles of the Civil Law], art. 75, para. 2.

[18] In the long run, compensable damages in environmental pollution cases may contain compensatory damages, mesne profits, consequential damages and exemplary damages.

It should be noted that civil liabilities cannot replace administrative and criminal responsibilities. People who bear civil liability cannot be exempted from administrative responsibility or criminal responsibility if necessary.[19] The Civil Procedure Law (1991)[20] provides the legal procedure for citizens or organizations to file a case against a polluter.

15.2.5 Civil Remedies

As the old Latin legal maxim goes: '*ubi jus ibi remedium*', which means 'where there is a right, there must be a remedy'. Civil remedy is a pillar of the Civil Law system. The term of 'civil remedy', as defined by the *Black's Law Dictionary*, refers to 'the means of enforcing a right or preventing or redressing a wrong; legal or equitable relief.'[21] Article 134 of the General Principles lists ten types of civil remedies: (1) cessation of infringements; (2) removal of obstacles; (3) elimination of dangers; (4) return of property; (5) restoration of original condition; (6) repair, reworking or replacement; (7) compensation for losses; (8) payment of breach of contract damages; (9) elimination of ill effects and rehabilitation of reputation; and (10) extension of apology.[22] Similar provisions can also be found in Article 15 of the Tort Law.

Civil remedies can, generally, be divided into three categories: (a) Preventive remedies: for example, (1)–(3) listed above could be applied when the tortuous activities continue and they aim to prevent the further damages. (b) Compensatory remedies: for example, (4)–(7) are remedies for tortuous activities that have already taken place and aim to compensate the victims' lawful rights, generally economic losses. (c) Punitive remedies: payment of breach of contract damages is a typical punitive remedy, and the only reason for this remedy is non-performance contract.

Several of the aforesaid remedies can be applied in environmental cases. Tortfeasors are required to restore the damaged environment to its original status and make compensation for losses of the victim. Article 15

---

19 《中华人民共和国民法通则》[General Principles of the Civil Law], art 110.

20 《中华人民共和国民事诉讼法》[Civil Procedure Law] (promulgated by the National People's Congress, Apr. 9, 1991 revised by the Standing Comm. National People's Congress, October 28, 2007, effective April 1, 2008) Issue No. 35 Serial No. 1250 ST. COUNCIL GAZ. (December 20, 2007).

21 Bryan A. Garner and Henry Campbell Black, *Black's Law Dictionary* (West, 9th ed, 2009) p. 1436.

22 《中华人民共和国民法通则》[General Principles of the Civil Law], art. 134.

of the Tort Law provides that the above preventive methods and remedies for tort liability may be applied individually or jointly.[23] At the same time, specific environmental laws also set forth certain forms of remedies. For example, the Water Pollution Law provides that an entity or individual damaged by water pollution may claim the cessation of infringements and compensation for the damages against the polluter. However, at present, punitive compensations are not available in pollution compensation cases.[24]

15.3 ENVIRONMENTAL ADMINISTRATIVE LIABILITIES

15.3.1 Definition

Before we discuss the administrative liabilities regarding environmental protection issues, the term 'environmental administrative offense' should be defined. Under China's legal system, an environmental administrative offense is commonly defined as illegal action carried out by administrative organs, administrative law enforcement officers and the concerned person, raised environmental pollution and damages or infringe on other types of administrative relationships.[25] Main features of an administrative offense are as follows: (1) it is an illegal action because the environmental related administrative laws or regulations are breached; (2) administrative organs, administrative law enforcement officers and the concerned persons (citizens, legal persons or other organizations) may commit the administrative offense; (3) there are two types of administrative offense: illegal actions of the administrative organs, for example, an administrative sanction without due procedure; and illegal actions of concerned persons, for example, unlawful discharge waste water or other forms of environmental pollution activities.

Environmental administrative liability is a legal obligation arising from an environmental administrative offense. According to above analysis,

---

[23] Article 15, para. 2.

[24] The establishment of punitive remedy has been discussed by scholars for years. At the same time, remedies such as 'partial injunction' (部分排除侵害) and 'Damages in lieu of injunction' (代替排除侵害之赔偿) have also been recommended by leading researchers. See, for example, Jin Ruilin, Environmental Tort and Civil Remedy – also on Problems in Environmental Legislation, *China Environmental Science*, 1997(3).

[25] Lv Zhongmei, *Environmental Law*, Law Press, 2004, pp. 160–61.

such liabilities can be divided into two categories. The first one is for liabilities for environmental related administrative organs, in most cases the local governments and local Environmental Protection Bureaus (EPBs) at different levels. The other is for liabilities imposed by environmental administrative authorities – the Ministry of Environmental Protection (MEP) and local EPBs – against violators which include citizens, legal persons or other organizations.

15.3.2 Scope of the Liability

Environmental administrative liabilities provisions are scattered throughout all the major environmental laws and the numerous administrative regulations and rules. Theoretically, such liabilities may, for both governmental bodies and individual persons, fall into two categories: punitive liabilities and remedial liabilities. For the relevant administrative organs and involved officers, punitive liabilities include public reprimand, administrative sanction and administrative penalty.[26] The scope of liability is broad and includes: make a formal apology, rehabilitate reputation, eliminate the ill impact, quash an illegal decision, warning, demerit, gross demerit, demotion, dismissal from post and expulsion, revocations of license or permit, and orders to shut down and terminate operations and so forth.[27] Some liabilities should be imposed on administrative organs and involved officers only, for example, warning, demerit and orders to stop operation or use; some liabilities, however, can be imposed on all parties, for example, issuing a public reprimand.

15.3.3 Disciplinary Sanctions

Environmental disciplinary sanction refers to administrative sanctions imposed upon the national administrative institutions and their staff or staff in enterprises or agencies authorized by national administrative institutions, for breaching laws and disciplinary rules regarding to environmental protection. Where a national administrative institution

---

26 See ibid. See also Cao Mingde et al (eds), *Environmental Resource Law*, ZhongXin Press, March 2004, 85–7. Some environmental law textbooks state that there are two main types of environmental administrative liabilities which include administrative sanction and administrative penalty. See Shi Xueying, *Environmental Law*, Tingha University Press, 2006, pp. 100–3.

27 《中华人民共和国公务员法》 [Civil Servant Law of the People's Republic of China], adopted at the 15th Session of the Standing Committee of the Tenth National People's Congress on April 27, 2005. art. 56.

violates any laws or disciplinary rules on environmental protection, the institution in question should ensure the administrative punishment is given to the head of the institution or other persons who are directly in charge of the institution, or relevant staff who violated the laws or disciplinary rules. Environmental disciplinary sanction could also be imposed on the head of the enterprise, agency or other persons directly in charge if enterprises or agencies committed the violation.

Major sources of the environmental disciplinary sanctions include various of the environmental laws of the State, the Civil Servant Law (2005); the Regulations on the Punishment of Civil Servants of Administrative Institutions, which was promulgated by the State Council in 2007; and the Interim Measures for the Punishment on the Violation of Laws and Disciplinary Rules on Environmental Protection (Interim Measures hereafter), which was jointly promulgated by the Ministry of Supervision and the former State Environmental Protection Administration (SEPA) in 2005.[28] The Interim Measures provides details for the specific application of disciplinary sanction. For example, when organizing an environmental impact assessment (EIA), if national administrative institutions or their staff colluded in deception that resulted in serious inaccuracy in the assessment, or where they fail to compile environmental impact reports and instructions according to law, or where they failed to serve planning drafts of the environmental impact reports, the persons directly in charge shall be subject to warning, record of a demerit, or record of a serious demerit; under some more severe or extreme circumstance, people who are directly in charge shall be subject to demotion or even be dismissed. The supervisory institution shall investigate and deal with the civil servants of administrative institutions who are suspected of violating laws and disciplinary rules as provided for in the Law on Administrative Supervision (as revised in 2010).

15.3.4 Administrative Penalties

Environmental administrative penalties refers to administrative liabilities that should be imposed on citizens, legal persons or other organizations for their violations of the order of environmental administration. However, in practice, a narrower concept of administrative liability is commonly accepted. That is, the term administrative environmental liability refers to the liabilities for private parties only. Or, in another word, it

28 《环境保护违法违纪行为处分暂行规定》[Interim Regulations on Punishments for Illegal Acts and Disciplinary Offences in Environmental Protection] (promulgated by the Ministry of Supervision and SEPA, February 20, 2006).

refers to the administrative penalties. Many administrative regulations and rules and all the major environmental laws contain separate penalty sections. For example, the Administrative Penalty Law[29] specifies seven types of administrative penalty, which include: (1) disciplinary warning; (2) fine; (3) confiscation of illegal gains or confiscation of unlawful property or things of value; (4) ordering the suspension of production or business; (5) temporary suspension or rescission of permit or temporary suspension or rescission of license; (6) administrative detention; and (7) others as prescribed by laws and administrative rules and regulations.[30]

Environmental administrative liabilities under major environmental laws are more specific. Take the PRC Water Pollution Prevention and Control Law for example, for a company violator, EPB may order the company to take treatment measures to eliminate pollutants within a specified period or designate a qualified company to carry out treatment or remediation work at the polluter's cost. If the correction fails to be made within the specified period, a fine of higher than RMB 10,000 and less than RMB 100,000 shall be imposed.[31] In the case of a serious water pollution event, subject to the approval by a competent people's governmental, EPB may order the polluter to shut down, impose fines on the polluter of 30 percent of the direct losses caused by the pollution event, and impose fines on individuals directly responsible for the pollution of up to 50 percent of the income the person received from the polluter for the preceding year.[32]

EPBs are the entities that are delegated with the authority to impose, or at least initiate, most of the sanctions in China's environmental laws and regulations. In 2009, MEP promulgated its most comprehensive regulation for a better implementation of environmental administrative penalties.[33] This Regulation embeds most types of administrative penalties under the Administrative Penalty Law. However, differences still exist between those provisions. Administrative penalties categorized by this regulation are: (1) a warning; (2) a fine; (3) an order to suspend production pending rectification of the violation; (4) an order to stop

---

[29] 《中华人民共和国行政处罚法》[Administrative Penalty Law] (promulgated by the National People's Congress, March 17, 1996, effective October 1, 1996).

[30] Ibid, art. 8.

[31] 《中华人民共和国水污染防治法》[PRC Water Pollution Prevention and Control Law], art. 72.

[32] Ibid., art. 83.

[33] 《环境行政处罚办法》[Environmental Administrative Penalties Regulation] (promulgated by the MEP on December 30, 2009, effective March 1, 2010).

production and close down the operations; (5) a temporary suspension or cancellation of environmental licenses or permits; (6) the confiscation of illegal property or gains; (7) administrative detention; and (8) any other types of administrative penalties provided by law.[34]

According to this regulation, administrative penalties should be imposed on polluters under certain circumstances: (1) refusal to report or make fraudulent reports on the items with respect to water pollutant discharge required to be filed and registered by the environment protection authority of the State Council; (2) failure to install automatic monitoring equipment for water pollutant discharge as required or fail to be networked with the monitoring equipment of the environmental protection authority as required and ensure the normal operation of the monitoring equipment; (3) failure to monitor the discharged industrial wastewater and preserve the original monitoring records as required.

MEP recently issued the Opinions on Regulating the Use of Discretion in Environmental Administrative Penalties.[35] These Opinions offer guidance to EPBs concerning the imposition of administrative sanctions in environmental cases. Several notable options have been reiterated in this document, which may greatly facilitate the imposition of penalties and other administrative sanctions in environmental cases.

(1) Focus on corrective action (para. 9). The Opinions note that punishment is not the ultimate objective of environmental enforcement and that special attention should be paid to the correction of existing violations and prevention of future violations. For first offenses in ordinary, non-emergency situations, the appropriate course of action is to order correction of the violation immediately or within a reasonable length of time (the 'correction within a time limit' principle). Diligent and strong follow-up inspection actions should ensure compliance with the corrective action order.
(2) Severe punishment (para. 13). Violations that are intentional, have serious consequences, impact 'sensitive' areas, and/or are committed by repeat offenders should be punished severely. The Opinions give several examples of 'intentional' or 'malicious' violations: use of secret discharge pipes; use of dilution to achieve compliance with water discharge limits; unauthorized facility construction; obstruction by facility operators of site inspections by regulatory

34 Ibid., art. 10.

35 《规范环境行政处罚自由裁量权若干意见》[Opinions Regulating the Use of Discretion in Environmental Administrative Penalties] (issued by the Ministry of Environmental Protection, February 20, 2009).

personnel; unauthorized changes to monitoring equipment; and forgery of monitoring data.

Violations with 'serious' consequences include those that lead to an interruption of drinking water supplies and/or cause serious harm to human health. Those that impact 'sensitive' areas include violations that affect drinking water source protection zones, nature reserves, scenic spots, and farmland protection areas. A 'repeat offender' is defined as an entity that commits a new violation within 12 months of being previously sanctioned.

(3) Lenient punishment (para. 14). Where a violator acts promptly to correct the violation, eliminates or mitigates the consequences of the violation, actively cooperates with the regulatory authorities to correct matters, and/or where the ecological harm caused by the violation is minor, 'lighter' punishments may be imposed.
(4) Entities Penalized (para. 15). Penalties for environmental violations can be imposed on both the enterprise committing the violation and the individuals directly responsible for the violation.
(5) Daily penalties (para. 16). Where environmental violations are of a continuous nature or a violator refuses to correct a violation within the period of time fixed by the regulators, the regulators may impose cumulative daily fines according to the duration of the unlawful act or the period during which the unlawful act fails to be corrected. This is a very significant development since the penalties in China's environmental statutes have traditionally been applied on a one-off basis.
(6) Combination of penalties with other economic sanctions (para. 19).

Where an entity is charged with a serious pollution violation, the environmental regulatory authorities should report the violation to the People's Bank of China, commercial banks and credit institutions, securities industry regulatory bodies, and/or the Securities and Futures Commission as required by the applicable regulations to prevent the approval of loans to the violating entity or access to the stock market. The Opinions reiterate existing MEP penalty policy that requires the transfer by EPBs of some specific violation situations to other agencies to handle.[36]

---

[36] See China Environmental Law Blog, *China's New Environmental Penalty Opinion*, March 27, 2009, available at: http://www.chinaenvironmentallaw.com/2009/03/27/chinas-new-environmental-penalty-opinion/.

Conditions and procedural provisions for the penalties and other sanctions are prescribed by specific administrative laws and regulations, which will discuss in the Chapter 16 ('Settlement') of this book.

15.4 ENVIRONMENTAL CRIMINAL LIABILITIES

For a long time, the Criminal Law of China did not include any provisions relating to environmental pollution and ecological damages. Gradually, some 'new' forms of crimes relating to the environment were found to be out of the control of the legislation: the absence of overarching criminal provisions relating to environmental protection resulted in a failure to respond to some new kinds of crimes. For example, in the 1980s, the environmental resources supply shortage and tempting illegal profits caused an increase in the crime rate of illegal logging and the killing of protected, rare and endangered wildlife.[37] In the meantime, in some districts, people's life and health were severely threatened by significant environmental pollution incidents. The environmental authorities realized that environmental laws and regulations of the time could not effectively deter criminals. The enactment of the Criminal Law 1997 and its eight amendments have greatly changed the landscape.

15.4.1 An Overview of Environmental Crime

Under China's legal system, there is no specific criminal environmental law or an overarching environmental law that is entitled 'environmental criminal law'. Instead, environment criminal law is a sum of the relevant legal norms concerning the protection of the natural environment and resources in the China's Criminal Law and subsidiary criminal laws.[38] China's Criminal Law 1997 expressly provides for environmental crimes

---

[37] Louis Kotze et al, *Compliance and Enforcement in Environmental law: Toward More Effective Implementation*, The IUCN Academy of Environmental Law series (Edward Elgar, 2011) 436.

[38] The only separate environmental criminal law in China's environmental legislation history was approved by the Standing Committee of the National People's Congress and was enforced in 1988 on the protection of rare and endangered wildlife, stipulating the killing of rare and endangered wildlife as a kind of crime. The separate environmental criminal law has been incorporated into the Criminal Law 1997 and abolished since the enactment of the Criminal Law 1997. See Michael G. Faure and Hao Zhang, 'Environmental Criminal Law in China: a Critical Analysis' (2011) 41(1) *Environmental Law Reporter: News & Analysis* 10024; Shizhou Wang, 'Environmental Crime and Environmental

and specific penalties. The subsidiary environmental criminal law means criminal provisions in the civil law, administrative law, and other laws and regulations. Those provisions prescribe criminal liabilities by referring to the specific provisions of the Criminal Law. The integration of China's Criminal Law 1997 and subsidiary criminal laws constitutes China's environmental criminal law. Judicial practice reflects that the combination of administrative and criminal law is a more powerful instrument combat against environmental offenses.

15.4.2 Statutory Environmental Crimes

15.4.2.1 Environmental crimes under the Criminal Law 1997

As the major source statutory environmental crimes, the Criminal Law 1997 provides that environmental pollution actions that severely damage the environment, such as dumping hazardous waste, should be charged criminal penalties. Environmental crimes under the Criminal Law 1997 are prescribed in following sections:

(1) Section VI (Articles 338–346) of the Chapter VI, which is entitled 'impairing the protection of environment and resources', it is devoted to crimes related to the obstruction of the administration of public order. If these crimes are committed, the units (including company, enterprise, institution, organ, or public organization) which committed them may be fined,[39] and the persons with direct responsibility and other personnel directly responsible for such violations are to be fined and/or imprisoned;[40]
(2) Section V of the Chapter VI, which is entitled 'crimes against public health';
(3) Section II of the Chapter III, 'crimes against smuggling' and 'crimes against the socialist market economic order'; and
(4) Chapter IX, which is entitled 'crimes of dereliction of duty'.

With a total of 15 articles of 25 charges, those provisions constitute the main body of the environmental criminal law in China. Box 15.1 below lists all relevant articles of environmental criminal law under the Criminal Law 1997.

Criminal Law in the People's Republic of China' (2004) 12(2) *European Journal of Crime, Criminal Law and Criminal Justice* 150.

[39] PRC Criminal Law 1997, art. 30.

[40] Ibid, art. 346.

BOX 15.1 OVERVIEW OF ENVIRONMENTAL CRIMES IN THE CRIMINAL LAW 1997 OF CHINA

- Crime of smuggling rare animals and rare animal products (Chapter II, Article 151, Paragraph 2);
- Crime of smuggling of rare plants and rare plant products (Chapter III, Article 151, Paragraph 3);
- Crime of smuggling waste (Chapter VI, Article 339, Paragraph 3);
- Crime of illegal transfer of land use rights (Chapter III, Article 228);
- Crime of escaping the quarantine of animals and plants (Chapter VI, Article 337);
- Crime of major pollution incident (Chapter VI, Article 338);
- Crime of illegal disposal of imported solid waste (Chapter VI, Article 339, Paragraph 1);
- Crime of unauthorized imports of solid waste (Chapter VI, Article 339, Paragraph 2);
- Crime of illegal fishing of aquatic products (Chapter VI, Paragraph 340);
- Crime of killing rare and endangered wildlife (Chapter VI, Article 341, Paragraph 1);
- Crime of illegal acquisition, transport, sale of precious and endangered species of wild animals and their products (Chapter VI, Article 341, Paragraph 1);
- Crime of illegal hunting (Chapter VI, Article 341, Paragraph 2);
- Crime of illegal occupation of arable land (Chapter VI, Article 342);
- Crime of illegal mining (Chapter VI, Article 343, Paragraph 1);
- Crime of destructive mining (Chapter VI, Article 343, Paragraph 2);
- Crime of illegal logging and the destruction of valuable trees (Chapter VI, Article 344);
- Crime of illegally chopping down trees (Chapter VI, Article 345, Paragraph 1);
- Crime of illegal denudation (Chapter VI, Article 345, Paragraph 2);
- Crime of illegal acquisition of timber through illegal logging and deforestation (Chapter VI, Article 345, Paragraph 3);
- Crime of illegal issuance of tree-cutting licenses (Chapter IX, Article 407);
- Crime of neglect of duty concerning environmental monitoring (Chapter IX, Article 408);
- Crime of illegal approval of requisition and occupation of land (Chapter IX, Article 410);
- Crime of illegal sale of use rights of state-owned land with low price (Chapter IX, Article 410);
- Crime of practicing favouritism and committing irregularities in quarantine of animals and plants (Chapter IX, Article 413, Paragraph 1);
- Crime of neglect of duty concerning quarantine of plants and animals (Chapter IX, Article 413, Paragraph 2).

15.4.2.2 Environmental crime under the environmental laws

As mentioned above, there is no overarching environmental law that is entitled 'environmental criminal law' in China. However, as the major source of subsidiary criminal law, environmental laws also play important roles in practice. These provisions do not prescribe the criminal charge, punishment or the range of penalties. Instead, they follow a similar pattern by indicating how to apply the corresponding provisions in the Criminal Law 1997.[41] Typical environmental crimes included in major environmental laws are as follows:

Article 61 of the PRC Air Pollution Prevention and Control Law: Should a serious atmospheric pollution accident occur that leads to any grave consequences of heavy public or private property losses or serious personal injuries or deaths, and if the act constitutes a crime, the criminal liability shall be investigated in accordance with the provisions of Article 338 the Criminal Law.[42]

Article 90 of the PRC Water Pollution Prevention and Control Law: Any person or entity which violates this law and thus constitutes a violation of the public security administration rules, such person or entity shall be subject to penalty under the public security administration rules. If a crime is constituted, such person or entity shall be penalized for criminal liability.[43]

Article 67 of the PRC Solid Waste Law: In violation of this law, if the competent administrative department of environmental protection under the local people's government at or above the county level or other supervisory and administrative departments of preventing and controlling environmental protection by solid waste commits any of the following acts, the people's government at the corresponding level and relevant competent administrative departments at the next higher level shall order correction and give administrative sanctions to the liable persons in charge and other directly liable persons according to law; if the situation

---

41 Generally, such provision provides that if acts are committed that constitute crimes, they should be 'investigated' and penalties therefore should be applied. One typical pattern of a criminal article under the environmental protection law stipulates that: 'acts which constitute a crime will be held criminally responsible in accordance with the Criminal Law'.

42 PRC Air Pollution Prevention and Control Law, art. 61.

43 PRC Water Pollution Prevention and Control Law, art. 90.

constitutes a crime, the concerned persons shall be investigated for criminal liabilities.[44]

While specific criminal liabilities are being considered, the law provides penalties of different severity. For example, if one engages in the acts of 'dumping, piling up, or treating within the territory of China of solid waste from abroad',[45] the penalties will be a 'fixed-term imprisonment of not more than five years[46] or criminal detention'[47] and an unspecified fine.[48]

15.4.3 Elements of Environmental Crime

The term 'elements of crime' refers to the constituent parts of a crime.[49] In order for it to be demonstrated that someone is guilty of a crime, the series of components must be present.[50] Different legal systems have different standards for the elements. Under the common law system, four key components must be present to secure a conviction: intent (*mens rea*), conduct (*actus reus*), concurrence, and causation.[51] Without one of these elements, a case can start to fall apart. China has adopted the Soviet Union's criminal law theories about the elements of crime from the 1950s; they are quite different to the common law theories. According to China's traditional criminal law theories, elements of crime also consist of four key components, namely the subject of crime; the criminal intent or guilty mind (similar to *mens rea*); the object of crime and the objective elements of crime. Although these elements are based on different standards, the essence of each element is similar to that under the common law system.

In China, both the individual offenders (with an age restriction of over 16) and unit offenders (companies, enterprise and other entities as listed in Article 30 of the Criminal Law) can be the subject of an environmental

---

44 PRC Solid Waste Law, art. 67; see also, arts 78, 83.

45 PRC Criminal Law 1997, art. 339.

46 Ibid, art. 45.

47 Ibid., art. 42.

48 Ibid., art. 52.

49 Garner and Black, note 21 above, p. 597.

50 In a criminal case, the prosecution must provide supporting evidence to demonstrate that all of the elements of a crime are present in a given case and on the contrary, the defence can challenge the validity of a case on one or more elements.

51 Charles Wellington Thomas and Donna M. Bishop, *Criminal Law: Understanding Basic Principles*, Law and criminal justice series Vol 8 (Sage Publications, 1987).

crime.[52] China's Criminal Law defines the subject of a crime as the person who is able to bear criminal responsibility for the commission of the forbidden acts stipulated. Article 30 of the Criminal Law 1997 provides that: 'a company, enterprise, institution, organ, or public organization that conducts an act harmful to society, where such an act is stipulated as a crime, shall bear criminal responsibility.' Today, most environmental crimes in China are committed by unit offenders.[53] If a company is found guilty of giving rise to serious pollution accidents or damages, both the company and persons who are directly responsible for the offense, for example, a general manager, safety manager, board director, etc., will be punished in accordance with relevant provisions. Other than the subject of a crime, other elements of crime, as we will discuss in the following paragraphs, are related to the intention, mental state and several objective factors.

Criminal intent refers to mental element, or the defendant's state of mind at the time of the offense, normally we called this term the 'guilty mind' or '*mens rea*'. Under the common law system, the term *mens rea* stems from the ancient maxim of obscure origin, '*actus reus non facit reum nisi mens sit reas*', which means 'the act is not guilty unless the mind is guilty.'[54] Generally speaking, criminal intent is always a necessary component to prove a criminal act has been committed.[55] Criminal intent of environmental crime varies depending on the offense. For environmental crime, it requires proof that the act was committed with mental elements such as knowingly or wilfulness or recklessness. Article 14 of the Criminal Law 1997 provides that 'an intentional crime' is 'a crime committed by a person who clearly knows that his act will produce socially dangerous consequences but who wishes or allows such consequences to occur.'[56] At the same time, Article 15 defines the 'negligent crime' referring to a crime committed by a person who should have foreseen that his act would possibly produce socially dangerous consequences but who fails to do so through negligence or, having foreseen the consequences, readily believes that they can be avoided, the result being

---

52 PRC Criminal Law 1997, art. 17.

53 Jin Wang, *Environmental Law*, Pekin University Press (2006), 627–32.

54 Richard J. Bonnie, *Criminal Law*, University casebook series (Foundation Press, 1997) 116.

55 See, for example, Xianping Wu, 'On the Perfecting Criminal Legislation of Environmental Crime in China' (2008) 8(5) *Journal of Kunming University of Science and Technology (Social Science and Law Ed)* 1; see also Chen Quanasheng, *Principles of Environmental Law* (Law Press, 1997) 12.

56 PRC Criminal Law 1997, art. 14, para. 1.

that these consequences do occur.[57] All the offenders of intentional crimes should bear criminal responsibilities,[58] while offenders of negligent crimes only bear criminal liabilities if the law provides so.[59]

In practice, it is not easy to differentiate the crime of an intentional crime or merely a negligent one, because not every crime is clearly expressed by the Criminal Law 1997 and its amendments as requiring criminal intent or not – although such differentiation could substantially impact the judicial result. Some environmental crime, for example, the 'illegal acquisition of timber through illegal logging and deforestation', is definitely prescribed as an intentional crime. On the other hand, debates have risen over some crimes regarding the required criminal intent. For example, no consensus has been reached among lawyers or academic researchers with respect to the role of criminal intent for the crime of the major pollution incident mentioned in Article 338 of the Criminal Law 1997.[60]

15.4.4 Liability Standards

As we noted above, four elements are frequently used as standards in deciding if an act is an environmental crime or not. However, in practice, giving rise to 'serious consequences' is a substantial requirement for many environmental crimes. Article 338 of the Criminal Law 1997 states that 'Whoever, in violation of the State provisions, discharges, dumps, or disposes of any radioactive waste, any waste containing pathogens of any infectious disease, any poisonous substance, or any other hazardous substance, which has caused serious environmental pollution', should assume criminal liabilities.[61]

---

[57] Ibid., art. 15, para. 1.

[58] Ibid., art. 14, para. 2.

[59] Ibid., art. 15, para. 2.

[60] Thomas Richter notes that the required criminal intent for Article 338 is debated, while most authors believe that Article 338 is a crime for which negligence and lower recklessness may be sufficient. See Thomas Richter, Umweltstrafrecht in der Volksrepublik China [Environmental Criminal Law in the People's Republic of China], 78–136 (2002) (dissertation). See also Michael G. Faure and Hao Zhang, 'Environmental Criminal Law in China: a Critical Analysis' (2011) 41(1) *Environmental Law Reporter: News & Analysis* 10024.

[61] PRC Criminal Law 1997, arts 338, 339. As a general principle in Chinese criminal law, if the violation of the law in question was 'clearly minor' and the 'harm is not severe', the act will not be deemed a crime. Ibid., art. 13. Chinese criminal law also contains a *mens rea* requirement. Ibid., arts 14, 15.

On July 28, 2006, the Supreme People's Court (SPC) issued a Judicial Interpretation[62] that sets a relatively low threshold for the application of Articles 338 and 339 in the case of 'major environmental pollution accidents.' The Judicial Interpretation provided detailed consequences of different severity.

(1) Serious consequences of heavy losses of private or public property. As defined, those kind of serious consequences include:[63]
   - private or public property losses not less than 300 000 RMB (approximately US$45 000);[64]
   - the permanent destruction or loss of use of not less than 5 Mu[65] basic farm or forest land or not less than 20 Mu of other land; or
   - the death of not less than 40 cubic meters of forest lands, or the death of not fewer than 250 young trees.

(2) 'Serious consequences of personal injuries or harm to human health' include:[66]
   - the death of one or more people;
   - serious injury of not fewer than three people; or
   - 'light wounds' to not fewer than ten people.

(3) 'Extremely serious' consequences that increase the range of applicable prison terms include:
   - private or public property losses of not less than 1 000 000 RMB (approximately US$ 150 000);
   - the permanent destruction or loss of use of not less than 15 Mu of basic farm or forest land or not less than 60 Mu of other land; or
   - the death of not less than three people, or serious injury of not less than ten people, or the 'light wounding' of not less than 30 people;

---

62 《最高人民法院关于审理环境污染刑事案件具体运用若干法律问题的解释》 [Supreme People's Court Interpretation of the Trial of Criminal Cases of Environmental Pollution] (released by the Supreme People's Court on July 21, 2006, effective July 28, 2006).

63 Ibid., art. 1.

64 Article 4 of the Environmental Crime Judicial Interpretation clarifies that these losses 'include actual losses due to the destruction or damage of property directly resulting from environment pollution and any reasonable expenses incurred which are necessary to prevent the spread of pollution or clean the pollution'.

65 Mu is a unit of area, 1 mu≈0.164 acres.

66 Environmental Crime Judicial Interpretation, Art 2.

- giving rise to the pollution of water or evacuation of people that can be characterized as an environment pollution accident at Level II or above in the National Plan for Handling Urgent Environment Pollution Accidents.[67]

15.5 CONCLUDING REMARKS

After several years' development, China's environmental legislation has formed a strong base and is now actively developing effective implementation strategies.[68] Over last 30 years, a relatively mature environmental liability system has been established in China. Three main forms of environmental liabilities – civil liabilities, administrative liabilities and criminal liabilities have received significant progresses during China's long march towards 'rule of law'. The enactment of the Tort Law of China has greatly enhanced the legislative bases of civil environmental liabilities. It is foreseeable that those innovative provisions will greatly change the ecosystem of environmental litigation and civil liability research in China.

Another progress that has been achieved is that the enforcement of liability has been strengthened. In recent years, prosecutors have become more active in environmental related crimes and become more creative in the claims they pursue. Generally speaking, criminal sanctions have not traditionally been imposed in pollution accidents with small social economic impacts. However, this situation changed in recent years. As evidence shows, between 1997 and 2003, of the 387 pollution accidents that would have constituted an environmental crime, only 20 involved criminal prosecutions. However, in 2006, the People's Procuratorate initiated 12 240 prosecutions for environmental pollution, illegal mining,

67 《国家突发环境事件应急预案》[National Plan for Handling Urgent Environment Pollution Accidents] (promulgated by the Central Office of the State Environmental Protection Agency January 24, 2006). According to the Plan, environment pollution accidents at Level II include: (1) the death of no less than 10 but no more than 30 people, or the serious injury of not less than 50 but no more than 100 people; (2) the evacuation of not less than 10 000 people but no more than 50 000; or (3) the pollution of a major river or lake or the cut-off of the water supply in a city above the county level.

68 Wang, see note 53 above, p. 27.

and other environmental crimes[69] and filed 53 745 cases in 2007.[70] The pace of criminal prosecution has considerably quickened.

However, China is still facing challenges in terms of environmental law enforcement. As Professor Wang Canfa noted, many relevant issues remain unresolved and require urgent attention.[71] Where the problems of environmental law enforcement in China were concerned, Professor Wang gave the following reasons: (1) problems with implementation; (2) superficial enforcement of environmental mechanisms; (3) lax investigation and delayed punishment of illegal activities; (4) unavailability of adequate compensation for pollution victims; (5) environmental violators often receiving administrative punishments instead of criminal penalties; (6) the lack of authority within relevant environmental protection administrations.[72] Essentially, all those problems are related to the environmental liability issues. What reason (1) reveals is the weak implementation, or at least an inconsistent practice of criminal liability. For example, as we noted above, when a large and well-publicized pollution accident occurs, officials of the facility should be criminally prosecuted. However, the company officials at the facility that caused the notorious Songhua River spill in 2005 seem to have escaped criminal liability.[73]

Therefore, in order to overcome current deficiencies, reforms of environmental law particularly environmental liability regimes should never be allowed to slow down.

---

69 《最高人民检察院工作报告》 [Supreme People's Procuratorate Work Report], March 13, 2007, available at http:/ /www.spp.gov.cn/site200612008-03-14/0001817297.html.

70 《最高人民检察院工作报告》 [Supreme People's Procuratorate Work Report], March 10, 2008, available at http://www.spp.gov.cn/site2006/2008-06-05/0001818747.html.

71 Wang Canfa, 'Chinese Environmental Law Enforcement: Current deficiencies and suggested reforms' (2007) 8(2) *Vermont Journal of Environmental Law* 59.

72 Ibid.

73 For more information about this case, see UNEP, Songhua River Spill, China – Field Mission Report, December 2005. Available at: http://www.unep.org/PDF/China_Songhua_River_Spill_draft_7_301205.pdf.

16. Environmental dispute settlement in China

Zhao Xiaobo and Zhang Jianwei

16.1 INTRODUCTION

Environmental disputes refer to disputes caused by infringement of environmental related rights and the distribution of environmental obligations. Among others, the main reasons for environmental disputes include environmental pollution or the infringement of property rights and ownership in connection with natural resources.

In China, environmental disputes may arise between different parties with quite different contexts: (1) disputes between polluters and the victims of environmental pollution; (2) disputes among the regulated community; and (3) disputes with the environmental protection authorities and between members of the public and the government. These types of disputes can be solved or settled by different means jointly or respectively, which primarily include environmental litigation and Alternative Disputes Resolution (ADR).

Environmental litigation, under China's current legal system, is a trifold judicial method that includes civil litigation, administrative litigation and criminal litigation. Environmental ADR refers to ways of settling disputes other than through the court: the most common of which are by mediation and arbitration. However, with the impact of China's specific social and culture traditions, mediation in China is often through court mediation, people's mediation and administrative mediation. This regime is quite different to mediation in other jurisdictions. In addition, another frequently used environmental ADR is the use of so-called 'letters and visits', which has been used for over 50 years in China and has proved an effective way of environmental dispute settlement.

Concomitant with the rapid economic growth and deteriorating environmental problems, environmental disputes have dramatically increased in the past decades in China. On the one hand, there has been substantial growth in the number of environmental civil actions in China in the last ten years.[1] The number of environmental lawsuits filed with the courts has had an average annual increase rate of 25 percent since 1998.[2] In recent years, more than 100 000 applications for environmental lawsuits were filed in the people's court every year.[3] On the other hand, statistics reveal that environmental disputes that end with the environmental protection authorities in the form of 'letters and visits' in China has continuously increased over the past two decades.[4] Leading researchers have also pointed out that the number of environmental cases is expected to rise as China's economy grows.[5] These trends suggested a growing environmental awareness of the general public, which has resulted in a dramatic growth in reported environmental disputes.[6] More importantly, they reflect the growing challenges faced by courts and environmental administrative departments involving the environmental dispute resolutions in China.

This chapter introduces legal frameworks of environmental dispute resolutions in China and primarily examines the methods for resolving disputes between polluters and victims of pollution. First, it introduces the environmental court as a foundation of environmental litigation in China; it then discusses the role of environmental litigation with an aim to assessing the effectiveness of this in resolving disputes. The main features of civil acts, administrative acts and criminal litigation are examined in this section. After that, there is a brief look at the environmental ADRs, the role of mediation, including people's mediation, administrative mediation and judicial mediation, examined in the

---

[1] The number of decided civil lawsuits in 2009 is nearly four times those of 1981; the courts received over 8.8 million applications for civil and administrative lawsuits in 2009. Supreme People's Court 2009 Annual Report to China's National People's Congress, (March 11, 2010).

[2] Tun Lin, Canfa Wang et al, "Green Benches: What can the People's Republic of China Learn from Environment Courts of Other Countries?", *Asian Development Bank*, 5, (2009).

[3] Adam Moser, Esq and Professor Tseming Yang, *Environmental Tort Litigation in China*, May 5, 2010.

[4] The number increased from 114 982 in 1996, 268 592 in 1999, 309 800 in 2000, 447 731 in 2001, to 525 766 in 2002. Ministry of Environmental Protection (former State Environmental Protection Administration, SEPA) has published the National Environmental Statistics Gazette since 1985.

[5] If it continues to rise at the current rate of 25 percent per annum, the number of first-instance environmental cases will increase 2.4 times in five years and 7.4 times in ten years. See Tun Lin, Canfa Wang et al, above note 2.

[6] SEPA, National Survey Report on Public Environmental Awareness (China Environmental Science Press, 1999).

context of environmental disputes settlement. This is followed by analysis to the 'letters and visits', which is one of most frequently used environmental dispute settlement methods. It concludes with suggestions for a more effective and equitable dispute settlement mechanism in China.

16.2 ENVIRONMENTAL COURTS IN CHINA

16.2.1 Court Structure and Hierarchy

Courts are the most significant place for disputes settlement. In China, the People's Courts are the judicial organs of the State, which can exercise judicial power independently, in accordance with the provisions of the law, and are not subject to interference by any administrative organ, public organization or individual.[7] As the highest judicial organ of the state, the Supreme People's Court is directly responsible to the National People's Congress (NPC) and its Standing Committee. Local people's courts (LPC) at various levels are responsible to the organs of state power, which created them.[8] There are three levels of LPCs: the Higher People's Courts are established at provincial level, the Intermediate People's Courts at a prefecture level, and the Basic People's Courts at a county level.

Beyond this three-level system, there are several special courts, which include the military courts, the maritime courts, the railway transport courts, the forestry courts and the agricultural reclamation courts.[9] Special courts are established to meet the needs of sectoral or professional enterprises, whereas local people's courts were established in line with the geographical area of the administrative jurisdictions of the local people's governments.[10] All these courts have played important roles in resolving environmental cases. For example, the maritime courts are responsible for commercial and civil cases dealing with marine business relating to coastal waters and watercourses that flow into the sea. The

---

[7] PRC Constitution Law, arts 123, 126.

[8] Ibid., art. 128.

[9] 《中华人民共和国法院组织法》 [Organic Law of the People's Republic Courts] (promulgated by National People's Congress, July 1, 1979, last revised by the Standing Commission of National People's Congress, October 31, 2006), art. 12.

[10] Louis Kotze et al, *Compliance and Enforcement in Environmental law: Toward More Effective Implementation*, The IUCN Academy of Environmental Law series (Edward Elgar, 2011) 423.

forestry courts may deal with civil, administrative and criminal matters relating to the harvesting, use and conservation of forests and forest products. The railway transport courts are also involved in environmental matters. Most cases dealt by the railway courts are related to noise nuisance emanating from railways. The military courts are empowered to resolve only criminal cases linked with the activities of members or entities of the People's Liberation Army. In the context of environmental protection issues, the military courts can deal with criminal cases related to activities directed to the compliance with and enforcement of the Regulations Regarding Environment Protection of the Chinese People's Liberation Army (1990).[11]

16.2.2 Creation of the Environmental Courts

There have been numerous attempts to create environmental courts in China. In 1988, an environmental tribunal was established in Qiaokou District, Wuhan City. Unfortunately, it was soon cancelled because it was declared that it lacked legitimacy and violated the institutional rules of the Organic Law of the People's Republic Courts 1983.[12] After more than 20 years of silence, special environmental courts have gradually been established in China since 2007. So far, environmental court divisions have been established in more than 12 cities within the structure of the People's Court system.[13] Major environmental courts created in China during April 2002 to May 2010 have been listed as follows.

- The Environmental Protection Tribunal of the People's Court of Dongling District of Shenyang, Liaoning Province (April, 2002);
- The Circuit Court of the People's Court of Shahekou District of Shenyang, Liaoning Province (April, 2004);
- The Environmental Protection Court of Jizhou Municipality of Shijiazhuang, Hebei (2004);

---

[11] 《中国人民解放军环境保护条例》 [The Regulations Regarding Environment Protection of the Chinese People's Liberation Army], promulgated by the Central Military Commission of the People's Republic of China, July 10, 1990; revised in 2004. So far, a very limited number of environmental cases in the military sector have been reported in China.

[12] Kotze et al, note 10 above, 423.

[13] For example, environmental court divisions exist at the Intermediate People's Courts of Guiyang, Guizhou Province, Wuxi, Jiangsu Province, and Kunming, Yunnan Province.

- The Circuit Court of Environmental Protection of Shiping County of Liaocheng, Shandong Province (2006);
- The Environmental Protection Court of the People's Court of Tiexi District, Shenyang, Liaoning Province (June, 2006);
- The Environmental Protection Trial Court of the Intermediate Court of Guiyang, Guizhou Province and the Environmental Protection Court of the Court of Qingzhen Municipality under its jurisdiction (November, 2007);
- The Circuit Court of Environmental Protection of Jianye District, Nanjing, Jiangsu (February, 2008);
- The Environmental Protection Tribunal of the Intermediate Court of Wuxi Municipality (May, 2008);
- The Circuit Court of the People's Court of Xinbei District, Changzhou, Jiangsu Province (August, 2008);
- Trial Division of Environmental Protection of the Intermediate People's Court of Kunming Municipality, Yunnan Province (November, 2008);
- The E.P. Tribunal of Shangma Court of Chengyang District of Qingdao in Shandong Province (April, 2010);
- The Tribunal on Ecology and Resources at the Intermediate Court of Zhangzhou Municipality in Fujian Province (May, 2010).

The powers of these special courts varies depending on the jurisdiction where they have been established. Generally, they are responsible for all civil and administrative cases and even criminal cases involving environmental protection.[14] In some cases, the courts can break down existing local court divisions and they can enforce their own judgments rather than having to resort to the enforcement division of the court.[15]

16.2.3 Reasons for Creating Environment Courts

The primary reason for the creation of environmental courts is to resolve the increasing load of environmental disputes in China. The traditional

---

[14] Some jurisdictions have established environmental crime teams. For example, in Kunming, Yunnan Province, a 60-strong police force has been formed under the municipal public security bureau. It is responsible for dealing with criminal acts in environmental pollution within the city, as well as assisting the environment bureau with administrative law enforcement. See 'Green' Crime Team Formed, *China Daily*, November 28, 2008.

[15] Environmental Protection Courts: Incubator of Environmental Public Interest Litigation or Just a Decoration?, *Greenlaw*, October 5, 2008.

court system seems to be incapable of dealing with the explosion of environmental cases in recent years.[16] Secondly, a trial for environmental cases is highly professional work; judges getting involved in environmental cases require specialized knowledge. Although short-term training may help judges in acquiring such knowledge, in the long run it is not practical to train all of them. New judges being recruited for the environmental court should, generally speaking, have knowledge of environmental law. This may prepare teams of highly specialized judges prepared to meet the technical demands of adjudicating environmental cases. Thirdly, the environmental pollution cases are often disciplinary issues which involve law, environmental science and other subjects, therefore, special agencies may facilitate the coordination of those issues.

16.2.4 Problems of the Existing Environment Courts

Despite the dire need, the development of environment courts in China has been slow. The current state of the PRC's environment courts reveals a variety of problems, such as a lack of responsible organizations, professional expertise, and constructive policies. Leading research carried out by the Asian Development Bank in 2009 showed that the development of China's environment courts are confronting major challenges.[17]

First, the number of environment courts is still limited. Debates about the question for or against establishing special environmental courts are continuing in China. Therefore, to some extent, existing environmental courts are only experimental projects; the total number of environmental courts is very small compared with ordinary courts. Second, judges have hardly received any training in environmental laws so they can refuse to accept environmental cases or make inconsistent decisions. Third, there is insufficient training of most judges in environmental law. Fourth, the lack of a driving force for some victims to file cases in the environmental courts. The survey of 2009 showed that most victims still preferred solving problems via non-litigious means, such as reaching an agreement in private or turning to a third party such as the media, administrative agencies, or higher authorities.[18] Fifth, most courts are reluctant to accept environmental cases. A deeper reason for this phenomenon is the possibility that environmental cases will be influenced by outside forces,

---

16 Ibid.

17 See Tun Lin, Canfa Wang et al, note 2 above.

18 Survey carried by China University of Political Science and Law (CUPL), see also Tun Lin, Canfa Wang *et al*, ibid.

particularly class suits with a potentially serious impact on major enterprises. Administrative intercession is therefore preferred over litigation. Sixth, there are inconsistencies in environmental judgments. This is a common problem not only faced by the environmental courts in China. Inconsistency tends to occur between juridical and administrative agencies. Finally, difficulties in compliance with the courts' enforcement has long been a problem in China, and this is also faces the environmental courts. Furthermore, regional protectionism has been thought to be a primary reason.

16.3 ENVIRONMENTAL CIVIL ACTIONS

16.3.1 Overview

Generally speaking, Article 124 of the Civil Law of the People's Republic of China (General Principle hereafter) and the Article 58 of the 2014 Environmental Protection Law created the legal basis of civil litigation for environmental cases. Article 124 of the General Principles states that: 'Any person who pollutes the environment and causes damages to others in violation of state provisions for environmental protection and the prevention of pollution shall bear civil liability in accordance with the law.' At the same time, the newly revised Environmental Protection Law introduced public interest litigation, which is an important environmental civil action in China. We will discuss it in section 16.3.4 of this chapter.

16.3.2 Burden of Proof

As a well-established general rule of law, an actor must prove the facts on which he relies in support of his claim – *actori incumbit probation*. But this maxim cannot be applied in environmental pollution disputes for several reasons. One main concern is the disparity in the capacity between the plaintiff and defendant in the context of environmental pollutions cases. Generally speaking, it is too difficult for an individual plaintiff to prove what he claims; and, in most cases, the connection between the environmental pollution and damage it causes is extremely complicated. Therefore, the connection between defendant's acts and the damage can only be clarified with highly organized scientific experiments and professional analyses.

As a result, the reversal of the burden of proof for environmental pollution cases has been provided for by several environmental laws and civil procedure laws. For example, both the PRC Water Pollution Prevention and Control Law[19] and the PRC Solid Waste Law[20] specifically place the burden of proof on the defendant to demonstrate that there is no causal connection between its acts and the damage claimed by the plaintiff. At the same time, the Supreme People's Court (SPC) has issued several judicial interpretations that confirm this burden allocation principle. For example, the Several Provisions on the Evidence in Civil Litigation[21] provides that the burden of proof in environmental damage compensation claims should be borne by the discharger of the pollutants. The defendant is obligated to show that there are no statutory defences and prove that there is no causation between its act and the damages suffered by the claimant. In addition, this principle has also been confirmed by the Supreme People's Court's Judicial Interpretation on Several Problems in the Applicability of the Civil Procedure Law, under which it reaffirmed that the defendant has the burden of disproving any of the plaintiff's claims that it disputes.[22] Article 74 of the interpretation provides that: 'in lawsuits each party has liability to provide proof of what he/she claims for, except for in the following lawsuits where the defendant bears the burden of proof of the tort fact that the plaintiff lodges but he/she denies … (c) lawsuit for damages by environmental pollution.'[23]

16.3.3 Damages and Causality

There are two main features for compensable damages in China. First, punitive damages have not been a feature of Chinese civil litigation. Although they are permitted in certain situations under the Tort Law,[24]

---

19 《中华人民共和国水污染防治法》[PRC Water Pollution Prevention and Control Law], art. 86.

20 《中华人民共和国固体废物污染环境防治法》[PRC Solid Waste Law], art. 87.

21 《最高人民法院关于民事诉讼证据的若干规定》[Several Provisions on Evidence in Civil Litigation] (promulgated by the Supreme People's Court, December 21, 2001, effective April 1, 2002), art. 4.

22 《最高人民法院关于适用<中华人民共和国民事诉讼法>若干问题的意见》[Supreme People's Court's Judicial Interpretation on Several Problems in the Application of the Civil Procedure Law of the People's Republic of China] (promulgated by the Supreme People's Court, July 14, 1992, effective July 14, 1992).

23 Ibid., art. 74.

24 《中华人民共和国侵权法》[The Tort Law of the People's Republic of China], art. 47.

they are not specifically mentioned in the sections relating to environmental pollution responsibility. Generally, claims for damages to crops, animal husbandry, health and loss of income would have been supported by most courts in practice.[25] However, claims for losses relating to animals and human health injuries were not usually supported by the court because they were not technically feasible to prove. Another fact is that for a long time damages awards were relatively small in civil actions, and were, therefore, inadequate to deter future pollution. The newly revised Environmental Protection Law (2014) may change this situation. Article 59 of the law introduces the Continuing Daily Penalty mechanism. It states that companies, units, other producers or operators who illegally discharge pollutants, should be fined and an order for correction should be issued. Offenders refusing to make improvements should pay for the accumulated fine based on a daily calculation. The amount of the fine should be determined on the basis of the costs for operating the pollution prevention facilities, the direct economic losses, or illegal profits from the illegal acts.[26]

Causation is a fundamental issue in deciding an environmental case. Causation basically refers to the causal connection between act and damage under a tort claim. According to the traditional tort law theory, the following tests are thought to be essential for the establishment of causation: the act of the respondent is a tort; the defendant's act is the cause de facto of the harmful consequences; the defendant's act is the legal cause of the damage.[27] For environmental cases, the Tort Law shifts the burden of proof from plaintiff to defendant.[28]

---

[25] However, it is difficult to find out a technical method to measure the actual damages in practice. For example, in the case of *Four Villages of Datong County of Qinghai Province v The Cement Manufactory of Qinghai Province* (damage to property and health arising from dust pollution), the plaintiff had endured dust pollution from the defendant for almost ten years and spent huge amount on medical expenses. In this case, the court used scientific reports and expert laboratory results as its reference in measuring the plaintiff's loss in crops and animal husbandry, and upheld the plaintiff's crop loss claim. See Zhang Kunmin (ed), *Handbooks of China's Environmental Law Enforcement* (Beijing: Publishing House of China University of Law and Politics, (1993), 411.

[26] Environmental Protection Law (2014), art. 59.

[27] See Chen Congfu, Legal Causation in Tort Acts, A Collection of Legal Studies in National Taiwan University, 29(2): 191–2, 2000.

[28] 《中华人民共和国侵权责任法》 [The Tort Law of the People's Republic of China], art. 66.

16.3.4 Joint Actions (Collective Actions)

China's Civil Procedure Law has provided for joint actions,[29] by which the court can handle the claims of two or more people with common litigation objects in one case. The joint action refers to one party who is named to represent the interest of the joint claimants with the authority to bind the joint group.

Although the 2014 Environmental Protection Law provides for environmental interest litigation, it offers no further interpretation about this scheme; although scheme has been confirmed by a number of local environmental regulations.[30] As a result, a study of these local regulations may deepen our understanding of the environmental public interests litigation. For example, in 2009, the Wuxi Municipal Intermediate People's Court of Jiangsu Province and the Wuxi Municipal People's Procuratorate of Jiangsu Province jointly promulgated the Regulations on the Handling of Civil Environmental Public Interest Litigation Cases (for Trial Implementation).[31] Article 2 of this Regulation provides that 'civil environmental public interest litigation' as referred to in these regulations refers to litigation activities implemented by people's courts and people's procuratorates in accordance with their functions and division of work and by such methods as handling and supporting lawsuits, supervising and prompting lawsuits, and bringing civil public interest litigation cases to deter and curb unlawful actions that infringe on the environmental public interest and protect the public's environmental interests.[32]

According to this Regulation, when people's courts and people's procuratorates are handling the civil environmental public interest litigation cases, they should adhere to following principles: (1) the necessity principle. When handling civil environmental public interest litigation cases, rigorous analysis and argument must be conducted to make sure that the lawsuit is indeed necessary, the claims are well founded, and adjudication is indeed feasible. (2) the legality principle. In civil environmental public interest litigation cases, the provisions of the relevant

---

[29] 《中华人民共和国民事诉讼法》 [PRC Civil Procedure Law], arts 53–55.

[30] For example, the Wuxi City, Jiangsu Province, and the Kunming City, Yunnan Province.

[31] *Regulations on the Handling of Civil Environmental Public Interest Litigation Cases (for Trial Implementation)* [Xi jian hui (2008) no.2], promulgated by the Wuxi Municipal Intermediate People's Court of Jiangsu province and the Wuxi Municipal People's Procuratorate of Jiangsu province, November 2008.

[32] Ibid, art. 2.

procedural laws and substantive laws must be strictly observed and responsibilities are to be fulfilled by law. (3) the exceptionality principle. In the initiation of civil environmental public interest litigation procedures, the litigation status of people's procuratorates is different from that of ordinary civil litigation plaintiffs, and special adjudication procedures different from those of ordinary civil litigation procedures applying to people's courts.

Before 2006, joint actions were rarely used in environmental litigation.[33] However in recent years there has been a trend for them becoming more frequent. Other than the Civil Procedure Law, the PRC Water Pollution Prevention and Control Law has specifically provided for joint actions.[34]

16.3.5 Defences

There may be occasions where statutory provisions can be used as a defence that may absolve the discharging entity of liability. Provisions about defences can be found in environmental laws and the civil laws. For example, Article 63 of the PRC Air Pollution Prevention and Control Law and Article 85 of the PRC Water Pollution Prevention and Control Law have force majeure provisions. In water pollution cases, if the injured party intentionally caused the 'water pollution harm', it shall not recover; if it negligently caused the harm, its damages are to be reduced. Moreover, if the water pollution harm was caused by the acts of the third party, the discharging party has the right to recover damages from the third party, after compensating the victims. The Tort Law also prescribes that polluter bears no liability if the pollution is caused by a force majeure event, and if the polluter took reasonable measures to avoid such pollution.[35] Defences under the Tort Law are as follows: (1) the polluter's liabilities may be mitigated if the victim is at fault; (2) if the pollution is caused by the victim's wilful conduct, the polluter bears no liability; (3) if the pollution is caused by a third party, the entity or individual damaged by the pollution may claim damages against either the polluter

---

33 《中华全国律师协会关于律师办理群体性案件指导意见》[Guiding Opinion on Handling Mass Cases] (issued by the China All Lawyers' Association, March 20, 2006, effective April 27, 2006).

34 《中华人民共和国水污染防治法》[PRC Water Pollution Prevention and Control Law], art. 88.

35 《中华人民共和国侵权法》[The Tort Law of the People's Republic of China].

or the third party; (4) if the polluter pays for the damages, it can seek indemnification from the third party.[36]

16.4 ENVIRONMENTAL ADMINISTRATIVE ACTIONS

Environmental administrative actions consist of the significant part of environmental administrative enforcement, the purpose of which is to secure the implementation of environmental laws by EPBs. There are basically two types of environmental administrative actions: environmental administrative review (or reconsideration) and the environmental administrative litigation. The main contents of environmental administrative actions include actions towards the issue of environmental administrative order; the imposing of environmental administrative punishment; the management of environmental administrative licensing; and the execution of coercive enforcement.

16.4.1 Environmental Administrative Review

Administrative review is also called administrative reconsideration in China.[37] Citizens, legal persons and other organizations who believe a concrete administrative action has been infringed, or is infringing, their legal rights and interests may apply for administrative review of an administrative organ.[38] As a supervision regime initiated by the administrative counterparts, environmental administrative review corrects the internal mistakes made in environmental administrative law enforcement through the internal examination of the administrative organs involved. The goal of environmental administrative review is to avoid illegal or inappropriate performance of environmental administrative organs and their staff.

The following laws and regulations set the legal foundations for the environmental administrative review. The NPC enacted the Administrative Review Law in 1999. In 2007 the State Council promulgated the Regulation on the Implementation of the Administrative Review Law. In order to direct the application of this regulation, the Ministry of Environmental Protection (MEP) promulgated the Measures for Environmental Administrative Review in 2008. The scope, time limit, conditions and

---

[36] Ibid., art. 68.

[37] He Haibo, English Translation of "Some Key Words in China's Administrative Law", *Administrative Law Review*, 2011(3) 18.

[38] 《中华人民共和国行政复议法》 [The Administrative Review Law] (1999), art. 2.

examination methods for reviews have been provided by these laws and regulations.

An important feature of the administrative actions against the government in China is that scope of administrative review has been strictly restrained. There are 11 categories of 'concrete administrative actions' under the Administrative Review Law (1999).[39] Five of those categories can be applied for administrative review in the context of environmental cases being involved, which include: (1) administrative penalties (sometimes also referred as sanctions), such as warnings, fines, confiscation of illegal gains or property, orders to suspend production or business, suspension or rescission of license or permit, administrative detention and other forms of administrative penalties; (2) compulsory administrative measures, such as restriction of personal freedom or the sealing up, seizing or freezing of property; (3) an administrative decision of altering, suspending or discharging certificates, such as a license, permit, credit certificate, credential; (4) an administrative decision confirming ownership or right to use of natural resources, such as land, mineral resources, rivers, forests, mountains, grasslands, un-reclaimed land, beaches, maritime waters; and (5) situations in which citizens, legal persons or other organizations believe that their legal rights were infringed by administrative decisions, including situations in which administrative organs infringed the legal rights of independently operated businesses; changing or cancelling agricultural leasing contracts; illegal collection of funds, the taking of properties, imposing fees or illegally requiring the performance of duties by administrative organs; illegally refusing to issue permits, licences, and other certifications which administrative organs should issue according to the law; non-performance by administrative organs in the protection of personal rights, property rights and the right to receive education; and other situations.[40]

The following key issues relating to environmental administrative review have been addressed by the relevant laws and regulations.

(1) Time Limits of the Application. Article 9 of the Administrative Review Law sets up a time limit for the application for administrative review, this restriction will be automatically applied in environmental administrative review cases.[41] Claims must be filed within 60 days from the date that the applicant knew of the complained of

[39] Ibid., art. 6.
[40] Ibid., art 6, paras 1–5.
[41] Ibid., art. 9, para. 1.

concrete administrative action. However, there are exceptions to this time period, for example, where a different period has been specifically prescribed by trade or other laws.

(2) Administrative Review Institutions. According to the Regulation on the Implementation of the Administrative Review Law and Measures for Environmental Administrative Review, this can occur where a citizen, legal person or any other organization believes that a specific administrative act of the local EPBs has impaired their legitimate rights and interests. An application could therefore be submitted to the people's government at the same level or higher for administrative review. If they believe that a specific administrative act of the State EPBs impairs their legitimate rights and interests, they may apply to the State EPBs for administrative reconsideration.[42] However, a reviewing application for a decision of a government department at or above county level should be made to the government department at one level higher, while a decision of the State Council or provincial government should be petitioned to the department of the State Council against which the complaint was made or to the government of the province, respectively.[43]

(3) Respondents. If the administrative counterpart refuses to accept a specific administrative act made by EPBs and applies for administrative review, the department that made the specific administrative act shall be the respondent. If a specific administrative act is made jointly by EPBs and other organization(s) or relevant departments as authorized by any law or regulation, departments involved shall be co-respondents. If a specific administrative act is jointly made by the SEPA and other organization(s), the environmental protection administrative department shall be the respondent. In addition, in cases where the subordinate department, internal body, or any other organization established by EPBs, makes a specific administrative act in its own name, without authorization of any law or regulation, the EPB shall be the respondent.

(4) Fees and Expenses. No fees should be charged by the environmental administrative review organ from any applicant. The necessary expenses for administrative review should be included in the institution's operational fees and be guaranteed by the financial department at the same level.

---

42 Ibid., art. 13.

43 Ibid., art. 14.

(5) Possible results. Results of the administrative review may include: maintaining the decisions made by the lower administrative organs; ordering the performance of the legal responsibility by the non-action administrative organ within a prescribed deadline; cancelling or changing the reviewed decision, or declaring it illegal and ordering the lower administrative organ to make a decision again.[44]

16.4.2 Environmental Administrative Litigation

Environmental administrative litigation could be brought to the court if a citizen, a legal person or other organization thought their lawful rights and interests were infringed by a specific administrative act of administrative organs. If the administrative review is an 'internal review', environmental administrative litigation is a way of judicial review, the purpose of which is to correct mistakes made in environmental administrative law enforcement through a litigation procedure. The following laws constitute the legal basis of an environmental administrative litigation, including: the Administrative Litigation Law (1989),[45] the Administrative Punishment Law (1996),[46] the Administrative Review Law (1999) and the Administrative Compulsion Law (2011).[47]

(1) Standing: who can sue? According to the Article 2 of the Administrative Procedure Law, citizens, legal persons, or organizations have the right to litigate in accordance with the law when they consider that their lawful rights and interests have been infringed upon by a specific administrative act. As the standing to sue has been considered, the law prescribes four conditions that must be met to successfully file for an administrative litigation. These are: (1) the

---

[44] An administrative decisions could be cancelled or changed or be declared illegal under following circumstances: (1) the main facts are unclear and lack evidence; (2) mistakes have been made in the application of the legal basis; (3) procedures prescribed by law have been violated; (4) an abuse of power has occurred; and (5) improper concrete administrative actions have been taken. Ibid., art. 28.

[45] 《中华人民共和国行政诉讼法》[Administrative Litigation Law] (1989) (promulgated by National People's Congress, April 4, 1989, effective October 1, 1990), Art 53.

[46] 《中华人民共和国行政处罚法》[Administrative Punishment Law (1996)].

[47] 《中华人民共和国行政强制法》[Administrative Compulsion Law of the People's Republic of China] (2011), adopted at the 21st meeting of the Standing Committee of the 11th National People's Congress of the People's Republic of China, June 30, 2011, into force on January 1, 2012.

plaintiff (a citizen, legal person or other organization) believes that their legal rights or interests were infringed by a concrete administrative action; (2) there must be a specific defendant; (3) specific requests and factual basis must be detailed; and (4) the case must be within the scope of administrative litigation and the jurisdiction of the court which hears the case.[48]

In addition, if these disagree with the decision after administrative review, they have the right to file an administrative litigation in a court according to law, except those cases in which the decisions of administrative review are prescribed as final findings by law.[49]

(2) Acceptance of environmental administrative litigation. Administrative lawsuits should be filed in the people's courts covering the jurisdiction in which the administrative unit issuing the original decision or administrative reconsideration decision is located.[50] The Administrative Litigation Law (1989) requires the courts to provide correct and timely decisions in administrative litigation. The law prescribes that citizens, legal persons or other organizations have the right to file litigation against a concrete administrative action of administrative organs, if they believe that the concrete action infringes their legal rights or interests.[51] The reviewing court must review the legitimacy of the concrete administrative actions.[52] There are two levels of trials. The second level of trial is the final level of trial of an administrative litigation.[53] Parties of an administrative litigation have the right to appeal the decision to a lower court or the court of higher level if they believe an effective judgment or finding violated the law.[54] In addition, the people's procuratorate have the right to counterplea an effective judgment or finding of the court if they believe the court's decision violates the law.[55]

(3) Scope of environmental administrative litigation. The Administrative Litigation Law (1999) has narrowed the scope of administrative litigation within eight categories of concrete administrative actions

48 The Administrative Litigation Law (1989), art. 41.
49 The Administrative Review Law (1999), art. 5.
50 The Administrative Litigation Law (1989), art. 17.
51 Ibid., art. 2.
52 Ibid., art. 5.
53 Ibid., art. 6.
54 Ibid., art. 62.
55 Ibid., art. 64.

or situations which include: (a) administrative decisions on administrative detention, fines, cancellation of permits or licences, suspending production or business, and confiscating property; (b) administrative decisions on limiting personal freedom, sealing up or seizing or freezing property; (c) administrative decisions deemed to have infringed the rights of independently operated businesses; (d) administrative decisions on re/using to issue a permit or licence or an administrative organ which does not reply to an application for a permit or licence; (e) administrative decisions on refusing to provide protection for personal rights or property rights of tire applicant citizens or organisations or an administrative organ which does not reply to the application; (f) an administrative organ which does not issue a pension according to law; (g) an administrative organ which illegally requires citizens or organisations to carry out a duty; and (h) administrative organs deemed to have infringed personal or property rights of citizens or organisations.[56] The law excludes from review any state actions taken in national defence and diplomacy; and administrative regulations, provisions or decisions and orders with general binding force adopted by administrative organs; as well as the final findings of an administrative organ prescribed by law, from administrative litigation.[57]

16.4.3 Relevant Procedures

The Administrative Litigation Law (1989) establishes the jurisdictions and procedures for administrative litigation. The law prescribes that a judgment regarding an administrative decision must be based on national law or State Council regulations or local law.[58] The provisions of the State Council and commissions and ministries of the State Council adopted according to national law and State Council regulations can be used as references by the courts in trials of administrative cases.[59] The law prescribes that the courts can revoke or partially revoke an administrative decision on, or require the administrative organ to make, an administrative decision again in the following circumstances: (1) inadequacy of essential evidence; (2) erroneous application of the law or

---

56 Ibid., art. 11.
57 Ibid., art. 12.
58 Ibid., art. 52.
59 Ibid., art. 53.

regulations; (3) violation of legal procedure; (4) exceeding authority; and (5) abuse of powers.[60]

A people's court shall pass a judgment of first instance within three months from the day of filing the case.[61] The extent of the time limit necessitated by special circumstances shall be approved by a higher people's court, the extent of the time limit for handling a case of first instance by a higher people's court shall be approved by the SPC.[62] Judgments not appealed within the time limit become legally effective.[63] The court at the next highest level should render a final judgment within two months of the filing of the appeal.[64]

An appealed case should be handled by a people's court according to following provisions: (1) if the facts are clearly ascertained and the law and regulations are correctly applied in the original judgment, the appeal shall be rejected and the original judgment sustained; (2) if the facts are clearly ascertained but the law and regulations are incorrectly applied in the original judgment, the judgment shall be revised according to the law and regulations; or (3) if the facts are not clearly ascertained in the original judgment or the evidence is insufficient, or a violation of the prescribed procedure may have affected the correctness of the original judgment, the original judgment should be rescinded and the case remanded to the original people's court for retrial, or the people's court of the second instance may amend the judgment after investigating and clarifying the facts. The parties may appeal against the judgment or order rendered in a retrial of their case in the original people's court.[65]

16.5 CRIMINAL LITIGATION

Criminal litigation generally refers to the process of going to trial in a criminal court to either prosecute or defend oneself in a criminal matter. Major environmental crimes have been discussed in Chapter 15, but here we briefly touch on the procedures of environmental criminal litigation. Administrative actions cannot replace the imposition of criminal liabilities on offenders. Where these are concerned EPBs are obligated to transfer cases where there is a suspicion of a violation of environmental

60 Ibid., art. 54, para. 2.
61 Ibid, art. 57.
62 Ibid.
63 Ibid., art. 58.
64 Ibid., art. 60.
65 Ibid., art. 61.

protection laws to the public security institutions or the people's procuratorates. In 2007, the former SEPA, together with the Ministry of Public Security and the Supreme People's Procuratorate, jointly promulgated the Several Provisions on the Transfer of Cases of Suspected Criminal Violations of Environmental Protection Laws by Environmental Administrative Departments.[66]

On the one hand, this Regulation requires EPBs at or above county level to make a comprehensive consideration over the amount of losses of public and private property, human casualties, harmful consequences, amount of smuggled wastes, consequences of environmental damages and relevant factors, and where these meet the requirements of an environmental crime, the case should be handed over to the public security institutions and offenders should therefore be subjected to criminal liabilities. On the other hand, if EPBs found that their staff members have violated the relevant provisions in Chapter 9 of the Criminal Law during the process of investigation, the cases should be prosecuted. Staff of national institutions who commit similar offences should also be prosecuted.[67]

While the administrative departments of environmental protection are conducting investigations, the following material should be collected as evidence, including: (a) investigation reports over environmental offences; (b) investigation records and inquiry records; (c) environmental monitoring reports or expert conclusions; (d) audio-visual materials of the on-site investigations; (e) other physical evidence or expert conclusions which can be stored; and (f) where an administrative penalty decision has been made over the environmental offences, a letter for the penalty decision and evidence for decision-making shall be transferred simultaneously.[68]

In some cases, such a transfer might be rejected by public security institutions. Under such circumstances, an administrative penalty shall be applied. That is to say, the disciplinary responsibilities of the Party and governments will not automatically be dismissed after the rejection. Materials such as procuratorial proposals and relevant documents shall be handed over to the disciplinary inspection and supervision institutions.

---

66 《关于环境保护行政主管部门移送涉嫌环境犯罪案件的若干规定》 [Several Provisions on the Transfer of Cases of Suspected Criminal Violations of Environmental Protection Laws by Environmental Administrative Departments], 2007.

67 Ibid., art. 3.

68 Ibid., art. 4.

16.6 ALTERNATIVE DISPUTE RESOLUTION

16.6.1 Overview

Alternative dispute resolution (ADR) is a collective term for the ways that parties can settle disputes, with (or without) the help of a third party. It includes dispute resolution processes and techniques that act as a means for disagreeing parties to come to an agreement short of litigation. The ADR methods generally include negotiation, mediation, collaborative law, arbitration, and sometimes also conciliation.

Instead of an independent form of environmental dispute settlement, ADR is an accepted part of the civil litigation process.[69] There is a growing tendency for courts and tribunals to direct or refer parties to one or more ADR processes, with or without the parties' consent, and even for judicial officers and registrars to conduct the sessions. Mediation, in particular, has been adopted in civil disputes as a viable alternative to costly and high-risk litigation. Legislation has even been introduced to make mediation mandatory in the resolution of certain types of disputes.

The rationale for these programs is the saving in the time it takes to dispose of matters brought before the courts, reducing the workload of the court, and the savings in costs for litigants. ADR tempers the rigidity of the formal legal system and most legal processes combine aspects of both formal adjudication and consent-based processes. Judges frequently incorporate ADR into case management, either in the form of judicially supervised ADR or judicial referral to an appropriate ADR process to ensure that parties exhaust every possible alternative to a court hearing.

16.6.2 Conciliation

In China, environmental disputes may be settled between the disputing parties through consultation and negotiation.[70] Normally, conciliation occurs prior to the more formal administrative or judicial proceedings, but it remains available to the parties in dispute even after the initiation

---

[69] Lv Zhongmei, "Establishing and Complete Environmental ADR Mechanism", *QiuShi*, http://www.qstheory.cn/zxdk/2008/200812/200906/t20090609_1298.htm; Qi Shujie, "On the Reconstruction of Environmental Dispute Resolution in China", *Journal of Law Application*, 2006(9) 26.

[70] Yuhong Zhao, "Environmental Dispute Resolution in China", *Journal of Environmental Law*, (2004) 16 (2) 157.

of the judicial process.[71] The settlement agreement becomes effective as soon as the parties reach consensus if conciliation occurs prior to any administrative or judicial process. However, the settlement agreement becomes effective only when it is approved by the relevant dispute resolution body if conciliation occurs during an administrative or judicial process.[72] For example, Article 16 of the PRC Land Management Law[73] provides that disputes over property right or land use right shall be resolved by the parties through consultation. Where consultation fails, the people's government will make a decision.[74] Where the disputing parties are not satisfied with the people's government's decision, they may bring the case to the people's court within 30 days of receiving such decision.[75] Similarly, PRC Water Law[76] provides that disputes over water resources between different regions shall be resolved by conciliation. Where conciliation cannot resolve the dispute, the people's government at a higher level shall make a decision.[77]

Conciliation can help parties involved in an environmental pollution dispute to settle the dispute at an early stage and has proved to be both effective and efficient. Although conciliation is probably the most speedy, flexible, inexpensive and efficient way of resolving environmental disputes if the two parties are willing to reach compromise, it has its own shortcomings as noticed by several researchers.[78] First, there is a high

---

[71] Article 51 of the Civil Procedure Law of the People's Republic of China provides that parties to a lawsuit may conciliate to settle the dispute.

[72] Supreme People's Court's Interpretation of the Civil Procedure Law (1992), art. 191. See also Xie Zhenhua (ed.), *Encyclopaedia on Environmental Law Enforcement in China* (*Huanjing Zhifa Daquan*) (Hongqi Publishing, 1997) 169. See also Zhao, note 70 above, 159.

[73] PRC Land Management Law was first passed by the Sixth National People's Congress Standing Committee at its sixteenth meeting on 25 June 1986. The latest amendment was made in 2004.

[74] Article 16 of the PRC Land Management Law further specifies that the disputes between work units will be dealt with by the people's government above county level. While disputes between individuals or individual and work units shall be dealt with by the people's government at or above township level or county level.

[75] PRC Land Management Law , art. 16(3).

[76] The PRC Water Law was first passed by the Sixth National People's Congress Standing Committee at its 24th meeting on 21 January 1988. The law was substantially revised by the Ninth NPC Standing Committee at its 29th Meeting on 29 August 2002 and was implemented from 1 October 2002.

[77] Ibid., art. 56.

[78] Chen Maoyun and Ma Xiangcong, *Ecological Law* (Shaanxi People's Education Publishing, 2000) 307; see also See also Zhao, note 70 above, 160.

moral risk involved in conciliation since there is no external binding force upon the two parties. Any party's disrespect of the settlement agreement would lead to a further dispute on an aggravated scale. Second, the unequal bargaining power of the two parties may lead to a conciliation result that is lacking in justice and fairness. Generally speaking, victims are the parties without sufficient knowledge of the law or proper legal assistance. As a result, it is quite difficult for the victims to get the proper compensation via negotiation.[79] Third, in practice, conciliation sometimes postpones the problem rather than solves it. Most of the cases that ended up in the more formal administrative or judicial process had gone through conciliation at earlier stages. One example is a noise dispute recently resolved by a court in Henan Province that was pre-dated by conciliations lasting for over 20 years.[80]

16.6.3 Environmental Mediation

As a primary environmental dispute resolving method in China, environmental mediation reflects one of typical China's culture traditions of terminating lawsuits and diminishing fights in a society, where harmony is cherished with utmost value.[81] Moreover, the inefficiency of judicial procedure and the uncertainty and cost of the litigation are also contributing factors for people's choice of mediation as an environmental dispute resolving method.

Although the terms mediation and conciliation are used as synonyms in some literatures, they differ from each other because the mediation is conducted with a third party serving as a facilitator.[82] Based on who plays the role of a mediator, mediation in China can fall into following categories: people's mediation, administrative mediation and judicial mediation.

People's mediation is carried out with a mediator who has no administrative or judicial role. So far, most people's mediation occurs at the People's Mediation Committees (PMC) established under the Residents'

---

[79] Ibid., Maoyun and Xiangcong, 307.

[80] Zhao, note 70 above, 157.

[81] With ongoing debates about whether its popularity during the imperial era was attributable more to cultural factors, such as the Confucian emphasis on harmony, or institutional constraints, such as the limited budgets provided magistrates for resolving civil disputes. See Randall Peerenboom and He Xin, *Dispute Resolution in China: Patterns, Causes, and Prognosis*, http://www.fljs.org/uploads/documents/Peerenboom_He%20Xin%231%23.pdf.

[82] Ibid.

Committees in urban areas and Villagers' Committees in rural areas. Normally speaking, the majority of disputes handled by the PMCs involve family and marriage issues and compensation for damage and neighbourhood disputes. In the context of environmental disputes, people's mediation is mainly restricted to the resolution of disputes arising between township or community enterprises, solely-owned workshops or stalls and their neighbouring residents over the nuisance generated by the manufacturing and/or operation process.[83]

Administrative mediation is carried out by the relevant administrative organs at the request of either or both parties to a dispute and helps the parties reach a legally binding agreement. In practice, the EPBs at various levels have played a major role in resolving environmental disputes, although other relevant administrative bodies are also delegated with the power to carry out administrative mediation.[84] The local EPBs, together with those delegated departments, plays an important role in resolving disputes via mediation at an early stage.

Judicial mediation was formally institutionalized in 1982 with the promulgation of the Civil Procedure Law (for Trial Implementation), which provided that judges should stress mediation while adjudicating cases. To rectify coercion and unlawfulness problems, the Civil Procedure Law (1991) emphasizes the principles of voluntariness and compliance with the law in mediating cases.[85] The people's courts may conduct mediation in resolving civil disputes upon a party's request. A settlement agreement must be reached voluntarily, without any coercion, between the two parties and in accordance with the law.[86] Judicial mediation has been approved as an effective way of environmental dispute settlement in China.[87]

---

[83] Zhao, note 70 above, 157.

[84] Up to 1990s, 75 percent of the environmental disputes have been resolved by the environmental protection agencies. See Zhenhua, note 72 above, 170.

[85] 《中华人民共和国民事诉讼法》 [Civil Procedure Law of the People's Republic of China] (1991), art. 6.

[86] Ibid., arts 85, 88.

[87] According to statistics, in 2001, the court of first instance concluded 3 457 770 civil disputes, of which 1 270 556 were resolved by mediation (about 37 percent of the total cases accepted); and 1 158 702 economic disputes, of which 351 776 were resolved by mediation (about 30 per cent of the total cases accepted). See *Law Yearbook of China*, Press of Law Yearbook of China (2002) 1239.

16.6.4 Letters and Visits

The term 'letters and visits' is also called *Xinfang* in the Chinese language. It refers to the process by which private citizens may file petitions with letters and visits to offices of various government agencies at successively higher levels of government to seek administrative intervention and redress for grievances against the government bureaucracy or other entities or persons.[88] The letters and visits system has persisted as an important pathway for common citizens to seek relief when other options have failed.

The Regulations on Letters and Visits[89] promulgated by China's State Council in 2005 and the Options of Environmental Letters and Visits[90] promulgated by the former SEPA of China in 2006 are the two most important regulations on governing the Environmental related letters and visits. Article 2 of the Regulations on Letters and Visits defines the term 'letters and visits' as:

> citizens, legal persons or other organizations give information, make comments or suggestions or lodge complaints to the people's governments at all levels and the relevant departments of the people's governments at or above the county level through correspondence, E-mails, faxes, phone calls, visits, and so on, which are dealt with by the relevant administrative departments according to law.[91]

In the context of environmental letters and visits, the 'relevant administrative departments' refer to all levels of EPBs and other relevant environmental protection departments under the people's governments at or above the county level.[92] Those departments are required to perform following duties:

(1) to accept the letter and visit application regarding environmental issues presented by a letter-writer or visitor;

---

[88] Carl Minzner, Xinfang: "An Alternative to Formal Chinese Legal Institutions", 42 *Stanford Journal of International Law* 103 (2006).

[89] 《国务院信访条例》 [Regulations on Letters and Visits], State Council of the P.R.C No. 431, adopted at the 76th Executive Meeting of the State Council on January 5, 2005, came into force in May 1, 2005.

[90] 《环境信访办法》 [Rules of Environmental Letters and Visits], promulgated by the SEPA in Jun 24, 2006, came into force July 1, 2006.

[91] The Regulations on Letters and Visits, art. 2.

[92] Ibid., art. 6.

(2) transmit the application to another environmental administrative organ, or assign another organ to handle it;
(3) to handle applications assigned by environmental administrative organ at higher levels;
(4) to coordinate efforts in handling important letter-or-visit matters;
(5) to urge and examine the handling of letter-or-visit matters;
(6) to study and analyze letters and visits, conduct investigation and study and, in a timely manner, make suggestions on improving policies and work to the environmental administrative organ at the corresponding level;
(7) to provide guidance to other relevant environmental administrative organ at the corresponding level and the departments or environmental administrative organ for letters and visits at lower levels in their work regarding letters and visits; and
(8) to develop annual reports and submit the report to environmental administrative organ at the corresponding level and the departments at one level higher.

Although letters and visits petitions generate responses from the government, only a small number of them can finally lead to positive remedies for the petitioners. In practice, this system received a lot of critiques in recent years. Among others, its inefficiency and a lack of proper monitoring have been noted as among the main reasons by many researchers.[93]

16.7 CONCLUDING REMARKS

China has established an advanced environmental disputes settlement system, which covers litigious methods and ADRs. On the one hand, substantive and procedural provisions relating to civil actions and administrative actions have been prescribed by laws, regulations and governmental documents; environmental litigation is flexible and the combined application of those methods has greatly facilitated the access to justice for victims of environmental catastrophes. On the other hand, the distrust of the legal system, combined with the traditional roots of the petitioning system has raised a general preference for mediation as a method of dispute settlement in China. This has greatly reduced the rise in environmental tort cases.

---

[93] For example, see Qi Shujie, "On the reconstruction of Environmental Dispute Resolution in China", *Journal of Law Application*, 2006(9) 26.

ADR processes, particularly mediation and conciliation, can improve the efficiency of a formal court hearing by helping to clarify and narrow the issues that are in dispute in order to reduce the length of a hearing. However, ADRs are not a panacea, and its use in environmental disputes should not undermine the overriding function and goal of administrative law to maintain government accountability. The challenge for the future will be to improve rules of procedure on environmental disputes settlement. The existing processes of litigious and ADRs should be further refined in order to build on the existing high rate of settlement, without adding to the costs of the parties or detracting from the public confidence in the justice system.

Meanwhile, in view of the current development of environment courts in China, it is too early to draw any conclusions about their efficacy in improving the enforcement of environmental laws. However, it is hard to see any downside to their creation up to date. In order to refine the environmental courts regimes, China may need to take the following steps to fully realize its goal of an effective nationwide environment court system. The first step is to develop more environment courts with different models as pilot projects; the second step is to elaborate a system of regulations for nationwide replication; the final step is to strengthen the regulatory and legislative foundation of the environment courts.

In brief, each method has its own advantages and pitfalls. As a result, it is important to understand the interplay of all those instruments. As the continual efforts have been made, there is every reason to expect a better environmental disputes settlement regime in China.

17. China's position on international environmental issues*

Liu Nengye

17.1 INTRODUCTION

In 2010, China overtook Japan as the world's second biggest economy.[1] This marks a milestone in China's rise as an economic superpower. As the world's most populous country and a leading economic power, China has a natural place at the heart of global dialogue and cooperation. A rapid development in China has however also led to global environmental problems. For example, in 2006, China overtook the United States as the largest emitter of greenhouse gases.[2] The impact on the global environment created by China's economic growth has resulted in widespread concern in the rest of the world.

China's first foray into the international environmental arena was at the 1972 United Nations Conference on the Human Environment (the Stockholm Conference). China's "open door" policy commenced in 1978 and since then, China has gradually become an active participant in international environmental issues. This chapter presents research based on official documents published by the Chinese Government about China's positions towards international environmental issues. It first provides an overview of the development of China's official positions on international environmental issues. The author's comments can be found in the concluding remarks.

* Part of this chapter (Section 17.2.4) is reprinted from Nengye Liu, *Chinese Government's Latest Position on Global Environmental Issues*, IUCN Academy of Environmental Law eJournal (2014), 126–33.

1 (2011) 'China overtakes Japan as world's second-biggest economy', www.bbc.co.uk/news/business-12 427321, accessed 31 Jan 2013.

2 David Teather (2010) 'China overtakes Japan as world's second-largest economy', www.guardian.co.uk/business/2010/aug/16/china-overtakes-japan-second-largest-economy1, accessed 31 Jan 2013.

17.2 CHINA'S POSITIONS TOWARDS INTERNATIONAL ENVIRONMENTAL ISSUES (1990–2012)

17.2.1 1990 China's Principles and Positions on Global Environmental Issues[3]

The first official document regarding China's position on global environmental issues was published in 1990 by the State Council of China (hereinafter "1990 Official Document"). The Chinese Government recognised for the first time that a guiding document concerning China's position on international environmental issues was necessary for environmental cooperation in the international sphere. The 1990 Official Document was issued before the 1992 United Nations Conference on Environment and Development (UNCED) in Rio de Janeiro. The document represents China's official position at the Rio Conference. It reflects China's perception of itself as a developing country and its view that it could represent developing countries on the international stage.

17.2.1.1 General principles

By 1990 China had begun to see itself as an active player on international environmental issues. China saw global environmental protection campaign as an opportunity and external force for the improvement of China's environment and use of natural resources. China was willing to share a "reasonable" burden and make an "appropriate" contribution to the protection of global environment.[4]

The relationship between economic development and environmental protection is the first concern of China.[5] Economic growth lays its foundation on sustainable development. However, global environmental problems could only be solved by economic development. China has been promoting a "new international economic order" since the 1980s.[6] It is believed by China that global environmental problems also link to the

---

[3] Published by the Environmental Protection Committee of the State Council of P. R. China, 26 October 1990.

[4] Para. 1, Part 2, 1990 Official Document, 2.

[5] Para. 3, Part 2, 1990 Official Document, 2.

[6] 'China's Suggestions on the Establishment of a New International Political and Economic Order', news.xinhuanet.com/ziliao/2003-01/19/content_696057.htm, accessed 4 February 2013. (in Chinese).

injustice of international economic order established by developed countries. International environmental cooperation should go hand in hand with international economic cooperation.[7]

It is China's opinion that developed countries should take the major responsibility for global environmental problems.[8] The industrialization of developed countries in the past centuries has resulted in the deterioration of the global environment. Developed countries made free use of natural resources for their development and they now have better technology and funding to meet a greater part of the burden of the protection of global environment.[9]

China has endorsed Principle 21 of the 1972 Declaration of the United Nations Conference on the Human Environment,[10] and believes that States have, in accordance with the Charter of the United Nations and the principles of international law, the sovereign right to exploit their own resources pursuant to their own environmental policies.[11] China is against the intervention in a country's internal affairs through international environmental cooperation.[12]

There is a further belief that the voice of developing countries, including China's, are rarely heard in the international arena and that this situation must be changed.[13]

China hopes that the international community will develop a special concern for the environmental problems in developing countries.[14] The deterioration of the environment in developing countries is a regional problem but it has global impact; and the lack of funding in developing countries means that they lack the technology to deal with many of the environmental problems caused by industrialization.

China maintains a strong position against setting environmental protection as a trade barrier and also opposes development aid being loaded with additional conditions such as environmental protection.[15]

---

[7] See n. 5 above.

[8] Para. 4, Part 2, 1990 Official Document, 2.

[9] Ibid.

[10] (1972), 'United Nations Conference on the Human Environment: Final Documents', *International Legal Materials*, **6** (11), 1416–1469.

[11] Para. 5, Part 2, 1990 Official Document, 3.

[12] Ibid.

[13] Para. 6, Part 2, 1990 Official Document, 3.

[14] Para. 7, Part 2, 1990 Official Document, 3.

[15] Para. 8, Part 2, 1990 Official Document, 3.

China has called for developed countries to provide funding in addition to development aid to developing countries.[16] It is envisaged that this funding would be used to help developing countries participate in international environmental protection or compensate them for economic loss resulting from environmental protection. China called for developed countries to transfer environmental friendly technology to developing countries in a non-commercial way;[17] and insisted that the transfer of technology in a non-commercial way from developed countries to developing countries should be included in international environmental conventions.[18] China is against developed countries making huge profits from selling environmental protection technology to developing countries.[19]

China believes that a strengthened international law is necessary for environmental protection,[20] although it is willing to actively participate in international law-making processes on environmental protection, believes that international environmental law should take care of the interests of developing countries.[21]

It seems that in 1990 China was slightly skeptical of the "precautionary principle",[22] China was unadventurous over environmental issues without sufficient scientific support and as it declared, comprehensive scientific research was needed as a precondition for international environmental law-making.[23]

---

16 Para. 9, Part 2, 1990 Official Document, 3.

17 Ibid.

18 Ibid.

19 Ibid.

20 Para. 10, Part 2, 1990 Official Document, 3.

21 Ibid.

22 Rio Declaration on Environment and Development 1992, Principle 15 – the Precautionary Approach, The Rio Declaration: In order to protect the environment, the precautionary approach shall be widely applied by States according to their capabilities. Where there are threats of serious or irreversible damage, lack of full scientific certainty shall not be used as a reason for postponing cost-effective measures to prevent environmental degradation. For discussions, see for example, Jonathan B. Wiener, 'Precaution' in Daniel Bodansky, Jutta Brunnée and Ellen Hey (eds), *The Oxford Handbook of International Environmental Law* (OUP 2010) 598–612.

23 Para. 11, Part 2, 1990 Official Document, 3.

17.2.1.2 Specific positions

Climate change The United Nations Framework Convention on Climate Change was adopted in 1992.[24] As can be seen from the 1990 Official Document, China's position on the work of Intergovernmental Panel on Climate Change (IPCC) was quite positive.[25] However, at that time suggested that the IPCC could create more opportunities for the participation of developing countries.[26] China, as one of those countries, saw the work of IPCC being dominated by developed countries.[27]

China suggested that developed countries should take the lead on the reduction of green house gas (GHG) emissions,[28] first, because they are mainly responsible for the global warming; and second, because they also have more resources and technology to prevent and mitigate global climate change. Additional funding was requested from developed countries to help China mitigate and adapt to climate change.[29] As part of that assistance it was felt that there should be a mechanism for the transfer of green technology[30] which developing countries should be entitled to on favorable terms.[31]

In the 1990s, China was already paying much attention to climate change negotiations. However, it was doubtful of the concept of setting mandatory articles for the reduction of GHG emissions in developing countries.[32] Moreover, China put economic development as its priority by declaring that any CO_2 reduction plans must not damage the economic growth of developing countries,[33] and admitted that the GHG emissions in China would increase in the coming years as the country was on its way to industrialization and urbanization. Nevertheless, it still argued that GHG emissions per capita in China were much lower than in developed countries.[34]

---

[24] (1992), 'United Nations Conference on Environment and Development: Framework Convention on Climate Change', *International Legal Materials*, **4** (31), 849–73.

[25] The IPCC's work is appreciated by China. *See* para. 7, Part 3, 1990 Official Document, 4.

[26] Ibid.

[27] Ibid.

[28] Para. 8, Part. 3, 1990 Official Document, 4.

[29] Ibid.

[30] Ibid.

[31] Ibid.

[32] Para. 9, Part. 3, 1990 Official Document, 4.

[33] Para. 10, Part. 3, 1990 Official Document, 4.

[34] Para. 11, Part. 3, 1990 Official Document, 4.

Protection of the ozone layer China adopted the Vienna Convention for the Protection of the Ozone Layer (Vienna Convention) in 1989, one year after it entered into force. In 1990, China was a contracting party of the Montreal Protocol on Substances that Deplete the Ozone Layer (Montreal Protocol), which entered into force in 1989.[35]

China is quite supportive of the Vienna Convention and Montreal Protocol. However, in the 1990 Official Document, it once again blamed developed countries for causing the ozone depletion and called for an international special fund for developing countries as well as the transfer of technology.[36] China's intention was to be able to produce substitutes for the ozone depletion substances instead of importing from developed countries.[37] China wanted to build a good image within international community and hoped to get international aid as well as technology.[38] The Montreal Protocol was finally adopted by China in 1991.

Biodiversity According to the 1990 Official Document, China is not convinced that biodiversity is a "common heritage for mankind."[39] Rather, it states that biodiversity is a regional issue and an integral part of a country's natural resources and a country has sovereignty over biodiversity within its jurisdiction.[40] In order to use biodiversity in a sustainable way, China called again for the funding and technological support from developed countries to protect its biodiversity.[41] It emphasized that the success of action plans for the protection of biodiversity depended on the awareness and active participation of people from local communities[42] and in order to effectively protect biodiversity, the economy and interests of local community shall be fully considered before making any implementation plans.[43] China ratified Convention on Biological Diversity (CBD)[44] in 1993 and published its first National

35 The texts of Vienna Convention and Montreal Protocol can be found on the official website of United Nations Environmental Programme, Ozone Secretariat: montreal-protocol.org, accessed on 5 February 2013.

36 Para. 14, Part. 3, 1990 Official Document, 5.

37 Para. 16, Part. 3, 1990 Official Document, 5.

38 Ibid.

39 Para. 19, Part. 3, 1990 Official Document, 6.

40 Ibid.

41 Ibid.

42 Ibid.

43 Ibid.

44 United Nations Conference on Environment and Development: Convention on Biological Diversity, (1992) 31 (4) *ILM* 818–41.

Action Plan for the Protection of Biodiversity in 1994. Moreover, China Agenda 21 was published in 1996, with Chapter 15 specifically focusing on biodiversity.

Transboundary movement of hazardous wastes The Basel Convention on the Control of Transboundary Movements of Hazardous Wastes and their Disposal (Basel Convention)[45] was adopted in 1989, with China signing it in 1990. China was seriously concerned about the transboundary movement of hazardous wastes and chemicals from developed countries to developing countries and saw The Basel Convention as a good initiative to prevent moving hazardous wastes from developed countries to within its own borders.[46] However, China lacked the experience and the capacity to prevent and control hazardous wastes; moreover, at that time, its domestic legislation was not sufficient to fully implement the Convention. China therefore hoped that developed countries could help it to establish institutions that could monitor and control hazardous wastes,[47] as it needed the technology and equipment that could test, analyze, assess and dispose of hazardous wastes.

From 1978 China had already started its economic reform and "open door" policy and foreign investments were therefore warmly welcomed. However, China paid special attention to any foreign investment in the chemical industry that might cause serious environmental problems; strict environmental impact assessments would be applied before approval was given for new chemical projects.[48]

Marine pollution It is mentioned in the 1990 Official Document that three key issues regarding the protection of marine environment were debated between developed and developing countries. Developing countries were against the disposal of radioactive wastes and burn wastes at sea; nor were they interested in adopting a legally binding international convention regarding the prevention and control of land-based marine

---

[45] (1989), 'United Nations Environment Programme Conference of Plenipotentiaries on the Global Convention on the Control of Transboundary Movements of Hazardous Wastes: Final Act and Text of Basel Convention', *International Legal Materials*, 3 (28), 649–86.

[46] Para. 24, Part. 3, 1990 Official Document, 7.

[47] Para. 26, Part. 3, 1990 Official Document, 7.

[48] Para. 27, Part. 3, 1990 Official Document, 7.

pollution.[49] China especially believed that mandatory control of land-based marine pollution might affect its economic growth.[50]

China declared that the high seas are a common heritage of mankind and should not become a "common tragedy",[51] and stated that countries have the sovereignty on the protection and use of resources within their internal waters, territorial seas and all other sea areas under their jurisdiction.[52] Countries must be prohibited from transferring pollutants or causing pollution damage to sea areas under other countries' jurisdiction.[53] As always mentioned in the 1990 Official Document, China asked developed countries to take more responsibility and help developing countries by providing funding and technology.[54]

17.2.2 1997 National Report on Sustainable Development

China published its first National Report on Sustainable Development in 1997 (hereinafter '1997 National Report'), just before the Earth Summit Rio+5. The State Council of China adopted the China Agenda 21 in 1994. This document assessed China's implementation of the Agenda 21[55] from 1992 to 1996. The 1997 National Report could be seen as a supplementary document to the China Agenda 21.[56] Chapter 5 of the 1997 National Report presents China's principles and positions on international environmental issues.

17.2.2.1 China's views on international environmental protection

In the 1997 National Report, China took a positive view on international efforts for the implementation of the Agenda 21. Principle 4 of the 1992 Rio Declaration on Environment and Development (1992 Rio Declaration)[57] states that: "In order to achieve sustainable development, environmental protection shall constitute an integral part of the development

---

49 Para. 30, Part. 3, 1990 Official Document, 7.

50 Ibid.

51 Para. 31, Part. 3, 1990 Official Document, 7.

52 Ibid.

53 Ibid.

54 Ibid.

55 'Agenda 21', www.unep.org/documents.multilingual/default.asp?documentid=52, accessed 7 February 2013.

56 (1994), 'Circular on the Implementation of China Agenda 21', *State Council of P. R. China Gazette*, **16** (765), 710.

57 (1992), 'United Nations Conference on Environment and Development: Rio Declaration on Environment and Development', *International Legal Materials*, **4** (31), 874–80.

process and cannot be considered in isolation from it." China believes that Principle 4 lays the foundation for international cooperation on social, economic and environmental development.

China was however dissatisfied with the progress of international environmental cooperation. Its view was that the Global Environment Facility (GEF) played too limited a role in international environmental cooperation.[58] Furthermore, China criticized developed countries for not fulfilling their promise to help developing countries in the protection of their environment.[59]

17.2.2.2 Specific positions

Funding The 1997 National Report referred to the 33.15 of Agenda 21:

> For developing countries, particularly the least developed countries, Official Development Assistance (ODA) is a main source of external funding, and substantial new and additional funding for sustainable development and implementation of Agenda 21 will be required. Developed countries reaffirm their commitments to reach the accepted United Nations target of 0.7 per cent of Gross National Product (GNP) for ODA and, to the extent that they have not yet achieved that target, agree to augment their aid programmes in order to reach that target as soon as possible and to ensure a prompt and effective implementation of Agenda 21.

Although Agenda 21 is not a legally binding document, China criticized developed countries for not fulfilling their commitments to provide ODA to developing countries[60] and consistently maintained its position that developed countries should share more of the burden for global environmental protection.[61] China is disappointed with the fact that except for Denmark, Finland, Sweden, Norway and Netherlands, the ODA provided by other developed countries never reached the UN target of 0.7 percent of their GNP. It was hoped that those developed countries could reach the UN target in 2000.[62]

---

[58] Para.5.6, Section 1, Chapter 5, 1997 National Report, 93.

[59] Para.5.7, Section 1, Chapter 5, 1997 National Report, 93.

[60] Para.5.27, Section 3, Chapter 5, 1997 National Report, 99.

[61] The 1997 National Report also referred to the Para. 9, UN General Assembly Resolution 44/228, United Nations Conference on Environment and Development, 22 December 1989: "Notes that the largest part of the current emission of pollutants into the environment, including toxic and hazardous wastes, originates in developed countries, and therefore recognizes that those countries have the main responsibility for combating such pollution."

[62] Para.5.29, Section 3, Chapter 5, 1997 National Report, 99.

Transfer of technology China has criticized developed countries for not following Chapter 34 (Transfer of Environmentally Sound Technology, Cooperation and Capacity-Building) of Agenda 21.[63] It has maintained that developed countries use intellectual property concerns as an excuse to set barriers for transferring technology in a favourable way to developing countries.[64] China is also worried that developed countries see the transfer of environmental sound technology to developing countries as business opportunities.[65] It seems that China relied on non-binding documents such as Agenda 21 to request funding and technology from developed countries and declared that ODA and environmentally sound technology were key issues for the implementation of the Agenda 21 and the establishment of "new global partnership" called for by the UNCED.[66]

Trade and environment Regarding the relationship between trade and environment, China paid special attention to Principle 12 of the Rio Declaration.[67] China is strongly against developed countries setting environmental protection standards for discriminating or restricting the market access of goods and commodities from developing countries.[68]

Pattern of production and consumption China has expressed the view that the major cause of the continuing deterioration of the global environment is the unsustainable pattern of production and consumption, particularly in industrialized countries.[69] It urges developed countries to

---

[63] Para.5.7, Section 1, Chapter 5, 1997 National Report, 94.

[64] Ibid.

[65] Ibid.

[66] Para.5.30, Section 3, Chapter 5, 1997 National Report, 99.

[67] It reads:

> States should cooperate to promote a supportive and open international economic system that would lead to economic growth and sustainable development in all countries, to better address the problems of environmental degradation. Trade policy measures for environmental purposes should not constitute a means of arbitrary or unjustifiable discrimination or a disguised restriction on international trade. Unilateral actions to deal with environmental challenges outside the jurisdiction of the importing country should be avoided. Environmental measures addressing trans-boundary or global environmental problems should, as far as possible, be based on an international consensus.

[68] Para.5.32, Section 3, Chapter 5, 1997 National Report, 100.

[69] UN General Assembly Resolution 44/228, United Nations Conference on Environment and Development, 22 December 1989.

change their pattern of production and consumption,[70] and moreover, believes they should provide funding and technology to help developing countries to make similar changes.[71] China hopes to develop its economy in a sustainable way rather than "pollution first, restoration later."[72]

Climate change It has been noted by China that the largest share of historical and current global emissions of GHG originates in developed countries, but that the per capita emissions of developing countries are still relatively low although their share of global emissions will have to grow to meet their social and development needs.[73] China is not willing to meet new obligations to reduce GHG.[74] Funding and transfer of technology from developed countries are the major concerns of China.[75] In the 1997 National Report, China referred to Article 4(7) of the UNFCCC to strengthen its views on climate change:

> The extent to which developing country Parties will effectively implement their commitments under the Convention will depend on the effective implementation by developed country Parties of their commitments under the Convention related to financial resources and transfer of technology and will take fully into account that economic and social development and poverty eradication are the first and overriding priorities of the developing country Parties.

Biodiversity China reiterated its statement from the 1990 Official Document that countries have sovereignty over the natural resources within their jurisdiction[76] and that in order to help developing countries effectively implement the CBD,[77] developed countries should provide new additional funding as well as transfer technology in a fair and most favorable way to developing countries.[78] With respect to the biosafety

---

70 Para.5.33, Section 3, Chapter 5, 1997 National Report, 100.

71 Ibid.

72 Ibid.

73 Para.3, Preface, United Nations Framework Convention on Climate Change (UNFCCC).

74 Para.5.36, Section 3, Chapter 5, 1997 National Report, 101.

75 Ibid.

76 Para.5.38, Section 3, Chapter 5, 1997 National Report, 101.

77 (1992), 'United Nations Conference on Environment and Development: Convention on Biological Diversity', *International Legal Materials*, 4 (31), 818–41.

78 Para.5.38, Section 3, Chapter 5, 1997 National Report, 101.

issue, China suggested adopting a protocol that could regulate the transboundary movement of genetically modified organisms (GMOs).[79]

Forestry China declares that countries have absolute sovereignty over their forestry.[80] When it comes to the discussions of forestry issues, countries' sovereignty over their forest resources should be respected[81] and they are entitled to protect, manage, develop and used their forestry according to their own social and economic situations.[82]

Basel Convention China remains supportive of the Basel Convention, which it ratified in 1990. Afterwards, China adopted the PRC Solid Waste Law[83] to implement the Convention domestically. China is also willing to support the adoption of the Basel Protocol on Liability and Compensation. It is China's view that countries producing and exporting hazardous wastes should compensate for damage resulted from transboundary movement and disposal of hazardous wastes.[84]

Sustainable development of small islands developing states Established by UN General Assembly Resolution 47/189, the UN Global Conference on the Sustainable Development of Small Islands Developing States (SIDS) was held in Bridgetown, Barbados, from 25 April to 6 May 1994. Some 125 States and territories participated in the conference, 46 of which were small island developing states and territories. The Conference adopted the Barbados Program of Action on the Sustainable Development of SIDS (BPOA), a 14-point program that identifies priority areas and indicates specific actions necessary for addressing the special challenges faced by SIDS. China is willing to provide funding and technical support to SIDS for achieving the goals set in the BPOA,[85] but has no specific plan on how to help the SIDS.

---

79 Ibid.

80 Para.5.40, Section 3, Chapter 5, 1997 National Report, 102.

81 Ibid.

82 Ibid.

83 PRC Solid Waste Law, *Standing Committee of National People's Congress Gazette*, 7 (1995), 62–73.

84 Para.5.43, Section 3, Chapter 5, 1997 National Report, 102.

85 Para.5.44, Section 3, Chapter 5, 1997 National Report, 102–3.

17.2.3 2002 National Report on Sustainable Development

The second National Report on Sustainable Development was published in 2002 (hereinafter 2002 National Report), before the World Summit on Sustainable Development (Earth Summit Johannesburg 2002). Chapter 4 of the 2002 National Report stated China's principles and positions towards international environmental issues.

17.2.3.1 China's views on international environmental cooperation

In the 2002 National Report, China's views on international environmental issues are as follows:

First, economic development is the priority for developing countries such as China,[86] which contends that such development lays the foundation for environmental protection. China argues that without economic capacities, a country is not capable of protecting its environment and the international community should make efforts and create a good environment to help developing countries with their debts, trade and funding.[87] Developing countries need their help to achieve sustainable development.

Secondly, international environmental cooperation should be based on the equality and mutual respect between countries.[88] China insists that independence and sovereignty are the prerequisite for international cooperation, including environmental cooperation.[89] Countries should enjoy equal rights to participate in international environmental issues; and can freely adopt and implement their own policies for economic development and environmental protection. International environmental cooperation should not be used as an excuse for interfering with other countries' sovereign affairs. But at the same time, countries must also take the responsibility for not damaging another country's environment by the exploration and exploitation of their own natural resources.

Thirdly, the common but differentiated responsibility principle is cherished by China. It is stated that although the international community has to protect the global environment, developed countries should take more responsibility.[90] China continues to believe that the current global environmental problems results from pollutants discharged mainly by developed countries[91] that have been consuming global natural resources

---

[86] Para.4.2.1, Section 2, Chapter 4, 2002 National Report, 47.
[87] Ibid.
[88] Para.4.2.2, Section 2, Chapter 4, 2002 National Report, 47.
[89] Ibid.
[90] Para.4.2.3, Section 2, Chapter 4, 2002 National Report, 47.
[91] Ibid.

for hundreds of years feeding their industrialization. They should, therefore, be obliged to provide additional funding and technology to improve the environment in developing countries.[92]

Fourthly, China emphasizes that peace is important for achieving sustainable development;[93] war or turmoil damages not only the ecological environment, but also a countries' capacity to develop in a sustainable way and disputes between countries should, therefore, be settled in a peaceful way.

Finally, short-run and long-term interests of countries should be equally considered for dealing with global environmental problems. Some regional environmental problems need to be prioritized: these include the shortage of water, urban air pollution, soil erosion, desertification and natural disasters in developing countries.[94]

17.2.3.2 Specific positions

Transfer of funding and technology China argues that most developing countries are not able to achieve the sustainable development targets set in the UNCED 1992 because of their poor economic situation.[95] The transfer of funding and technology from developed countries to developing countries is the fundamental issue of international environmental cooperation.[96] Once again China urges developed countries to provide ODA that meets the 0.7 percent target of their GNP set by the UN.[97] China formerly was not fond of ideas such as private investment or new/innovative financing mechanism suggested by developed countries, however, in a slightly different stance from the 1997 National Report, China is no longer opposed to those ideas and expresses its willingness to discuss any new money-raising mechanisms with developed countries.[98] Furthermore, China hopes the International Monetary Fund (IMF), World Bank and other UN bodies will play an active role in helping transfer funding and technology to developing countries.[99]

---

92 Ibid.
93 Para.4.2.4, Section 2, Chapter 4, 2002 National Report, 47–48.
94 Ibid.
95 Para.4.3.1, Section 3, Chapter 4, 2002 National Report, 48.
96 Ibid.
97 Ibid.
98 Ibid.
99 Ibid.

Poverty The alleviation of poverty is a serious issue for the world. Although globalization contributes to the decrease of poor populations, the gap between the rich and poor is widening in China. Poverty is not only a social problem but may cause destruction to natural resources as well; it is seen as one of the major reasons for causing the deterioration of the environment in developing countries. China believes that poverty is the biggest obstacle for developing countries to achieve sustainable development[100] and that developed countries should, therefore, take measures to improve the trade environment and reduce the foreign debt of these countries.[101] It is China's idea that the alleviation of poverty in developing countries will in turn make positive contribution to the environmental protection.[102]

Rural and agricultural development Seventy-five percent of the world's population is found in the rural areas of developing countries. Their lives rely heavily on natural resources so that any environmental deterioration or resources depletion has a huge impact on them. China states that sustainable agriculture should be the priority of sustainable development[103] and that the international community should take affirmative action to support agriculture in developing countries[104] with measures such as the application of new agricultural technology, infrastructure improvement; and raising the productivity to achieve sustainable agriculture.[105]

Trade and environment China believes that trade and the protection of the environment can be mutually beneficial.[106] The development of trade and export could be helpful for the economy of developing countries as a better economy can contribute to improved environmental protection. China is strongly opposed to setting environmental protection as a trade barrier by developed countries.[107]

---

100 Para.4.3.2, Section 3, Chapter 4, 2002 National Report, 48.
101 Ibid.
102 Ibid.
103 Para.4.3.3, Section 3, Chapter 4, 2002 National Report, 48.
104 Ibid.
105 Ibid.
106 Para.4.3.5, Section 3, Chapter 4, 2002 National Report, 48.
107 Ibid.

Consumption model China blames developed countries for their unsustainable consumption model as the main reason causing the deterioration of the global environment.[108] China argues that developed countries should take the lead in changing the consumption model. China hopes its own economic development might learn from the experience of developed countries and avoid the consumption model of "pollution first, restoration later."[109] However, as we already know from other chapters of this *Handbook* about the current situation of the Chinese environment, China so far has not been successful in finding a different way to develop its economy from developed countries.

Climate change China reaffirms that developed countries are mainly responsible for the GHG emissions and global warming and that developing countries are the victims of climate change[110] China declares that there are huge differences regarding capacity and CO_2 emissions per capita between developing countries and developed countries and that it is not fair or realistic for developing countries to share the burden of reducing/limiting GHG emissions.[111] China does, however, support the entry into force of the Kyoto Protocol.[112]

Desertification China adopted the UN Convention to Combat Desertification[113] in 1994. China has been investing funding and human resources to deal with its own desertification problem for years but has, however, declared that its work is not proving effective[114] and is, therefore, arguing that desertification is especially in need of funding and technology from developed countries.[115]

Forestry China consistently declares that countries have absolute sovereignty over forestry within their territory.[116] It is China's opinion that

108 Para.4.3.6, Section 3, Chapter 4, 2002 National Report, 49.
109 Ibid.
110 Para.4.3.7, Section 3, Chapter 4, 2002 National Report, 49.
111 Ibid.
112 Ibid.
113 United Nations: 'Convention to Combat Desertification in those Countries Experiencing Serious Drought and/or Desertification, Particularly in Africa', *International Law Materials*, **5** (33) 1994, 1328–82.
114 Para.4.3.8, Section 3, Chapter 4, 2002 National Report, 49.
115 Ibid.
116 Para.4.3.9, Section 3, Chapter 4, 2002 National Report, 49.

funding, transfer of technology, trade and environment are key issues for dealing with global forestry problem.[117]

17.2.4 2012 National Report on Sustainable Development

The United Nations Conference on Sustainable Development (Rio+20) took place in Rio de Janeiro, Brazil from 20 to 22 June 2012. The Chinese Government published its third National Report on Sustainable Development in 2012 (hereinafter 2012 National Report), right before the Rio+20. Chapter 7 (International Cooperation) and 8 (Principles and Positions) of the 2012 National Report provide China's latest positions on international environmental issues.

17.2.4.1 Cooperation with developing countries

For decades China has been promoting the transfer of funding and technology from developed countries to developing countries. In the 2012 National Report, China published its work on cooperation with other developing countries. As mentioned above, it is believed that economic development and poverty alleviation are the primary tasks for developing countries as poverty can be seen as one major reason that could result in the deterioration of environment in developing countries. Until 2010, China offered zero tariff treatment to more than 60 percent of the products from 38 least developed countries.[118] China has also provided other developing countries with 287 billion yuan of financial assistance and waived the 30 billion yuan debt of the 50 heavily indebted poor countries and least developed countries.[119] In recent years, in order to help other developing countries cope with the international financial crisis, China has provided some African countries with 10 billion U.S. dollars in preferential loans and is committed to providing 15 billion U.S. dollars in credit to the least developed country members of the Association of Southeast Asian Nations (ASEAN) (Laos, Cambodia and Myanmar) to support their infrastructure construction projects.[120] It has also signed "Memorandums of Understanding on Poverty Reduction Cooperation" with Mexico, Argentina, Venezuela, Colombia and other Latin American countries to jointly promote the eradication of poverty.[121]

---

117 Ibid.
118 Para.2, Section 1, Chapter 7, 2012 National Report, 72–3.
119 Ibid.
120 Ibid.
121 Ibid.

Moreover, the Chinese Government has conducted personnel training programs for developing countries in more than 20 areas such as agriculture, health, education, economics and environmental protection. By 2010, a total of 130 000 management and technical personnel in developing countries had been trained in China.[122] China signed documents such as "the Memorandum of Understanding for Cooperation in Technology and Mechanism Concerning Africa's Environment", and "the Implementation Agreement of Environmental Cooperation Projects in Africa" in order to promote cooperation among developing countries.[123]

17.2.4.2 Cooperation with developed countries

The Chinese Government has established a regular exchange and cooperation mechanism with developed countries in environmental protection, climate change, energy and resource conservation and sustainable use, disaster prevention, so as to jointly promote global sustainable development.

China has signed several memoranda of understanding with developed countries such as the United States, Canada, the EU, Germany, the UK, France and Singapore on buildings' energy efficiency, green building and low-carbon eco-cities.[124] One recent example is China and Japan signing a "Memorandum of Understanding on the Continuous Cooperation in Energy Saving and Environmental Protection." China keeps dialogue open on environmental protection issues with several developed countries: for example, in 2001, China and the EU agreed to establish a ministerial-level dialogue mechanism on China-EU environmental policies and so far the ministerial meetings have been held four times. In 2008, China and the United States held the fourth Strategic Economic Dialogue, signed a "Ten-Year Framework for Cooperation on Energy and Environment." In addition, China has established the China Council for International Cooperation on Environment and Development to study the major issues of environment and development, and to share and spread the successful international experience.

17.2.4.3 China and international organizations

China is willing to be actively involved in activities of various international organizations and institutions[125] and is interested in strengthening multilateral international exchanges and cooperation on

---

122 Para.4, Section 1, Chapter 7, 2012 National Report, 73.
123 Para.5, Section 1, Chapter 7, 2012 National Report, 73.
124 Para.2, Section 2, Chapter 7, 2012 National Report, 74.
125 Para.1, Section 3, Chapter 7, 2012 National Report, 75.

environmental protection,[126] because it realizes that the funds and technology of international organizations and institutions are important for domestic economic and social sustainable development.[127]

China benefits greatly from working together with international organizations on the environmental protection; it has made full use of loans from the World Bank, the Asian Development Bank, the European Investment Bank, the International Fund for Agricultural Development and other financial organizations to build a large number of demonstration projects covering the fields of agriculture, forestry, soil and water, energy, environment, urban construction, disaster prevention and mitigation.[128] From 2001 to 2010, the GEF approved a total of 77 projects in China and promised 565 million U.S. dollars in grants to improve China's ability to comply with international environmental conventions.[129] In addition, the Chinese Government has also worked with United Nations Development Program (UNDP), Food and Agriculture Organization (FAO), World Wildlife Fund (WWF) and was granted more than 20 million U.S. dollars.[130]

17.2.4.4 China's views on sustainable development

In the 2012 National Report, China pays much attention to the concept of the "green economy", because it believes that this is positive in the alleviation of poverty in developing countries.[131] However, developed countries should take the lead in the development of a green economy and set a model for developing countries; moreover, they should help developing countries establish a green economy by providing funds, technology, capacity building and widening market access for goods from developing countries.[132] The international community should take all necessary measures to compensate for the cost of economic transition towards a green economy in developing countries[133] and should not use it as an excuse for trade barriers or a prerequisite for providing funding or technology.[134]

---

126 Ibid.
127 Ibid.
128 Para.3, Section 3, Chapter 7, 2012 National Report, 75.
129 Ibid.
130 Ibid.
131 Para.2, Section 1, Chapter 8, 2012 National Report, 82.
132 Ibid.
133 Para.3, Section 1, Chapter 8, 2012 National Report, 82.
134 Para.4, Section 1, Chapter 8, 2012 National Report, 82.

It has been suggested by China that an effective institutional framework for sustainable development is important for the full implementation of "Agenda 21" and "the Plan of Implementation of the World Summit on Sustainable Development" and the response to new and emerging challenges.[135] Such an institutional framework should coordinate economic development, social development and environmental protection, increase the voice and decision-making power of developing countries and solve their practical difficulties concerning capital, technology and capacity building.[136]

When it comes to how to establish an effective institutional framework, China focuses on the role of the United Nations (UN). It is necessary to give the core leadership role of the UN,[137] the policy guidance and coordination functions of the UN need to be strengthened, so that it can coordinate and guide the various agencies of the international community, multilateral institutions and treaty mechanisms to take consistent actions for sustainable development.[138] The existing role of the UN's specialized agencies should be strengthened as well:[139] for example, the role of the United Nations Economic and Social Council, the Commission on Sustainable Development should be reinforced so as to promote the implementation of Agenda 21 and the Plan of Implementation of the World Summit on Sustainable Development.[140] The role of United Nations Environment Program (UNEP) should be enhanced in global environmental governance and more capital and technical support shall be rendered to it.[141]

China is also willing to contribute to the multi-level global environmental governance. It is believed by China that "Agenda 21" should be used as the basic framework to strengthen governance, encourage all states to develop their comprehensive strategies to strengthen the coordination of various government departments, and mobilize public participation and improve the implementation capacity.[142] China suggests that international financial institutions, the World Trade Organization and the multilateral development banks should incorporate the agenda on sustainable development into their planning and projects, and coordinate and

---

135 Para.5, Section 1, Chapter 8, 2012 National Report, 82.
136 Ibid.
137 Para.6, Section 1, Chapter 8, 2012 National Report, 83.
138 Ibid.
139 Ibid.
140 Ibid.
141 Ibid.
142 Para.7, Section 1, Chapter 8, 2012 National Report, 83.

cooperate with relevant UN bodies to form synergies and support the sustainable development governance at the regional, national and local levels.[143]

17.2.4.5 Specific positions

Funding and transfer of technology Transfer of funding and technology from developed countries has always been the priority of China's policy because it believes that the international community should take full account of the differences between developing countries and developed countries in terms of development stages and basic needs.[144] It is necessary to establish and implement long-term, effective funding and technology transfer mechanisms between developed and developing countries.[145]

Alleviation of poverty China is seriously concerned about its poverty problem, believing that poverty is still the biggest obstacle for developing countries in achieving sustainable development.[146] The international community therefore should fully understand this problem in developing countries, strengthen cooperation and take action to alleviate and eventually eliminate poverty. China understands that developing countries themselves bear the primary responsibility for solving their own poverty problems,[147] but holds that it is necessary to accelerate the transformation of the economic development pattern, adjust the economic structure and layout, strengthen the economic competitiveness, and implement development strategies and policies in favor of poor areas and the impoverished population.[148] Developed countries should to keep their ODA commitments and look beyond short-term commercial interests to reduce the technological monopoly.[149] International organizations should develop a fair assessment framework to comprehensively assess the progress made by countries in reducing poverty and coping with challenges, and carefully evaluate the implementation of the ODA commitments and contributions to poverty reduction.[150]

---

143 Ibid.
144 Para.1, Section 2, Chapter 8, 2012 National Report, 83.
145 Ibid.
146 Para.2, Section 2, Chapter 8, 2012 National Report, 84.
147 Ibid.
148 Ibid.
149 Ibid.
150 Ibid.

Rural and agricultural development Like the 2002 National Report, China reiterates the viewpoint that the international community should take concrete actions to support the efforts of developing countries and help them increase investment in agriculture, adopt new agricultural technologies, improve rural infrastructure and increase agricultural productivity, so as to promote sustainable rural and agricultural development and improve food security.[151]

Urbanization Since the beginning of its market economy and open door policy, China has made swift progress towards urbanization. It hopes that developed countries could provide financial and technical support for developing countries to help them achieve sustainable urbanization.[152] In the process of urbanization, China suggests that developing countries should pay great attention to energy and resource conservation and environmental protection. The role of national planning in guidance and restraint should be highlighted, but the historical and cultural backgrounds of developing countries should also be taken fully into account.[153] As a country currently in a stage of rapid urbanization, China is willing to further cooperate with the international community to integrate the urban and rural development, improve urban planning, construction management and service levels, strengthen the housing guarantee, energy efficiency for buildings and green building development, traffic management, urban and rural greening, and historical and cultural protection, develop low-carbon ecocities and improve the living environment.[154]

Water China adopted its most stringent water management system[155] to date on 12 January 2012. The objective is to achieve the rational development, efficient use, comprehensive management, optimal allocation, comprehensive conservation, protection and scientific management of water resources.[156] In the meantime, it hopes that developed countries will support developing countries and improve those countries' capacities

---

151 Para.2, Section 2, Chapter 8, 2012 National Report, 84.

152 Para.3, Section 2, Chapter 8, 2012 National Report, 84.

153 Ibid.

154 Ibid.

155 State Council's Opinion on the Implementation of the most stringent water management system, State Council of P. R. China Gazette, 6 (2012), 5–8.

156 Para.6, Section 2, Chapter 8, 2012 National Report, 85.

to cope with flood and drought disasters and achieve sustainable hydrological development.[157]

Ocean For ocean governance, China hopes the UN might encourage member states to develop and implement sustainable marine development strategies in line with their national conditions, take joint actions to ensure the fair, sustainable use of marine resources and maintain or restore the structure and functions of marine ecosystems.[158] The international community should support the development of marine economy of developing countries.[159] It is also necessary for developed countries to cooperate with developing countries in the restoration of marine ecosystems, the protection of marine environment, responses to sea level rise and ocean disaster prevention and reduction, with an aim of improving the capacity of developing countries in the sustainable use of marine resources.[160]

Climate change China is fully supportive of the United Nations Framework Convention on Climate Change and the Kyoto Protocol. China follows the principles of fairness and "common but differentiated responsibilities." China's position in the 2012 National Report does not significantly differ from its 2002 National Report, but continues to declare that developed countries should take the responsibility for their historical emissions and current high per capita emissions and make a change to their unsustainable lifestyles and consumption patterns.[161] Developed countries should take the lead in substantially reducing greenhouse gas emissions, ensure a proper space for development for developing countries, and at the same time, provide funds and transfer technology to the developing countries.[162] At the same time, developing countries need to take active measures and actions for climate change mitigation and adaptation, which, China believes, should be given equal attention for dealing with climate change.[163]

The Chinese Government acknowledges that China benefits greatly from the international cooperation on the reduction of GHG emissions. By 2010, China had ratified 3 241 clean development mechanism

157 Ibid.
158 Para.7, Section 2, Chapter 8, 2012 National Report, 85.
159 Ibid.
160 Ibid.
161 Para.8, Section 2, Chapter 8, 2012 National Report, 85.
162 Ibid.
163 Ibid.

projects, of which 1 718 projects successfully registered with the United Nations Clean Development Mechanism Executive Board.[164] For the registered projects, the certified emission reductions are expected to be about 351 million tons of carbon dioxide equivalence, accounting for 63.78 percent of the global total.[165]

It is worth mentioning that the Chinese Government started publishing an annual report on China's Action and Policy to Combat Climate Change from 2009. In the latest 2013 Report, the Chinese Government emphasizes that it is keen to actively participate in climate change negotiation under the UNFCCC. It also provides specific positions on the Warsaw Climate Change Conference 2013, with a focus on transfer of funding from developed countries.[166]

Disaster prevention and mitigation For disaster prevention and mitigation, China promotes the idea of international cooperation. It has suggested that countries should exchange information, participate in relevant scientific and technological research projects of international organizations as well as initiate and participate in global, regional disaster prevention cooperation programs.[167] Efforts should also be made to promote the sharing of scientific and technological resources in this regard, improve bilateral and multilateral scientific and technological collaborative mechanisms, enhance the overall levels of national disaster prevention, so as to create synergy in disaster prevention and mitigation worldwide.[168] Developed countries should support developing countries in strengthening disaster response and disaster risk management, as well as disaster monitoring, prediction and warning.[169]

Biodiversity Unlike the 1997 National Report, China does not stress the sovereignty issue over biodiversity within its jurisdiction. It only mentions that biological diversity conservation is a common responsibility of mankind.[170] China reaffirmed that developed countries should support developing countries in biodiversity conservation without mentioning any

---

164 Para.4, Section 4, Chapter 7, 2012 National Report, 79.

165 Ibid.

166 China's Policy and Action to Combat Climate Change, 2013 Annual Report, National Development and Reform Commission, 39–42 (in Chinese).

167 Para.9, Section 2, Chapter 8, 2012 National Report, 86.

168 Ibid.

169 Ibid.

170 Para.10, Section 2, Chapter 8, 2012 National Report, 86.

specific suggestions such as transfer of funding and technology.[171] It is also willing to promote the research and development of sustainable development technologies of biological resources to realize the scientific and rational use of biological resources, and promote the access to and benefit-sharing of biological genetic resources and associated traditional knowledge.[172]

In addition, China is willing to cooperate with both developing and developed countries on the implementation of CBD. According to the fifth National Report on Implementation of Convention on Biological Diversity, China successfully completed a six-year EU-China Biodiversity Protection (ECBP) project in 2011, which significantly contributed to the protection of biodiversity in China.[173] Furthermore, nine projects with different partner countries have been approved under the GEF China Biodiversity Partnership and Framework for Action (CBPF) Programme.[174]

Desertification China suggests that relevant UN agencies should strengthen coordination and cooperation and make full use of their institutional strengths to support the implementation of the UN Convention to Combat Desertification.[175] Developed countries should help developing countries improve the quantitative performance monitoring and evaluation system for the implementation of the convention and the national reporting capacity.[176] China also believes that governments should incorporate the control of desertification into national economic and social development plans and strategies, so as to provide funds and policy support for desertification control.[177] Moreover, it calls for setting goals of global desertification control, establishing a powerful technological support mechanism, strengthening fund-raising, ensuring compliance through effective use of regional coordination mechanisms and promoting experience-sharing and technical exchanges.[178]

---

171 Ibid.

172 Ibid.

173 5th National Report on Implementation of Convention on Biological Diversity, Ministry of Environmental Protection, 2014, 42 (in Chinese).

174 Ibid.

175 Para.11, Section 2, Chapter 8, 2012 National Report, 86.

176 Ibid.

177 Ibid.

178 Ibid.

Forestry As in the 2002 National Report, China states that each country has absolute sovereignty over its own forest resources.[179] It suggests that the international community should promote the intergovernmental consultation process on forest issues. The launch of international forest instruments is necessary to strengthen global forest resources and ecological management systems[180] and China is willing to participate in the bilateral, multilateral and intergovernmental consultations on international forest issues.[181]

Wetland China believes strongly that international cooperation to supporting developing countries to carry out wetland conservation should be strengthened.[182] China is willing to put more effort into protecting natural wetlands, restoring degraded wetlands and maintaining the health and safety of the wetland ecosystem.[183]

17.3 CONCLUDING REMARKS

China has always seen itself as a developing country. The transfer of funding and technology from developed to developing countries has been China's key concern for the past 30 years and it hopes to gain more funding, technology and other capacity building resources from developed countries so as to improve its work on environmental protection. China initially criticized developed countries for not providing the promised ODA to developing countries, but these criticisms disappeared in the 2012 National Report. That report also acknowledged that China benefits significantly from international environmental cooperation and has, moreover, also expressed a willingness to assist other developing countries.

Economic development has been China's priority for decades. China's stance on relations between environmental protection and economic development is clear. Since it first adopted its market reform and open door policies, China has clearly stated its belief that a good economy provides the foundation for better environmental protection, but although China would like to have avoided the western model of 'pollution first,

179 Para.12, Section 2, Chapter 8, 2012 National Report, 86.
180 Ibid.
181 Ibid.
182 Para.13, Section 2, Chapter 8, 2012 National Report, 87.
183 Ibid.

restoration later', it has failed to create a new path to develop the economy while protecting the environment.

China's position on climate change has not changed for 30 years: it has insisted that developed countries bear more responsibility for the reduction of GHG emissions. Meanwhile, the Chinese Government has argued that developed countries should provide funding and technology to help developing countries establish a green economy. To some extent, developed countries are responsible for their historical emissions and should play a lead role in promoting a greener economic model, however, China has become the world's biggest GHG emitter and it is now time for it to make a more significant contribution to combating global warming. Domestically, it is essential to pay more than lip service to environmental protection and the concept of sustainable development.

18. China's participation in major international environmental agreements

Jiang Xiaoyi

As a populous and leading developing country, China attaches great importance to environmental issues and plays an indispensible role in the international environmental regulatory regime. For decades, China has participated in various international environmental agreements, covering areas such as sustainable development and general environmental agreements; international atmospheric environmental protection; international freshwater resources utilization and protection; international marine pollution control; international biological resources protection; international land resources protection; environmental protection of polar regions; environmental protection in outer space; world natural and cultural heritages protection; international hazardous substances and activities management; international waste management; control of the weapons of mass destruction and environmental protection; and international trade and environmental protection. Against this background, this chapter introduces and explores China's participation in the major international agreements on the above-mentioned areas respectively.

18.1 SUSTAINABLE DEVELOPMENT AND GENERAL ENVIRONMENTAL AGREEMENTS

18.1.1 The United Nations Conference on the Human Environment

The United Nations Conference on the Human Environment (also known as the Stockholm Conference) was an international conference convened under United Nations auspices held in Stockholm, Sweden from June 5–16, 1972. It was the UN's first major conference on international environmental issues, and marked a turning point in the development of international environmental politics.[1]

[1] John Baylis and Steve Smith, *The Globalization of World Politics* (3rd ed.) (2005), Oxford: Oxford University Press, 454–5.

Attended by the representatives of 113 countries, 19 inter-governmental agencies and more than 400 inter-governmental and non-governmental organizations (NGOs), it is widely recognized as the beginning of modern political and public awareness of global environmental problems.[2] It focused on human activities in relationship to the environment and laid the foundations for environmental action at an international level. The conference acknowledged that the goal of reducing human impact on the environment would require extensive international cooperation, as many of the problems affecting the environment are global in nature.

The meeting agreed upon a Declaration containing 26 principles concerning the environment and development; an Action Plan with 109 recommendations, and a Resolution. Following this conference, the United Nations Environmental Programme (UNEP) was launched in order to encourage UN agencies to integrate environmental measures into their programs.

Although the representatives of China also attended the conference, the Chinese Government did not pay much attention to environmental issues at that time, their main priority concerned political issues and environmental issues were neglected. In spite of that, under the influence of the Stockholm Conference and its Declaration, the Chinese Government began to take action to translate the Declaration and the Action Plan into domestic policies and rules. The first National Conference on Environmental Protection was convened in 1973 and drew up the Some Regulations on Protecting and Improving Environment, which was subsequently issued by the State Council. This political document actually functioned as the first comprehensive administrative regulation on environmental protection in China. The State Council also issued the first administrative regulation on pollution prevention and control. Furthermore, China revised the PRC Constitution[3] and put environmental protection into it for the time in 1978. The PRC Environmental Protection Law (for trial implementation) was issued in 1979 and a series of specific laws and regulations on pollution prevention and control and natural resources were formulated in 1980s. In spite of these regulations and rules, however, the environmental protection remained weak.

---

2 Ibid.

3 The *PRC Constitution 1982*, last revised in 2004, art 9, http://english.people.com.cn/constitution/constitution.html (last accessed 5 May 2014).

18.1.2 Sustainable Development and the UN Conference on Environment and Development

In 1987, the UN released the *Brundtland Report: Our Common Future*, which included what is now one of the most widely recognized definitions of sustainable development: "Sustainable development is development that meets the needs of the present without compromising the ability of future generations to meet their own needs."[4] In addition, it suggested the UN formulate a general declaration on the environment and sustainable development and hold an international conference on environment and development issues.

Against this background, the United Nations Conference on Environment and Development (UNCED), also known as the Earth Summit was held in Rio de Janeiro from 3 June to 14 June 1992. 172 governments, including the Chinese Government, participated in the conference. The UNCED resulted in the following documents: Rio Declaration on Environment and Development; Agenda 21; Convention on Biological Diversity; Forest Principles and Framework Convention on Climate Change (UNFCCC).

The conference expressed new ways of thinking about the sustainable development of human society and called for each nation to develop and put into effect their individual national strategies and plans to promote sustainable development.[5] The priority for China during that period was still economic development and establishing the socialist market economy, but after attending the UNCED, the State Council approved ten countermeasures to environment and development in China, pointing out the importance of sustainable development and considering it as a right choice and reasonable model to address the key issues of economic development and environmental problems. In addition, based on its national circumstances, China unveiled its own Agenda 21[6] in 1994, which is the first national strategy for promoting sustainable development. China has also strengthened the sustainable development through integrating its Agenda 21 into concrete successive national development

---

[4] Report of the World Commission on Environment and Development: Our Common Future (1987), Conclusion.

[5] See UN Conference on Environment and Development, United Nations, http://www.un.org/geninfo/bp/envirp2.html (last accessed 4 February 2014).

[6] *China's Agenda 21 1994*, http://www.acca21.org.cn/english/index.html (last accessed 3 May 2014).

plans. Furthermore, PRC Environmental Protection Law[7] was issued in 1989 and a series of specific laws on pollution prevention and control and natural resources were revised with sustainable development at their core.

18.1.3 The World Summit on Sustainable Development

The Johannesburg Summit 2002 is a third landmark on the road of international environmental law development. This Summit – the World Summit on Sustainable Development – brought together tens of thousands of participants, including heads of state and governments, national delegates and leaders from NGOs, businesses and other major groups in Johannesburg, South Africa on August 26–September 4, to focus the world's attention on, and direct action towards, meeting difficult challenges, including improving people's lives and conserving natural resources in a world that is growing in population, with ever-increasing demands for food, water, shelter, sanitation, energy, health services and economic security.[8]

The major outcomes of the Summit include the Johannesburg Declaration on Sustainable Development: From Our Origins to the Future; Plan of Implementation of the World Summit on Sustainable Development; and Summary of the Partnershp Initiatives. After attending the Summit, the Chinese Government also began paying more attention to natural resources conservation. With a view to conservation and establishing the economic society, China promulgated a series of laws and regulations, for example, PRC Cleaner Production Promotion Law 2002[9] and PRC Circular Economy Promotion Law 2008,[10] and revised existing laws.

---

[7] PRC *Environmental Protection Law 1989*, http://www.china.org.cn/english/environment/34356.htm (last accessed 3 May 2014).

[8] For more details, see Johannesburg Summit 2002, http://www.johannesburgsummit.org/ (last accessed 3 May 2014).

[9] PRC *Cleaner Production Promotion Law 2002*, http://www.chinacp.com/EN/PolicyDetail.aspx?id=39 (last accessed 3 May 2014).

[10] *PRC Circular Economy Promotion Law 2008*, http://www.chinaenvironmentallaw.com/wp-content/uploads/2008/09/circular-economy-law-cn-en-final.pdf (last accessed 3 May 2012).

18.1.4 The United Nations Conference on Sustainable Development (UNCSD)

After the Johannesburg Summit 2002, a series of international conferences have been held, one of the most significant was the United Nations Conference on Sustainable Development (UNCSD) in 2012. Rio+20 – the short name for the UNCSD – took place in Rio de Janeiro, Brazil, in June 2012 and was an historic opportunity to define pathways to a safer, more equitable, cleaner, greener and more prosperous world for all.[11]

Sustainable development was the main the topic of the conference. The official discussions focused on two main themes: how to build a green economy to achieve sustainable development and lift people out of poverty, including support for developing countries that will allow them to find a green path for development; and how to improve international coordination for sustainable development. It resulted in a focused political outcome document that contains clear and practical measures for implementing sustainable development. In Rio, member states decided to launch a process to develop a set of Sustainable Development Goals (SDGs), which would build upon the Millennium Development Goals and converge with the post-2015 development agenda.

China was a member state of the conference. The Chinese representatives outlined China's Progress on Sustainable Development and Expectations on the Conference.[12] China's position on sustainable development was clear and constant, it has been making efforts to pursue the goal of sustainable development on the premise of adherence to the principle of "common but differentiated responsibilities". Sustainable development, however, remains to be translated into its domestic policies, regulations and laws.

18.2 INTERNATIONAL ATMOSPHERIC ENVIRONMENTAL PROTECTION

The global atmospheric environment is worsening, and is present in air pollution centered upon cities, acid rain, ozone depletion and climate change caused by global greenhouse effect. The deterioration of the

---

11 See RIO+20, United Nations, http://www.uncsd2012.org/index.html (last accessed 4 February 2014).

12 For more details, see RIO+20, United Nations, http://www.uncsd2012.org/index.php?page=view&nr=133&type=1000&menu=126 (last accessed 4 February 2014).

atmospheric environment has attracted worldwide attention. In order to address this situation, the international community reached global and regional agreements. China participated in the 1992 UNFCCC and its 1997 Kyoto Protocol as well as the 1985 Vienna Convention for the Protection of the Ozone Layer and its 1987 protocol.

18.2.1 Climate Change

In light of the urgency of addressing climate change issues, the Intergovernmental Panel on Climate Change (IPCC) was established in 1988 with a view to improving the understanding of the extent of anthropogenic causes of climate change and its implications. The latest report of the IPCC concluded that global warming is real and mostly human-induced. Under this scenario, irreversible adverse consequences will occur through global warming, unless a solution is found to effectively address the problem. Humanity already possesses the fundamental scientific, technical, and industrial know-how to solve the carbon and climate problem,[13] it should, therefore, be possible to combat global warming but what is needed is immediate action.

The international community began to take GHGs and global warming into account in the 1980s. By the late 1980s climate change was already firmly on the international agenda and in 1988 the UN General Assembly (UNGA) passed Resolution 43/53 on the protection of the Global Climate for Present and Future Generations of Mankind.[14] It declared the issue to be one of "common concern to mankind" and endorsed the establishment of IPCC.[15] Two years later, in 1990, UNGA Resolution 45/212 established an intergovernmental negotiating committee to develop a legal instrument on climate change.[16] The outcome of a further two years of strenuous negotiations was the 1992 UNFCCC.

The text of the Convention was adopted at the UN Headquarters, New York on 9 May 1992; it was open for signature at the earth Summit in

---

13 See especially Stephen Pacala and Robert Socolow, 'Stabilization wedges: Solving the climate problem for the next 50 years with current technologies' (2004) 13 *Science*, 968.

14 *Protection of the Global Climate for Present and Future Generations of Mankind,* GA Res 43/53, 70th plen mtg, UN Doc A/Re/42/53 (1988).

15 See ibid.

16 David Freestone, 'Introduction: The UN Framework Convention on Climate Change, the Kyoto Protocol and the Kyoto Mechanisms' in David Freestone and Charlotte Streck (ed), *Legal Aspects of Implementing the Kyoto Protocol Mechanisms: Making Kyoto work* (2005), 3, 3.

Rio de Janeiro from 4 to 14 June 1992, and thereafter at the UN Headquarters from 20 June 1992 to 19 June 1993. By that date the Convention had received 166 signatures. The Convention entered into force on 21 March 1994.[17] It now enjoys a near universal membership, with 194 countries having ratified it.

Under the UNFCCC, all convention parties are required to develop national inventories of anthropogenic emissions by sources and removals by sink of all GHGs and launch national strategies for climate change mitigation and adaptation to expected impact. They should also take climate change into account in their relevant social, economic, and environmental policies; cooperate in scientific, technical, and educational matters; and promote technology transfer, sustainable management, education, public awareness, and the exchange of information relating to climate change.[18]

In addition, Annex I countries, which essentially comprise developed countries and economies in transition, committed themselves to adopting policies and measures with the aim of returning their GHG emissions to 1990 levels by the year 2000 and the richest countries providing new and additional financial resources and facilitating technology transfer.[19]

When the Convention was adopted, governments knew that their commitments would not be sufficient to seriously tackle climate change. In order to develop more concrete obligations and a more precise time frame for reducing GHGs emissions produced by the industrialized countries in Annex I, after two and a half years' intense negotiations, the Kyoto Protocol was adopted in Kyoto, Japan, on 11 December 1997.

The Kyoto Protocol shares the Convention's objective, principles and institutions, and significantly strengthens the Convention by committing Annex I Parties to individual, legally-binding targets to limit or reduce their GHG emissions within a specific time frame. The individual targets for Annex I Parties are listed in the Kyoto Protocol's Annex B, which add up to a total cut in collective emissions of six GHGs[20] by 5.2 per cent from 1990 levels in the commitment period 2008–12. However, as the legitimate priority needs of developing countries at the current phase are

---

[17] See United Nations Framework Convention on Climate Change, http://unfccc.int/essential_background/convention/status_of_ratification/items/2631.php (last accessed 3 May 2014).

[18] Ibid.

[19] Ibid.

[20] The six gases are to be combined in a "basket", with reductions in individual gases translated into "CO_2 equivalents" that are then added up to produce a single figure.

the achievement of sustainable economic growth and the eradication of poverty, they are free of reduction obligations during this period.

After strenuous negotiations, the Kyoto Protocol eventually entered into force on 16 February 2005 with 141 countries ratifying it, including the most major industrialized countries – except the United States, Australia and Monaco.[21] To date, the US is the only industrialized country that has not ratified the Kyoto Protocol.[22]

China ratified the UNFCCC and its Kyoto Protocol. As a party to the UNFCCC and its Kyoto Protocol and a developing country, China is under obligations to:

- develop national inventories of anthropogenic emissions by sources and removals by sink of all GHGs;
- launch national strategies for climate change mitigation and adaptation to expected impacts;
- take climate change into national policies; and
- promote activities for emissions reductions.

China claims that it seriously fulfills its commitments and adheres to its principles under the Convention and the Kyoto Protocol, which are considered a major legal framework for the international community to address climate change. The National Development and Reform Commission accomplished the Initial National Communication on Climate Change of the PRC in November 2004 and subsequently submitted it officially to the Conference of Parties of the Convention (COP), which was the first action that the China took to perform its obligations under the UNFCCC. Apart from this, China announced its emission reduction targets and has also released national policies and dozens of laws and

---

[21] Article 25 of Kyoto Protocol stipulates that:

> This Protocol shall enter into force on the ninetieth day after the date on which not less than 55 Parties to the Convention, incorporating Parties included in Annex I which accounted in total for at least 55 per cent of the total carbon dioxide emissions for 1990 of the Parties in Annex I.

The US which is responsible for about a quarter of the emissions that have been blamed for global warming formally withdrew from the protocol in 2001, claiming it would damage the US economy, and major developing nations like China and India are exempt. After the strenuous negotiations, the Russian Federation eventually ratified the protocol and the Kyoto Protocol came into effect.

[22] It should be noted that Canada left the Kyoto Protocol in December 2011.

regulations in order to fulfill its obligations and translate the agreement into domestic actions.[23]

As the first commitment period of Kyoto Protocol expired in 2012, the international community has been working together to discuss the future of international climate regime. In spite of unremitting efforts, the new agreement regarding emission reduction targets and responsibilities has not been reached because of the divergence of major countries.

First, all the countries have recognized the urgency of reducing carbon emissions and are involved in the post-2012 negotiations and although these negotiations have not been concluded, most countries have set their individual numerical targets for addressing emission reduction beyond 2012. Moreover, they are taking, or have promised to take, measures to reduce their domestic emissions in different forms.

Second, national interests are the root cause of different positions on the post-2012 regime. The divisions between developing and developed countries and between the EU and the US originate in different national interests and according to different national circumstances.

Third, China's and the US's positions play a decisive role in designing a post-2012 framework. In terms of its rapid economic development and large emissions, China is the focus of negotiations on mitigating global warming for the post-2012 era. China set up a model for other developing countries and where China leads other developing countries are almost certain to follow. In addition, the US's position influences the other countries' stances with regard to their obligations in the post-2012 regime.

Finally, divisions between developing countries and developed countries, especially between the US and China, are the critical factor impeding the post-2012 negotiations. The nature of these divisions are various. Should countries share their reduction obligations on the basis of historical emissions or future emissions? Should countries share their reduction obligations based on per capita emissions or nationwide emissions. The major developing countries, which have both relatively low historical and per capita emissions, are expected to produce massive emissions in future decades because of their rapid economic growth. By contrast, the major developed countries, which are the main contributors to the current global warming, will decrease their shares in global carbon emissions with their relatively low economic growth rates. In this scenario, most developed nations believe that for the next global agreement to be meaningful, it must contain GHG reduction commitments

---

23 For more details, see Chapter 10.

from China, India and the other large developing economies. The developing countries, however, are reluctant to deal in specific targets because of the restrictive effects that such targets may have on their industrial development. Consequently, although the developed countries under the Kyoto Protocol are urging the US and China to accept mandatory emission cuts in a post-2012 regime, neither of them are willing to move.

18.2.2 The Protection of the Ozone Layer

The problem of ozone depletion has attracted worldwide attention since the 1970s. In 1974 scientists published their first scientific hypotheses that chemicals being produced could harm the stratospheric ozone layer.[24] The ozone layer protects the earth against excessive ultraviolet radiation, which could cause damage and mutations in human, plant, and animal cells. The scientists found that the chlorofluorocarbon gases (CFCs), which were widely used and regarded as harmless, could migrate to the stratosphere, remain intact for decades or even centuries, and by releasing chlorine, break down the ozone layer.

In 1977 UNEP concluded a World Plan of Action on the Ozone Layer, which called for intensive international research and monitoring of the ozone layer, and in 1981, the UNEP acted on a proposal to develop a global convention on the ozone layer.

With 196 parties, the Vienna Convention was adopted in 1985 and entered into force on 22 September 1988. In 2009, the Vienna Convention became the first convention of any kind to achieve universal ratification. The objectives of the Convention were for parties to promote cooperation by means of systematic observations, research and information exchange on the effects of human activities on the ozone layer and to adopt legislative or administrative measures against activities likely to have adverse effects on the ozone layer.[25] The obligations are general and contain no specific limits on chemicals that deplete the ozone layer.

A working group under the UNEP began negotiations on a protocol, and The Montreal Protocol on Substances that Deplete the Ozone Layer

---

[24] Edith Brown Weiss (2009), United Nations Audiovisual Library of International Law, http://untreaty.un.org/cod/avl/ha/vcpol/vcpol.html (last accessed 3 May 2014).

[25] The text of the Convention is available at http://ozone.unep.org/pdfs/viennaconvention2002.pdf (last accessed 3 May 2014).

(Montreal Protocol)[26] was concluded in September 1987, only nine months after the formal diplomatic negotiations had opened in December 1986. It came into effect on January 1, 1989. A state must be a party to the Vienna Convention in order to become a party to the Montreal Protocol. The Vienna Convention and the Montreal Protocol established the precedent in UNEP for completing a framework agreement, followed later by one or more Protocols. This precedent has been used frequently since then, as in the Kyoto Protocol to the United Nations Framework Convention on Climate Change and the Cartagena Protocol on Bio-safety to the Convention on Biological Diversity.

China entered into the Vienna Convention on 11 September 1989 and ratified the 1990 London Amendment to the Montreal Protocol and 1992 Copenhagen Amendment to the Montreal Protocol on 13 June 1991 and 22 April 2003 respectively. In accordance with the Montreal Protocol, the Chinese Government formulated the National Plan on the Phase Out of Ozone Depleting Substances in China (hereinafter referred to as the National Plan) in 1993 and its revision in 1999. As the basic action guideline for implementing the Montreal Protocol, the National Plan, approved by the State Council and recognized by the Multilateral Fund Executive Committee of the Montreal Protocol, provides comprehensive regulations and principles for phasing out ozone-depleting substances. China made commitments in the National Plan that on the precondition of transferring alternative technology through providing necessary capital and favorable conditions by multilateral fund, it would phase out ozone substances and consumption according to the requirements under the Montreal Protocol and established the official strategy and the relevant policy and legislative system of the phase out of ozone depleting substances.

The National Plan also plays an essential role in the relevant policy and legislative system. Under the guide of the National Plan and based on PRC Air Pollution Prevention and Control Law,[27] the policy and legislative system of import and export management, production control, consumption control, monitor management, multilateral fund management, etc. In order to implement the Vienna Convention and Montreal Protocol, the Chinese Government set up the Chinese Ozone Protection

[26] The text of the Convention is available at http://ozone.unep.org/Ratification_status/montreal_protocol.shtml (last accessed 3 May 2014).

[27] *PRC Air Pollution Prevention and Control Law 1995*, last revised in 2000, http://www.china.org.cn/english/environment/34422.htm (last accessed 3 May 2014).

Leading Group compromising different governmental functional departments, responsible for organization and coordination of the performance of convention and its protocol. The Ministry of Environmental Protection is the national administrative management organ for ozone protection.

18.3 INTERNATIONAL FRESHWATER RESOURCES UTILIZATION AND PROTECTION

International freshwater, that is, rivers and lakes which serve as boundaries between States or which traverse the territories of two or more States, have provided a source of conflict between states throughout history.[28] In the history of international law, the customary rules on international freshwater protection developed with the development of national practices. The first great landmark on the development road of international freshwater resources protection legal system is the Helsinki Rules on the Uses of the Waters of International Rivers (hereinafter referred to as the Helsinki Rules).[29] In addition, the international community agreed upon international, regional or bilateral treaties, the major of which include the Convention on Law of Non-navigational Uses of International Watercourses (hereinafter referred to as the UN Watercourse Convention)[30] and the Agreement on the Cooperation for the Sustainable Development of the Mekong River (hereinafter referred to as the Mekong River Agreement).[31]

18.3.1 Customary International Law on Freshwater Resources

The Helsinki Rules were adopted by the International Law Association (ILA) at the 52nd conference held at Helsinki in August 1966. It is an international guideline regulating how rivers and their connected groundwaters that cross national boundaries may be used. In spite of its adoption by the ILA there is no mechanism in place that enforces the

---

28 Owen McIntyre, *Environmental Protection of International Watercourses under International Law*, 2007, London UK: Ashgate Publishing, 9.

29 The text is available at http://webworld.unesco.org/water/wwap/pccp/cd/pdf/educational_tools/course_modules/reference_documents/internationalregionconventions/helsinkirules.pdf (last accessed 3 May 2014).

30 The text is available at http://assets.panda.org/downloads/8_3_1997.pdf (last accessed 3 May 2014).

31 The text is available at http://www.ancetogo.org/resources/freshwater%20-%20mekong.pdf (last accessed 3 May 2014).

rules, but despite the guideline's lack of formal status, its work on rules governing international rivers was pioneering and had great influence upon international freshwater resources utilization and protection. It led to the creation of the UN Convention on the Law of Non-Navigational Uses of International Watercourses in 1997.

On August 21, 2004, the ILA, meeting in Berlin approved a superseding agreement, the Berlin Rules on Water Resources as a summary of the modern customary international law applicable to fresh water resources. The Helsinki Rules crystallized the rule of equitable and reasonable utilization as the basic rule of international law applicable to the transboundary use and development of waters.

In spite of having no binding effect, China accepts the Helsinki Rules and the Berlin Rules on Water Resources and is willing to solve the relevant issues based on the principle of "not to cause significant arm to other riparian's" and the principle of "reasonable and equitable utilization enshrined in the Helsinki Rules and the Berlin Rules."

18.3.2 Global Agreement on International Freshwater Resources

Water is the earth's most important resource. In view of the global increase in the demand for water and climate change, the sustainable use and distribution of water and the conservation of the water resources such as lakes, wetlands, rivers and aquifers are the central mission of our society. The UN Watercourses Convention provides a regulatory framework for common and cooperative management for water systems crossing or forming international borders. The UN Watercourse Convention is a document that was approved by the United Nations General Assembly (UNGA) on 21 May 1997. This was the first global water law, which applies to uses of international watercourses and of their waters for purposes other than navigation and to measures of protection, preservation and management related to the uses of those watercourses and their waters.

However, China did not ratify the UN Watercourse Convention. As early as 1970, the UNGA requested the ILC to take up the study of the law of the non-navigational uses of international watercourses. When the draft articles were sent to governments to elicit their comments and observations, the substantive legal principles governing the utilisation of international rivers and the protection of related ecosystems had been very controversial. Due to ongoing controversies, the Working Group could not accomplish the final text and did not submit it to the UNGA until 1997. It took more than 25 years for the Convention be adopted on May 21, 1997. A majority of states voted in favour (103 in number), which indicates that the rules embodied in the convention were acceptable; only three states voted against, including China and 27 abstained. Currently, 16 countries have signed up to the Convention.[32] The main reason for the reluctance for ratification is because China thinks the Convention does not recognize and protect the legitimate rights and interests of upper riparians, China and a minority of states being upper riparians.

18.3.3 Regional Agreement on International Freshwater Resources

The Mekong River (known in Tibet as Dza-chu, in China as Lancang Jiang and in Thailand as Mae Nam Khong), is a major river in south-eastern Asia. It is the longest river in the region. From its source in China's Qinghai Province near the border with Tibet, the Mekong flows generally south-east to the South China Sea through China, Myanmar, Thailand, Laos, Cambodia and Vietnam. For thousands of years, the Lancang-Mekong River has been providing beneficial floods, fish, alluvial soil, fresh water and food for the people living alongside its route and in its basin.

On 5 April 1995, Cambodia, Laos, Thailand, and Vietnam signed the Agreement on Cooperation for the Sustainable Development of the Mekong River Basin that created the Mekong River Commission (MRC). These countries agreed on joint management of their shared water resources and development of the economic potential of the river. In 1996, China and Myanmar became Dialogue Partners of the MRC and the countries now work together within a cooperation framework. Parties agreed to cooperate in all fields of sustainable development, utilization, management and conservation of the water and related resources of the Mekong River Basin including, but not limited to irrigation, hydro-power, navigation, flood control, fisheries, timber floating, recreation and tourism, in a manner best suited to optimizing the multiple-use and mutual benefits of all riparians and to minimize the harmful effects that might result from natural occurrences and man-made activities.

China has participated actively into the Cooperation on Lancang-Mekong since the 1990s. The "National Lancang-Mekong Development Early Research Coordination Group" was set up in 1994. China thinks the development of international navigation is the priority of joint cooperation and signed the Lancang-Mekong Passengers and Luggage

---

[32] For more details about the negotiations on the Convention, http://water wiki.net/index.php/Convention_on_the_Law_of_the_Non-Navigational_Uses_of_International_Watercourses (last accessed 3 December 2014).

Transport Agreement with Laos and Myanmar respectively in 1994 and 1997. In addition, China also promotes the cooperation through providing hydro information, signing understanding memorandum concerning establishing hydro power station with other riparians, strengthening the basic research and increasing the official dialogue with the MRC.

18.4 INTERNATIONAL MARINE POLLUTION CONTROL

The international marine pollution control regulatory system has two levels. One consists of global agreements on marine environmental protection, including global framework conventions and conventions for certain types of marine pollution issues; the other covers regional marine environmental protection conventions, including the regional marine environmental protection conventions by UNEP and the other regional conventions.

As a member state of the International Maritime Organization (IMO), China participated in the third UN Conference on the Law of the Sea (UNCLOS III), which took place from 1973 through 1982 and the draft of UN Convention on the Law of the Sea (UNCLOS),[33] and finally joined UNCLOS. In addition, China has joined many international marine environmental protection agreements including: 1969 International Convention for the Prevention of Pollution of the Sea by Oil[34] and its 1973 Protocol; 1972 Convention on the Prevention of Maritime Pollution by Dumping of Wastes and Other Substances;[35] 1974 International Convention for the Safety of Life at Sea;[36] 1973/1978 International Convention for the Prevention of Pollution from Ships;[37] and the Convention as modified by the Protocol of 1978; 1989 International

---

[33] The text is available at http://www.un.org/Depts/los/convention_agreements/texts/unclos/unclos_e.pdf (last accessed 3 May 2014).

[34] The text is available at http://sedac.ciesin.org/entri/texts/pollution.of.sea.by.oil.1954.html (last accessed 3 May 2014).

[35] The text is available at http://www.admiraltylawguide.com/conven/dumping1972.html (last accessed 3 May 2014).

[36] The text is available at http://indonesianmla.com/resources/SOLAS+$281974$29.pdf (last accessed 3 May 2014).

[37] The text is available at http://sedac.ciesin.columbia.edu/entri/texts/pollution.from.ships.1973.html (last accessed 3 May 2014).

Convention on Salvage;[38] and 1990 International Convention on Oil Pollution Preparedness, Response and Cooperation.[39]

China is also the member state of the East Asian Seas Action Plan the Northwest Pacific Action Plan under the Regional Seas Program of the UNEP. In order to implement China's Agenda 21, UNCLOS and the other international agreements, China National Oceanic Administration formulated China's Agenda 21 on Seas in 1996. It drew up plans for marine natural environmental protection, including the establishment and management of marine natural protection zones and marine special protection zones, marine biodiversity protection, marine environmental protection and other aspects.

The *PRC* Marine Environmental Protection Law[40] was adopted on 23 August 1982, promulgated on 1 March 1983 and revised on 25 December 1999. This law is formulated in order to protect the marine environment and resources, prevent pollution damage, maintain ecological balance, safeguard human health and promote the development of marine programmers. Article 97 stipulates that:

> Where an international treaty regarding marine environment protection concluded or acceded to by the People's Republic of China contains provisions differing from those contained in this Law, the provisions of the international treaty shall apply; however the provisions about which the People's Republic of China has declared reservations shall be excepted.

In order to implement the Marine Environment Protection Law and the relevant international agreements, a series of laws and regulations on marine environment protection has been formed, most of which include the Regulations on the Prevention and Control of Land-Based Marine Pollution; the Regulations on the Prevention and Control of Marine Pollution from Coastal Construction Projects; the Regulations on the Administration of Dumping into the Sea; the Regulations on the Administration of Environmental Protection in the Exploration and Development of Offshore Petroleum; the Regulations on the Prevention and

---

[38] The text is available at http://www.admiraltylawguide.com/conven/salvage1989.html (last accessed 3 May 2014).

[39] The text is available at http://www.admiraltylawguide.com/conven/oilpolresponse1990.html (last accessed 3 May 2014).

[40] *PRC Marine Environmental Protection Law 1982*, last revised in 1999, http://english.mep.gov.cn/Policies_Regulations/laws/environmental_laws/200710/t20071009_109912.htm (last accessed 3 May 2014).

Control of Vessel-Source Marine Pollution; and the Law of the PRC on the Administration of the Use of Sea Areas 2001.[41]

18.5 INTERNATIONAL BIOLOGICAL RESOURCES PROTECTION

The existing international agreements on biological resources protection can be divided into the following three categories: global agreements on biological resources protection; regional agreements on biological resources protection; and other agreements as well as documents on special biological resources protection. China has placed importance on biological resources protection and participates actively in international legal practices of international biological resources protection. The main agreements that China has joined include the 1973 Convention on International Trade in Endangered Species of Wild Fauna and Flora (CITES);[42] 1973 Convention on Wetlands of International Importance Especially as Waterfowl Habitat, also called Ramsar Convention;[43] and 1992 Convention on Biological Diversity (CBD).[44]

18.5.1 CITES

CITES is an international treaty drawn up in 1973 to protect wildlife against over-exploitation, and to prevent international trade from threatening the survival of certain species. CITES is an agreement to which states adhere voluntarily and those that have agreed to be bound are known as parties. Although CITES is legally binding on the parties – in other words they have to implement the Convention – it does not take the place of national laws. Rather it provides a framework to be respected by each party, which has to adopt its own domestic legislation to ensure that CITES is implemented at the national level. CITES now has 180 parties.

---

41 *The Law of the People's Republic of China on the Administration of the Use of Sea Areas 2001*, http://www.chinalawedu.com/news/23223/23228/22597.htm (last accessed 3 May 2014).

42 The text is available at http://www.cites.org/eng/disc/text.php (last accessed 3 May 2014).

43 The text is available at http://www.ramsar.org/cda/en/ramsar-documents-texts/main/ramsar/1-31-38_4000_0__ (last accessed 3 May 2014).

44 The text is available at http://www.cbd.int/convention/text/ (last accessed 3 May 2014).

China jointed CITES in 1981 and it came into effect the same year. Being a member State, China has been participating actively in Convention affairs and working on strengthening international and regional cooperation. According to Article IX of the Convention,[45] the Chinese Government has designated "The Endangered Species Import and Export Management Office of the PRC" (affiliated to National Forestry Bureau) and Chinese Academy of Sciences as the Management and Scientific Authorities respectively.

In addition, China has increasingly enhanced the legal system concerned with the import and export of endangered species: PRC Wild Animal Protection Law;[46] Regulation on Wild Plants Protection; and Law on the Entry and Exit Animal and Plant Quarantine.[47] According to these laws and regulations, China strictly manages imports and exports. The Catalogue of Imported and Exported Animal and Plants Products was formulated to provide a standard for the management. The Criminal Law of the PRC[48] and Customs Law[49] also have similar rules, the Criminal Law of which stipulates that "If the circumstances are especially serious … can be sentenced to life imprisonment or death, with forfeiture of property …".

18.5.2 Ramsar Convention

The Ramsar Convention is an intergovernmental treaty that provides the framework for national action and international cooperation for the conservation and wise use of wetlands and their resources. It is the only global environmental treaty that deals with a particular ecosystem. With the objectives of stemming the progressive encroachment on, and loss of, wetlands, the treaty was adopted in the Iranian city of Ramsar in 1971 and the Convention's member states cover all geographic regions of the planet.

---

[45] For more details, see *supra* note 42.

[46] *PRC Wild Animal Protection Law 1988*, http://www.china.org.cn/english/environment/34349.htm (last accessed 3 May 2014).

[47] *Law on the Entry and Exit Animal and Plant Quarantine 1991*, http://www.chinalawedu.com/news/23223/23228/24144.htm (last accessed 3 May 2014).

[48] *Criminal Law 1979*, last revised in 1997, http://hk.lexiscn.com/law/criminal-law-of-the-peoples-republic-of-china-last amended -in-1997.html?eng=0 (last accessed 3 May 2014).

[49] *Customs Law 1987*, last revised in 2000, http://www.chinaembassy.org/eng/ywzn/lsyw/vpna/faq/t710007.htm (last accessed 3 May 2014).

China joined the Ramsar Convention in 1992 and its competent authority is the Wetland Convention Implementation Office under the National Forestry Administration, which is responsible for organizing and coordinating wetlands protection at national and international levels. Furthermore, a system of natural protection zone for wetlands has been set up in China to give effective protection.

18.5.3 Convention on Biological Diversity (CBD)

Signed by 150 government leaders at the 1992 Rio Earth Summit, the CBD is dedicated to the promotion of sustainable development. It entered into force on 29 December 1993 and has three main objectives: the conservation of biological diversity; the sustainable use of the components of biological diversity; and the fair and equitable sharing of the benefits arising out from the utilization of genetic resources.

Afterwards, a series of protocols have been made to complete the CBD, which play an important role in protecting biological diversity.

The Cartagena Protocol on Biosafety to the CBD was adopted on 29 January 2000 and entered into force on 11 September 2003.[50] It is an international agreement which aims to ensure the safe handling, transport and use of living modified organisms (LMOs) resulting from modern biotechnology that may have adverse effects on biological diversity, also taking into account risks to human health.

The Nagoya–Kuala Lumpur Supplementary Protocol on Liability and Redress to CBD was adopted on 15 October 2010. It provides for international rules and procedures on liability and redress for damage to biodiversity resulting from LMOs, including the definition and nature of the damage, the valuation of damage to biodiversity and to human health, the threshold of damage, causation, channeling of liability, roles of parties in import and export, standards of liability, mechanisms of financial security and rights to bring claims.

The Nagoya Protocol on Access to Genetic Resources and the Fair and Equitable Sharing of Benefits Arising from their Utilization to the CBD, a supplementary agreement, was adopted on 29 October 2010 in Nagoya, Japan. It provides a transparent legal framework for the effective implementation of one of the three objectives of the CBD: the fair and equitable sharing of benefits arising out from the utilization of genetic resources.

---

50 For more details, see http://bch.cbd.int/protocol/background/ (last accessed 3 May 2014).

China is a country with the richest biodiversity and it places great importance on biodiversity. The Chinese Government participated in each negotiation about the CBD and contributed to its governing body, the Conference of the Parties (COPs) as well as to other meetings. China was one of the states that ratified and approved the CDB at the earliest opportunity, the Chinese Government ratified the CBD in 1992 and it came into force in China in December 1993.

In response to the CDB, China has carried out a series of plans and makes a contribution to sustainable development and biological diversity protection. The "Coordination Group for Implementing the CBD in China" led by the Ministry of Environmental Protection (MEP) was launched to provide administrative function for biological diversity protection. At the same time, the Chinese Government established a relationship with the UNEP, UN Development Program, World Bank and Global Environmental Fund and extensive bilateral relationships with other developed countries. By doing these, China obtains the relevant know-how and capital, enhances capacity building and increases the public protection awareness.

Although there is no specific legislation on biodiversity, China issued and revised laws and regulations to promote sustainable development and biological diversity protection, which include: the Environmental Protection Law;[51] the Regulation on Natural Protection Zone; the Law on Entry and Exit Animal and Plant Quarantine; Seed Law;[52] the Plant Variety Protection Regulation; the Wild Plant Protection Regulation; the Regulation on Safety Management of Agricultural GMO; the Forest Law (revised);[53] the Marine Environmental Protection Law (revised);[54] and the Fisheries Law (revised).[55] Furthermore, concrete action plans are introduced into national plans and China also takes measures to enhance on-site and off-site protection of biodiversity. Unlike some developed countries, which want to protect wild animal and plant resources through

---

[51] *Environmental Protection Law 2014*, http://www.china.org.cn/english/environment/34356.htm (last accessed 3 May 2014).

[52] *Seed Law 2000*, last revised in 2004, http://review.jcrb.com/200803/ca689818.htm (last accessed 3 May 2014).

[53] *Forest Law 1984*, last revised in 1998, http://www.ccchina.gov.cn/en/NewsInfo.asp?NewsId=5382 (last accessed 3 May 2014).

[54] PRC, *Marine Environment Protection Law 1982*, last revised in 1999, http://english.mep.gov.cn/Policies_Regulations/laws/environmental_laws/200710/t20071009_109912.htm (last accessed 3 May 2014).

[55] *Fisheries Law 1986*, last revised in 2004, http://www.china.org.cn/english/environment/34340.htm (last accessed 3 May 2014).

retraining trade, the Chinese Government is in favor of the principle of sustainable utilization of wild animal and plant resources.

For biosafety, China plays a positive role in promoting research, exploration and industrial development of modern biological technology and also places much importance on biosafety problems that might be caused by biological technology. China ratified the Cartagena Protocol on Biosafety on 8 August 2000 and it entered into effect in China on 6 September 2005.

So far China has made efforts to implement the Protocol. First, China conducts research on biosafety. Second, the Biosafety Management Office was set up as the Competent National Authority. Third, China actively formulates laws, regulations or guidelines on biosafety and the preliminary framework of a legislative system on biosafety has been formed. In spite of this, the following aspects of biosafety need to be given priority: biosafety expertise; capacity building needs and priorities; news and information disclosure; and reports on assignment and risk assessment.

18.6 INTERNATIONAL LAND RESOURCES PROTECTION

Desertification is one of the most critical challenges the global land resources are facing today. Desertification, along with climate change and the loss of biodiversity, were identified as the greatest threats to sustainable development during the 1992 Rio Earth Summit. Adopted in Paris on 17 June 1994 and entering into force in December 1996, UN Convention to Combat Desertification (UNCCD)[56] is the sole legally binding international agreement linking environment and development to sustainable land management. The Convention addresses specifically the arid, semi-arid and dry sub-humid areas, known as the drylands, where some of the most vulnerable ecosystems and peoples can be found.[57] As the dynamics of land, climate and biodiversity are intimately connected, the UNCCD collaborates closely with the other two Rio Conventions; the CBD and the UNFCCC, to meet these complex challenges with an integrated approach and the best possible use of natural resources.

---

[56] The text is available at http://www.unccd.int/en/about-the-convention/Pages/Text-overview.aspx (last accessed 3 May 2014).

[57] For more details, see UNCCD http://www.unccd.int/en/about-the-convention/Pages/About-the-Convention.aspx (last accessed 3 May 2014).

China suffers from the problem of desertification. It ratified the UNCCD on 14 October 1996 and it came into force in China on 19 May 1997. Since ratification, China has taken various actions towards, and has made a great contribution to, combating desertification. First, management organizations at different levels were set up. The Chinese Government established "China Coordination Group to Combat Desertification", also known as the "China Committee for Implementing the Convention to Combat Desertification" in 1994. At the provincial level, the coordination Groups were also set up in 14 places that are prone to desertification. Second, the Chinese Government formulated a national strategy and action plans to implement the CCD, including 1995 National Action Plan for Implementing the CCD. The central and regional governments also combine the desertification combat with poverty eradication and providing sufficient financial support. Third, the Law on Prevention and Control of Desertification[58] was adopted on 31 August and entered into effect on 1 January 2002. It is the first legislation concerning desertification prevention and control. Some local governments also promulgated regional regulations on desertification in order to better implement the law. Fourth, China also plays an active role in international, regional and sub-regional cooperation.

18.7 ENVIRONMENTAL PROTECTION IN POLAR REGIONS

Environmental protection agreements on the South Polar Region and North Polar Region are quite different. There is a multilateral Antarctic Treaty System for the South Polar Region, while there is no universal force agreement on environmental protection covering the North Polar Region. The Antarctic Treaty was signed in Washington on 1 December 1959 by the 12 countries whose scientists had been active in and around Antarctica. It entered into force in 1961 and has since been acceded to by many other nations. The total number of parties to the Treaty is now 50.[59] The main purpose of the Antarctic Treaty is to ensure "in the interest of all mankind that Antarctica shall continue forever to be used exclusively

---

[58] *Law on Prevention and Control of Desertification 2001* (the People's Republic of China) http://www.china.org.cn/china/LegislationsForm2001-2010/2011-02/14/content_21915867.htm (last accessed 3 May 2014).

[59] For more details, see http://www.ats.aq/e/ats.htm (last accessed 3 May 2014).

for peaceful purposes and shall not become the scene or object of international discord."

China is a party to the Antarctic Treaty and participates actively in Antarctic and Arctic issues mainly through conducting research and scientific explorations in Polar Regions. The China Antarctic Great Wall Station was set up on 26 February 1985 and the China Antarctic Zhongshan Station on 28 July 2004. Also, the first permanent scientific exploration station – Huanghe Station was established in the North Polar Region on 28 July 2004. They provide importance platforms for scientific research on polar regions.

18.8 ENVIRONMENTAL PROTECTION IN OUTER SPACE

There has been no specific treaty on protecting the environment of outer space, and the only relevant scattered articles can be found in some agreements concerning space exploration and utilization activities. China is a leading country in respect of outer space exploration and utilization; has been a member state of the Committee on the Peaceful Uses of Outer Space since 1980 and plays an active role in international cooperation and communication. China ratified a series of the relevant treaties and also advocates drawing up a universal and comprehensive convention on international outer space law and also maintains the concept of demilitarized management of outer space.

In order to perform the obligations of protecting outer space environment, the Chinese Government has taken various measures. First, it ratified the Outer Space Treaty[60] and enhances the research and regulation of reducing the effect of space debris. Second, the government ratified the 1972 Convention on International Liability for Damages Caused by Space Objects[61] and it provides that a launching state shall be completely liable to pay compensation for damage caused by its space objects to the surface of the Earth or to aircraft, and also liable for damage due to any of its faults in space. Thus, China is working on improving the legal system of liability for damages caused by space objects. Third, the Chinese Government ratified the 1975 Convention on

[60] The text is available at http://www.oosa.unvienna.org/oosa/SpaceLaw/outerspt.html (last accessed 3 May 2014).

[61] The text is available at http://www.oosa.unvienna.org/oosa/SpaceLaw/liability.html (last accessed 3 May 2014).

Registration of Objects Launched into Outer Space[62] and plays an active role in performing the obligation of registering objects launched into outer space.

18.9 WORLD NATURAL AND CULTURAL HERITAGES PROTECTION

Noting that the cultural heritage and the natural heritage are increasingly threatened with destruction not only by the traditional causes of decay, but also by changing social and economic conditions which aggravate the situation with even more formidable phenomena of damage or destruction, a Convention concerning the Protection of the World Cultural and Natural Heritage was adopted by the UN Educational, Scientific and Cultural Organization (UNESCO) General Conference at its 17th session in Paris on 16 November 1972.[63] The Convention came into force in 1975. The Convention aims to promote cooperation among nations to protect heritage around the world that is of such outstanding universal value that its conservation is important for current and future generations.

China ratified the Convention on 12 December 1985. So far 41 of China's natural and cultural heritage has been inscribed on the World Heritage List making it one of the countries leading the list. According to the relevant article, states that are parties to the Convention agree to identify, protect, conserve, and present world heritage properties. States recognize that the identification and safeguarding of heritage located in their territory is primarily their responsibility and they agree to do all they can with their own resources to protect their world heritage properties. Although China has recognized the importance of protecting its natural and cultural heritage and makes great efforts to implement the Convention, there are many actual problems needing to be solved. First, China does not have a unified administrative authority managing its world heritage sites at national level. The protection and management of its world heritage is relatively scattered and remains weak. Second, with regard to domestic legislation, there is no specific law on heritage protection and management. Finally, there are other problems awaiting solutions, some of which include lack of qualified staff, a disordered management institution and the over-development of tourism.

---

[62] The text is available at http://www.unoosa.org/pdf/publications/STSPACE11E.pdf (last accessed 3 May 2014).

[63] For more details, see http://whc.unesco.org/en/conventiontext/ (last accessed 3 May 2014).

18.10 INTERNATIONAL HAZARDOUS SUBSTANCES AND ACTIVITIES MANAGEMENT

The hazardous substances and activities referred to are hazardous chemicals, radioactive substances and the use of living modified organisms that are considered severely harmful to human health and the environment as well as the activities of using, operating, transporting, handling and disposing these substances. Many of them are commonly used substances that are harmless in their normal use but are quite dangerous when released. There are many international treaties and legal documents concerning hazardous substances and activities in international community. However, the existing international regulations are unsystematic and operate at a low level, they still lack a framework convention and most of the regulations are from soft law documents.

China has signed many agreements on hazardous substances and activities, including the Rotterdam Convention: On the Prior Informed Consent Procedure for Certain Hazardous Chemicals and Pesticides in International Trade (Rotterdam Convention);[64] the Stockholm Convention on Persistent Organic Pollutants (Stockholm Convention);[65] a series of conventions on nuclear safety; and the Cartagena Protocol on Biosafety to the Convention on Biological Diversity (Cartagena Protocol on Biosafety).[66]

18.10.1 Rotterdam Convention

The Rotterdam Convention was adopted on 10 September 1998 by a Conference of Plenipotentiaries in Rotterdam, the Netherlands, and entered into force on 24 February 2004. The objectives of the Conventions are to promote shared responsibility and cooperative efforts among parties in the international trade of certain hazardous chemicals in order to protect human health and the environment from potential harm and to contribute to the environmentally sound use of those hazardous chemicals, by facilitating information exchange about their characteristics, by

---

64 The text is available at http://www.pic.int/TheConvention/Overview/TextoftheConvention/tabid/1048/language/en-US/Default.aspx (last accessed 3 May 2014).

65 The text is available at http://chm.pops.int/Convention/ConventionText/tabid/2232/Default.aspx (last accessed 3 May 2014).

66 The text is available at http://bch.cbd.int/protocol/text/ (last accessed 3 May 2014).

providing for a national decision-making process on their import and export and by disseminating these decisions to parties.[67]

China is a leading country producing and using pesticides, thus the safety of the pesticides is essential. China ratified the Rotterdam Convention on 22 March 2005; participation in which influences pesticide production and exports in China because some of the pesticides it produced were inhibited by the Convention. The Regulation on Environmental Management of the First Import of Chemicals and the Import and Export of Hazardous Chemicals was enacted and has been implemented since 1994. In this case, the environmental management of the import and export of hazardous chemicals in China had been following the prior informed consent procedure as stipulated in the Rotterdam Convention. After ratifying the Convention, the Chinese Government also revised the list of forbidden and/or strictly controlled chemicals and began to manage them in accordance with the Rotterdam Convention.

18.10.2 Stockholm Convention

The Stockholm Convention is a global treaty to protect human health and the environment from chemicals that remain intact in the environment for long periods; become widely distributed geographically; accumulate in the fatty tissue of humans and wildlife; and have adverse effects to human health or to the environment. In response to this global problem, the Stockholm Convention, which was adopted in 2001 and entered into force in 2004, requires parties to take measures to eliminate or reduce the release of Persistent Organic Pollutants (POPs) into the environment. The Convention is administered by the UNEP and is based in Geneva, Switzerland.[68]

China ratified the Convention on 22 May 2001 and it was approved on 25 June 2004. The Chinese Government places great importance on POPs issues. The Leading Group for Implementing the Convention under the Ministry of Environmental Protection was established and implementing the Stockholm Convention brings opportunities and challenges for China to reduce economic loss and risk of environmental health.

---

[67] For more details, see http://www.pic.int/TheConvention/Overview/tabid/1044/language/en-US/Default.aspx (last accessed 3 May 2014).

[68] For more details, see http://chm.pops.int/Convention/tabid/54/Default.aspx (last accessed 3 May 2014).

18.10.3 Conventions on Nuclear Safety

The Chinese Government places great importance on nuclear safety and ratified and approved the Convention on Physical Protection of Nuclear Material; the Convention on Early Notification of a Nuclear Accident; the Convention on Assistance in the Case of a Nuclear Accident or Radiological Emergency, and the Convention on Nuclear Safety; etc. The nuclear industry commenced in China in 1955 and the "Safety First" principle is at the top of development strategy and plans. China decided to establish National Unclear Safety Administration in 1986, began to issue laws and regulations on unclear safety in 1986 and has endeavored to set up a monitoring and management system.

18.11 INTERNATIONAL WASTES MANAGEMENT

The problem of wastes is a great challenge faced by many countries in the world, especially by developing countries. There are two reasons for concern. First, the developing countries have relatively less developed infrastructures, technology or capital to handle or dispose of wastes. Second, developed countries are more willing to export and dispose their wastes to developing countries. Thus, the transboundary movements of hazardous wastes and their disposal have become a controversial topic.

Against this background, the Basel Convention on the Control of Transboundary Movements of Hazardous Wastes and Their Disposal (Basel Convention)[69] was adopted on 22 March 1989 by the Conference of Plenipotentiaries in Basel, Switzerland, in response to a public outcry in the 1980s, following the discovery of deposits of toxic wastes imported from abroad, in Africa and other parts of the developing world. The Convention entered into force on 5 May 1992 and now has 179 parties. The overarching objective of the Basel Convention is to protect human health and the environment against the adverse effects of hazardous wastes.[70]

China places great importance on the transboundary movements of hazardous wastes and their disposal. China ratified the Convention on 22 March 1990 and approved it on 4 September 1995. Shortly after the

---

[69] The text is available at http://www.basel.int/TheConvention/Overview/TextoftheConvention/tabid/1275/Default.aspx (last accessed 3 May 2014).

[70] For more details, see http://www.basel.int/TheConvention/Overview/tabid/1271/Default.aspx (last accessed 3 May 2014).

approval, PRC Solid Waste Law, 1995[71] was adopted on 30 October 1995 and revised on 29 December 2004. This law provides basic rules and principles on production, use and disposal of solid wastes, including forbidding or controlling wastes import and export and transboundary movements of hazardous wastes and their disposal. The crimes of the illegal disposal of imported solid waste; of importing solid waste materials without authorization; and of smuggling solid wastes were put into the amendments to the Criminal Law.

In addition, China has made great efforts to implement the Convention and to translate it into domestic laws and actions. First, regulations and standards on controlling the import of wastes are issued. Second, the import of hazardous wastes is strictly controlled. Third, the national list of hazardous wastes has been drawn up. Fourth, the MEP is designated as the competent authority and a liaison office is also designated. Fifth, hazardous wastes training and technology transfer centers have been established. Sixth, all cases concerning illegal transboundary movements of wastes are dealt with.

18.12 CONTROL OF WEAPONS OF MASS DESTRUCTION AND ENVIRONMENTAL PROTECTION

A weapon of mass destruction is one that can kill and/or bring significant harm to a large number of humans (and other life forms) and/or cause great damage to man-made structures (e.g. buildings), natural structures (e.g. mountains), or the biosphere in general. In order to forbid and limit the research, production and use of such weapons and safeguard world peace and security, the international community has agreed upon some treaties, most of which are on chemical, biological, radiological, and nuclear weapons. Although the main objective of these treaties is not environmental protection, they have influence upon the environment.

The Chinese Government first issued the White Paper on China's Non-Proliferation Policy and Measures in December 2003 which advocates the prevention of the proliferation of weapons of mass destruction and their means of delivery. In order to promote and improve the non-proliferation system, China ratified all the international agreements

---

[71] PRC Solid Waste Law 1995, last revised in 2004, http://www.fdi.gov.cn/pub/FDI_EN/Laws/GeneralLawsandRegulations/BasicLaws/t20060620_50961.jsp (last accessed 3 May 2014).

concerning non-proliferation and participated in the relevant international organizations. China joined the International Atomic Energy Agency in 1984 and ratified the Treaty on the Non-Proliferation of Nuclear Weapons[72] in 1992. China played a positive role in negotiations on the Comprehensive Nuclear-Test-Ban Treaty[73] and ratified it in 1996. It also ratified and approved the Treaty for Prohibition of Nuclear Weapons in Latin America;[74] the South Pacific Nuclear Weapons Free Zone Treaty;[75] the African Nuclear Weapons Free Zone Treaty;[76] the Treaty on the Southeast Asia Nuclear Weapons Free Zone[77] and their Protocols. With regard to biological weapons, China has ratified the Convention on the Prohibition Of the Development, Production and Stockpiling of Bacteriological (Biological) and Toxin Weapons and on Their Destruction[78] in 1984 and has been performing the obligations under the Convention strictly. In the field of chemical weapons, China made contribution to negotiations on the Convention on the Prohibition of the Development, Production, Stockpiling and Use of Chemical Weapons and on Their Destruction,[79] ratified it in 1993 and approved it in 1997. The Chinese Government has taken various measures to ensure the effective implementation of these agreements.

18.13 INTERNATIONAL TRADE AND ENVIRONMENTAL PROTECTION

The relationship between international trade and environmental protection has become a hot topic attracting worldwide attention since the

[72] The text is available at http://www.un.org/en/conf/npt/2005/npttreaty.html (last accessed 3 May 2014).

[73] The text is available at http://www.ctbto.org/fileadmin/content/treaty/treaty_text.pdf (last accessed 3 May 2014).

[74] The text is available at http://www.iaea.org/Publications/Documents/Treaties/tlatelolco.html (last accessed 3 May 2014).

[75] The text is available at http://www.armscontrol.org/documents/rarotonga (last accessed 3 May 2014).

[76] The text is available at http://www.armscontrol.org/documents/pelindaba (last accessed 3 May 2014).

[77] The text is available at http://www.aseansec.org/2082.htm (last accessed 3 May 2014).

[78] The text is available at http://www.opbw.org/convention/conv.html (last accessed 3 May 2014).

[79] The text is available at http://www.opcw.org/chemical-weapons-convention/ (last accessed 3 May 2014).

1990s with the occurrence of two incidences. One is the 1992 UN Conference on Environment and Development, promoting the development of environmental protection; the other is the 1993 Uruguay Round of Multilateral Trade Negotiations and the establishment of the World Trade Organization (WTO), representing the development of liberalization and globalization of international trade.

Nowadays, international trade and environmental protection are becoming more interdependent. First, the liberalization and globalization of international trade exerts positive or negative influences on environmental protection. On the positive side, trade liberalization may promote green trade, poverty eradication and clean technology transfer. On the negative side, trade liberalization may bring about excessive consumption of natural resources, transboundary environmental pollution and potential safety hazard caused by international transportation.

Under the multilateral trade system, there are many clauses relating to the environment. For instance, Articles 1, 3, 11, 20 of the General Agreement on Tariffs and Trade 1994 (GATT) are involved with environmental protection.[80] Article 1:

> any advantage, favour, privilege or immunity granted by any contracting party to any product originating in or destined for any other country shall be accorded immediately and unconditionally to the like product originating in or destined for the territories of all other contracting parties

and Article 3 of national treatment principle are made with a view to preventing the misuse of environmental policy. Article 11 provides for the general elimination of quantitative restrictions that are an origin of the environment related cases. In addition, Article 20 stipulates some general exceptions, which include (b) necessary to protect human, animal or plant life or health; and (g) relating to the conservation of exhaustible natural resources if such measures are made effective in conjunction with restrictions on domestic production or consumption.

With the purpose of environmental protection and trade promotion, the Marrakesh Agreement Establishing the WTO stipulates that:

> Recognizing that their relations in the field of trade and economic endeavour should be conducted with a view to raising standards of living … while allowing for the optimal use of the world's resources in accordance with the

---

[80] The text is available at http://www.wto.org/english/docs_e/legal_e/06-gatt.pdf (last accessed 3 May 2014).

> objective of sustainable development, seeking both to protect and preserve the environment ...[81]

Generally speaking, the relevant international trade provisions are made to eliminate potential trade barriers that would be brought by environmental protection as well as to promote environmental protection.

Second, the environment provides a basis and resources for trade, and thus has direct impact on international trade. There are many multilateral environmental agreements related to international trade through restrictions on importation and exportation between the parties. The agreements include but are not limited to the following: Basel Convention on the Control of Transboundary Movements of Hazardous Wastes and Their Disposal (Basel Convention); Convention on International Trade in Endangered Species of Wild Fauna and Flora; Convention on Biological Diversity; and the Montreal Protocol on Substances that Deplete the Ozone Layer. The agreements are reached with a view to reducing the potential environmental harms that could be brought by international trade.

China has been a member of WTO since 11 December 2001. The problems concerning trade and environment that China faces today can be attributed to two aspects. First, liberalization and globalization of international trade bring about over-exploration and use of resources and pollution transfer. Second, strict environmental standards increase the cost of exported products, impairing the competitiveness of Chinese products in international markets. In this context, China is facing two challenges. One is how to eliminate the potential side effects on the environment brought about by international trade and realize the objective of international and domestic environmental protection through reasonably regulating and restricting trade. The other is to regulate and adjust the international trade restriction environmental policy and measures to avoid the situation of environmental protection becoming an umbrella over trade protectionism and to maximize the elimination of potential trade barriers that would be brought by environmental protection.

Faced with this situation, China has taken measures combining international cooperation with domestic policy and legislation and imperative rules with guided conditions to establish, in the short term, a policy system of trade and environment. China is making an effort to promote

---

[81] The text is available at http://www.wto.org/english/docs_e/legal_e/04-wto.pdf (last accessed 3 May 2014).

international trade and environmental protection through adopting policies on the following aspects: foreign investment, environmental management of products import and export, environmental management of wastes import, management of technology import and export, environmental services trade and environmental label.

18.14 CONCLUSION

China has gone through a series of economic and political reforms, enabling rapid economic growth and significantly increasing its international status. Nowadays, China is attempting to become a more influential player in the international community. As the environmental issue is one of the hottest topics attracting worldwide attention, it is sensible for China to play a more active role in international environment regime with a view to making its voice better heard in the international community.

In addition, environmental issues have been put at the top of agenda. On one hand, China is one of the countries that suffers severely from environmental problems; on the other hand, China is making more contributions to the current situation of environmental problems due to rapid economic development and relatively low level environmental protection awareness and basis. Thus, in spite of being a developing country, China is expected to take on more environmental protection responsibilities and thus will be under considerable international pressure to address its environmental issues without undermining its economic development. In this scenario, China has actively participated into various international environmental agreements and negotiations to possibly safeguard and extend its legitimate rights.

Facing the challenge of environmental problems and in order to increase its international status, China seriously fulfils the due obligations under the international environmental agreements and translates the relevant international provisions into its national policy, regulations and laws.

19. Conclusion

Zhou Chen and Qin Tianbao

Since the inception of "Open and Reform Policy" at the end of the 1970s, China has welcomed a booming economic development which although it eases poverty, provides employment and lengthens life expectancy has aroused significant side effects in the ecological domain. Moreover, its environment is worsening with natural resources depletion and serious pollution of air, water and soil, etc. This has not only impacted on human health but also on the potential for maintaining fast economic growth.

The Chinese leadership realizes that the current pattern of economic growth is not environmentally sustainable. In this regard, they have taken top-down actions to build an overarching regulatory and institutional framework for a full, sound and effective environmental management system, above all, environmental protection has been set out as a basic national policy. The State Environmental Protection Committee was established in 1984 particularly to improve legislation and almost immediately the first Environmental Protection Law (EPL) was issued in 1989. In the meantime, Chinese environmental legislation was often portrayed in an attempt to meet international trends. After the United Nations Conference on Environment and Development in 1992, China was one of the first countries to formulate and carry out a strategy of sustainable development. Within this guidance, China began to frame environmental objectives into the Five-year Plans, which are designed to identify, coordinate and implement public policy priorities. For instance, the most recent twelfth Five-year Plan envisaged a set of regulatory and institutional measures specializing in environmental targets such as improving supporting laws and legislation and promoting evaluation on the work of administrative levels.[1]

[1] Twelfth Five-year Plan for Environmental Protection (2011–15) sets out a basic principle of "accelerating the transformation of economic growth based on carrying capacities of resources and the environment". Apart from two parts mentioned above, it consists of nine parts as follows: I, the national environmental situation; II, the guiding ideology, basic principle and main targets; III, further emission reductions of major pollutants; IV solving the most prominent environmental problems; V, strengthening control of environmental

Accordingly, institutional construction has been strengthened over the last three decades. The restructure of the institutional framework, by the end of the 1990s, led to the creation of a State Environmental Protection Administration (SEPA) placed under the State Council. More recently in 2008, the central government further promoted the SEPA into the Ministry of Environment Protection (MEP) that reports directly to the Vice Premier in charge of environmental protection and participates in State Council meetings when environmental matters are discussed. At the sub-national level (sector and region), enforcement centers have been coined to reinforce supervision and adherence. It was of vital importance that attention was devoted recently to the relationship between institutional capacity and the enforcement of environmental laws in China.[2] Increasing finance and improving personnel are considered essential to assist in overcoming the obstacles to enforcement of regulations, e.g. in relation to the reduction of pollution.

From a regulatory perspective, China's environmental law framework is recent but dynamic, with the 1989 Environmental Protection Law (EPL) at its center. Over the past 25 years, the country has not only become the world's second-largest economy but also its biggest carbon emitter, and the decades of breakneck economic growth have left its environment scarred. Confronting the disjoint with the recent reality, potential conflicts with single environmental protection laws (i.e. pollution prevention and control laws) and poor implementation, the 1989 EPL was unable to fulfill its legislative goals and called for amendment. The official start of amendment was in 2011 and three years later Chinese environmental protection business welcomed the news that the revised EPL is adopted and came into force on January 1, 2015. The new law has made constructive achievements in certain significant aspects such as state obligations, enterprise pollution control and public interest litigation; but it leaves some unsolved issues, for instance the confirmation of the right to environment, the restructure of current environment supervision and governance system.

To date, the state has promulgated more than 30 laws for natural resources conservation, pollution control, and the management of the environmental aspects of productions and consumption patterns. These

---

risks in focused areas; VI, optimize the system of environmental public services; VII, implement eight priority and other environmental protection projects.

[2] See Wanxin Li and Eric Zusman, 'Translating Regulatory Promise into Environmental Progress: Institutional Capacity and Environmental Regulation in China', 8 *News & analysis* 36 ELR (2006), p. 10617.

laws are concurrently supported by more than 40 State Council regulations, approximately 500 standards and more than 600 other regulatory documents. By very example, environmental protection authorities have publicized over 100 national environmental protection regulations and more than 1000 local ones.[3] In the meantime, a host of existing legal statutes were revised (i.e. the 1989 EPL) in accordance with the fast social-economical development. In spite of the comprehensiveness, however, some issues still remain outside the central framework and are, therefore, not yet regulated. These include: soil pollution prevention; comprehensive waste reduction and management; environmental permits; damage compensation; and addressing the liability for past pollution.[4]

The Chinese environmental law system is meanwhile supported by a number of specific regulatory instruments. Basically, command-and-control regulations and economic incentives are applied hand in hand, as the proverbial "stick" and "carrot".[5] In a Chinese context, regulatory measures like standard-based limitations are adopted as a priority;[6] this is particularly the case in pollution control, e.g. environmental quality and emission/discharge standards. Domestic incentive mechanisms are provided to increase private conservation; this is most apparent with regard to the material-based aspects of the environment like forestry and grasslands, ocean resources – all deemed to be the objects of conservation. "Environment legislation has acquired special importance as a result of the leadership's recognition of the contribution of material incentives and the profit motivation to economic growth."[7] Whatever the command-and-control regulations and economic incentives, China firmly carries out the "prevention first policy" by obligating the state to provide preventive measures that effectively control and mitigate

---

3 China.org.cn, Green strategy, available at http://english.gov.cn/2006-02/08/content_182528.htm.

4 'Environmental Compliance and Enforcement in China', *An Assessment of Current Practices and Way Forward*, Secretary-General of the OECD, 2010, p. 50.

5 See Nazrul Islam, Isabel Martínez and Wang Xi, etc., 'Environmental law in developing countries, selected issues', IUCN Environmental Policy and Law Paper nr. 43, 2001, pp. 144–7.

6 See ibid., p. 144.

7 See Wang Jin, *The Chinese Path to Environmental Legislation: Introspection and Exploration*, China Environmental Science Publisher, 2011, pp. 4–9. According to Wang, the effectiveness of policy instruments (including standards, permitting and economic instruments) should be enhanced by designing their optimal mixes to tackle different environmental problems and different segments of the regulated community.

negative impacts on natural resources to a level at which human health is protected and sustainable development is achieved.[8]

As a response to its importance as a player in the international legal regime, China has signed abundant Multinational Environmental Agreements (MEAs). This, on one side, suggests an effort to resist and/or transform international standards and norms.[9] On the other side, as we have noted throughout this book, normative assimilation remains uncertain. China's environmental diplomacy is very much intensified in the new emerging domains like global climate change and biodiversity degradation.[10] Its growing integration into the international society, in particular through environmental aid from global organizations, is bound to support the country's sustainable development.

19.1 TRENDS AND PROSPECTS

How stringent Chinese environmental laws are and to what extent they are robustly applied in practice is the central question we have attempted to answer in this *Handbook*. Considering the country's short environmental law history, "respectable achievements have been made in a short period of time".[11] A comprehensive legal system has been created in China and continues to expand, but there is apparent evidence that the current system holds limited influence and seems far from ideal: China has not been able to control the further deterioration of the environment as a whole, even with localized areas of improvements, due to inadequate and superficial compliance. There is little doubt that the implementation of environmental laws and regulations in China has not been as successful as their formulation and many legislative objectives remain unachieved. In fact, environmental laws suffer from the same inadequacies and problems that characterize contemporary Chinese law in general. Statuary deficiencies like vague language, potential conflicts and timid standard bars generally persist. However, China has now realized this and is trying to increase

---

[8] Environmental Protection Law, arts 16, 24, 25, 27 and 30.

[9] See Pitaman B. Potter, *China and International Legal System: Challenge of Participation*, in China's Legal System: New Developments New challenges (edited by Donald C. Clarke), Cambridge University Press, 2008, p. 145.

[10] In these new areas, there is a tendency for China's position in the North-South issue to be questioned.

[11] See Stefanie Beyer, 'Environmental Law and Policy in the People's Republic of China', *Chinese Journal of International Law,* Vol. 5, No. 1, 2006, p. 196.

rates of compliance: for instance, by the stricter non-compliance responses of the revised Criminal Law making provision for criminal sanctions in cases of serious harm to the environment and/or natural resources.

Looking towards the future, this, at least, will have to be addressed. We can also sketch some promising tendencies that remain untried and speculative.

First, the adoption of the new revised EPL illustrates that although the tensions between economic development and environmental protection continue to prevail in China, it is likely to reduce gradually henceforth. Until recently, green GDP was not a priority in that political willingness was primarily driven by national concerns for economic competitiveness rather than environmental considerations.[12] Although there are improvements along with the increased appeals over public health and the frequency of environment crises, environment performances in the past appear less optimistic.[13] However, the situation turns out to be brighter since the EPL was revised and successfully adopted in 2014. This legislative effort releases a very positive signal that the state seeks to inject more investment into national and local environmental protection. Legal/administrative resources and economic supports are expected to be in place in due course.

Secondly, environment protection agencies are, and will be, confronting huge challenges under the new context of the 2014 EPL. As described at the very beginning, China's legal regime is based on "the Combination of Legislative and Executive Powers", which, by its very nature, integrates the process of decision-/law-making into implementation/enforcement in a highly consistent term.[14] On the whole, China's sustainable development and environmental protection is top-down deployed and environment protection agencies, as a major organ of governance, management and supervision, play a primary role in effectively implementing and enforcing the revised EPL. However, currently, it is difficult for environment protection agencies in China to shoulder this task, in particular for the Central

---

[12] See Julian L. Wong, 'The Challenge of China's Green Technology Policy and Ohio's Response', Centre for American Progress Action Fund, 2010, p. 2.

[13] They are too easy to be influenced by macro-economic context. Here is an example: conflicts between resource use and preservation have so far been minimal due to the low level of economic development. The hundreds of nature preserves that have been established so far exist largely in name only and, in any event, are expected to coexist with substantial economic activity within their boundaries.

[14] Chapter 1, section 1.1.2: The evolution of Chinese institutional construction, Chapter 2: The Chinese legal system.

EPA. Their subordinate status as well as the institutional incapacity of the EPA in reality leads to poor performance, undermining to a great extent, the effectiveness of implementation and enforcement. Now, there are an increasing number of appeals to restructure the EPA.[15] There are opinions on both slight adjustment and fundamental reformation. As far as local environment protection agencies are concerned, a specific-regional and regional-cooperation approach is required to be in place in order to reduce implementation gap and to enhance supervision and scrutiny of law enforcement.[16]

Finally, there could be a great opportunity for China to achieve a professional, nationwide environmental judiciary. Two major reasons account for this: the induction and development of the concept of environmental rights and the reconstruction of civil litigation procedures. Recently, the concept of the right to the environment has entered Chinese thought, having, as might be expected, its effect on legislation. As an individual and collective right, the right to the environment is assumed to forego in the name of less tangible, spiritual values, enforcing substantive and procedural environmental rights, and even conflict resolution. Where there is a violation a citizen could thus resort to remedy. The public interest litigation has thus been written into the basic environmental law, providing a legal channel for citizens and community groups to participate in environmental protection. For a long time, most of environmental litigation traditionally fell under the jurisdiction of civil courts in China. Up until 2007 when the first environmental law division was established in the Guiyang municipal intermediate people's court of Guizhou Province.[17] At the time of writing, more than 90 environmental courts have been established on a national scale and 11 of them have been in operation long enough for preliminary analysis of their experiences to be possible. It is usual that practice comes in advance of legislation and the

---

[15] Ministry of Environmental Protection of the People's Republic China, 'The Institutional Reformation of EPA', available at http://rss.mep.gov.cn/jggg/, also see, 'The Top Design of Institutional Reform on the EPA Is to Be Enacting', Xinhua News, 03 March 2014, available at http://news.xinhuanet.com/energy/2014-03/30/c_126329017.htm.

[16] See Zhu Ningzhu, 'China to Enhance Environmental Protection Legislation', 04 March 2013, available at http://news.xinhuanet.com/english/bilingual/2013-03/04/c_132207161.htm. Recent examples of this trend include introduction by regional authorities of pollution charges, bans and waste minimization and recycling measures such as "pilot Projects".

[17] The State Council's *Decision on the Implementation of Scientific Development and Strengthening of Environmental Protection* specifically mentioned the "promotion of environmental public interest litigation", 2005.

establishment of public interest ligation on one side legally confirms local efforts, while on the other side it is likely to promote the process of a professional and specialized Chinese environmental judiciary.

In a nutshell, China's response to public health and environment crises and its legal efforts illustrate a demonstrable case. Concurrently, there are ongoing political, legal and economic reformations nationwide, which, and will continue to influence the local environmental protection business to a less or greater extent. However, economic development on a more environmentally sound basis than the People's Republic of China has encountered before is certainly a brighter prospect. If it intends to achieve the ambitions of "The Dream of Beautiful China" and stride towards a more sustainable model of development, the stringent law, robustly applied, will be a critical part of that success.

Annex: Timeline of the great events of the Chinese Environmental Protection Law

PRC Environmental Protection Law (for Trial Implementation), 1979.

PRC Environmental Protection Law, 1989.

PRC Environmental Protection Law (1989), listed in The Revising Plan of 11th NPC, 2011.

First Review, The Draft of Amendment to PRC Environmental Protection Law, 28th Section of The Standing Committee of the 11th NPC, August 2012.

Open for public opinions, advice and suggestions, 31 August–30 September 2012.

Second Review, The Draft of Amendment to PRC Environmental Protection Law, 3th Section of The Standing Committee of the 12th NPC, June 2013.

Open for public opinions, advice and suggestions, 19 July–18 August 2013.

Third Review, The Draft of Amendment to PRC Environmental Protection Law, 5th Section of The Standing Committee of the 12th NPC, October 2013.

Fourth Review, The Draft of Amendment to PRC Environmental Protection Law, 8th Section of The Standing Committee of the 12th NPC, April 2014.

PRC Environmental Protection Law (2014), passed by 8th Section of The Standing Committee of the 12th NPC, 24 April 2014.

PRC Environmental Protection Law, 2014.

Index